Refugee Scholars in America

REFUGEE SCHOLARS IN AMERICA

Their Impact and Their Experiences

Lewis A. Coser

Yale University Press   New Haven and London

Designed by Nancy Ovedovitz and set in VIP Baskerville type by
Graphic Composition Inc., Athens, Georgia. Printed in the United
States of America by Vail-Ballou Press, Binghamton, New York.

Library of Congress Cataloging in Publication Data
Coser, Lewis A., 1913–
   Refugee scholars in America.
   Includes bibliographical references and index.
   1. Jews—United States—Biography. 2. Refugees, Jewish—
United States—Biography. 3. Refugees, Political—United States—
Biography. 4. Scholars—United States—Biography. I. Title
E184.J5C66 1984   973'.04924022 [B]   84–40193
ISBN 0-300-03193-9 (alk. paper)

10 9 8 7 6 5 4 3 2 1

For Irving Howe

Contents

Preface

The aim of this book is to analyze and assess the contributions to American scholarship and culture made by European refugees who arrived here between 1933 and the end of World War II, mainly but not exclusively from Germany and Austria. Their achievements were made possible by the interplay between cultural patterns and social structures that existed before they arrived and the new elements that they brought to their various disciplines and lines of endeavor in this country.

The impact of the flow of ideas from a point of origin to a point of destination can be assessed in two distinct ways. One may utilize such "objective" measures as citation indexes or various types of content analysis. Although such measurements have sometimes yielded impressive results, this is not the method I have followed here. I believe that a crucial dimension gets lost in an approach that neglects human agency, the interaction of human beings in the process of intellectual exchanges. In the last analysis, the history of ideas, like all history, is about people and their interrelationships with their fellows. To be sure, a great deal of cultural transmission comes about via impersonal channels such as the printed media and, more recently, by electronic means. However, such impersonal processes have always been supplemented by personal contacts between human agents. It makes a great deal of difference whether you read somebody's book, correspond with him by mail, talk to him on the telephone, or consult with him in the office next door. Modern structuralist arguments to the contrary notwithstanding, intellectual history is largely about the interaction of human beings. The experience of being taught by a great scientist or a great humanist scholar cannot be duplicated by even the most diligent perusal of published works or by listening to even a major paper at an occasional international meeting.

If it is true that many of the most formative influences on the life of the mind arise through personal contacts and exchanges of ideas,[1] a study of the infusion of European cultural elements into the American mainstream through several thousand European intellectuals who arrived on these shores after the rise of Hitler seems worth undertaking. In order for cultural materials to be transmitted successfully, there must exist an audience that is at least potentially receptive to new messages. What has to be studied, then, is not a simple flow of messages from originators to consumers but a two-way flow between potential transmitters and potential receivers. Messages remain without effect if they are not listened to. That is why this study focuses not only on what the refugee intellectuals had to offer but also on the social and cultural conditions in the country of refuge which, as it were, fostered or impeded the reception of their teachings. There were undoubtedly periods in American history when receptivity to new sets of ideas was much less pronounced than it was in the New Deal era during which the refugees arrived here. Americans, whether intellectuals or not, were more receptive listeners in the period of social and intellectual turmoil during the Great Depression and the New Deal effort at reconstruction than they would have been in the complacent years that followed the First World War.

Even in periods of general receptivity, different intellectual domains or academic disciplines are likely to show differential inclinations to accept novel ideas from the outside. As shall be shown, certain disciplines in the American scholarly world, such as academic psychology, proved more resistant to the impact of refugee scholars than others, such as psychoanalysis. Various degrees of readiness to listen to new voices and the differential receptivity in various scholarly and cultural circles will hence have to be attended to if the impact of the refugees is to be traced and assessed. Moreover, and in tune with what has been said about the central importance of human agents in the diffusion of culture, an effort has to be made to trace the specific persons within the American context who helped foster or impede these new human contacts. A good deal of attention will have to be paid to various networks of influence and the interpersonal ties that came to link newcomers to those already settled in specific intellectual territories.[2]

When I first conceived the idea of writing a book on this subject, I was momentarily stymied by the vastness of the enterprise. How, short of producing an encyclopedia, could one do justice to the many groups and individuals of various backgrounds, disciplinary interests, statuses, and achievements who clamored for inclusion? What seemed to be called for was the collective effort of a number of scholars rather than the labors of one individual. When I finally decided nevertheless to take a stab at this enormous subject, I did so by adopting and adhering more or less to a self-denying ordinance. I would restrict myself to certain categories

of persons and certain cultural subject matters, eschewing the temptation to tell the whole story.

In the first place, I decided not to deal with the natural sciences and
the arts. This was partly because my expertise in these areas is limited
and partly because a fairly extensive literature in these areas already
exists. This book, hence, deals largely with the social sciences and the
humanities, although I have devoted a short section to belles lettres.
Even within these cultural areas, I have not dealt with a number of
scholarly disciplines. In some cases they are fields, such as anthropology,
upon which European refugees had no discernible impact. In other cases,
such as that of international law, which was indeed deeply influenced by
European scholars, I regretfully concluded that treatment in these pages
would force me to deal with the intricacies of a highly specialized field
removed from the concerns of all but relatively few readers.

Generally, then, as a glance at the table of contents will indicate, I have
limited myself to those major areas in the humanities and the social sciences that are relatively familiar and of central interest to the nonspecialist reader. I nevertheless do not doubt that many of my readers will
complain that I have neglected this or that particular area of special
concern to them. In the last analysis, I know of no foolproof objective
criterion in such matters, so that I had to rely on the partially subjective
evaluation of what I consider significant. I have tried to eschew purely
idiosyncratic criteria of choice of subject matter, but I am well aware
that, unless one attempts encyclopedic coverage, a measure of personal
taste and orientation cannot be entirely avoided.

The matter of choice becomes even more salient in regard to the selection of particular individuals to be included in this study. I decided
from the outset that I would include only persons who received their
major education in Europe. Since my topic is the transmission of knowledge and cultural elements across the Atlantic, it stands to reason that I
have had to exclude young refugees who pursued a significant part of
their higher education in this country. A large and brilliant array of such
scholars—let me mention only Peter Gay in history or Peter Blau and
Reinhard Bendix in sociology—has had great impact on American
scholarship, but I shall not deal with them in these pages. Although
their careers in this country might well be a very important subject of
study for students of contemporary American culture, only those scholars who arrived here with at least a completed university education or,
as in most cases, with a junior or senior position in a European academic
institution are discussed in this book.

I deal largely with men and women who arrived in this country after
Hitler's assumption of power in early 1933. Yet I have broken my rule
in a few cases by including some persons who were already in this coun-

try at the time, as guest professors or holders of fellowships. I judged in these cases that the likelihood was high that they would have come to America as refugees had they not already been here.

I have assumed that in order to make a major impact on the culture of the receiving country, refugee scholars need a fairly extended period of acclimatization and adjustment. I have therefore excluded a number of individuals who spent relatively few years in this country. Most French scholars and intellectuals who came here after the fall of France have not been dealt with, since almost all of them speedily returned home after the liberation. I have also not dealt with persons who died after a relatively short stay in America. This was a hard decision to make, and it again involves a measure of personal choice. It seemed rather unproblematic to exclude the prominent German psychologist William Stern, who taught for only four years at Duke University before his death in 1938 and who had little impact on American colleagues. The matter was more complicated with the great neo-Kantian philosopher Ernst Cassirer, whose influence on American philosophy was considerable. But the fact that he taught in this country—at Yale and Columbia—for only four years before his death in 1945 made me decide to exclude him from consideration. Generally, then, I have dealt only with men and women who remained in America for a sufficiently long period to become imbedded in relatively stable and enduring networks of relationships with American colleagues and students.

Perhaps my most complicated problem when deciding whom to include and whom to exclude had to do with the nature of the intellectual influence that individuals or groups of individuals exerted when they came to their new cultural environment. It might be argued, for example, that the influence of a particular scholar derived simply from transmitting sets of ideas acquired in his home country to colleagues and students from his country of refuge who were acquainted with them. In this view, the transmitter need only be a kind of retailer of knowledge without himself contributing creatively in his own work. There is no doubt that many refugee intellectuals in fact played such a role and that their influence in America was consequential. Such is the case with those, for example, who chose, or were forced to choose, to teach in small Southern colleges both black and white, and who were often the first ambassadors of European scholarship and cosmopolitan culture in these settings. They remain the unsung heroes of American higher education. I nevertheless decided not to concern myself with such persons, even though I feel that there is an urgent need to assess their impact. I decided instead to focus on those who, while serving as conduits of previously acquired knowledge, made independent creative contributions in their areas of interest and competence which had a discernible impact in their adopted country.

The decision to concentrate on persons who were able to make significant cultural or scholarly contributions in America has the drawback of implying a kind of bias in favor of those who had successful careers here. But *success* in this context only means receiving a hearing. By definition, then, only those who received a hearing (were successful) could have an impact, while those who, for whatever reason, were denied success were not listened to even though they may have had an important message to convey. The reasons for success or lack of success in an American setting will be discussed at some length later in this introduction. Here suffice it to say that, while I have dealt largely with those persons who left a mark on American scholarly and cultural developments, I have also included, for purposes of contrast, the case of the eminent psychologists Charlotte and Karl Buehler, whose careers in America were marked by utter failure even though their previous work in Europe was outstanding and secured for them an important niche in the annals of psychology. The section on creative writers also deals with some failures as well as with successes.

As will be readily apparent, the various chapters of this book are by no means standardized. Some are considerably longer than others. In particular, some deal in a certain degree of depth with the European careers of the subjects, while others pass over the European background rather lightly. This is so because I judged in a number of cases that only a relatively extensive description of European antecedents would allow assessment of these persons' subsequent careers in this country; in other cases, such background information seemed of minimal value for the purposes of this study. There are also more mundane reasons for the differences in format among individual chapters. In some cases a good deal of biographical or autobiographical information was readily available, but in others such information was scarce. It may be that for those in the latter category archival resources would have disclosed additional information, but such research proved not feasible for me and awaits exploration by a subsequent generation of historians of ideas.

Acknowledgments

Strange as it may seem, given the fact that I myself am a refugee, the first impetus for writing this book came from a suggestion made by my friend Peter Rose of Smith College, a native-born American sociologist. I am most grateful to him. His forthcoming book on the various rescue organizations that helped refugees to come to this country will be a fine complement to my efforts.

Work on this book was begun while I was a Fellow of the Center for Advanced Study in the Behavioral Sciences, Palo Alto, in 1979–80. It was completed during a stay at the Maison des Sciences de l'Homme, Paris, in 1983–84. I am most grateful to both institutions for their support, for access to clerical and library staff, but above all for the close contact with colleagues which they provided. These men and women proved to be willing listeners and active critical sounding boards for ideas which needed nurturing in a congenial atmosphere.

A number of colleagues in several disciplines were good enough to provide critical readings of one or more chapters of this work. Their help was especially appreciated when it came to areas in which my knowledge is limited. I especially wish to thank Moses Abramovitz, Werner Angress, Paul Benacerref, William M. Calder III, Alexander Erlich, Victor Erlich, Creighton Gilbert, William J. Goode, Robert Heilbroner, Mary Henle, Alex Inkeles, David Morrison, Robert K. Merton, Hans Speier, Michael Walzer, and Hans Zeisel. Others, too numerous to mention, offered help in a variety of ways. Many colleagues who were kind enough to help me in the research for different chapters are acknowledged in the notes.

The critical and exacting editorial standards and acumen of my wife, Rose Laub Coser, tempered by enduring empathy and love, have been as centrally important for the completion of this work as they have been for all of my previous writings.

Very special thanks are due to my editor, Gladys Topkis. Her faith in this work when it was still in an embryonic stage sustained me, her superb editorial skills when the book was nearing completion were indispensable.

Lewis A. Coser

Paris
October 1983

I
Introduction

The Refugees: Loss and Generation of Prestige

The refugee intellectuals who arrived from central Europe between 1933 and the end of World War II, though scarred by their recent experiences, nevertheless seem to have been revitalized by their arrival in this country. They usually testified to the truth of Francis Bacon's statement that "The fortune of an exiled man . . . has quickened in him all seats of observation and industry."[1] Yet they soon discovered the truth in Marx's dictum that "men make their own history, but not as they please."[2] That is, they found that their aspirations encountered obdurate constraints imposed by American culture and the American social structure. Their aspirations tended to be high, but their attainments during the initial period of adjustment and acculturation were often disappointing.

The hosts' receptivity to new messages is only one side of the equation between transmitters of cultural messages and their recipients. The other side concerns the characteristics of the cultural agents—that is, the refugee intellectuals themselves.

At this point, a major difference between immigrants, exiles, and refugee intellectuals must be noted. Immigrants leave their country for the most part voluntarily to make a permanent change of residence—although, to be sure, some of them may later decide to return. Exiles, in contrast, are forced to leave, yet hope, at least in the beginning, to return to their country of birth "as soon as the political regime changes." The great majority of the refugee intellectuals I deal with here, most of them Jewish, decided from the beginning to make this country their new permanent home. They were thus more like new immigrants, although some of them, as the following pages will show, can more properly be considered—and considered themselves—to be exiles.

But the refugee intellectuals differed from other immigrants in at least one significant respect. Immigrants, with some exceptions, tend to come from low socioeconomic status positions; refugee intellectuals, in contrast, usually came from positions fairly high on the status ladder, where they had lived in relative comfort and were accustomed to receiving a certain deference and respect. While the immigrants, despite discrimination and exploitation, generally experienced their position in the new country as an advance, most refugee intellectuals suffered, at least at first, from the fact that their status in the new country was inferior to what they had felt as their due at home. The status of the professoriat, for example, is higher in central Europe than it is here. In addition, even when refugee scholars attained professorial rank here, it was most likely not in the most prestigious academic institutions. Adjustments to new conditions was hence likely to pose some problems for refugee intellectuals that were not shared by ordinary immigrants. While the point of reference for the latter will initially be friends and associates at home who rank fairly low in the status hierarchy, the refugees have as their point of reference former colleagues and associates who continue to hold fairly high-status positions at home. Thus there are built-in sources of frustration for refugee intellectuals that normally do not come into play among ordinary immigrants. In addition, just because the refugees were in many respects so very like their native counterparts and yet were treated here, at least at first, as very unlike them, they felt relatively deprived.[3]

The refugees of the 1930s differed significantly from most previous groups of emigrés in their extraordinary heterogeneity. The Byzantine scholars who came to Italy shortly before and after the fall of Constantinople were part of a unified cultural stratum. The German intellectuals who came to America as political exiles after the failure of the Revolution of 1848 were perhaps not quite so similar in social origin, but at least they were similar in their political allegiances. The Huguenots driven out of France after the revocation of the Edict of Nantes, and the Jews and Marranos who fled to Amsterdam, Salonika, Venice, and Leghorn to seek refuge from the Grand Inquisition, largely came from similar strata with like occupational and class backgrounds. In contrast, the refugees of the 1930s were widely diverse both in background and in their reasons for coming here. They were moved by political, racial, and moral forces—and some came for two or all three of these reasons. Their political coloration comprised the whole gamut from conservative to Communist, even though liberals predominated. Many of them fled because of racial persecution; Jews, half- and even one-quarter-Jews, who might or might not have opposed the regime of their homeland had it not been for their racial characteristics, comprised the largest group. Others came because of their moral revulsion from the Fascist regimes of central and southern Europe. In addition, the professional and occupational backgrounds of the refugees differed considerably, even among those who may loosely be called intellectuals.[4] This great diversity helps account to some extent for their variant modes of adaptation to American conditions.

Refugees, immigrants, exiles, and even ordinary travelers face a critical physical problem: how much is it worthwhile to carry from the old setting to the new? But more important than the physical baggage is the intellectual and moral baggage they are able to carry. Prestige and skill are central in this respect. Whatever bits of prestige or social esteem have been accumulated during a lifetime seem crucial for the future, yet it is not always possible to carry these across the Atlantic. Refugees may take along a few letters of recommendation; they may try to reactivate acquaintances with native scholars met at international meetings or on previous visits, yet all but the few truly great international figures soon realize that much of their prestige and esteem remains in the minds of those they have left behind.

Among scholars, any one who moves to a new work setting faces the problem of transferring status and prestige acquired in one environment to another. This is especially pronounced for those who are "local" rather than "cosmopolitan" in their orientation—that is, those who derive their status mainly from recognition by their immediate colleagues and are hence attuned to the local scene, as contrasted to those who are attuned to the wider intellectual world and who attempt to gain recognition from a wider public of fellow intellectuals. The problem is even more pronounced for refugees, who not only must move from one specific reference group to another but are faced with adjusting to a whole new culture and society. Under these conditions, rates of failure are likely to be higher, at least initially, than for those who move within the same culture. What, then, are the conditions under which people's reputations can be successfully carried with them into a new country?

A central factor in such transfers of prestige and esteem is the degree of similarity between the native land and the country of refuge in intellectual requirements—what might be called the "rules of the game." A tennis champion, say, will find the same rules at home and abroad. He needs no relearning in a new country in order to maintain his ranking. The games of intellectuals, however, present significant differences from nation to nation. For many refugees much frustration stemmed from their feeling that many of the skills, talents, and achievements they had to their credit could not be displayed under the new rules. They often found themselves in the paradoxical situation of feeling superior to the members of the group whose approval or esteem they sought, while the members of the new group frequently perceived them as inferior for not knowing the rules of the game. Unfortunately for the refugee, it is usually the natives who define how the game is to be played and determine who wins.

The nature of the intellectual skills that the refugees brought to this country was one of the major determinants of their relative success or failure in finding a niche in America. To the extent that such skills were transferable, adjustment was facilitated. Engineers, physicists, some chemists, and other technically trained specialists found it easy to gain employment and status. Since "blueprints have no language," and the language of the natural sciences is largely mathematical and not bound to the vernacular, language barriers proved to be minimal obstacles for them.[5] Moreover, the international culture of science, with its many international congresses and seminars and its rich tradition of collaboration between scientists of different nationalities, allowed refugee scientists to profit from networks that they had already been a part of before they came to this country. In a similar way, for the Austrian economists of the so-called marginal-utility school, working in the tradition of mathematical economics and neoclassical approaches, it was relatively easy to establish themselves in leading universities, where they found colleagues who shared with them their language of mathematics as well as agreement as to the central problems of economic thought.

In contrast, those whose intellectual skills were more deeply rooted in the national traditions of their countries of origin faced greater obstacles. While Austrian economists highly trained in mathematics and neoclassical economics faced few difficulties, their German colleagues, having been trained largely in historical economics, found the going much rougher. Few of them managed to gain entry into major departments of economics in this country. Both types of economists often found an initial haven at the New School for Social Research, which was atypically hospitable to all types of European thought; but those with mathematical and neoclassical orientation soon moved on, whereas many of the others stayed there.

Or consider the fairly large number of lawyers and jurisprudents who came here as refugees. They were trained in Roman law and knew little about Anglo-Saxon common law. As a consequence, with the exception of the handful who managed to teach the history of Roman law, they were faced with the necessity of starting afresh. Many of them eventually became professors of political science or of international relations, while others drifted into occupations that had scant connection with their skills.

In other cases, such as medicine, Europeans could not automatically establish new practices but had to spend a year as interns and pass licensing examinations. Physicians who had held mature status and reputations in their native land felt that examinations and certification procedures were degrading rites.

Most academic men and women outside the natural sciences and engineering found that they had to reduce their high expectations if they were to find a position in the academic hierarchy. Many who had hoped for an appointment at Columbia or Berkeley found that Purdue or

Southern Methodist proved the only realistic alternative. As William J. Goode puts it, "Refugees of high rank have often had to decide that since people in the United States would not pay them all the deference they had been accustomed to in their own country, they would have to lower their demands in order to be accepted socially. They had to predict by how much they should lower the overt respect asked for in order to obtain a needed social circle of adequate rank."[6]

Related to the issue of differential skills are previous prestige and age. No matter what their age, persons of extraordinarily high international status like Thomas Mann or Albert Einstein or Kurt Goedel, found no obstacle to assuming positions in this country commensurate with their previous status. The matter was problematic, however, for refugees below this top rank. For them, previous positions could not so readily be translated into their American equivalents. Men and women who had already attained the rank of professor in their homeland soon found that they had relatively few chances to join the faculties of major American universities. One reason for this was the prevailing market.

The main flow of refugees arrived here at the time of the Great Depression, when the academic market was tight; the newcomers were resented by many native aspirants, who complained about unfair competition. Those refugees who were Jews frequently faced anti-Semitic prejudices, which were still virulent in many academic quarters.[7] It was rarely realized that the newcomers came here with a completed education, so that the host country could make use of them, so to speak, cost-free. Their educational expenses having been borne at home, they would be able to make contributions that were a net credit to the host country.

In addition to competition between natives and refugees, another factor created difficulties for the newcomers. The status claims of European intellectuals were by no means automatically endorsed by American colleagues, who in many cases rejected the orientations of the Europeans. For example, at a time when American psychology was dominated by behaviorism, none of the three key figures in Gestalt psychology received a major university appointment.

It is part of the wonderful irony that attended so much of the early reception of refugee scholars in America that most of them were hired at first by colleges or minor universities, where teaching rather than research was at a premium. The experience of teaching in an undergraduate institution was often disastrous for both the refugees and their hosts. In the first place, Europeans had had no exposure to the classroom routines of undergraduate teaching in America, found them exceedingly demanding, and often were just not very good at them. In addition, although accomplishments in research are relatively easy to appraise because the visible work is available in print and can be consulted, the work of a teacher is not directly visible to colleagues. His reputation is contingent upon the testimony of members of previous networks.

Many such institutions hired refugees out of compassion and felt that they had a right to expect gratitude in return. Yet the refugee scholars frequently felt degraded by such offers, as the schools that employed them were lower in rank than the ones from which they had come. School administrators frequently felt that they were paying the new European faculty member a great compliment by the attention they were giving him or her, while the recipient of the intended compliment felt demeaned. Many refugee teachers failed to realize that one's prestige ranking is largely determined by the community to which one belongs, so that if one leaves one's community of origin it is necessarily the new community that will decide, usually by a process of trial and error, how high a rank one will be able to attain.

Further, the refugees frequently had an aloof and condescending personal and scholarly style that did not sit well in the more open and democratic atmosphere of America. Their stiffness, distance, and rigid insistence on being addressed by their full professorial titles often made them the butt of nasty jokes and aggressive comments, although the same traits would often be found endearing once their colleagues had become accustomed to their foibles.

Refugee scholars usually received a warmer reception in the Middle West and in California than in the older intellectual centers of the Eastern seaboard. Similarly, when emigré scholars moved to Washington during the war years, few of them found niches in the old established government departments such as the Pentagon, the Treasury, or the Foreign Service, but many were received with open arms by newly established agencies such as the Office of Strategic Services (OSS), which valued the refugees' skills.[8]

When one turns from an older generation that had already attained some eminence in Europe to younger academics who had as yet reached only the lower ranks in academic hierarchies or had only recently received the doctoral degree, one notes that by and large the younger scholars met fewer obstacles on their academic pathways. They did not claim as much deference as their elders. They may actually have been relieved at not having to maintain the hierarchical forms of etiquette they had learned to expect at home. They were less rigid in their orientations, less burdened by family responsibilities, and, since they had no immediate expectations of joining prestigious institutions, more prepared to climb the academic ladder in ways similar to those of their native-born colleagues. They had time to develop networks of colleagues and to learn the patterns of ingratiation and making oneself known among the powers-that-be.

Scholars of the older generation often found it hard to build networks that would help enhance their prestige and their likelihood of success in America. Even those who attempted to reestablish ties carried over from Europe typically did not have many ties to exploit. Hence these older refugees, even if they had the needed abilities, were not always known to be available, and they in turn did not know about existing opportunities. The refugees' network and the network of potential employers did not overlap enough for adequate communication.

The field of knowledge of the refugees was strongly related to their fate in the host environment. The influence they would have was largely determined by the status and prestige they would gain here, but these were not equally accessible in the various branches of knowledge. The refugees seem to have been most influential in areas of study where they filled a perceived need not previously met, or in fields in which they encountered an already established tradition to which they felt affinity so that they could build on already established scholarly traditions. Matters became difficult in areas where there was little fit between the newcomers' skills and native American intellectual traditions and requirements. Psychoanalysis falls unambiguously into the first category; social psychology and philosophy, into the second. Art history falls between the first and second categories; academic psychology falls largely into the last.

Prior to the 1930s, psychoanalysis was either a stepchild within the academy and the medical schools or was excluded entirely. Only a few academic or medical institutions paid any attention to it. Psychiatry was largely hostile to it. That all this has changed is largely owing to the coming of refugees and their eager reception by a new generation of psychiatrists and academics.

In contrast, philosophy had a long history in America, and American philosophers had already produced major works long before the arrival of the refugees. Yet no historian of philosophy would deny that the coming of Rudolf Carnap and other members of the Vienna Circle deeply influenced the subsequent course of philosophical inquiries in this country. The members of the Vienna Circle quickly gained a hearing largely because they fitted into networks of American philosophers, whether they were pragmatists or followers of the Russell or early Wittgensteinian tradition in England. Most Vienna Circle philosophers gained prestigious university positions and were able to make major contributions to American philosophy of science and to symbolic logic. By contrast, European philosophers of the phenomenological school, which had only a few isolated upholders in America, found openings only in universities of lesser rank or at the New School for Social Research.

Similarly, social psychologists such as Kurt Lewin and Paul F. Lazarsfeld found a thriving, although undeveloped, tradition when they arrived here, and yet were instrumental in transforming the field, not only by making major contributions, but by training a large number of students who have continued to walk in their footsteps.

Art history, as I have said, falls somewhere in between. "Its native tongue," as an American scholar said to Erwin Panofsky, "is German."[9] It came into its own in America only after World War I, but it was already thriving by the time Panofsky and other gifted art historians, many of them trained at the Warburg Institute, arrived in this country. Yet these scholars, largely sustained by networks of American colleagues, made consequential contributions to American art history.

Finally, in general psychology, where the behaviorist tradition held unquestioned sway in America, European psychologists, who were judged to be upholders of outdated "mentalist" conceptions, found a cool and often hostile reception.

Marginality and Critical Perspective

I have put much stress on the success or lack of success of refugees in their various fields of study not because I consider the bitch goddess a particularly admirable deity but because success seems clearly related to acculturation in American society and hence to the ability to make creative contributions here. The higher the status that accompanies success, the higher the degree of acculturation.[10] Those who gained recognition from superiors or peers rooted themselves more easily and more deeply in American soil.

The impact of refugee intellectuals on America can best be summarized by what H. Stuart Hughes has called the deprovincialization of the American mind.[11] To be sure, the great figures in American intellectual history of the past had not confined their attention to things American. Many of them had drawn sustenance from European thought through study abroad or through attention to European ideas. Yet it is undeniable that the American mind was much stretched through its encounters with the refugee intellectuals. One need only ponder the impact of, to cite at random, Hannah Arendt, Bruno Bettelheim, Erik H. Erikson, Herbert Marcuse, or Vladimir Nabokov, in addition to others already mentioned.

The refugees could deprovincialize the American mind and upgrade American culture largely because they remained marginal. This made it possible for them to throw a novel and more searching light on American society and scholarship than was usually the case with those born and bred in the pieties of their tradition. Steeped in historical and critical traditions that often clashed with the present-mindedness and optimism that pervaded so much of American culture, from the vantage point of their status as marginal scholars they exercised their privilege to think otherwise and so to become salutory disturbers of America's intellectual peace.

The marginality to which I have alluded stemmed from at least two different motivations and had two different types of consequences. In order to understand this fact, it seems important to remember that refugee scholars fell into two broad categories: those who saw themselves as exiles—that is, who did not wish to stay permanently in America— and those who intended and wished to stay, even though they never managed to become more than marginal natives.

A minority saw America as only a temporary refuge which they would leave for their homeland as soon as political conditions permitted. These men and women regarded themselves as exiles rather than immigrants, even though some of them acquired American citizenship. Such persons, as Mary McCarthy has written, "are more like birds than plants, perching wherever they are, ready for homeward flight. Even when they have funds to buy a little house, take a long lease on a flat, they prefer transient accommodations."[12] The eminent political scientist Arnold Brecht, who taught for decades at the New School, lived for the whole of his stay in a series of furnished hotel rooms near Central Park. He and his wife rearranged the hotel furniture to their taste, cooked on a hotplate, and, not having a kitchen sink, washed their dishes in the bathroom. Figuratively, if not literally, their luggage was always packed.[13] Hannah Arendt and her husband, Heinrich Bluecher, lived for a long time in an uncomfortable New York hotel "because," said one of their friends, "they felt it was unbecoming for people like [them] to have an apartment with furniture of [their] own." When this friend, the refugee writer Henry Pachter, bought a second-hand car, they remonstrated "as though [he] had betrayed them."[14]

Exiles always live in tense expectation of impending political change in the homeland. This prevents them from taking the initiative to find a secure niche in their country of refuge. When the former premier of Italy, Francesco Nitti, who had been overthrown by Mussolini, was asked what he was doing in Paris, he answered, "I am waiting."[15] Such persons typically felt that the Fascists who had driven them from their homeland were aberrations whose reign could not possibly last. The philosopher Ernst Cassirer once explained to Henry Pachter, "You know, this Hitler is an error of history; he does not belong in German history at all. And therefore he will perish."[16] Such an attitude may have been extreme, but it was shared to one degree or another by many of those who considered themselves to be exiles in America. Such persons typically never sought much contact with native American intellectuals and preferred to live in cocoons of their own weaving. The great Austrian writer Hermann Broch lived for over a decade in Princeton without establishing any significant contacts with native American writers or scholars. A compulsive letter writer, he had hardly any native-born correspondents. When asked whether he was not influenced by American writers, he responded that he surely was, but that he was also influenced by Tolstoi and Dostoevski but didn't have to live in Russia for that purpose. The Bavarian poet and novelist Oscar Maria Graf lived for over twenty years in New York City without learning any English, and though he was deeply influenced by Whitman, Hemingway, and other American authors, he read them only in German translation. Since such writers did not profit from contemporary, living culture in America, they could also not contribute to it. The exiles' contribution to American culture was, at best, indirect.

While self-conscious exiles among the refugee scholars oriented themselves to points of reference across the ocean, whether real or nostalgic, the majority of the refugee intellectuals made efforts to integrate themselves in a cultural American setting that they expected to be their significant environment for the rest of their lives. Some of them started out with the mentality of exiles but were gradually caught up within the network of American cultural life, so that, wittingly or unwittingly, they were sooner or later absorbed into the American intellectual world.

Yet degrees of absorption differed considerably. Political scientist Franz Neumann insightfully distinguished among three types who were determined to make their life career in America: (1) those scholars who were willing to abandon their previous intellectual positions and accept their new orientations without qualification; (2) those who wanted to cling to their own thought structure and either believed they had a mission totally to revamp the American pattern or withdrew with disdain and contempt into islands of their own; and (3) those who attempted an integration of new experience with old tradition. This third position, Neumann believed, and I concur, was the most difficult but also the most rewarding, solution.[17]

Neumann's insights can be amplified when it is realized that these three modalities are not due to happenstance but have their roots in the variant positions of these men and women in the social networks in which they were enmeshed and the social positions they variously occupied in America.

Those who found their niches in social locations which they shared with many fellow refugees, such as those belonging to the Horkheimer circle and, less pronouncedly, those who taught at the New School, tended to be parochial in their orientations. Largely living in the Gemeinschaft-like groups where they were surrounded by like-minded peers and students, they developed only a limited capacity to deal with native-born scholars who had different vantage points. These refugees tended to think in linguistic categories, in which, as the British social psychologist Basil Bernstein has written, "The intent of the other person can be taken for granted as the speech is played out against the backdrop of common assumptions, common history, common interests."[18] Speaking largely to the initiated rather than to a larger and more diversified audience, they tended to a particularistic approach—that is, one that was context-bound to local relationships and a local structure. Even though they were not totally insulated from the surrounding intellectual community, they tended to restrict their contact with it. In such an environment, persons who belonged to Neumann's second type—those who clung to their own thought structure—were likely to find optimum conditions for sustenance.

Neumann's first and third types, consisting of those who wished to shed their previous intellectual baggage and those who wished to integrate the old and the new, seemed to thrive best under conditions in which they were forced to build a new world of ideas under the stimulus of a variety of colleagues and associates of differing backgrounds. Under such circumstances, they could no longer use the restricted language they used with intimates but had to develop elaborate speech patterns in an effort to come to grips with the diverse perspectives they encountered among associates when making contributions of their own. As Rose Laub Coser, to whose conceptualization this train of thought is largely indebted, has argued, "The various intentions of others have to be gauged, and one's own actions have to be adapted to one's expectations of the different ways in which those others are going to behave."[19] In settings in which the refugee intellectuals found themselves in mixed scholarly company, they were best able to transcend their previous style of thought. They might in some cases have tried to shed their previous identity and identifications completely and become more American than the native-born, or they might have made deliberate efforts to integrate previous with current perspectives acquired through intercourse with colleagues from different backgrounds.

H. Stuart Hughes, in a lecture at the Smithsonian Institution, observed that one of the preconditions for satisfactory integration of refugee intellectuals and for their creative influence on American scholars concerns the critical mass of the emigrés themselves. In order to bring their influence to bear, they needed to be concentrated in sufficient numbers. By the same token, there needed to be enough of them in each place or institution to provide mutual support, whether intellectual or emotional. But the optimum situation was when the mass was not overwhelming. In a setting where Central Europeans outnumbered the native-born, life was deceptively easy and familiar for them. The balance between enough and too many is always delicate.[20]

Settings in which refugee intellectuals were neither isolated, overpowered by native-born colleagues, nor ensconced in a close group where they mostly talked to each other were most likely to encourage types of scholarship that enabled them to integrate their previous training with perspectives that had grown on native soil. Under these conditions, it would seem, they could serve effectively as "bridges" between the learning of the old world and the new, even though they, too, paid the price of marginality, whether they wanted it or not.

No matter what their specific subjective dispositions or objective location, almost all refugee intellectuals were to one extent or another strangers in the land of their refuge. All of them, or almost all, fit Georg Simmel's classical depiction of the stranger:

> He is, so to speak, the *potential* wanderer: although he has not moved on, he has not quite overcome the freedom of coming and going. He is fixed within a particular spatial group or within a group whose boundaries are similar to spatial boundaries. But his position in this group is determined, essentially, by the fact that he has not belonged to it from the beginning, that he imports qualities into it, which do not and cannot stem from the group itself. The unity or nearness and remoteness involved in every human relation is organized, in the phenomenon of the stranger, in a way which may be most briefly formulated by saying that in relationship to him, distance means that he who is close by is far, and strangeness means that he who is also far, is actually near.[21]

The sociologist-philosopher Alfred Schutz has elaborated on Simmel's acute observations in an essay also called "The Stranger."[22] Strangers cannot share with the native-born the memories of youth. Many of the natives' ties stem from having gone to the same college or even high school, having known each others' boyfriends or girlfriends, and remembering many common youthful experiences, both joyful and sad. Refugees, to use a term coined by the French sociologist Maurice Halbwachs, cannot participate in the nation's collective memories.[23] In addition, not having been part of networks that youthful natives find so useful for selecting graduate schools and establishing their subsequent careers, refugees have few acquaintances and networks they can call upon when the occasion demands it. Being deprived of a collectively shared past is a significant impediment in present conduct as well as future planning.

People usually accept the ready-made scheme or cultural pattern handed down by parents, associates, teachers, and authorities as largely unquestioned guides for conduct in the social world. Yet the stranger, having been reared in a different pattern, does not share the basic assumptions of his present associates. Strangers question much that seems to be unquestionable to members of the host group. To them, "the cultural pattern of the [new] group does not have the authority of a tested system of recipes, and this, if for no other reason, because [they do] not partake in the vivid historical tradition by which it has been formed."[24] Seen from the perspective of the new group, they are people without history. They may, of course, learn about the new country's past as a means of anticipatory socialization, but this is learned, not experienced, history.

But, as I have noted, inability to share fully the experience of their hosts brings considerable advantages even as it may impose a great burden. Finding it hard to gain their bearings in a world they never helped to make, refugees are compelled to cultivate a detached form of knowledge that will help them along paths not marked by traditional signposts. They are structurally compelled to use analytical reasoning, where for the insiders custom and habit are sufficient guides to conduct. If the new group abhors and rejects such analytical reasoning, the strangers may be expelled or ostracized, but if it values such knowledge, it will extend them recognition.

American culture by and large prizes and values objective and analytical thought. It therefore welcomed the contribution of refugee intellectuals, even if it was also a little distrustful of their cold intelligence, unregardful, as it often seemed, of received verities and pieties. The refugee intellectuals therefore found America, by and large, willing to listen to their voices, although they were often held at a distance. Those among them who wished to make their home in America therefore became acculturated relatively quickly. But only their sons and daughters were likely to become fully assimilated. Strangers may learn to speak the language of their new community with considerable fluency, but they are unlikely to speak it without at least a slight accent, which remains the stigma of otherness. Their children speak without an accent.

II
Psychology and Psychoanalysis

Introduction

Refugee academic psychologists and psychoanalysts suffered contrasting fates after coming to America. The psychologists as a group were only minimally successful, both in their personal careers and in the reception of their teachings; the psychoanalysts were phenomenally successful in both respects.

The dominant orientation among American psychologists in the 1930s and 1940s was behaviorism in one or another form. Therefore, the American psychological establishment viewed with a good deal of suspicion European refugees who were, so it was thought, still committed to some kind of "unscientific," "mentalistic" approach to the study of human conduct. As a result, when the three founders of the Gestalt tradition of European psychology, Wolfgang Koehler, Max Wertheimer, and Kurt Koffka, came to America, none of them was enabled to keep this tradition alive as an independent focus of inquiry. They were never able to find positions in graduate departments of psychology and were therefore unable to train disciples in their image. Many of the findings of the Gestalt tradition were incorporated piecemeal into the general corpus of American psychology, especially in cognitive studies, and a few Americans made significant contributions; but the Gestalt tradition has by and large petered out in this country. Psychologists Heinz Werner and Kurt Goldstein also never achieved full recognition. Fritz Heider enjoyed and continues to enjoy a great deal of influence, but he is not, technically speaking, a refugee.

Other European psychological orientations suffered an even worse fate in that they found practically no hearing at all. The tragic fate of Charlotte and Karl Buehler, eminent representatives of Viennese child psychology and of the so-called Wuerzburg school, found no university position in America. They were forced to teach in small, unprestigious colleges and suffered a life of isolation and neglect. This may account in large part for their sterility after coming here. Theirs is, to be sure, an extreme case, but it nevertheless seems emblematic of many other cases in which the European psychologists' lack of acceptance of behaviorist premises curtailed their impact or hampered their careers.

There is, however, one conspicuous exception. The social psychologist Kurt Lewin, coming from a milieu and adhering to an orientation closely related to the Gestalt tradition, was eminently successful during his years in this country. When he arrived in America, social psychology, as distinct from other branches of psychology, was not dominated by behaviorism, which thrived mostly in experimental fields. It had no unified orientation and was still partly dominated by various forms of instinct psychology, which had lost its hold in other areas. Kurt Lewin, although denied a major university appointment in psychology until the last period of his life, nevertheless managed almost single-handedly to recast social psychology in the image of his theory of group dynamics. The generation of American social psychologists who began to attain eminence in the 1940s and 1950s was largely trained by Lewin, and today a third generation, mostly trained by Lewin's students, is still the dominant force in a branch of psychological investigation that has now come of age.

The impact of refugee scholars in psychoanalysis differed sharply from that of their colleagues in academic psychology. Theirs was an almost unqualified success story. Even though Sigmund Freud had some ardent disciples in America before World War I, and even though psychoanalysis commanded widespread attention in the 1920s, it remained during those early years a loosely organized congeries of practitioners who adhered only partially to the guiding ideas expounded by the Viennese and European psychoanalytic pioneers. In the late 1920s and early 1930s, some native Young Turks began to advocate more rigorous standards of training, closer ties to academic medicine, and more "orthodox" methods of investigation and treatment.

The European analysts who arrived here from Austria, Germany, and Hungary, allying themselves with some of the Americans, managed within a few years to transform the institutional structure and the practice of psychoanalysis in America. Surrounded by the aura of close association with the founding fathers, they imposed their vision on their American colleagues. At the present time American analysts trained by refugees still largely dominate the psychoanalytic establishment.

Orthodox analysts, while surely having an impact on general culture, largely confined themselves to the theory and practice of the treatment of patients. Others, diverging from orthodoxy to a greater or lesser degree, moved on to concentrate attention on psychoanalytically informed cultural and social analysis. Bruno Bettelheim, Erik H. Erikson, Erich Fromm, and Karen Horney, among others, became leading figures on the American cultural scene, with a general impact far transcending the relatively narrow world of psychiatry. They helped transform the cultural atmosphere of the postwar years. Even if psychoanalysis of both the orthodox and the unorthodox variety seems in something of an eclipse in psychiatry today, its impact on American cultural life, in the social sciences, the humanities, and among the public at large, cannot be questioned. As distinct from general psychologists, the story of refugee psychoanalysts in America is one of triumphant achievement.

Kurt Lewin (1890–1947) and the Renaissance of Social Psychology

When Kurt Lewin arrived in the United States in 1933 as a refugee, he already had significant accomplishments to his credit.[1] He had served as a privatdozent (lecturer) and later as an associate professor of psychology at the University of Berlin and had been for many years a central figure in that university's Psychological Institute. He and his students had published on various subjects in experimental psychology, and he had already developed the key elements of his "field theory," a theoretical approach that stressed the need to study individuals not in terms of genetic factors or biological drives but in terms of the field of forces in the here-and-now in which persons pursue their goals. Not past experiences, as in most psychoanalytic thinking, but present situations and future expectations within environmental fields, so Lewin taught, largely determine the behavior of individuals. Dynamic concepts alone, he felt, such as vectors, tensions, and valences, rather than the static concepts of most current psychology, could do justice to the peculiar nature of human conduct.

Lewin had been an effective teacher in Berlin, and many of his students—Tamara Dembo, Bluma Zeigarnik, and Maria Ovsiankina, for example—had published studies that became in time classical contributions to the study of, for example, the effect of interrupted tasks. Some twenty of his students, he proudly stated, had contributed to no fewer than forty different topics in psychology in the 1920s and early 1930s.

When Lewin came to America, some of his papers were already known to American psychologists in English translations. He had previously served as a visiting professor at Stanford and had given an important programmatic paper at the International Congress of Psychology at Yale

I am deeply grateful to Grace and Fritz Heider for a detailed critical reading of this profile and for much additional information.

in 1929. Moreover, a few Americans who had studied with him at Berlin had made efforts to publicize his work in introductory papers and detailed evaluations.

Nevertheless, Lewin's first experiences in America proved somewhat discouraging. Despite the efforts of Edwin Boring, Lewis Terman, and other prominent psychologists, he did not get a position in a prestigious university department and had to be content with a temporary appointment at the Cornell School of Home Economics. In fact, Lewin never managed during all his years in America to move into the inner sanctum of the psychological establishment. Although he had close ties to many eminent psychologists, the American Psychological Association never selected him for an assignment or appointed him to any important committee. His most significant work, after the Cornell stay, was done on the periphery of the American academy, at the Iowa Child Welfare Research Station, and toward the end of his career, at a research center in the Massachusetts Institute of Technology, largely established with funds that he had raised on his own initiative.

Even though most knowledgeable observers agree that anti-Semitism quite often hampered the attempts of refugee scholars to secure academic positions in America, it is usually rather difficult to document this. In Lewin's case, there exists at least one solid piece of evidence. The Boring papers at Harvard contain a letter from Lewis Terman of Stanford seeking some information before even a visiting appointment could be arranged for Lewin at Stanford. Terman asked Boring "whether Lewin is a Jew. It would not necessarily be fatal to his appointment here if he were, but it would be best for me to know the facts if I were recommending him. The few Jews we have on our Stanford faculty have no trace whatever of the objectionable traits usually attributed to Jews, and against this kind I haven't the slightest prejudice in the world." Lewin received the appointment even after it was established that he was indeed a Jew, and Terman subsequently became one of his great admirers, but such a letter nevertheless throws a rather brutal footlight on the academic mores of the 1930s.[2]

With all these hampering factors, Lewin nevertheless succeeded in building a brilliant career in America and in raising a whole generation of graduate students who dominated social psychology for several decades. He left an indelible mark on American psychology. Only the psychoanalysts can be compared with him in their influence on their fields in America. What accounts for this "success story" in the face of the relative lack of institutional backing?

Lewin managed soon after his arrival to build a number of bridges to influential colleagues. Jerome Frank, a psychologist and psychiatrist who had been one of his students in Berlin, and Lawrence K. Frank, a psychologist who had become a foundation executive, befriended Lewin soon after he came to America and often served as "brokers" to the powers-that-be. Lawrence Frank, in particular, found positions for Lewin and his students, arranged salaries for him and his associates, and gave him all sorts of personal support. Lewin's appointments at both Cornell and Iowa were due to Lawrence Frank's efforts. Leading American psychologists, such as Henry A. Murray, Edward Tolman, Gardner Murphy, and Gordon Allport, soon recognized Lewin's genius, profited from his work, and were eager to repay him for his stimulation by familiarizing American psychologists with his work. Two former students of his, Donald K. Adams and Karl Zener, translated a few of his most important articles and published this collection under the title *A Dynamic Theory of Personality* in 1935.[3] A year later, Fritz Heider and his American-born wife, Grace Heider, translated Lewin's *Principles of Topological Psychology.*[4] A number of reviews were unfavorable, largely because of misunderstandings of Lewin's novel system, but these books now allowed many more American psychologists, senior and junior, to become familiar with Lewin's thought. Not only psychologists but anthropologists such as Margaret Mead and Ruth Benedict, and other social scientists and business types too, were early drawn to Lewin and his work.

Beginning in 1933, Lewin was mainly responsible for creating a loosely organized discussion group, known as the Topology Group, which met once a year in different settings to consider major themes suggested by Lewin's work. In addition to some of Lewin's former students and his old Gestalt psychology colleagues from the Berlin days, a number of prominent American social scientists—Margaret Mead, Ruth Benedict, Edward Tolman, Henry A. Murray, Gardner Murphy, and Gordon Allport, among others—participated in these annual meetings, which continued to be held for some years even after Lewin's death. In this way, Lewin, although denied a major professorial appointment that could be used as a platform from which to spread his message, created such a platform *ab ovo*.

Nor were the meetings of the Topology Group the only occasion for Lewin to meet with native-born colleagues in the social sciences. He spent part of the war years in Washington, D.C., with the Office of Strategic Services, and it was under the auspices of that organization that he collaborated with Margaret Mead and others in the now-famous studies on changes in food preferences.[5] When wartime shortages highlighted the problem of how best to persuade Americans to eat varieties of meat that they had previously spurned, Lewin enlisted the aid of many colleagues in developing experimental settings that would show what method of persuasion would be most effective. (It proved to be open-ended discussions rather than lectures or "authoritative" demonstrations.)

Just as these studies in the change of personal preferences were first suggested to Lewin by his wartime services, so his later work within industrial settings was initially suggested to him by an encounter with Alfred Marrow, who eventually became his biographer. Marrow was working for his doctorate in psychology in 1935 when he came to see Lewin in Connecticut, just before Lewin was to leave for Iowa. Marrow, as it happened, was not an ordinary student but a wealthy owner of factories in the South. It was Marrow who aroused Lewin's interest in industrial psychology, which led to the many studies carried out by Lewin and his students both in Iowa and at MIT and brought him much renown in the world of progressive management.

Meetings with senior social scientists and with public as well as private decision-makers proved to be important to Lewin, but his major impact on the American scene probably came not from them but from the many students he soon gathered around himself at Iowa. How this recent refugee from Europe, who still spoke English with a marked accent, managed to attract an admiring galaxy of rising young native-born stars, and in Iowa, is still something of a mystery. In the nine years that Lewin spent in Iowa he raised a whole generation of social psychologists who were to dominate the field for several decades. Dorwin Cartwright, Ronald Lippitt, Alexander Bavelas, and Leon Festinger, to mention just a few, were trained at Iowa, as were Morton Deutsch, Stanley Schachter, John R. P. French, and Harold Kelley a few years later. What accounts for this astonishing feat?

To begin with, Lewin had an open, "democratic" method of teaching, far different from the professorial rigidity of many of his fellow refugees. This appealed to the American temperament. His stress on present-day experiences in shaping personality, his rejection of approaches seeking for clues to current behavior in past events, was congenial to many young Americans to whom historical experiences seemed remote and alien. His conviction that psychology would win acceptance only if it could contribute to desirable social change was also congenial to reform-minded young Americans reared in the Depression years and immediately after. This teaching fitted well into the atmosphere of the New Deal, with its stress on social engineering.

Above all, perhaps, it was Lewin's teaching style and infectious enthusiasm that appealed to his young disciples. He was always bubbling over with ideas, ever open to new suggestions, ever exploring new frontiers. One of his students, Donald MacKinnon, has remarked, and Edwin Boring has elaborated, that "Lewin seems not to have required loyalty [as Freud did] yet to have received it. There used to be the communal meetings in which Lewin . . . was always the central figure. . . . We shall not understand Lewin's place in American psychology . . . except in relation to the enthusiasm which his generous, friendly, insistent zealotry created."[6] Iowa soon became not only a training ground and the locale for many experimental studies but the dovecote from which Lewin began to send his disciples to many corners of the academic world bearing his message. The Iowa research monographs, some of them authored or coauthored by Lewin, many more signed by his students, began to exercise a wide influence in psychological circles and beyond.

In the Iowa days, Lewin turned from his Berlin concentration on individual behavior and its determinants to study groups and their effects on individual participants. Books and papers on the consequences of different leadership styles on group performance, of frustration in a group context, of the determinants of group cohesion, of patterns of aggressive behavior, and many more, rapidly followed. After Lewin moved his group to MIT, many more studies were completed. It is not an exaggeration to say that these series of research reports determined the direction American social psychology was to take in the following two or three decades. Other influential studies, such as those by Festinger on cognitive dissonance or by Cartwright and Harary on graph theory, while going a good deal beyond what Lewin taught, would hardly have been conceivable without the groundwork he provided.

It has already been noted in connection with the Topology Group that when Lewin did not find adequate institutional support for his ideas he proceeded to create an institutional framework himself. When further stay in Iowa seemed restrictive, Lewin managed to raise funds to establish a successor to the Iowa group at MIT's Research Center for Group Dynamics, where he did most of his work until his death. When his interest in social action became preponderant in the last years of his life, he managed again to raise private funds to establish the Commission on Community Interrelations in New York, mainly sponsored by the American Jewish Committee, and to find niches there for those of his students who were drawn to "action research." Finally, when the powers-that-be in the American Psychological Association did not avail themselves of Lewin's advice and counsel, he helped to establish the Society for the Psychological Study of Social Issues, which is still today the major gathering ground for social psychologists interested in the application of psychological knowledge to current affairs.

It would seem that toward the end of his life, Lewin was somewhat overinvolved in a great variety of activities, both theoretical and practical, within organizational settings that he had helped to bring into being. His premature death from a heart attack in 1947 may even have been a result of his constant flurry of activity. But be this as it may, Lewin's enthusiastic involvement in many intellectual and practical causes and his participation in a great number of networks on the American scene seem to have been preconditions for his success and for his enduring impact, directly and through his many students. He gave himself most generously and completely to the cause and promise of American democracy, whether as a director and inspirer of research, as counselor, government adviser, or liberal activist. The general public may perhaps best remember him as the originator of "leadership training" in the so-called T-(training) groups which he initiated at the National Training Laboratories in Bethel, Maine, shortly before his death. This initiative was later to lead to the emergence of many sensitivity training groups, some serious and others rather less so, that emerged in the 1950s and 1960s. Even in such a conventional city as Boston, T-groups became part of the training programs for psychiatric residents. While this line of development of Lewin's ideas may have received excessive attention, other research areas, inherently more important, continue unmistakably to carry the mark of his genius. He helped make social psychology into an experimental science. He and his collaborators produced research results that inspired the work of at least one, and perhaps more, subsequent generations. His impact on general psychology, on child psychology, and on action research was perhaps not quite as deep as he had hoped, but it was consequential nevertheless. His influence on the American cultural scene, while hard to measure in precise detail, was certainly significant.

The fact that a number of Lewin's technical terms—"time perspective," "gate keepers," "level of aspirations," "life space," among many others—have penetrated into the vernacular testifies to this fact. This refugee intellectual, located on the periphery of the academic world, succeeded in transforming a significant corner of its map. Edward Tolman, in an assessment of Lewin's work, is probably correct when he says: "Far more important than any final more precise evaluation of the details of Lewin's theoretical system was its extreme fruitfulness."[7] And one of his students, John R. P. French, has remarked that: "Somehow he seemed to be able to transmit to others a little of his own enormous creativity."[8] We may perhaps add that Lewin was able to do this because he was forever weaving new networks of associations and relations, new ties and bonds to his American students and peers. He communicated his creative vision through many channels, whether from Iowa or from Cambridge. In this way, this "outsider" contributed creatively to an "inside" cultural tradition. Many European observers after the war, ignorant of Lewin's European background, commented on the particularly "American" character of his open, democratic, and pragmatic vision.

Wolfgang Koehler (1887–1967), Kurt Koffka (1886–1941), and Max Wertheimer (1880–1943): The Gestalt Triumvirate in America

Eminent representatives of several European schools in the social sciences found refuge in America, but Gestalt psychology was unique in one aspect: all three of the major figures in its development came to this country. Gestalt psychology is also exceptional among scientific schools in that its three founding members worked so closely together that it is often difficult to decide to whom a particular contribution should be attributed. As Grace M. Heider has put it, "The men whose names were originally connected with [the Gestalt movement] formed a close-knit triumvirate, and to some extent it is impossible to attribute particular aspects of the theory to one rather than another."[1] This being the case, it seemed best to deal with the three founders of Gestalt psychology, Koehler, Koffka, and Wertheimer, in a composite section.

Max Wertheimer, the oldest of the triumvirate, is generally credited with having been the founder of the school. Koffka was the systematizer and also the most successful popularizer of the movement. Koehler, who outlived the others and thus had a longer time span in which to influence American students, was probably its most accomplished experimentalist.[2] Yet it is impossible to go beyond such generalizations when assessing their relative contributions.

Gestalt psychology aimed at a revolution in psychology. It rejected the entire theoretical tradition of German experimental psychology of Wilhelm Wundt and G. E. Mueller at the same time as it rejected all aspects of associationist psychology (the mainly British doctrine that all complex

I am most grateful to Grace and Fritz Heider, who not only saved me from several egregious mistakes in the first draft of this paper but also provided a great deal of crucial information.

ideas or perceptions are formed through association) and the various forms of the broad behavioral tradition that had dominated American psychological thought ever since John B. Watson. It advocated the study and description of whole psychological configurations and large perceptual units. Rejecting received notions of unconscious processes, past experiences, and associations as explanations of perceptual and ideational processes, it suggested instead that psychological phenomena be investigated in terms of the immediately given experience by proceeding *von oben nach unten* (from above to below) rather than *von unten nach oben* (from below to above).[3] In contradiction to the prevalent analytical and summative approach, which attempted the comprehension of wholes through the analysis of component pieces, it stressed that wholes are not simply the sum of such pieces but have characteristics peculiarly their own. Order and structure need not be imposed on events; they resided in the events themselves. What the Gestaltists taught in perceptual psychology but also in other fields was the genetic and logical primacy of the whole.

Related to this stress on configurations and whole structures was the Gestalt school's emphasis on, as Koehler once put it, "the world as we find it, naively and uncritically."[4] No matter where later developments of their theory may have led them, the description of direct experience was always at the center of the Gestalt school's program. In this it had affinities with phenomenology and differed fundamentally from the approaches of behaviorists and associationists alike.

The inception of the movement dates from 1912, when Max Wertheimer published his seminal paper "Experimental Studies on the Perception of Movement."[5] The paper had grown out of discussions between its author and Koehler and Koffka in the preceding two years. Koehler and Koffka were two subjects in the experiment—a third was Koffka's wife.

Wertheimer was born in Prague in 1880. He first studied law and then turned his interest to philosophy and psychology, which he studied in Prague, Berlin, and Wuerzburg. A man of catholic interests, he wrote not only on psychological topics but also on problems of logic, on the music and language of primitive peoples, on ethics, and on various other subjects. Never a person to immerse himself totally in one area of specialization, he endeavored throughout his life to range broadly over several fields of knowledge. Nevertheless, in Frankfurt, where he became a privatdozent in 1912, and later at the University of Berlin and at Frankfurt, he worked largely in the field of psychology. Flanked during most of these years by his close collaborator Koehler, who had a somewhat more down-to-earth cast of mind, Wertheimer was, so to speak, the "seer" of the movement. He never wrote a systematic treatise, yet without him the treatises of Koffka and Koehler that helped spread the message of Gestalt psychology might never have been written.[6]

Wolfgang Koehler, Wertheimer's close associate over a lifetime, nevertheless differed considerably from him in temperament.[7] He was hardly a "seer" but rather an experimental doer, whose major aim was to combine field theory in physics with the Gestalt idea of psychology. Born in Reval, Estonia, of German parents (it might be worthy of note that two members of the triumvirate of rebels against the psychological establishment were born outside the boundaries of the German Reich, although they came from otherwise quite different cultural milieux) in 1887, Koehler studied psychology and natural science in Tuebingen, Bonn, and Berlin, and received his Ph.D. from the University of Berlin in 1909. Though his was a well-furnished mind, he seemed not to have been drawn to the wide-ranging studies that marked Wertheimer's early career but concentrated on psychology and to some extent on the natural sciences, especially field theory in physics. Koehler became an assistant in the department of psychology at Frankfurt in 1909, and this is where he, Koffka, and Wertheimer met. The collaboration was interrupted in 1913 when Koehler accepted an appointment to become director of the anthropoid station which the Prussian Academy of Science had established on the island of Tenerife. The outbreak of World War I kept him there until 1920 and led to the writing of *The Mentality of Apes*,[8] a major breakthrough in the psychology of thinking, as well as to his major theoretical treatise *Die Physischen Gestalten in Ruhe und in Stationaeren Zustand*.[9] In 1920, Koehler became acting director of the Psychological Institute in Berlin, and two years later he assumed the chair of psychology at Berlin, which he occupied until his emigration to America in 1935. (His courageous stand against the Nazi domination of the university was exemplary.)[10] Since Wertheimer was also in Berlin during most of the Weimar period, their Frankfurt collaboration was resumed. It was also in Berlin that the journal that broadcast the message of the Gestalt school, *Psychologische Forschung*, was founded in 1921. The original editorial board consisted of the triumvirate plus two close allies.

Kurt Koffka, born in Berlin in 1886, did not come as a refugee to America but settled here before Hitler came to power.[11] It would nevertheless be excessively purist to exclude him from treatment here. Koffka came from a family of lawyers and might have followed the family tradition had it not been for an uncle who aroused his interest in science and philosophy. Before entering the University of Berlin, he spent a year at the University of Edinburgh, where he not only acquired his mastery of English academic vocabulary but also developed his enduring anglophilia in intimate contacts with a number of British scientists and scholars. Returning to Berlin in 1904, he first resolved to study philosophy, but gave this up because, as he put it, he was "too realistically minded to be satisfied with pure abstractions," and turned to psychology instead.[12] His doctoral dissertation on the perception of rhythm already adumbrated problems that were later treated in Gestalt theory, but his thinking came to full fruition only after his encounter with Wertheimer a few years later. After working at the University of Frankfurt, where he collaborated with Wertheimer and Koehler, Koffka moved to the University of Giessen, where he stayed for over a decade. In those years, he contributed some eighteen papers to the newly founded Gestalt school's house organ, *Psychologische Forschung,* and produced one of the major works in the Gestalt tradition, later translated into English as *The Growth of the Mind* (1928).[13] His survey of experimental work over a broad field in psychology published under the title *Principles of Gestalt Psychology* (1935)[14] was built on studies done during his stay in Giessen and on later experimental work done at Smith College. The more theoretical parts of the book were elaborated in America and grew in part through fruitful intellectual interchange with American scholars, especially Edward Tolman.

Koffka came to the United States in 1924, teaching first as a visiting professor at Cornell, later at the University of Wisconsin, and then, in 1928, as a research professor at Smith College, where he occupied a chair that had recently been established in honor of the president of the college, William Allan Neilson. The original plan was to make incumbency of the chair a five-year appointment during which some world-renowned scholar would be provided with a staff and whatever facilities he might need to pursue his own work but would have no prescribed teaching or other duties. It was thus an honorable appointment that Koffka gladly accepted, especially since he was eager to leave Giessen. Koffka's position as Neilson Professor at Smith was entirely independent of any department, although the people most interested in his coming were mainly members of the departments of education and psychology. It was assumed that at the end of his five-year tenure the Neilson Professor would be "snapped up" by some prestigious university department with a major graduate school. But Koffka was never offered such a position. He was, however, appointed to a regular chair in Smith's department of psychology. His masterpiece, *Principles of Gestalt Psychology,* grew out of class notes taken by a student appointed for each class session and read and discussed at the beginning of the next meeting of the class. The four volumes of the *Smith College Studies in Psychology* published under Koffka's editorship between 1930 and 1933 contained not only accounts of Koffka's laboratory work at Smith but also work by students he trained there. In the last few years of his life, Koffka moved to nonexperimental studies such as the psychology of art and the place of values in scientific inquiry. A manuscript on the impact of brain injuries on human behavior remained incomplete at the time of his death in 1941.

What strikes one when assessing the career and impact of the Gestalt triumvirate in America is the fact that, as one of their historians has put it, "they came through the back door."[15] Koffka went to Smith College largely through the influence of his translator, R. M. Ogden,[16] and, as has been seen, was without departmental connections during the first part of his stay there. Moreover, since Smith had no graduate school, Koffka had no occasion to teach doctoral students, although he taught M.A. students who later went elsewhere for their Ph.D.'s

The situation of the other two members of the triumvirate was similar. Wertheimer was always more interested in wide-ranging speculation than in the humdrum work of experimentation, but after he came to the New School in September 1933 he did no more experimental work whatsoever. The New School started training Ph.D. students in psychology only toward the end of Wertheimer's life, and it had no laboratory facilities. As a consequence, and also owing to the fact that Wertheimer's seminars attracted a mixed audience of beginners, graduate students from other institutions, and junior colleagues, Wertheimer was motivated to investigate a wide range of subjects, from social psychology to philosophy, and from current social and political affairs to investigations in problem-solving and the psychology of the process of thinking.[17] He was a much beloved figure at the New School, but his impact in New York came mainly through personal discussions and contacts rather than through publications.

The situation of Koehler at Swarthmore, though in some ways similar to that of his two friends, was yet somewhat different. There were no graduate students at Swarthmore either, but Koehler, like Koffka, had access to a fine psychological laboratory where he pursued his studies until the end of his career. Two of his fellow refugees from Berlin, Karl Duncker and Hans Wallach, worked with him. He also managed to attract a number of highly gifted postgraduate fellows, many of whom had a considerable impact on the subsequent history of the Gestalt message in America.

All three Gestalt theorists had held highly prestigious positions in Germany, yet none of them managed to attain such posts in America. They remained, instead, in peripheral or marginal institutional positions throughout their American careers. Even though some of their work had been published in English translations before they came here, and even though a number of Americans had studied with them in Europe, they were still perceived as strongly at variance with the main tenets dominating the largely behavioristically oriented American psychological establishment. Some heterodox American behaviorists, Edward C. Tolman in particular, were ready to engage in a serious theoretical dialogue with them in order to learn from their novel approach, but most orthodox behaviorists were not. Tolman's teachings on "purposive behavior" and "cognitive maps" owed a great deal both to Gestalt theory and to Karl Buehler's action orientation (see pp. 37–41). The Harvard department of psychology at one time considered appointing both Wertheimer and Koehler. But the former was judged not to have sufficient publications to his credit, and the latter, while he was supported by key Harvard philosophers such as Ralph Barton Perry, found little support among the psychologists, especially E. G. Boring, the Wundtian introspectionist psychologist and historian of psychology.[18] Koehler's appointment at Columbia was vetoed by a philosophy professor who considered him too rigidly Germanic.[19] One might entertain the contrafactual question whether American psychology would have taken a different course than it did, had Wertheimer and Koehler been ensconced at Harvard or Columbia rather than restricted to marginal professorships. The extremely successful career of Kurt Lewin, a younger associate of the Gestalt triumvirate, suggests that it was possible to exert considerable influence on American psychology even from relatively marginal locations. Yet it ought to be kept in mind that Lewin had many gifted graduate students, while the Gestaltists were barred from regular access to such students.

It also seems significant that Koffka and Wertheimer, whether because they did not wish to be involved or because they were not invited, seem to have participated but little in the institutional life of the American Psychological Association, even though they were quite active in its regional divisions and were rapidly accepted into the Society for Experimental Psychology. They died in the early 1940s, when the APA was not yet eager to honor "foreigners." Koehler, who outlived them and, incidentally, was not a Jew, on the other hand, was honored by that association toward the end of his career by being given its Distinguished Scientific Contribution Award in 1957 and becoming its president a year later. Koehler also received several other prestigious awards and honorary degrees. Koffka and Wertheimer were not elected to the National Academy of Sciences, but Koehler was.

Given their generalized hostility to the dominant trends in American psychology during their lifetime, the relatively marginal position of the Gestalt triumvirate is perhaps not surprising. It would, however, be a mistake to believe that the Gestalt theorists stuck inflexibly to their German positions after coming to America. To the contrary, as Mitchell G.

Ash has cogently argued, "They altered the shape of their argument in order to address their new American audience." Koffka made this explicit in his *Principles of Gestalt Psychology*, where he wrote: "When the first attempts were made to introduce Gestalt theory to the American public, that side which would most readily appeal to the German type of mentality . . . was kept in the background, and those aspects which had a direct bearing on science were emphasized. Had the procedure been different, we might have incurred the danger of biasing our readers against our ideas."[20] The Gestalt theorists, it would seem, were willing to be flexible in America, but many of their American colleagues still found them to be not flexible enough.

It also has to be kept in mind that, as distinct from Lewin, the Gestalt psychologists just did not fit into the framework of American departments of psychology. They had hardly any notion of the structure, the politics, the grading system of an American college or university. Moreover, each of the triumvirate had been *the* professor of psychology at his respective university in Germany. It was hence difficult to offer them lesser positions here, and American universities in the 1930s already had their native top men. Wertheimer had little if any sense of professorial dignity—it was said that he climbed up on his desk to lecture at the New School when he became enthusiastic—but the others had too much of it.[21] The following story may be apocryphal, but it is still worth telling: Once Koehler is said to have told a colleague, "Don't be so formal. Don't call me Professor Koehler." The colleague thought this meant that Koehler wished to be addressed by his first name. Instead, Koehler continued, "just call me Dr. Koehler." Altogether, it would seem that at the time the Gestalt triumvirate arrived in America, colleagues welcomed their coming, were happy if some other university offered them a position, but felt that they would not fit into their own department. No major department, it seems, wanted someone with that much status.

Historians of psychology still differ in their assessment of the impact of Gestalt ideas on the subsequent history of American psychology. Some have claimed that these ideas never succeeded in gaining a secure hold on America, and Koehler, in his presidential address to the APA seems to have agreed with them. Others have made more sanguine assessments.[22] Mary Henle of the New School's department of psychology, a student of Koffka, an associate of Koehler, and a committed Gestalt psychologist, has argued that "Gestalt psychology transformed the study of perception" but "was not given a real hearing" and has been misunderstood in other areas of research and theorizing.[23] Yet a veteran defender of the Gestalt approach, Harry Helson, entitled a research paper, "Why Did Their Precursors Fail and the Gestalt Psychologists Succeed?"[24]

An outsider had better refrain from judgment where the experts are so patently divided. But it would seem that Edwin Boring, a man not particularly disposed in favor of the Gestalt school and who possibly intended to be somewhat disparaging, nevertheless rendered a balanced assessment when he wrote in his *History of Experimental Psychology:* "Schools can fail, but they can also die of success. Sometimes success leads to 'failure' . . . Gestaltist psychology has been successful. . . . The movement has produced much new important research, but it is no longer profitable to label it as Gestalt psychology . . . Gestalt psychology has already passed its peak and is now dying of its success by being absorbed into what is psychology. It seems already a little Americanized as compared to what it was in Berlin and Frankfort."[25]

If Gestalt psychology is at present no longer a vital movement of its own, this is due to some extent, as Boring claims, to its growing absorption into the mainstream of American psychology. A brief overview of the careers of those Americans who studied under the triumvirate or were influenced by it as postgraduate students or junior colleagues will reinforce this impression.

Solomon Asch, who worked at the New School with Wertheimer and then became for many years an intimate collaborator of Koehler at Swarthmore, and still later his successor there, is probably the most prominent American Gestalt psychologist of the generation following the founders of Gestalt psychology. His work in social psychology is known to every undergraduate taking courses in that area, and his contributions to the psychology of association have also been influential. But few other native American Gestalt psychologists have achieved comparable stature. Molly Harrower, Koffka's only Ph.D. student, went into clinical psychology, though she has retained her interest in Gestalt psychology and is now working on Koffka's papers. Most of those who gravitated around Wertheimer at the New School, apart from Mary Henle, who still teaches there and upholds the Gestalt tradition, and the aforementioned Solomon Asch, went into private practice and clinical psychology and, lacking an academic affiliation, had little occasion to carry on Wertheimer's tradition. Yet men as divergent in their subsequent interests as the psychoanalyst David Rapaport and the humanist psychologist Abraham Maslow were much in debt to Wertheimer's New School teachings.

Apart from Asch, only those who worked with Koehler at Swarthmore seem to have had a major impact on American psychology. Social psychologists such as David Krech and Richard Crutchfield, general psychologists such as Ulric Neisser, Richard Held, and a galaxy of others spent some time with Koehler at Swarthmore and were influenced by him. In the last two decades of his life Koehler moved from the Gestalt psychologists' traditional concern with visual perception to physiology

and a physicalist interpretation of brain processes.[26] Few of those who
worked with him at Swarthmore were willing to follow him all the way;
they all seem to have felt a large debt to Koehler, but none wanted to be
identified as a Gestalt psychologist.

Gordon Allport, for many years one of the leading figures in Harvard's distinguished department of psychology, called Koffka's *Principles
of Gestalt Psychology*, upon its publication in 1935, "probably the most
significant treatise in mental sciences published thus far in the twentieth
century."[27] He was not alone among senior American psychologists to
have such an exalted opinion of the contribution of the Gestalt school.
Yet despite the fact that the Gestalt triumvirate touched many minds in
America and had a lasting impact, even if only through absorption by
incorporation, the history of Gestalt psychology in America is not as
triumphant a success story as that of Lewin's social psychology. Whether
this was due to institutional factors, such as the peripheral location of
the major exponents and their resultant lack of access to graduate students, or to factors intrinsic to the content of their theory, is still open to
question. But the fact remains that the Gestalt triumvirate wrote a chapter in the history of American psychology that cannot possibly be ignored by subsequent generations.[28]

Charlotte Buehler (1893–1974) and Karl Buehler (1879–1963): Casualties of Exile

The story of Karl Buehler and his wife, Charlotte, has tragic overtones. Though both Buehlers enjoyed reputations in the front ranks of European psychology, Karl, a leading theoretician and experimental psychologist, found no recognition in this country, had no students, and did not even see his major German works translated into English. He published next to nothing after coming here. Charlotte Buehler's reputation in Europe equaled her husband's in many respects. She was a pioneer in developmental psychology. A German journal recently referred to her, with a bit of exaggeration, as "the discoverer of the child," yet she too received little recognition in this country. Having remained silent for many years after coming to America, she resumed writing and produced several papers and books, but these later publications had much less impact here than had her earlier work. When she is cited at all in current textbooks, the citations refer almost always to her work in Europe. The Buehlers were casualties of the Atlantic passage; they did not manage to flourish in the American climate.[1]

Karl Buehler, the son of a railroad employee and peasant, was born near Heidelberg in 1879. After attending a Catholic gymnasium, he studied medicine and psychology. He received his M.D. degree from the University of Freiburg in 1903 and his Ph.D. from the University of Strassburg a year later. It would seem that the major influence on Karl Buehler's work did not come from those to whom he listened in preparation for his M.D. and Ph.D. degrees but from the leading figure in the so-called Wuerzburg school of psychology, Oswald Kuelpe. Buehler became Kuelpe's assistant as a postdoctoral researcher in 1906, soon after finishing his doctoral studies, and followed Kuelpe when the latter moved from Wuerzburg, first to Bonn and then to Munich. Having taught as an associate professor at Munich since 1913 and then having occupied a professorial chair at the Dresden Polytechnical College, Buehler moved

to Vienna in 1922 as a professor of psychology and remained there until
Hitler's invasion of Austria in 1938.

Charlotte (Machlowski) Buehler was born in Berlin in 1893, the
daughter of a well-to-do and highly cultivated architect. Though her
family was of Jewish origin, she was reared as a Protestant. Her family
considered it in the normal order of things that Charlotte as well as her
brother would go into academic careers, and so she went to gymnasium
and then became a university student, first at Freiburg, then at Berlin,
and finally at Munich. Although she had decided to become a psychologist early in her university career, she took courses in a variety of subjects, studying under, among others, the sociologist Georg Simmel, the
philosophers Heinrich Rickert and Edmund Husserl, and the art historian Heinrich Woefflin, before settling down to the study of psychology
under her most influential teacher, Oswald Kuelpe. She received her
Ph.D. degree in psychology under Kuelpe at the University of Munich
in 1918. In the meantime, the Buehlers had married in Munich, in 1916.
In 1920 both moved to the Polytechnical College at Dresden, he as a
professor and she as a freshly minted privatdozent. When the Buehlers
moved to Vienna, he to assume a chair in psychology at the university
and she, many years younger than her husband, as an associate professor, the most successful years of their joint careers began.

The Psychological Institute the Buehlers founded in Vienna largely
centered on the then much neglected field of the psychology of the young
and on developmental psychology. The creative teamwork of the two
Buehlers paid high dividends; the institute was successful almost from
its inception. Not only students from Austria and Germany but other
Europeans and Americans as well flocked there. Paul Lazarsfeld, Bruno
Bettelheim, Egon Brunswik, Else Frenkel (later Frenkel-Brunswik),
Katherine Wolf, Marie Jahoda, Herta Herzog, Fritz Redl, Hans Zeisel,
Fritz Redlich, René Spitz, and many others who later achieved recognition in American sociology, psychology, and psychoanalysis were trained
there. Many American-born psychologists spent some time working with
the Buehlers, among whom Edward Tolman, Goodwin Watson, Neal
Miller, David Klein, and Robert McMurray were perhaps the most outstanding. Charlotte Buehler has stated that the Vienna Institute awarded
degrees to students from eighteen different nations. The publications
of the institute were translated into most European languages, and both
Buehlers lectured widely throughout Europe. Both were given a good
deal of recognition among American psychologists. Karl served as a visiting professor at Stanford, Johns Hopkins, and Harvard in 1927–28
and at the University of Chicago in the following year. Charlotte taught
at Barnard College in 1929–30 and spent the year 1935 in America as a
Rockefeller Fellow. In 1930 Karl Buehler was offered the MacDougal

Professorship at Radcliffe College. Because they were both deeply attached to Vienna, he declined. (It is interesting to note that Charlotte
Buehler, despite her reputation, was deemed worthy of a visiting or regular professorship only at a woman's college.)

The Buehlers were so successful and felt so firmly ensconced in Vienna that even as late as 1938 Karl considered declining an invitation to
be a professor at Fordham University. (The offer was withdrawn in any
case, allegedly because the Roman Catholic authorities had been advised
that Karl Buehler, though born a Catholic, had been married in a Protestant ceremony and that the Buehlers' children were brought up Protestant.)[2]

The Buehlers' odyssey in America is especially tragic because it was
preceded by such important work in Europe. While Charlotte's contributions are intimately tied to her Vienna years, Karl, her senior by many
years, had already achieved a considerable reputation in his various positions in Germany as a major representative of the action- or goal-oriented
psychology of the Wuerzburg school. Early in his career he had made
major contributions to the psychological study of thought processes, and
these had led to a widely noticed polemic with the grand old man of
German psychology, Wilhelm Wundt. Soon thereafter, Karl Buehler
turned to the psychology of language and here again achieved considerable renown among his colleagues. Important work in the psychology
of perception soon followed. When he finally turned to developmental
psychology and the psychological study of children, their mental development, and the evolution of their linguistic capacities, he had already
made his reputation as an experimentalist theorist. Charlotte Buehler,
in contrast, limited herself almost exclusively to the study of childhood
development and to studies of the life cycle. Her careful observational
studies of, among others, to quote the titles of some of her writings, *The
Mind of the Young* (1929), *Childhood and Youth* (1928), and *The Social Behavior of the Child* (1930), earned her a major reputation. Both Buehlers
were considered leading authorities on the psychology of youth and the
sequential stages in childhood development. Charlotte Buehler's pioneering tests of infants' development laid the foundation for later work
in America by Arnold Gesell and others.[3]

When the Nazis invaded Austria, Karl Buehler was imprisoned. Even
though he was freed after a few months, mainly upon the intervention
of colleagues and political authorities in Norway, where Charlotte had
found temporary refuge, his prison experience seems to have had a
traumatic impact. He was a broken man. Yet, had he been received with
some enthusiasm when he arrived in America, he might well have re-
gained his forces. But Karl Buehler's reception was decidedly cool. Many
other psychologists in search of positions had arrived before him. Ford-

ham had withdrawn its offer of a professorship. Edward Tolman, a former student of the Buehlers, had managed to get a chair at Berkeley for one of Buehler's students, Egon Brunswik, and could find no niche for another Viennese refugee. A projected appointment at Clark University did not materialize. Buehler felt rejected as well as neglected. As one of his biographers put it: "He suffered greatly under the emigration, which he experienced as an expulsion and an insult. . . . His style of thinking, his manner of lecturing, even his entire concept of psychology found little understanding and [he was] neither willing nor able to adjust."[4] This feeling of rejection was reinforced when Buehler came to realize that his favorite student from the Vienna days, Egon Brunswik, had turned away from his teacher's orientation upon coming to America, had been converted to Tolman's heterodox behaviorism, and had come under the influence of the logical positivists of the Vienna Circle.

Charlotte Buehler's attempts to secure a position in a major university department proved as futile as her husband's. In Karl Buehler's case, his repeated rejections may be partly accounted for by the fact that he was sixty years old when he came here. But Charlotte was only forty-six. Be it as it may, both Buehlers finally managed to gain teaching positions at two excellent, but nevertheless minor, undergraduate colleges in Minnesota. Having been accustomed to invigorating contact with graduate students, both felt acutely deprived by having no chance to direct doctoral studies and no experimental settings at their disposal. Both attempted several times to move east. Karl managed for a while to teach at Clark University and Charlotte at the City College of New York. But these were only temporary positions, so that they were again forced to return to Minnesota. Karl Buehler attempted to work in applied psychology, but his refusal to consult American colleagues in that field led to failure.

Realizing that the chances for a regular university position in her field of developmental psychology were nearly nil, Charlotte decided to redirect her interest to clinical psychology, where it seemed easiest to gain a position. She turned her attention to psychoanalysis, which she had largely neglected in Vienna, and assumed a position in clinical psychology at the Minneapolis General Hospital and later, after the Buehlers moved to California, at the Los Angeles County General Hospital. The University of Southern California had promised Charlotte a professorship in the department of psychology, but this offer again came to naught. Karl Buehler worked for a while as a clinical psychologist at Los Angeles's Cedars of Lebanon Hospital, but finally the Buehlers, having been rebuffed again and again, decided to open a private clinical practice in Hollywood.

Karl Buehler did not produce any significant work either in Minne-

sota or in Los Angeles. Charlotte, who has said that she had been unable
to do any work in the first ten years of her stay in America, not even to
revise her chapter on the social behavior of children for a well-known
handbook, thereafter wrote a number of works, mostly in clinical psychology. She had now moved closer to a semipsychoanalytic perspective
in the tradition of Karen Horney but was also attracted by the so-called
humanistic psychology of Abraham Maslow and his associates. In addition, she became active in developing group psychotherapy in California
and served a term as president of the Group Therapy Association of
Southern California. Most of her publications in the last period of her
life were devoted to exploring the borderline territory between moral
philosophy and psychology; others were attempts at popularization. They
seemed far removed, both in method and in style of presentation, from
the careful observational and testing studies through which she achieved
her reputation. When Charlotte Buehler died at eighty-one years of age,
she had some two hundred publications to her credit. Her work in Vienna, even if it is no longer cited as often as it once was, has inspired
many students of the psychology of youth and the stages of the human
life cycle, though it would seem that not all of them have adequately
indicated their indebtedness to her. Her later studies are probably alive
only in the milieu of humanistic psychology, decidedly a small and marginal movement in American psychology.

It may be argued that Karl Buehler's work, given his age, was largely
done by the time he arrived in America. But the much younger Charlotte Buehler would almost surely have continued her highly productive
work in developmental psychology had she continued to work in an atmosphere where she could have profited from stimulating exchanges
with students and colleagues. This was denied her in America, and her
work suffered as a result. What is more, American psychology suffered.
Both Buehlers became casualties of the Atlantic passage.

European Psychoanalysts in America:
The Promised Land

Between 1933 and 1941 about forty European refugee psychoanalysts came to the United States. Within a few years almost all of them had managed to move to prominent positions in the American psychoanalytic movement. By 1941, sixteen of them had become training analysts for aspiring younger native-born analysts, and the other twenty-four taught at various newly established training institutes.[1] They had remunerative private practices as well. Moreover, they soon assumed leading roles in the regional and national psychoanalytic societies, and their contributions to both theory and clinical research were widely published in psychoanalytic and related journals. *A Guide to Psychiatric Books*, published in 1956 by the prominent native-born psychoanalyst Karl Menninger (who is said to have been not overly enamored of the refugee analysts), lists more titles by refugee authors than by the native-born or earlier immigrants.[2]

The refugee analysts came to dominate the psychoanalytic movement intellectually and succeeded in putting their stamp on it. Counterfactual statement must always be treated with some suspicion, but in this case it seems hardly open to question that had this handful of analysts not arrived in this country in the 1930s, American psychoanalysis would not have acquired the character and shape that it did. This amazing success story cannot be explained by the intellectual eminence of the new arrivals alone. It was largely due to the receptiveness to their contributions of their native-born colleagues. The refugee analysts arrived at the right place at the right time.

Even though some of them may have come with a perspective that was partly colored by Freud's jaundiced view of America and its culture, they nevertheless looked to her as a promised land in which the road to recognition, professional success, and high income would be relatively easy. The prominent refugee analyst Otto Fenichel used to tell an amusing story about a group of Central European analysts gathered in Prague, discussing their prospects in America. One of them read aloud from a guidebook about Chicago: "This city," so the reader claimed, "is an important bank note site," misreading the word *Bahnknotenpunkt* (railroad junction) for *Banknotenpunkt*.[3]

The American psychoanalytic movement had come into being soon after Freud gave his famous series of lectures at Clark University in September 1909. Its first adherents were neurologists and hospital psychiatrists who were discontented with the prevailing somatic interpretations of the neuroses and psychoses and were looking for functional and psychological interpretations of these disturbances. By that time a growing number of psychiatrists, abnormal psychologists, and neurologists had become concerned about the discouraging clinical results of prevailing modes of treatment and had been encouraged by William James, G. Stanley Hall, Morton Prince, and others to look for explanations in psychic phenomena rather than in the physiology of the brain. Some of them had already become familiar with bits and pieces of Freud's message before he came to America, but it was largely his personal appeal that was responsible for their conversion.

The early American psychoanalysts were hardly a cohesive and unified group. Many of them would not be considered psychoanalysts at all by current standards. They picked and chose from Freud's writings whatever suited their individual needs. Most of them took little interest in Freud's coherent theory but concentrated mainly on what they considered to be the "cathartic method" for the treatment of neuroses. Though they were perceived as most daring when they spoke of sexuality and its repression in the context of the etiology of mental diseases, they nevertheless muted Freud's emphasis on sexuality and aggression as well, making both less harsh and more amiable. They emphasized social adjustment and social conformity much more than Freud's early disciples in Europe did. Though they rebelled against the prevailing "civilized"—that is, repressive—American morality, they were nevertheless gentle rebels.

Most of the rebels were relatively young, about ten years younger on the average than their adversaries among the neurologists. In 1909, Abraham A. Brill, who was soon to become the chief spokesperson for the American analysts, was thirty-five, William Alanson White was thirty-six, Ernest Jones (a Canadian who later moved to England) was thirty, and Smith E. Jelliffe was forty-three. But they also had the advantage of counting in their ranks the highly respected neurologist James J. Putnam, a man of impeccable Boston Brahmin background, who had for a long time held a prestigious chair at Harvard and who at the time of his conversion was already sixty-three years old.

Their backgrounds were more diverse than those of the group around

Freud in Vienna. Putnam came from impeccable upper-class roots; Brill was an immigrant Jew who had had to make his way on his own after arriving in America as a young man. Some of the others came from small-town and rural backgrounds. Their intellectual horizons and assumptions were equally diverse. Some still lived in the afterglow of Emersonian idealism; others were strict positivists or Spencerians; some, such as White, were influenced by Bergson's vitalism; others cleaved more closely to Darwinian evolutionism. Almost all of them had some roots in the progressive tradition, though few of them were active social reformers.

Psychoanalysis almost immediately became a popular success. Within six years of the Clark conference it had eclipsed all other therapies in terms of coverage in the nation's popular magazines. Between 1910 and 1914 eleven articles about Freud and psychoanalysis were published in America. Between 1915 and 1918, about thirty-one appeared, of which twenty-five were favorable. By 1915, psychoanalysis had reached mass circulation in women's magazines.

Popular interest and appeal were paralleled by a measure of professional acceptance, at the same time that sharp polemical attacks against psychoanalysis from the Old Guard continued. William Alanson White became director of Washington's highly prestigious St. Elizabeth's Hospital. Other psychoanalysts directed psychiatric facilities in Boston and New York hospitals and served on the staffs of eminent medical schools. Under these conditions it is understandable that there was no dearth of private patients.

It is revealing that even though the early American psychoanalysts succeeded in moving into clinical work, their theoretical concerns were somewhat restricted. Many of them, though they practiced what they called psychoanalytical therapy, seemed relatively unconcerned with the overall theoretical structure that Freud had built. This was surely not the case with Jones or Brill, who translated much of Freud's work, but it seems to have been true of many others who relied on more eclectic theoretical foundations. This probably explains why Freud's books sold poorly in America, despite the popular acclaim and professional interest. Freud's most popular book, *The Interpretation of Dreams,* sold only 5,250 copies in America and Great Britain combined between its publication in 1910 and 1919. *Totem and Taboo* (1914) sold fewer than a thousand copies in its first eighteen years. Higher sales figures came only in the late 1920s and the 1930s.

Theoretical eclecticism was probably functional for the psychoanalytic movement in its early stages. It allowed neurologists, psychotherapists, and psychiatrists of various outlooks to collaborate amiably in the psychoanalytic associations that came to be organized in New York and Boston in the early years of the movement.

In the 1920s Morton Prince, the gentlemanly founder of the non-Freudian Boston school of psychotherapy, could write, "Freudian psychology has flooded the field like a full rising tide, and the rest of us were left submerged like clams buried in the sands at low water."[4] This success rested on twin pillars: the treatment of mental and nervous disorders through varieties of "cathartic methods" and the transformation of sexual morals during and immediately after World War I.

Although the early American psychoanalysts wittingly or unwittingly watered down some of Freud's emphasis on the sexual etiology of mental suffering, and although they seemed much concerned with helping their patients become healthy and adjusted, their emphasis on the ways in which the prevailing "civilized morality," with its repressive characteristics, warped the lives of "normal people" as well as neurotics found an echo outside professional circles, and especially among young intellectuals. These men and women were not disposed to ferret out the more puritanical views of Freud when it came to sexual morality but perceived only his polemical thrust against the restraints of prevalent moral standards. For them, Freud, often together with Havelock Ellis, was seen as the great liberator. And although the professional psychoanalysts were wont to counsel the need for sublimation of sexual drives much more strongly than Freud did, their patients and intellectual fellow travelers were not deterred from seeing psychoanalysis as their great ally in the revolt against genteel cultural restraints.

In the interwar period, American psychoanalysis gradually developed into a medical speciality and so became part of the medical establishment. While many of Freud's earlier disciples in Europe had no medical degrees and were trained in various branches of humanistic scholarship, American psychoanalysis after the formative period tended to reject practitioners who had no medical training. The reason for this divergence seems obvious. The powerful medical establishments of Europe largely opposed psychoanalysis in the early years and admitted only a handful of analysts into their ranks. In contrast, the American medical establishment, which was still weak and in the process of formation when the pioneers of psychoanalysis appeared on the scene, found it easier to accept analysts in its newly formed psychiatric research centers and medical schools, where professional specialization and certification were just then becoming more demanding. Once appointed, the analysts wished to show that they were true medical practitioners and shunned organizational ties with those who lacked medical degrees. While only two-thirds of Europe's psychoanalysts had been physicians, few orthodox

American psychoanalysts between the wars and after lacked a medical degree, even though a minority continued to oppose the medical orientation, and many heterodox psychoanalysts rejected the medical alignment of the orthodox.

The urge to professionalize on a medical model also led psychoanalysts after 1930 to tighten their standards and to do away with the pronounced eclecticism that had marked the early years of the psychoanalytic movement. Borrowing from a model that had largely been developed in the Berlin Psychoanalytical Institute in the interwar years, they created American institutes with control over the acceptance, training, and certification of members. No longer could one become a psychoanalyst merely by self-selection. The first systematic psychoanalytic texts, which began to appear in the 1930s, were written to serve the need for institute teaching. The various local institutes, most of them night schools where teachers and candidates met, became the center of the movement's intense in-group life, usually led by those members of the analytical elite who had achieved the high status of training analysts.

In all these ways, the charisma of the founding members was slowly eroded by a tendency to routinization and professionalization. And so, as American medicine generally was completing its transformation into a modern professional organization between 1910 and 1940, by stressing uniformity, specialization, monopoly, and high status, American psychoanalysts followed in its wake. Psychoanalysis became a medical field in the 1920s and was transformed into an elite speciality with a unified theoretical framework in the 1930s. By the late 1930s all candidates for psychoanalytic training were expected to have completed a psychiatric residence in an approved institution.

In 1930 there was not a single psychoanalytic institute in America, so that prospective analysts had to seek systematic training in Europe. But soon thereafter a new young elite, almost all of them trained in Europe, seized power from the elders grouped around Brill in New York and a more eclectic band around William Alanson White at St. Elizabeth's Hospital in Washington. These young Americans—such as Bertram Lewin, Gregory Zilboorg, Ives Hendrick, to mention just a few—insisted on tighter intellectual discipline, on an exclusively medical and psychiatric background, and on the foundation of institutes according to the European pattern.

The success of the European analysts becomes understandable once it is realized that they arrived in this country just as the Young Turks had largely won over the older generation. Most of those refugees who lacked a medical background were not admitted into the new institutes, and some were led to develop their own schismatic movements, but the majority became allies of the Young Turks in the foundation of institutes and the setting up of more demanding and rigid intellectual standards.

In 1933 the American Psychoanalytic Association assumed its present organizational form as a federation of local associations and institutes. Between 1940 and 1960 its membership increased more than fivefold. Six new societies were founded between 1940 and 1950. By the end of the 1960s there were twenty-nine local societies and twenty training institutes. This was surely the golden age of psychoanalysis in America, and the refugee analysts had come just in time to enter the swelling movement on the ground floor. In 1945 there were sixty-nine training analysts, and twenty-eight applications for training were accepted. Between 1945 and 1949, 490 candidates were accepted, or seventeen times the 1945 figures.[5]

Dr. Charles Brenner, a leading American psychoanalyst, makes the telling point that a proportionally equal number of European refugee analysts went to England, but without producing a great flowering of psychoanalysts there.[6] It was the fortunate conjunction of developments internal to the American psychoanalytic movement and the timing of the refugees' arrival that accounts for their tremendous success in this country. The conditions were ripe, but, as Dr. Brenner argues, "without [the refugees], I am sure, [psychoanalysis] could never have developed as it did."[7] I agree with Arnold Rogow, author of a fine research study on the characteristics of American psychiatrists and psychoanalysts, that "The list of refugee Jewish analysts is sufficiently impressive to justify the statement that the history of psychoanalysis in America, like that of atomic physics, would have been very different had it not been for Adolf Hitler."[8] But it needs to be added that in psychoanalysis, as in atomic physics, the ground was prepared by prior institutional developments in these fields of inquiry.

One additional development favorable to the growth of American psychoanalysis in general and to the influence of European refugees in particular still needs to be mentioned. As Dr. Brenner argues:

When the U.S.A. began to mobilize, before the outbreak of the war here, . . . Dr. William Menninger [a native-born psychiatrist] was appointed chief of psychiatry in the office of the surgeon general of the army and air force. Therefore, when young MDs were drafted, and trained as psychiatrists, they were trained by and large by teachers whom Menninger picked. The teachers were analysts. They taught a whole generation of young MDs who were interested in psychiatry enough about psychoanalysis so that several scores of them, when the war was over, went into psychoanalytical training. When they applied to the few institutes then functioning, there were European refugee analysts there ready to educate them. If not for Hitler, the analysts would not have been there in sufficient numbers and with good enough qualifications to make American analysis what it rapidly became—the best in the world. Without Menninger and his recruitment and organizational policies, the situation here would have been just what it was in England during and after World War II; there wouldn't have been any more people for analytical education than there had been in the 1930s.

I am inclined to believe that Dr. Brenner somewhat overestimates the influence of Menninger and that internal developments within American psychoanalysis prior to the war were at least as important, if not more so.[9] But be that as it may, the wartime developments surely reinforced tendencies that had already made themselves felt before the war.

After the war's end, European analysts, such as Heinz Hartmann, René Spitz, Sandor Rado, Rudolph Loewenstein, Annie Reich, Hermann Nunberg, Edith Jacobson, Ernst and Marianne Kris, in New York; Felix and Helene Deutsch, and Edward and Grete Bibring in Boston; Ernst Simmel, Otto Fenichel, and Martin Grotjahn in Los Angeles; Franz Alexander in Chicago; Robert Waelder in Philadelphia; Richard Sterba in Detroit; and Frieda Fromm-Reichmann at the Chestnut Lodge Sanitarium in Maryland, dominated the American psychoanalytic establishment. They served as training analysts, thus transmitting their message to a new generation. They headed local and national psychoanalytic associations and institutes, and they were instrumental in spreading the message of psychoanalysis to the wider audience of American psychiatry and the lay public.

When Arnold Rogow asked a sample of 113 general psychiatrists in 1966 to identify "the most outstanding living psychiatrists and psychoanalysts in terms of their contribution to theory and/or practice," the refugee Erik H. Erikson (see pp. 55–60) received 26 mentions, third only to Anna Freud and Karl Menninger; Heinz Hartmann came next with 21 mentions; and all others, whether native-born or not, received a much smaller number of mentions. When the same question was put to 31 psychoanalysts, Anna Freud headed the list with 21 mentions, followed by Hartmann with 20, Erikson with 16, and Loewenstein and Spitz with 7 each. Only one native-born American, Phyllis Greenacre, received as many as 7 mentions.[10] Whether one looks at citations in trade books or in books recommended for instructional use in training courses, one finds similar results.

The younger generation of American-born psychoanalysts had been very active in helping the immigration of European analysts, many of whom they had known in Europe as fellow analysts and/or teachers. They provided affidavits, travel tickets, and financial aid, as well as needed referrals, to the newcomers. They did so not only for humanitarian motives. They perceived a basic affinity between the refugees' orientations and their own. The older generation in America was much less receptive and sometimes even tended to see the refugees as unwanted competitors,[11] largely because they were aware of the discrepancy between the rigorous standards of the newcomers and their own more easy-going styles. The old-timers resisted the foundation of institutes and the imposition of strict training standards, realizing, correctly, that the Europeans would reinforce the new generation to emphasize rigor and medical orientations while at the same time accelerating the trend for analytically trained psychiatrists to move into private practice.

But purely intellectual divergencies also separated many of the older generation from the newly arrived Europeans as well as from some of the native-born Young Turks. Many of the newcomers and their American allies had developed considerable theoretical interest in what has come to be known as "ego psychology" within the broad psychoanalytic movement. Taking their point of departure from Anna Freud's influential work *The Ego and the Mechanisms of Defense* (1936), they argued that previous analytical thought, though recognizing the ego alongside the superego and the id as part of the basic structural triad of the psychic economy, nevertheless had slighted it in favor of the buried, unconscious forces of the id and the superego. They argued that the mechanisms of adaptation of the ego to the outside world, the relatively "conflict-free" ways in which the ego could deal with the environment through the process of perception and intention and strategies of adjustment, allowed healthy individuals enough "ego strength" to cope with social demands. The task of the analyst hence was to reinforce the ego strength of the patient. Heinz Hartmann, one of Freud's last analysands in Vienna, had already published two important papers laying out the principles of ego psychology shortly before coming to America. Together with his close theoretical allies Rudolph Loewenstein and Ernst and Marianne Kris, he developed ego psychology in a number of seminal publications soon after coming to America.[12] A number of Marxist analysts from Berlin, such as Fenichel and Annie Reich, while differing politically from Hartmann's group, agreed with his stress on the ego.

What made ego psychology so appealing to American psychoanalysts, and what accounts for the fact that in most surveys the ego psychologists are ranked as the most important innovators in the theory and practice of psychoanalysis, are two interrelated factors. The emphasis on the ego allowed psychoanalysts to build bridges to various academic psychological orientations that shunned the notion of the unconscious and Freud's instinct-based theorizing. Ego psychology held the promise that at some time in the future it would become possible to develop a general psychology bridging the gap between psychoanalytical and academic psychological assumptions. Hence, for example, ego psychologists could profit from the genetic psychology of Karl and Charlotte Buehler—with whom both Bruno Bettelheim and René Spitz had studied in Vienna—without relinquishing their claim that they operated within the basic theoretical framework elaborated by Freud. Once in America, the ego psychologists found it much easier to develop the rudiments of a common language with academic non-Freudians who shared their preoccupation with the mechanisms of defense even though they found other aspects of the Freudian system unacceptable. This was a most beneficial development, and suited those refugee and native-born analysts who wished to move closer to the medical schools and departments of psychology and psychiatry. Hartmann explicitly stated that ego psychology "would open up the no-man's land between sociology and psychoanalysis" and provide a "meeting ground with non-analytical psychology."

There is, however, another reason why ego psychology was well received and fitted the American temper. While remaining within the limits of Freudian orthodoxy, it stressed an outlook that was considerably more hopeful for the alleviation of psychic distress than were Freud's tragic view and despairing vision in the years after World War II. Although the ego psychologists did not go as far as psychoanalytical rebels such as Fromm and Horney (see pp. 69–82) in stressing the importance of environmental and cultural factors in the etiology of neuroses, they still afforded these factors a larger place than had previous analytical thought. Ego psychology held out the hope that patients could come to terms with their environment through therapy, and it also favored attempts to change that environment through benevolent strategies of sociopolitical intervention.

In these ways, through building bridges with nonanalytical psychology and psychiatry, and through an inflection of orthodox doctrine in a direction more in tune with America's optimistic temper, the European ego psychologists and their American associates moved into the intellectual forefront of American psychoanalytical thought and practice. In the process of removing some of the acerbity and sting of Freud's postwar pessimism, they made psychoanalysis more acceptable. As Nathan Hale puts it, in their hands "the death instinct was socialized, the ego was moralized," and "aggression was interpreted as an important drive in the mastery of reality."[13]

Survey Results, or Saying It in Figures

Throughout most of this book, I infer the success or lack of success of the refugee scholars discussed by such indirect measures as their occupancy of prestigious chairs, the impact of their publications, their ability to attract graduate students, and their achievement of recognition by professional and learned societies. An alternative mode of proceeding would have been to ask their colleagues directly through questionnaires or interviews what impact the refugee newcomers had on their respective professional fields. I rejected this approach not only because it would have required financial resources and research assistance that were not at my disposal, but also because it would necessarily slight the many qualitative details that would not be caught in the net of quantified data.

However, I have used this method in regard to refugee psychoanalysts. Since most of them were engaged almost exclusively in private practice, university appointments could not serve as indicators of status, nor could the number of graduate students serve as an indicator of their professional standing. In addition, the community of professional psychoanalysts is relatively small and has distinct boundaries so that it was feasible to send questionnaires to a major portion of all practicing psychoanalysts.

I therefore sent a questionnaire to all members of the New York, Boston, and San Francisco Psychoanalytic Institutes in late 1980.[14] The first two are the largest and most prestigious of all American institutes. The San Francisco Institute was added so as to have responses from a smaller yet also highly regarded group of psychoanalytical practitioners. The three institutes had at the time a combined membership of 692 persons. The return rates for the questionnaire were gratifyingly high: 58.8 percent for New York, 66.3 percent for Boston, and 62.2 percent for San Francisco. Such high response rates are considered exceptional in survey research. In all, we received 432 responses.

The questionnaire read:

1. Your name _____Date of birth _____

2. Place of birth _____

3. Check any that apply to you:

    a. Trained in Europe _____
    b. Trained in the U.S.A. by a native-born U.S. analyst _____
    c. Trained in the U.S.A. by a European refugee analyst _____
    d. Trained in the U.S.A. by an analyst of other national origins _____

4. Name of training analyst _____

5. Who do you think are the five leading psychoanalysts in this country, native-born or otherwise, in the last 50 years or so? Please list:

1. _____   2. _____

3. _____   4. _____

        5. _____

It might be thought that our responses were biased by the fact that ref-ugee psychoanalysts would be disproportionately motivated to answer the questionnaire, but this was probably not the case. If refugee analysts had been more likely to respond, New York, where 64.1 percent of all refugee analysts in our sample are located, should have the highest pro-portion of responses, with lower rates of responses from Boston and San Francisco (where 25.6 percent and 10.3 percent of our sample of refu-gees, respectively, are located.) But it turns out that the New York rate of response was the lowest and the Boston response rate was the highest. Hence I have reason to believe that there is little if any bias in the re-sponse rate in favor of refugee respondents.

Turning now to some background data, we found that refugee re-spondents were slightly older than the native Americans. About half of the 39 refugees who replied were born between 1900 and 1915, while about half of the Americans were born between 1916 and 1931. Some-what to our surprise, it turned out that most of the refugee respondents were not trained in Europe. Of the 432 respondents, 32 were trained in Europe, including 16 refugees—41 percent of the total.

Twelve percent of the respondents were women, but the younger gen-eration of psychoanalysts has fewer women than the older. In part—but *only* in part—the difference may be due to the fact that women live longer than men. (Of the analysts born before 1916, 19.7 percent were women, whereas women represented only 9.1 percent of the generation born in 1916 or after.)

When asked who they thought were the five leading psychoanalysts in this country, native-born or otherwise, in the last fifty years or so, our respondents named a total of 1,912 individuals, of whom no less than 1,304 (68.2 percent), or more than two-thirds, were refugees.

Ten of these leading figures were named sixty times or more: Heinz Hartmann (named 245 times), Ernst Kris (named 142 times), and Erik Homburger Erikson (131 times). The ten most often named included eight refugees!

The high standing and prestige of the refugee psychoanalysts were further established through answers of the respondents to the question of who had been their training analysts. Several respondents named more than one. In all, 179 training analysts were named, of whom 70 (39.1 percent) were refugees. Some training analysts were mentioned repeat-edly. This happened more often with those who were refugees than with those who were not. Those named more than twice included 25 native Americans and 28 (52.8 percent) refugees.

Three training analysts were named more than ten times; all three were refugees. Of four training analysts who were named eight or nine times, three were refugees. Indeed, the more frequently a training analyst was named, the more likely it was that the person was a refugee. (Of those named six or more times, 61.5 percent were refugees; of those named three to five times, 50 percent were refugees; of those mentioned twice, 42.5 percent were refugees, and of those named only once, 28.5 percent were refugees.)

Leaders and Trainers

It is noteworthy that those who transmit knowledge to the younger generation of future professionals are not necessarily the same as those who disseminate it to the public. Those who were named most frequently as leading psychoanalysts were not necessarily those who were named most frequently as training analysts, although both groups included a significant number of refugees. Only one of the leading analysts, or perhaps two, combined the two roles, as the following table indicates.

There is another way of finding out about the transmission of knowledge in psychoanalysis: namely, by looking at the number of publications by analysts in the authoritative bibliography. Table II shows the results of our count.

On the average, refugees published four times as many books and more than one and a half times as many papers in psychoanalytic journals as did their American-born colleagues. Refugee psychoanalysts have produced on the average 79 percent, 82 percent, 63 percent, and 52 percent, respectively, of books, articles in psychoanalytic journals, articles in psychological journals, and articles in popular journals.

All in all, the story of refugee analysts is indeed a success story. They are disproportionately represented among those whom their colleagues see as their leaders. They are disproportionately represented as trainers of a new generation of largely native psychoanalysts. Their publication

Table I. Frequency of being named as a leader or as a trainer

	Leader	*Trainer*
Heinz Hartmann*	245	4
Ernst Kris*	142	5
Erik H. Erikson*	131	3
Margaret E. Mahler*	92	3
Phyllis Greenacre	92	4
Ruth Jacobson*	78	3
Rudolph Loewenstein*	78	2
Otto Fenichel*	67	2
Helene Deutsch*	62	16
Bertram Lewin	60	9

* Asterisks indicate refugees.

Table II. Mean Frequency of Publications

Average number of publications	Books	Papers in Psychoanalytic Journals	Papers in Psychological Journals	Papers in Other Journals
Refugee analysts	1.97	14.74	5.97	6.77
American-born analysts	0.51	3.13	3.44	6.18
Refugees named at least once as leaders in the field	4.02	24.59	10.24	12.52
American-born analysts named at least once as leaders in the field	1.81	9.37	11.49	11.54
Ten people most frequently named as leaders	4.40	35.00	9.10	11.80

record as a whole is much higher than that of the native-born. The refugees in psychoanalysis published more books, contributed much more to psychoanalytic journals, and also were more frequent contributors to general, namely, "other" publications, which indicates that they have influenced the general culture as well as their professional colleagues.

Given the results of this inquiry, it can be asserted with some confidence that the coming of the refugees transformed not only American psychoanalysis, but also psychology and general culture. The present shape and stature of psychoanalysis were largely the result of the arrival of the refugee psychoanalysts at a moment when the intellectual climate within American psychoanalysis was sufficiently receptive to the influence they were able to assert as the bearers and inheritors of the original tradition of the European founding fathers.

Erik Homburger Erikson (1902–) and Wilhelm Reich (1897–1957): Creative Innovation and Sectarian Rebellion in Psychoanalysis

Erik Homburger Erikson

It might be argued that other refugees have had an equal or even a greater impact on the practice of psychoanalysis in America, but Erik Homburger Erikson without any doubt made the most consequential contemporary psychoanalytic contribution to general American culture. There are few undergraduate students with any cultural pretensions today who lack at least some acquaintance with his writing. His name crops up again and again in the mass media. He has influenced a variety of humanistic scholars, social scientists, cultural commentators, and, above all, psychologists and psychiatrists. He has made a mark on methods of child analysis and at the same time is the founding father of much of what has come to be called psychohistory. Certain of the terms Erikson has introduced—"ego identity," "moratorium," "identity crisis," for example—have passed from the technical literature into the vernacular. There are few psychologists and personality theorists who have not felt the need to come to grips with his theory of developmental stages in the life cycle. He has held prestigious professorships, has been associated with leading clinical and research centers, and has been honored on many occasions by academic and scholarly institutions and by eminent peers. His imprint on modern American culture is indelible.

Apart from his undoubted individual talent, Erikson's ability to be receptive to a number of diverse influences in the American setting and his refusal in his social and intellectual exchanges, to be limited to just one set of role-partners—i.e. professional psychoanalysts and psychiatrists—seem to have had much to do with facilitating his career in America and with laying the groundwork for his creativity. His contributions are rooted in his ability to transcend narrow intellectual grooves in favor of multifaceted involvement with a wide set of ideas. Hence, he has been able to bridge divergent perspectives on the problems of human growth and development, which have always been in the forefront of his concerns. While many of his peers from central Europe confined themselves to the relatively narrow group of their professional colleagues, whether native or European, Erikson from the beginning of his career in America moved in a variety of circles and involved himself with a series of intellectual issues that preoccupied his diverse role-partners.[1]

The circumstances of Erikson's background were not unconnected with his subsequent career in America. He was born in Frankfurt, Germany, where he grew up as the stepson of a Jewish pediatrician, Theodor Homburger. Erikson's natural father, a Dane, had abandoned his mother before the boy's birth. The young Erikson hence grew up in a set of complex circumstances and found it hard to gain a secure sense of identity. His German classmates tended to reject him as a Jew, while his Scandinavian features led the members of his stepfather's synagogue to dub him a "goy" and tend to be suspicious of him.

Erikson at first wished to be an artist, like his mother, and hence did not seek a university education. Instead, in 1927 he accepted an invitation to become an art teacher at a small Viennese private school. It so happened that this school was sponsored by leading psychoanalysts, so Erikson soon came to know Anna Freud, as well as her father. Largely because of Anna Freud's sponsorship, Erikson was introduced into the Vienna psychoanalytical circle. He was analyzed by Anna Freud. He then resolved to embark on a career in psychoanalytical practice. As shall be seen, problems of identity and adolescence remained in the center of his concerns as a therapist, as they had been in his own life.

Without university education or medical training, Erikson was an outsider in Vienna's psychoanalytic milieu, but in Vienna, unlike Germany, he was treated as a kind of "favored stepson" by the psychoanalytic establishment.

Erikson came to America after Hitler invaded Austria. Lacking academic credentials, he nevertheless had one asset that facilitated his acceptance in psychoanalytic circles: he had for several years moved in the intimate circle of Freud and his trusted disciples. When Erikson arrived in Boston, the analyst Hanns Sachs, whom he had known in Vienna and who had preceded him to this country, smoothed the way for him. Within a short time, Erikson was given a position at Harvard Medical School and Massachusetts General Hospital as a child analyst and had become a consultant to the Judge Baker Guidance Center, which pioneers in the diagnosis and treatment of emotionally disturbed children. He was also able to open an office in a high-status neighborhood of Boston, where he treated emotionally unsettled young persons.[2]

Though Erikson was to live for only three years in the Cambridge-Boston area, the Harvard intellectual community in which he was soon immersed exerted considerable influence on him. He established close intellectual contacts with one of the major figures in American academic psychology, Henry A. Murray. Murray soon saw to it that Erikson would work with the Harvard Psychological Clinic. At the same time, in the then flourishing interdisciplinary seminars at Harvard, Erikson met not only psychiatrists but also anthropologists such as Margaret Mead, Ruth Benedict, and Gregory Bateson, and social psychologists such as Lawrence Frank and his fellow exile, Kurt Lewin. It would seem that Erikson managed quickly to find intellectual and social roots in the Harvard milieu that others managed to establish only after many years, or not at all. Perhaps the fact that he did not belong to any academic discipline and thus felt free to have intellectual intercourse with persons in various fields contributed to this ease of integration. Just as Veblen has argued that newcomers on the industrial scene found it easier to respond to the challenge of modernization than those who had arrived earlier and were hence weighed down by the tradition they had once established, thus paying the penalty of once having taken the lead, so it might be argued that Erikson, unburdened by academic tradition, found it easier to respond to the new challenges that beckoned around the Harvard Yard.

Soon after publishing as articles the results of his child analyses and his clinical work with Harvard students (most of his early writings form the basis of his first major book, *Childhood and Society*), Erikson left for New Haven, having been offered a position at the Yale Medical School and the Institute of Human Relations. Again he soon established contacts with anthropologists, psychologists, and sociologists, as well as psychiatrists. He continued to do clinical work with disturbed children but also became interested in the research on the development of normal infants and young children then being carried on at the Yale Institute of Human Relations. When contact with anthropologists convinced him that some of the generalizations he had become accustomed to making about white middle-class children might not apply in other cultures, he resolved to see for himself and embarked on a study trip to observe Sioux children on a reservation in South Dakota. This openness to new experiences seems to have been a characteristic of the young Erikson; one can hardly imagine many central European analysts leaving their middle-class patients to study, of all things, Indians on a reservation.

Erikson's paper on Sioux education and the character structure of the Sioux child points to some of the major themes of much of his later work. It is written in the lucid and non technical style that was to become the hallmark of his later writings. By highlighting the impact of the cultural experiences and life space of the Sioux child on the formation of the Sioux personality, it points to Erikson's later rejection of a one-sided emphasis on the internal dynamics of personality development and to his heightened awareness of history and culture as central molders of character.

Soon after his work with the Sioux, Erikson moved again, this time to the University of California at Berkeley, where he was to stay for a decade. It was in the California years that he wrote *Childhood and Society*,[3] a series of interrelated essays ranging in topical variety from another study of Indians—done under the guidance of the dean of American anthropology, Alfred Kroeber—to studies of the childhoods of Hitler and of Maxim Gorky, in which the interplay between psychic forces and historical and cultural milieux were in the forefront. Above all, this book provides the first schematic version of Erikson's theory of the stages of human development. The book established his preeminent stature not only among psychoanalytic clinicians and theorists but also in much wider circles.

When during the McCarthy period the regents of the University of California started to require a special loyalty oath from their faculty as a condition of further employment, Erikson refused to sign. His statement on why he could not do so in good conscience is one of the most moving defenses of academic freedom ever penned. It seems important to note that this was written by a man who had no academic credentials and was hence by no means assured of further academic appointment anywhere; and by a man, to boot, who was acutely aware that he was not a native-born American. Perhaps Erikson's inner sense that he had nevertheless established for himself a secure position in a wide network of associations can account, at least in part, for his self-assured gesture of defiance.

Returning East, in 1951 Erikson joined the prestigious Austin Riggs Center for Psychiatric Treatment and Research in Stockbridge, Massachusetts, where for the next ten years he was a member of the senior staff and where he did much of his major work on the life cycle and the problems of ego identity. Between 1950 and 1960 he also lectured widely to a variety of audiences. He addressed, among others, the Judge Baker Guidance Center's staff, the American Psychoanalytic Association, the Academic Academy of Arts and Sciences, the World Health Organization, and the Children's Bureau of HEW, thus testifying again to the fact that he cared for a wide variety of responses from different audiences. He was especially well received by social workers and clinical psychologists, i.e. by professionals dealing mainly with short-term cases where his basically "optimistic" outlook was seen as more congenial than the "pessimistic" stance of orthodox psychoanalysis.

It also seems significant that during the years at Austin Riggs, where by and large he met only middle-class patients, Erikson also commuted to the University of Pittsburgh's Western Psychiatric Institute, where he could observe the children of working-class parents and of the unemployed. He also joined the staff of the Arsenal Health Center in Pittsburgh, working with Dr. Benjamin Spock and observing mother–child interactions among recent working-class immigrants. Erikson was always intent on escaping from narrow perspectives and exclusive concern with middle-class subjects and patients.

In 1960 came a major turning point in Erikson's career: he accepted a professorship at Harvard. It soon became apparent that he would make a significant mark on that university. Undergraduates flocked to his lectures by the hundreds, and he often had to turn away graduate students who wished to be admitted to his seminars. Like Paul Tillich before him (see pp. 313–19), Erikson appealed to a wide audience, many, perhaps most, of whom were not attempting to become professionals in the field in which he lectured. I have often encountered young men and women in sociology or history who have testified that exposure to Erikson's teaching was more consequential for their intellectual development than the courses they took in their own fields of specialization.

While at Harvard, Erikson continued to work in the areas of ego identity, youth, and the life cycle, but his major work turned in the direction of psychohistory. Since he now was removed from clinical practice and had all the intellectual resources of Harvard at hand, Erikson shifted from considering the influence of variant contemporary cultural orientations to the impact of different historical circumstances on the character development of historical actors. His two major studies in this vein, *Young Man Luther* (1958) and *Gandhi's Truth* (1969) (which won a Pulitzer Prize), are too well known to require a summary here. Suffice it to say that Erikson's unusual capacity to immerse himself in historical and biographical data, his sense of empathy, equal to that of the great historians and biographers of the past, augmented by his clinical knowledge, made these books landmarks in the field of psychobiography, which he was largely instrumental in founding, or at least in making respectable.

Erikson now lives in northern California in semiretirement. We may still hope for other significant contributions from him, but even if that should not be the case, his place in American intellectual life is secure, as secure as that of almost any of the refugees who came to this country in the 1930s.

It is interesting to note that, especially in the past ten or twenty years, Erikson's work has taken a turn that some critics have called conservative.[4] Perhaps because American society has been so receptive to him, he has been somewhat reluctant to be critical of its culture. He did not, for example, participate openly in the protests against the war in Vietnam which attracted so many of his students and colleagues. An additional reason for this apparent lack of critical impetus might be Erikson's reluctance to commit himself to any particular camp along warring ideological or academic factions. Although he clearly departed from the path of Freudian orthodoxy at least as much as many of those who founded rival psychoanalytic schools, he seems never to have wished to break with the official psychoanalytic establishment. He has kept open the lines of communication with various schools, academic disciplines, and ideological orientations, striving to reach multiple role-partners and variegated audiences, but never to be exclusively identified with any one of them. He was much aware of the importance of multiple ties to a variety of persons, even if many of these might be only relatively weak.[5]

To highlight the importance of many networks, role-partners, and criss-crossing bonds for the creative contributions of an individual, it might be profitable to contrast, even though briefly, Erikson's life and work in America with those of another man with impressive intellectual endowments, his fellow refugee psychoanalyst Wilhelm Reich.

Wilhelm Reich

Wilhelm Reich had major contributions to his credit when he arrived in this country in 1939. His career had been stormy. Freud and his intimates had accepted him into their inner circle in the early 1920s, even though he was still very young (he was born in 1897).[6] For a while he seemed to be the rising star of postwar psychoanalysis. But after a few years, it became evident that Reich was not willing to be Freud's heir apparent. He developed instead a number of heretical ideas on the importance of social transformations in securing an environment conducive to individual mental health. He established clinics for the emotional and sexual guidance of working-class children, first under the aegis of Vienna's Social Democratic party and later, after 1930, under the guidance of the Communist Party in Berlin. Moreover, Reich developed unorthodox ideas about psychoanalytical technique and theory. Giving an extreme materialistic twist to Freud's teaching, Reich argued that neuroses were largely to be accounted for by inadequate discharges of sexual or orgasmic energy, which led to an "armored" character structure, as manifested by rigidified muscular posture. Even though some of Reich's contributions, especially those that concerned "character analysis," were subsequently incorporated into the orthodox psychoanalytical canon, and even though some of his ideas were later adopted by students of "body language" and other types of nonverbal communication, the bulk of his unorthodox teachings was rejected, and he was expelled from the official psychoanalytical association.

After the Nazi victory, Reich moved to Scandinavia, where he established a network of clinics, publishing houses, and seminars to propagate his own more and more sectarian doctrines, which he now called *Sexpol* (for sexual politics). Gradually, Reich's teachings assumed a bizarre character. He came to assert that orgasmic energy not only regulated psychical and physical balance but also governed the universe. He claimed that "bions"—that is, units of orgasmic energy—could be observed at work in developing protozoa, as well as in the atmosphere and in outer space. Despite the increasingly outré character of his assertions, he found a willing group of disciples in Scandinavia and was able to found a sect of true believers that had a considerable impact on Norwegian, as well as Danish and Swedish, intellectual life.

When Reich arrived in America in 1939, he immediately made plans to build a laboratory in a rented house in Forest Hills, New York. Even though he lectured for a while at the New School for Social Research, he established few contacts with American psychiatrists or with fellow refugees, confining his intellectual and social intercourse largely to his disciples and adherents. At Forest Hills and later in Maine, where he moved the major part of his laboratory in 1950, Reich established various research institutes, publishing houses, and foundations—all destined to preach orgonomic theory.

There seems to be little doubt that Reich was becoming psychotic during this period, if he was not mad earlier, but this did not detract from his capacity to attract followers. He now proclaimed that he could treat cancer, make rain, and repel invading space ships by directing orgonomic energy. He bombarded the U.S. government and leading scientists, such as Albert Einstein, with increasingly harebrained projects. He finally developed the orgone box, a contraption which was supposed to recharge persons deficient in vital energies. When he started selling these boxes by mail across state lines, the Federal Drug Administration imposed an injunction, which Reich refused to abide by. He was subsequently tried, convicted, and imprisoned in the federal penitentiary in Lewisburg, Pennsylvania—where he died of a heart attack in November 1957.[7]

It would be absurd to claim that Reich's aberrations could be fully explained by the fact that he chose to limit his social and intellectual contacts to true believers and disciples. It has been hinted that his mental condition could be traced to some organic problems. It seems, nevertheless, that, whatever predispositions Reich may have had for his descent into delusion, they were allowed to flourish by the absence of any person in his network who could attempt to contradict his visions and by his own unwillingness to extend this network.

As it is, Reich's teachings, shorn of their manifestly absurd features, have had some continued influence in America. Major literary figures, such as the late Paul Goodman, were influenced by him. Many of the themes of liberation, relaxed life styles, and unfettered sexual discharge, were picked up by the liberation movements of the 1960s. Reich established a reputation, even though largely underground, that has persisted. Those aspects of his teachings that have entered the psychoanalytic canon, especially the notion of "character analysis," were developed during his days in Vienna and Berlin, when he kept up sustained contact with his colleagues and was still open to their critical appraisals. His later work, developed in isolation and only to the admiring applause of unquestioning adherents, failed to make an impact except in the adversary culture.[8] While Erikson, with his many-faceted involvement in a great number of networks, made contributions to American culture at large, Reich, encapsulated in a cocoon of self-chosen disciples, developed esoteric themes that could never have been accepted by the culture in general, though they did stimulate the imaginations of active minorities in revolt against the main tenets of American culture.

Bruno Bettelheim (1903–): Psychotherapist and Cultural Critic

When Bruno Bettelheim arrived in this country in 1939, after an excruciating year as an inmate of Nazi concentration camps, neither he nor anyone else would have predicted that he would have a central role in building the clinical and theoretical foundations for group and milieu therapy of disturbed children, or that he would address a wide lay audience in America as a highly influential social critic. His impact on both professional psychotherapy and general American culture turned out to be pervasive.

Bettelheim was born in Vienna in 1903. His parents were prosperous upper-middle-class Jews who had come from Eastern Europe and had rapidly been assimilated into the secular urban culture of prewar Vienna. Bettelheim did not attend a gymnasium as did many of his contemporaries, but rather a *Realgymnasium,* that is, a high school in which modern languages and science, as well as classical education, were the core of the curriculum.

Bettelheim received a Ph.D. in psychology and philosophy from the University of Vienna in 1938, but several years before receiving his degree he had already developed his interest in psychoanalysis and the practice of psychotherapy. What fascinated him in psychoanalysis was not so much the study of the individual psyche and the psychotherapy of individual patients but the uses of psychoanalytic techniques in the group treatment of emotionally disturbed children. He was led to these concerns by the combined influence of his major university teacher, Karl Buehler (see pp. 37–41), who in his action-oriented approach to psychology concentrated most of his attention on the life-course of children and adolescents, and of the psychoanalyst August Aichorn, who, almost alone among his colleagues, had developed a psychoanalytic approach to disturbed and delinquent adolescents. He was also influenced by Anna Freud and other psychoanalysts, who had begun to emphasize the psychology of the ego and its defenses in their theoretical and clinical work.

Finally, his close companionship with Fritz Redl, a like-minded, child-oriented student of delinquent adolescents (who later also came to America), stimulated Bettelheim's thought and interests.

Never content with narrow professional training and associations, the young Bettelheim built many bridges to diverse cultural circles in Vienna, not only in the world of scholarship but also in the art world. All these involvements in cultural networks came to a brusque end when Hitler occupied Austria in 1938 and Bettelheim was imprisoned in the concentration camps of Dachau and Buchenwald. When he came to America after his release, in contrast to most other refugee intellectuals, he did not settle on the Eastern seaboard but went to the Midwest, where there was less temptation and opportunity to limit social intercourse to fellow refugees and more of a chance to become acquainted with native-born academics and professionals.

From 1940 to 1942 Bettelheim worked as a research associate at the University of Chicago on a project dealing with art education and the psychology of art. He then became an associate professor of psychology at Rockford College, Illinois, returning to the University of Chicago as a faculty member in late 1944. Soon thereafter, he became the director of the University of Chicago's school for disturbed children, the Orthogenic School. He directed the school and remained at the University of Chicago until his retirement in 1973. Bettelheim now lives in semiretirement on the West Coast. His literary activities have become even more extended than before, and he continues to be a much sought-after speaker and discussant at various conferences and symposia, addressing both professional and literary audiences as well as the general company of educated men and women. He also appears frequently on the mass media.[1]

What strikes one when considering Bettelheim's career in America is his involvement with and impact upon two distinct circles, professional psychologists and psychoanalysts, on the one hand, and literary milieux and audiences, on the other. He successfully combined a double career as a major group therapist at the Orthogenic School and as a humanistic critic of the culture at large. While the great majority of psychoanalysts who are considered here spoke only to audiences of their peers and sought recognition mainly from fellow psychotherapists, Bettelheim reached out for wider response from other circles fairly soon after his arrival in America. It is interesting to note in this respect that, whereas most of his early writings were issued by a leading publisher of professional books, The Free Press, his later work appeared under the imprints of Macmillan and Knopf, more general publishers.

Bettelheim's first publication in America, his article "Individual and Mass Behavior in Extreme Situations," appeared in the *Journal of Abnor-*

mal and Social Psychology in 1943.[2] This journal addresses itself to a scholarly audience of teachers and researchers in social psychology. But soon thereafter the article was reprinted in Dwight Macdonald's *Politics,* a journal of opinion read by an audience interested in general cultural criticism. This account of the behavior of concentration camp inmates, based largely on personal observations, brought Bettelheim to the attention of an audience of nonprofessionals. Its inclusion in the leading reader in social psychology[3] helped disseminate Bettelheim's work to undergraduates. Its provocative thesis—that camp inmates were characterized by infantile regression and that older inmates tended to identify with the prison guards and developed a character structure willing and able to accept the values of the Nazi elite—has continued to fuel controversy inside and outside academia ever since.[4] The paper is still widely reprinted in readers in social psychology. This double reception of Bettelheim's paper was a token of things to come.

Bettelheim's first book, *Love Is Not Enough,*[5] provided a detailed account of his therapeutic efforts at the Orthogenic School. Written in his characteristically lucid style and uncluttered by psychoanalytic jargon, the book attracted an audience considerably larger than would normally be expected for works of this type. It is indicative of Bettelheim's ability to move without apparent effort from one topic to another that in the same year in which this book was published (1950), he also published, in collaboration with the University of Chicago sociologist Morris Janowitz, *Dynamics of Prejudice,*[6] a study of young World War II veterans and their susceptibility to various types of prejudice. In contrast to several theories of prejudice current at the time, such as those of Fromm (see pp. 69–75) and Adorno (see pp. 91–98), the authors concluded from their empirical findings that it is difficult to establish the existence of distinct authoritarian personalities, and that degrees of prejudice can instead be accounted for by situational factors such as social position, degree of upward or downward social mobility, and education, together with the strength of ego controls.

A few years later, in 1954, Bettelheim turned to a still different area of investigation. This time, and in tune with his general disposition to think within a framework of disputation and controversy, he took issue with what he considered the predominantly male-oriented outlook of most Freudian psychoanalysis. He argued, in *Symbolic Wounds: Puberty Rights and the Envious Male,*[7] that orthodox Freudian thought, by concentrating on penis envy and the alleged female sense of inferiority in regard to male accomplishments, was severely one-sided. The reverse, male envy of the female capacity for giving birth and nurturing, was equally pervasive.

It is interesting to note that the data on which Bettelheim built his thesis varied from book to book In his first work (*Love Is Not Enough*) clinical observation took pride of place; the second (*Dynamics of Prejudice*) was based on interviews with veterans; whereas *Symbolic Wounds* largely built on Bettelheim's extended knowledge of the anthropological literature. His next book, published only a year after *Symbolic Wounds*, returned to his work at the Orthogenic School. *Truants from Life*[8] describes the therapeutic features of his residential treatment of disturbed and autistic youth, stressing that children coming from disorganized families should not be treated in individual therapeutic sessions but instead need a new life space in a residential center with a minimum of coercive restraints. Only in such a setting can they fashion a new social identity in close involvement with a staff trained to give maximum emotional support. These themes were further developed in a 1974 book, *A Home for the Heart.*[9]

In a series of essay collections published after his major reports on his work at the Orthogenic School—*The Informed Heart* (1960)[10] and *The Empty Fortress* (1967)[11] in particular—Bettelheim drew on his concentration camp experiences as well as on his therapeutic knowledge and his broad acquaintance with cultural trends in America to develop a philosophical position that relies heavily on psychoanalytic doctrine yet is also often at variance with some of its main tenets. Freud, one gains the impression, is to Bettelheim a *maître à penser* but not an infallible guide. In these essays, Bettelheim carries on a variety of battles with, among others, authors who have taken a position differing from his own on the nature of the concentration camp experiences, on the character of modern mass society, on the situation of Jews in the modern world, and on many other salient issues. Rejecting an overly rationalist psychology, and stressing that unconscious and nonrational factors inevitably influence the actions and behavior of individuals, Bettelheim argues that one of the main failures of modern mass society has consisted in its inability to channel and control irrational forces and direct them into safe channels. Poised between Freud's thorough cultural pessimism and what Bettelheim considered the utopianism of the Left, he attempted to outline a middle path. Cultural despair would lead only to acquiescent passivity in the face of the disintegrating tendencies of mass society, but Rousseauist optimism about the essential goodness of the human animal is a rationalistic delusion. Bettelheim's position seems essentially that of an old-fashioned, nineteenth-century liberal individualist who, however, has lost his overoptimistic illusions in the post-Holocaust world.

Three later works of Bettelheim need to be mentioned if only to indicate the astonishing breadth of his interests. In *The Children of the Dream*,[12] based on an observation tour of Israeli kibbutzim, he argued, in a polemical stance against admirers of the kibbutz method of collective upbringing, that even though children reared in this setting were able to sustain a sense of collective responsibility that was in danger of vanishing in the West, they paid for this accomplishment by shallowness of personality and a lack of individual creativity. His next book, *The Uses of Enchantment* (1976)[13] again moved into new territory. It is an analysis of the symbolism in classical fairy tales, arguing that since these symbols have powerful appeal to the subconscious mind of the reader and tap the sources of unconscious strivings and desires, it is useless to try to suppress them because of their alleged cruelty, as many contemporary educators have urged. Access to the symbolic world through the resources of fairy tales, Bettelheim argues, can be used for beneficent as well as for maleficent purposes. Fairy tales can help children to master the world of adult reality. His detailed analyses of a number of these tales reveal a masterful knowledge of the uses of psychoanalytic interpretation.

Bettelheim's most recent book, *Freud and Man's Soul* (1983),[14] while not as memorable as some of his earlier works, is yet of great interest for students of the careers of refugee scholars. Bettelheim wrote the book in his eightieth year after spending more than half his life in the United States. The book shows that, despite his apparent adjustment to American society and culture, Bettelheim is still by no means fully at home in America.

He argues in this slender volume that American psychoanalysts, not having had the benefit of his own training in Vienna, and misled by the Victorian conventions of the standard translation, have severely misunderstood Freud's message. Not only have they converted psychoanalysis into a medical specialty, quite contrary to Freud's intention, but they have misunderstood much of Freud's message, partly because of not being familiar with the German distinction between *Naturwissenschaft* and *Geisteswissenschaft* and thus ignorant of Freud's insistence that he had made contributions to the science of the spirit rather than to natural science. They have also absorbed Freud's message in translations, including the "official" Strachey translation, which distort his original meanings. The German word *Masse,* for example, does not mean "group"; *Trieb* does not mean "instinct"; and Freud's *Ich, Es,* and *Ueber-Ich* should be rendered as "I," "it," and "over-I" or "upper-I" rather than as "id," "ego" and "superego."

Most reviewers of the book found it somewhat quixotic. They pointed out that the Standard Edition of Freud's work in English had been approved by Freud's daughter and intellectual heir, that no translation can ever be free of error and distortion, and that Bettelheim's proposed changes are as open to question as some of the earlier translations. As the eminent literary critic Frank Kermode has pointed out, "Bettelheim in this work looks back after a lifetime of achievement in an alien culture and an alien language to the happiness and security of the Gymnasium, the city and the language of his youth."[15]

Reflecting on the reasons for Bettelheim's outstanding success on the American scene, despite his reservations and misgivings, one must note his characteristically lucid style of presentation and his flexible command of idiomatic English. There is no trace in his writings of psychoanalytic jargon or of the Germanic tendency to sacrifice readability in favor of "profundity." A second factor has surely been Bettelheim's willingness and ability to learn from American sources—from pragmatic philosophy, for example—and not to rely exclusively on the European fund of knowledge that he brought with him from Vienna. But the importance of these factors seems in the last analysis to be overshadowed by still another: Bettelheim's capacity to shuttle back and forth between groups and intellectual settings of widely different character. He can address his fellow psychologists and psychoanalysts on one occasion and then switch to the universe of discourse of philosophers or literary people on another. He can write for, and appeal to, *The New Yorker* audience as much as to fellow practitioners of child therapy. His is a strong and highly opinionated voice, whether it attempts an assessment of the concentration camp experience and its implications for the modern world or probes the psyche of autistic children. Not only is he extremely versatile in his choice of subjects for his writing, but he has also addressed different networks of audiences and publics. A pugnacious and acerbic critic, he has enlivened debate on crucial cultural issues even as he has contributed to the science and art of healing the wounds of children and adolescents. Like a great juggler, he is always able to keep many balls in the air. One is hard put to think of many other refugee intellectuals who have contributed with such apparent ease to so many crucial areas of American life and experience.

Erich Fromm (1900–1980): Neo-Freudian Psychoanalyst and Social Critic

More than any other psychoanalyst of his time, Erich Fromm, who came to America as a refugee in 1933, enjoyed a large audience among laypersons. Yet he also gained a considerable hearing among professional psychoanalysts and psychologists. Even though his more orthodox psychoanalytic colleagues deplored his departure from Freud's teachings, they nevertheless profited from his writings, especially from his notion of social character. In addition, Fromm was closely associated with the neo-Freudians around the prestigious William Alanson White Institute of Psychiatry, where he served for a number of years as chairperson of the faculty. Finally, not content with the elaboration of psychoanalytic thought and with psychotherapeutic practice, Fromm wrote a series of highly successful books in an Old Testament prophetic voice which established him as a leading social critic. In these books, he decried the wickedness of the times and pointed to the urgent need for redemption through a return to justice and love. In all these ways, Fromm had a significant impact on the American culture of the 1940s and 1950s.

Fromm was born in Frankfurt-am-Main in 1900, to a middle-class family. In contrast to most of the German-Jewish families that produced distinguished sons and daughters in the early part of the century, Fromm's family adhered to strict religious orthodoxy. As a result, he was brought up in an environment in which the Old Testament in general, and the prophetic writings in particular, had pride of place. Even though Fromm lost his religious faith in his late twenties, this background remained a potent influence throughout his career. His Talmudic teachers in adolescence and early manhood shaped his life. After studying with several such teachers—some of them mystics, others socialists—and also with the great Kabbalah scholar Gershom Scholem, Fromm planned to become a rabbi.[1] But soon after high school, he was exposed to very different winds of doctrine. During his studies in psychology, sociology, and philosophy at the universities of Frankfurt and Heidelberg, he be-

gan to associate with secular students and teachers whose influence soon
overshadowed his previous intellectual background. His dissertation on
the psychological structure of the members of three Jewish groupings,
in which he examined, inter alia, the differing religious orientations of
Chassidim and modern Reform Jews, indicates that he was still poised
between the world of Judaism and that of modern secular thought. But
soon after completing this dissertation and receiving his Ph.D. from the
University of Heidelberg at the age of twenty-two, Fromm made a defi-
nite move away from his religious fundamentalism.

Gershom Scholem says in his autobiographical account that in the
Frankfurt of the 1920s there existed "another remarkable institution
[beyond the Jewish House of Studies] which created a stir among young
academicians. . . . This was the 'torahpeutic' sanatorium, as the wags called
it, located in Heidelberg, where the strictly orthodox psychoanalyst Frieda
Reichmann . . . was attempting to combine Torah and Freudian therapy.
Some of my best students . . . such as . . . Fromm . . . were being treated
at this sanatorium on an outpatient basis. All of them, with the exception
of one, had their Orthodox Judaism analyzed away."[2] A few years later,
Fromm married Frieda Reichmann, pursued additional studies in psychiatry and psychology at the University of Munich, and began his psychoanalytic training. Upon graduating from the Berlin Psychoanalytic
Institute (where he was analyzed by Hanns Sachs) in 1931, he became
one of its members and practiced psychoanalysis in Berlin. During this
same period, commuting between Berlin and Frankfurt, he also founded
the Frankfurt Psychoanalytical Institute with Fromm-Reichmann.

While psychoanalysis seems to have been the major intellectual influence that cut Fromm loose from his religious moorings, and while psychoanalytic practice seems to have been for him a substitute for the rab-
binical career on which he had first set his eye, still other intellectual
influences contributed to his mature world view. When still very young,
Fromm was passionately opposed to the world war. At an early age he
had already developed an internationalist outlook and a passionate concern with the conditions that might promote peace among nations. These
concerns were reinforced during his university days spent associating
with radical students of a Marxist cast of mind. During the mid-1920s
Fromm became a Marxist, though he never publicly identified himself
with Marxist political movements. Instead, he began to associate with
the unorthodox Marxist philosophers and social scientists who, under
the direction of Max Horkheimer, led the Frankfurt Institute for Social
Research. He was a member of that institute from 1928 to 1938, the
period when he and most of its members moved to the United States.

Fromm's early psychoanalytic practice was in the Freudian mode. But
largely under the influence of Marxist students and his work with the

Frankfurt Institute, Fromm soon attempted to incorporate Marxian ideas into his psychoanalytic framework. His contributions to *Autoritaet und Familie*,[3] a major collective work by the members of the Frankfurt Institute on the interrelations of economic structures and family relations, which were partly based on interviews with working-class families in the last years of the Weimar Republic, document that notions such as "character structure" and "sadomasochistic personality," which Fromm developed during his years in America, were adumbrated in his thinking as early as 1936.

In America, Fromm first set up a private practice in New York City. But not content with treating private patients, he broadened his network of associates as well as his intellectual concerns by moving into academic positions. He became a member of the faculty of Bennington College (1941–49) and later (1948–49) a guest professor at Yale, where he gave a seminar on social character and anthropology in association with the prominent anthropologist Ralph Linton. In 1949, for reasons of his (second) wife's health, Fromm moved to Mexico to accept a professorship at the National Autonomous University of Mexico, where he started a Department of Psychoanalysis at the university's Medical School. After his move to Mexico, Fromm commuted regularly to the United States, teaching at the William Alanson White Institute and at Michigan State University, where he was professor of psychology from 1957 to 1961, and finally at New York University. After his retirement in 1971 he moved to Switzerland, where he died nine years later.

Fromm's numerous writings fall largely into two distinct types that correspond at least roughly to the different audiences he addressed over time. His earlier writings, conceived in collaboration with other members of the Frankfurt Institute and culminating in his masterpiece, *Escape from Freedom*[4] in 1941, attempted a reformulation of psychoanalytical theory through the creative incorporation of major elements of Marxian thought. Though widely read by an interested general audience, these writings were intended primarily for social scientists and other professionals. His later writings were increasingly addressed to a wider audience and abandoned the scientific mode of discourse in favor of the prophetic.

At the center of Fromm's earlier writings is the concept of social character. Building on foundations laid by Wilhelm Reich and the Berlin group of Marxist psychoanalysts gathered around Otto Fenichel and Annie Reich, Fromm developed the notion much further. Accepting the theory of oral, anal, and genital stages in human development, Fromm nevertheless rejected Freud's libido theory and argued instead that variant social character types must be understood as typical responses to the class structure and socioeconomic conditions. Humans, so he argued, are "a freak of nature" in that they largely lack the instinctual equipment that guides the behavior of all other animals. As a consequence, human beings develop character structures that serve to give a measure of consistency to their responses to the environment. Character, then, is the relatively fixed way in which human energy is channeled and structured through the process of socialization. The social character is the nucleus of the individual character structure, and it is typically shared by most members of a culture or, in differentiated societies, of a social class. The dominant mode of production, in particular, has a crucial influence on character formation.

The family is seen by Fromm as the most important transmission belt that helps to inculcate character traits deemed to be functional requisites in particular types of societies or in particular social classes. It is within the family that maturing individuals learn to want to act as the society wishes them to act. It is within the family that they learn to channel their balance of pleasure and pain so as to find gratification in behaving in accordance with prevailing systems of values and functional requirements. Where orthodox Freudians, for example, talk about an anal character, Fromm uses the term *hoarding orientation* and argues—the point made was first developed in the Marxist groups of psychoanalysts in Berlin—that a predisposition for orderliness, punctuality, and saving began to be emphasized in the middle class in the nineteenth century to serve the functional needs of that class during a period of rapid industrialization, with its stress on productivity and economic advancement. In the twentieth century, in contrast, the social character required for the middle class in advanced societies deemphasized production in favor of consumption and bureaucratic adaptation and led to the emergence of a "marketing personality."

Fromm developed another fruitful concept: the sadomasochistic or authoritarian character. Drawing on interview data gathered in the last few years of the Weimar Republic, Fromm showed that large parts of the German middle classes, but also some working-class strata, developed a sadomasochistic or authoritarian character—that is, a predisposition to react to external restraints with the internal repression of "dangerous" impulses and rigid obedience to social controls. People with such a character structure achieve social adjustments largely through submission and by taking pleasure in being subordinate. They respect only the strong and, concomitantly, hate the weak. Authoritarians develop what the Germans call the "bicycle rider syndrome," which consists of bowing to those above and pushing around those below.

Fromm's character typology served him well when he wrote *Escape from Freedom,* an attempt to explain the rise of German fascism in psychoanalytic as well as Marxian terms. Arguing that authoritarian traits have long been a distinctive aspect of the family structure of the German middle classes, he stated that an authoritarian personality resulting from authoritarian upbringing was likewise a distinctive phenomenon throughout Germany at least until the early twentieth century. Yet as long as German society rested on secure foundations, such character types followed expected social routines and posed no threat to the orderly operation of an authoritarian society. However, when, as a result of inflation and depression, German society collapsed, it failed to provide its citizens, especially those with authoritarian predispositions, with a secure anchorage. Under these circumstances arose the tendency "to escape from freedom"—that is, to seek a solution to the disorientation in everyday life through submission to a powerful father figure who would exercise the authority the sadomasochist craves. By creatively linking psychoanalytic thinking and the study of social character with the Marxian emphasis on underlying socioeconomic conditions, Fromm forged an explanation of the rise of nazism that is still persuasive. What is most remarkable about this work is Fromm's success in linking these two schools of thought without doing violence to either and without falling into the trap of psychologizing sociological realities. Moreover, the book is also outstandingly successful in putting recent German developments into historical perspective by comparing the pervasive sense of insecurity and rootlessness in the contemporary German middle classes to a similar sense of the world's coming apart during the years preceding the Reformation in Germany.

A number of other papers Fromm wrote during his German period and in the first few years of his stay in America exhibit the same subtle blend of Marxist and Freudian ideas. Among these, the essay "The Dogma of Christ," written in Germany but published here only in 1963, is perhaps the most outstanding.[5] It is a remarkable attempt to understand the social psychology of Christ's disciples in the development of Christianity from a sect of true believers drawn from the lower social strata to a highly structured and organized church with a bureaucratically regimented set of rituals and ceremonies and a membership that comprised the high and mighty as well as the lowly. Theologians such as James Luther Adams have testified to the impact of this essay on their own thought and teaching, and knowledgeable sociologists of religion have seen it as one of the few successful attempts to deal with both psychological and sociological factors in the study of a religious movement.

After publishing *Escape from Freedom,* and after having severed his relations with Horkheimer's Institute for Social Research, Fromm increasingly moved away from his previous scientific work and addressed himself to the moral and philosophical problems of the hour. What seems to have been involved here is, in addition to a kind of return to the previously repressed concerns of his younger days, a strong feeling on Fromm's part that the crisis of our times required him to address wide audiences with his prophetic message of doom and redemption. Books such as *Man for Himself* (1947), *The Sane Society* (1955), *The Art of Loving* (1956), and *The Revolution of Hope* (1968)[6] brought him to the attention of a wide audience in quest of guidance and psychoanalytic advice. It is characteristic of all these books that even though Fromm sharply criticized modern culture, with its competitiveness, its loss of community, its greed, and its lack of moral standards, he nevertheless emphasized that modern men and women, once they became aware of the errors of their present ways, could always find their path to salvation. It is curious in how many ways these books came to reflect an outlook that was pervasive in the American inspirational literature of the nineteenth and early twentieth centuries—jeremiads in the American mode. These books, with their admixtures of Freud, Marx, and Zen Buddhism, surely do not exhibit the rigor of thought that was characteristic of Fromm's early work, but he would probably have remarked that it is foolish to insist on rigorous argumentation at a time when Rome is burning. It behooved the intellectual, so Fromm seems to have argued, to enter the public arena in defense of humanistic values, of peace, and of a more humane society, even if that meant abandoning some scholarly preoccupations.

In any case, Fromm became a modern guru to the middle classes in the postwar years. His books were eagerly bought not only in bookstores but from the racks of drugstores and airport newsstands. I can hardly remember looking at the private libraries of students and young professionals without finding at least one of the many prophetic books that Fromm wrote in the 1940s and 1950s. Even in the 1960s, the New Left, though more activist in its orientation than Fromm would allow, still considered some of his writings, especially those which stressed the need to return to the humanistic orientations of the young Marx, to be among their favorites. Being not overly discriminating in their taste, many young activists of the 1960s read both Fromm and Marcuse even though these former comrades-in-arms had long ago parted ways. Marcuse attacked Fromm for his optimistic reformism, and Fromm deplored Marcuse's "nihilism" and total rejection of all aspects of modern America.

Fromm's impact on American culture in general was strongly felt for several decades. That it will prove to be enduring seems more open to question. The message of salvationists tends most often to be so tied to the problems of the hour that it recedes from the collective consciousness when other problems become more salient. Whether this will be the fate of Fromm's prophetic writings, only time can tell.[7] But when it comes to the more rigorous work of his earlier years, one can be more certain. Concepts such as "social character" and "authoritarian personality" will continue to be consequential in social and psychological analysis for some time to come.

Karen Horney (1885–1952): Cultural Critic and Theorist of Feminism

When Karen Horney came to the United States in 1932, she had already been a successful psychoanalyst in Berlin for a number of years.[1] She had written a series of influential papers, particularly on the psychology of women and on problems in therapy, in which she had strayed from the orthodox view of women within the psychoanalytic movement. Yet it was only after coming here that she developed her own distinctive, culture-centered views, not only on feminine psychology and psychoanalytic therapeutic practice, but also on the theoretical structure of psychoanalysis as a whole. The American intellectual scene allowed Horney to develop her heretical ideas in a much more congenial setting than the German environment in which she had worked during the first period of her psychoanalytic practice.

Karen Danielson Horney was born in 1885. Her father was a Norwegian sea captain who later became a German citizen and commodore of a major German shipping line; her mother was of Dutch origin. Her father was a devout reader of the Bible, but her mother was a lifelong atheist. In her teens Horney apparently went through a period of religious enthusiasm, presumably inspired by her father, with whom she had made many sea voyages as a child. Yet her identification with her mother was much closer. She seems, in fact, to have come to hate her father.

At the turn of the century it was unusual for a woman to decide to become a physician. But Karen Horney seems not to have felt any inhibitions about the matter when, with the encouragement of her mother, she went to Berlin for medical and psychiatric studies at the university and, somewhat later, for training as a psychoanalyst. Soon after coming to Berlin in 1909 at the age of twenty-four, Karen Danielson married Oscar Horney, a Berlin lawyer, with whom she subsequently had three daughters. She received her medical degree in 1913 and did her psychiatric training from 1914 to 1918. Her training analysts at the Berlin

Psychoanalytic Institute were first Franz Alexander and then Hanns Sachs, both at the time prominent orthodox Freudians, and later fellow emigrés. From 1918 to 1932, Horney taught at the Berlin Psychoanalytic Institute and wrote a series of papers which, although they deviated in important respects from orthodox psychoanalytic doctrine on the psychology of women, were widely read and debated within the psychoanalytic movement.[2]

It is only after coming to America in 1932, at the invitation of Franz Alexander, who by then had become the head of the Chicago Psychoanalytic Institute, that Horney formulated her heretical ideals in systematic fashion. After two years in Chicago, she divorced her husband and went to New York as a psychoanalytic practitioner and writer. The two important works she published in that period, *The Neurotic Personality of Our Time* (1932) and *New Ways in Psychoanalysis* (1939),[3] brought her to the attention of a wide professional as well as lay public but also led to a break with the psychoanalytic establishment. In 1941 she was disqualified as a training analyst by the New York Psychoanalytic Institute and abruptly expelled from the New York Psychoanalytic Society. Soon thereafter she helped found the Association for the Advancement of Psychoanalysis, a meeting ground for neo-Freudian revisionists largely influenced by her teaching, but also by other such heterodox psychoanalysts as Harry Stack Sullivan and Erich Fromm.

In the Introduction to her *New Ways in Psychoanalysis,* Horney explained that the American intellectual climate had enabled her to break from Freudian orthodoxy. "The greater freedom from dogmatic beliefs which I found in this country," she wrote, "alleviated the obligation of taking psychoanalytic theories for granted, and gave me the courage to proceed along lines which I consider right." This seems indeed to have been the case, but it is remarkable that many roots of Horney's heretical beliefs can already be found in her German writings. It seems that, given the constricting circumstances of the psychoanalytic movement in Europe, Horney made an effort not to stray in principle from the orthodox paths although diverging in concrete particulars, especially in her view of feminine psychology. It was only in the less constricted, flexible, and open milieu of America that she found it possible to state openly her divergencies on issues of fundamental theory. This was so in part because other American approaches to dynamic psychology, particularly the work of Harry Stack Sullivan and of her fellow refugee Erich Fromm, proved congenial to Horney and facilitated the reception of her message among an American professional audience in psychiatry and clinical psychology, as well as among laypersons.

It is worthy of note that Karen Horney, in contradistinction to most orthodox psychoanalysts, managed very soon after her arrival to establish sustained intellectual contacts with American social scientists in neighboring disciplines. In Chicago she established friendships with the political scientist Harold Lasswell as well as with the orthodox psychoanalyst Karl Menninger. After the move to New York City, she was befriended not only by fellow heterodox psychoanalysts but also by the theologian Paul Tillich and the anthropologists Ruth Benedict and Margaret Mead. Margaret Mead later recalled that in 1932 Horney looked like a "typical Viennese intellectual" who judiciously neglected her personal appearance. But when Mead met her again six years later in New York City, Horney was sporting a fashionable hat and dress and seemed completely "Americanized."[4]

In the cultural and intellectual climate of New York in the 1930s and 1940s, the cultural relativism propounded by such prominent anthropologists as Benedict and Mead became widely diffused among professionals and laypersons alike. Biological interpretations of human nature were rejected, partly because of their association with the abhorrent race theories of the Nazis, and the view that the human psyche and human behavior are largely shaped by cultural influences became prevalent. These were the years of widespread discussions of the issue of nurture versus nature, with the former gaining the ascendancy, at least partly because of the intellectual impetus of the New Deal, with its basic optimism about changing social conditions and the human psychic economy.

Neurotic patients seeking relief from their troubles were not hard to find in the 1930s and 1940s. The demand for psychological help exceeded the supply of services, and psychoanalysts as well as clinical psychologists had no trouble finding eager patients. This situation made it difficult for orthodox psychoanalysts to control and monopolize the market. In Germany, in contrast, psychoanalysis had been a struggling sect that found difficulty in getting a hearing.

Horney's German work, largely on the psychology of women, diverged from orthodox psychoanalysis in important ways.[5] She found herself unable to accept Freud's view that women's fate is determined by their anatomy. Even in her early papers, Horney quarreled with Freud's largely biologically based libido theory as well as with his key notion in regard to feminine psychology: the concept of penis envy. Drawing in part on the writings of the sociologist Georg Simmel, she argued that only in an essentially masculine culture could penis envy be considered the key component of feminine psychology. Horney rejected the then prevalent belief in psychoanalysis that it was "natural" for women to be passive and masochistic and men active and sadistic in their drives. Nor was she willing to accept the idea that women were "naturally" envious of the male sex organ. On the basis of her wide clinical evidence from both women and men, she concluded that many men expressed "envy of pregnancy, childbirth, and motherhood, as well as of breasts and of the act of suckling," while many women suffered from repression of their active tendencies.[6] More generally, and in reaction against much Freudian thinking, Horney opposed physiologically based theories of the functioning of the human psyche. "The willingness to reduce complex psychological phenomena to physiological factors," she wrote, "[is] an assumption [that] is not only untenable but . . . makes the understanding of psychological phenomena even more difficult."[7]

In America Horney developed her notions into a full-fledged theoretical structure, with a strong emphasis on cultural factors in the fashioning of the human psyche and a concomitant deemphasis of biological determinants. In *New Ways in Psychoanalysis* she made a systematic critical evaluation of major theoretical constructs in psychoanalysis. Her critics pointed out that Freud was not as exclusively oriented toward biological interpretations as she made it appear, and that earlier, more orthodox psychoanalysts such as Ferenczi and Rank had already attempted to put more emphasis on the current life-situation of patients and hence the cultural fashioning of their personality; but the fact remains that these earlier theorists had not pushed these matters very far. Horney, in contrast, now argued that libido theory rested on a vague and mystical notion of biological constants and needed replacing by notions anchored in the culture that was the effective environment of the patient. This may have been, as her former teacher Franz Alexander argued, like trying "to expel Satan with Beelzebub,"[8] but it was perceived by the nonorthodox in America's melioristically optimistic 1930s and 1940s as a promising departure from received doctrine.

Horney not only attacked Freud's libido theory, with its alleged biological determinism, and the strictly sexual interpretation of the Oedipus complex. She also argued against the Freudian emphasis on instinctual energies feeding the id and the repressive superego. Such a view, she argued, deprived the ego of its directive powers and its relative autonomy. It is noteworthy that at the time Horney developed her view of the crucial importance of the powers of the ego, more orthodox analysts such as Anna Freud and Heinz Hartmann were developing an ego-oriented theory that bore some resemblance to Horney's. But these other theorists modified Freud's orientation without explicitly attacking its base. Hence they could remain within the ranks of the orthodox, while Horney was expelled.

It would seem that Horney's theoretical divergencies from the Freudian model would most likely have been restricted in their influence to professional psychoanalysts and psychotherapists, but in fact her success was with a wider public. This seems to be due to her attempts to account for the current crisis in modern culture and the concomitant anxieties besetting modern men and women. The source of all anxiety, Horney taught, is rooted in interpersonal relations; some of them are to be found in early family life while others have to be imputed to general cultural conditions.

What characterizes modern Western culture in general, and American culture in particular, Horney argued, is a high degree of competitiveness, as well as the contradictory pulls exerted by the dual desires to obtain success and to gain affection. These strains result not only in particular neurotic symptoms, she argued, but in neurotic personality types. Under these circumstances, neurosis is not just a temporary maladjustment but has a peculiar dynamism of its own that can dominate the personality as a whole. The strong stress on individualistic success and achievement in American culture creates a neurotic pattern in which competitive strivings are pervasive and create, in reaction, powerful feelings of anxiety, loneliness, isolation, alienation, insecurity, and barely repressed hostility. Under these conditions, neurotic patterns of defense largely replace a healthy quest for affection and love.

Horney's emphasis on the destructive effects of a competitive culture found a hearing among many who were torn between their striving for success and their yearning for security. The same public that took to Ruth Benedict's *Patterns of Culture,* with its at least implicit critique of the ravages of a competitive culture, also lent a ready ear to the more explicitly stated critique of Karen Horney. Perilously poised between the quest for success and upward mobility, and the New Deal yearnings for a more egalitarian and communitarian orientation of American culture, many of Horney's readers were touched by her message.

But here we face an interesting paradox. Many of Horney's comrades-in-arms, particularly Erich Fromm, used their criticisms of the competitive personality of our time as an argument for the reconstruction of society along brotherly and communal lines, but such political applications of her findings never claimed Horney's attention. She hence became an easy target of radical and left-wing critics, who argued that the neo-Freudians ultimately aimed at adjusting their patients to an unjust society rather than at making society more equitable and cooperative.

Horney's break with the official psychoanalytic establishment had some detrimental consequences for her later intellectual labors. She had previously elaborated her ideas in a continuing dialogue with more orthodox theoreticians, such as her former teacher Franz Alexander. This dialogue now ceased. As a result, she seems to have developed her own ideas in a somewhat more inflexible and doctrinaire manner. She now gathered a devoted group of followers around her in the Association for the Advancement of Psychoanalysis and its official publication, *The American Journal of Psychoanalysis.* It is my impression that her new associates, though gifted, were not of the caliber of her earlier associates in the orthodox psychoanalytic movement. This was not due to happenstance. Even though an establishment may repress unorthodox doctrine and limit theoretical flexibility, it does allow the opportunity for the exchange of ideas among equals. A small splinter group, on the other hand, while perhaps offering greater possibilities for innovation, also provides fertile ground for negative selection—that is, for attracting the disgruntled and malcontented rather than the most highly qualified. While the establishment restricts, the small splinter group may not offer the opportunities for adequate exchange of ideas with one's intellectual peers. This may be why Horney's work in the 1940s, while being sustained by the willing and eager audience of her associates and disciples, does not seem to have borne fruits as rich as her earlier writings.

Horney's neo-Freudian emphasis on cultural factors seems to have suffered a sea change in the cultural climate of America that followed her death in 1952. The New Deal meliorism and the postwar American Celebration, of which C. Wright Mills wrote so eloquently, were replaced by the strife, dissensions, and social confrontations of the 1960s and 1970s. In the tougher climate of these two decades, Horney's tenderminded views on the healing powers of therapeutic correction and self-analysis receded into the background or were replaced by frantic, and often irrational, quests for magical healing through cultish activities. Her modulated and reasonable message found a much less willing audience. The young were attracted to what they conceived to be "stronger stuff."

Horney's reputation would have suffered an even more serious eclipse in the 1960s had she not found a new audience among the feminists. Her early writings on the psychology of women and some of her later work began to be eagerly read by members of the women's liberation movement who were searching the psychological literature for support of their beliefs. Freud's pessimistic views, though they were defended by some feminist writers, repelled most of them by their apparent antifeminist stance. Anatomy, these feminists believed, was *not* destiny. Searching for cultural variables behind apparent biological constants, they rediscovered Horney just when she was in danger of being largely forgotten. The study of her work has now become a "must" among feminist psychologists and sociologists and also among many feminist lay readers. Even though she herself held out little hope for large-scale social and cultural transformation, her views on cultural variability have helped to provide a basis for those feminists who are unwilling to accept present-day patriarchal culture as eternal and God-given.

It is largely her feminist audience that sustains Horney's reputation today. Yet her work is still frequently referred to by clinical psychologists, especially those who, in opposition to Freud's views, argue that the human personality is essentially healthy even though some of its elements may be distorted by unhealthy cultural conditions. Nor is her influence forgotten among sociologists who, like Robert K. Merton and Peter M. Blau, have written about the dark side of the upward mobility and success strivings of Americans.

Curiously, Horney's success as a theoretician may well be accounted for by her making use of the opportunities available to insiders in one context and to outsiders in another.[9] Her perceptive view of the psychology of women owed a great deal to her position as an insider who could discern the male bias of Freud and other sexual outsiders to the world of women. On the other hand, her powers of observation as a refugee in America allowed Horney to discern defects in the American character that might well have remained hidden from most inside observers. Like those other outsiders, the Frenchman Alexis de Tocqueville and the Norwegian-American Thorstein Veblen, she put her finger on the hidden underside of the American character and thus contributed to a many-sided analysis of the effects of American culture.

This daughter of a sea captain helped to chart murky waters in the exploration of feminine psychology and America's competitive personality. Despite ups and downs in her reputation, it is likely that Karen Horney's impact on American culture and scholarship will not soon be forgotten.

III
Sociology and Social Thought

Introduction

The Nazi takeover in Germany led to a victimization of sociologists that was probably more thoroughgoing than in any other branch of learning, partly because a high proportion of sociologists were Jews and partly because many of them were politically left of center. About two-thirds of the professors of sociology were driven from their chairs. Moreover, the majority of younger sociologists who did not yet have regular academic positions were forced to leave the country.[1] There were roughly 55 teachers of sociology in Germany in the academic year 1932–33; only 16 remained in 1938. Of the 27 regular professors in 1933, 12 chose to emigrate, another 6 were dismissed but remained in Germany, and 9 continued to teach, but largely not in sociology. Thirteen of the 20 *Privatdozenten* chose to emigrate.[2] Sociology in Germany, and in Austria as well, was largely destroyed under the Nazis, and a high proportion of its representatives, both older and younger, came to the United States.

Under these circumstances, one would expect to find that refugees, since they represented a high proportion of German sociologists and included both eminent holders of chairs and highly promising younger people, had a major impact on the field in the United States. This was not quite the case, however, as the few examples I have chosen to deal with in detail testify.

As distinct from the situation in economics, for example, only a few refugee sociologists made significant contributions in their adopted country. Most of them became important as links between sociological scholarship here and in Europe, but without leaving a distinct mark as original thinkers. In other words, they served as transmission belts for sociological knowledge, especially sociological theory, but without adding to that knowledge in more than marginal ways. For instance, they were instrumental in providing translations, or inspiring translations, of such seminal thinkers as Georg Simmel, Max Weber, and Karl Mannheim. Their teaching in universities and colleges in the United States, and by no means only on the Eastern seaboard, familiarized large numbers of graduate students and also undergraduates with the theories and approaches of the European classics in the discipline. Even today one still encounters many native-born sociologists who are ready to testify that their European teachers were the ones to kindle in them the sociological imagination that led them to become social scientists.

What the European refugees brought to their student audiences, in addition to conveying the importance of the European classical sociologists, was a sense of history and of historical crises that was so often absent among their American colleagues. As Edward Shils has put it, "The refugees in the social sciences brought the awareness of the possibilities of decay of the social order, of the possibilities of disruption of what once seemed stable. They brought the exhilaration of intellectual melodrama—they brought Freud and Marx and a respect for the name of Max Weber."[3]

Why was it that refugee sociologists only rarely succeeded in contributing original knowledge once they arrived in the United States? At least part of the answer, I think, lies in the fact that American sociology in the 1930s was still largely, though not entirely, dominated by a relatively ahistorical and atheoretical orientation which most of the new arrivals found uncongenial. All this was to change rapidly a decade or two after most of the refugees arrived here, partly owing to their influence. Yet at the time, given the perceived "otherness" of American sociology, most of the refugees clung to a kind of adversary stance in regard to native scholarly trends. As a result, they often suffered from ossification of ideas. They tended to be unable to transcend the cultural stance that had been ingrained in them while still in Europe.[4]

The following chapters will deal with the exceptions, and they were largely exceptions, to this rule. Here I shall mention briefly some of those who acquired substantial merit as transmitters of knowledge.

Hans Gerth (1908–78), who taught for many years at the University of Wisconsin, not only translated, or inspired the translation, of much of Max Weber's work, but collaborated with his most prominent student, C. Wright Mills, in building links between the Weberian tradition and native American streams of thought, especially the pragmatist tradition of George H. Mead.[5] He also alerted his students to Mannheim's sociology of knowledge.

Kurt H. Wolff (1912–   ) provided translations of Georg Simmel which revived a long-dormant interest in this thinker and helped propel him into the rank of classical writers in sociology. Wolff was likewise active in stimulating renewed interest in the sociology of knowledge of Karl Mannheim by providing new translations as well as exegesis.[6]

Hans Zeisel (1905–   ), a close associate of Paul Lazarsfeld in Vienna, enriched the study of the sociology of law at the University of Chicago, as did his colleague Max Rheinstein (1899–   ), who, as a professor of comparative law, familiarized his American audience with the contributions Max Weber made to the sociology of law. Another German-born sociologist at the University of Chicago, Joachim Wach (1898–1955), developed a historical and phenomenological approach to the sociology of religion which moved in the wake of his teachers Ernst Troeltsch and Adolf von Harnack. His *Sociology of Religion* (1944)[7] was generally received as a kind of *summa* of a major strand of the European approach to the subject. Rudolf Heberle (1896–   ), who was on the faculty of Louisiana State University for many years, transmitted to American audiences, and applied to American data, the ecological approach to the study of politics that he had first developed in Germany.[8] Werner Stark (1909–   ), who taught at Fordham University, brought to America the sociology of knowledge of Max Scheler, an approach to the subject that differed in significant ways from the Mannheimian tradition that Gerth and Wolff were transmitting.[9]

The Russian-born, German-educated Alexander von Schelting (1894–1963) spent only a few years in the United States, most of them at Columbia University, but his *Max Weber's Wissenschaftslehre* (1934), a profound study of Weber's methodology which unfortunately has never been translated, exercised considerable influence on native interpretations, especially those of Talcott Parsons. Finally, one of the most creative students of Marx's ideas, Karl Korsch (1886–1961), has had considerable influence on recent American neo-Marxist thought. He taught only for a short time (in New Orleans) and was otherwise almost totally divorced from academic life in America, but he has continued to exert a kind of underground influence, partly through some younger American neo-Marxists who were privileged to know him or who "rediscovered" his work in the 1960s and 1970s.

The list of central European sociologists who made significant contributions to American social science as brokers and transmitters could easily be enlarged, but this book is not meant to be a compendium. In summary, let me reiterate that central European refugee sociologists performed the yeoman's task of helping to make American sociology a cosmopolitan enterprise, even though most of them made no enduring contributions of marked originality. It is to some of those who did make such contributions that we now turn.

The graduate faculty of The New School for Social Research, the academic home of the largest number of refugee social scientists in America, provided an almost indispensable haven for many of them, at least during the initial stage of their careers in this country. The New School's contributions in this respect have not yet been fully recognized, even though several major studies of its impact are now in the making. As time passed, many of those who had first taught at the New School moved on to other positions, but a strong contingent remained, whether by choice or necessity, to teach there until the end of their careers. These individuals comprised a critical group who were able to contribute to American social thought while still maintaining an intellectual and institutional life that strongly resembled that in European seats of learning.

To some extent, the New School provided a kind of gilded ghetto for those refugee social scientists who valued a protective bulwark against native-grown academic influences. Yet many of them were also willing and able to build many bridges to American-born colleagues while still nursing the feeling that they were teaching *in partibus infidelium*. Depending on one's views of the matter, one might feel that theirs was a somewhat ingrown mode of thought and way of life; or one might argue, to the contrary, that the New School, precisely because it was so different from other academic institutions, acted like an invigorating leaven in the world of American social thought.

In contrast, those Marxist scholars who were later to become known as members of the Frankfurt School self-consciously removed themselves almost completely during the first decade of their lives in America from American academic contacts, choosing instead to see themselves as a kind of saving remnant of German left-wing thought in the Babylonian captivity of New York City. At a later stage, some of them moved back to Germany, whereas others moved closer to American-style social thought, and still others contributed mightily to major strains of American adversary culture.

Among individual sociologists, not tied to either the so-called Frankfurt School or the New School, the name of Paul Lazarsfeld stands out. He was a major institutional as well as intellectual innovator whose mark is still deeply felt in the social sciences. He is somewhat comparable to Kurt Lewin, in that he managed, by cultivating native seeds, to open up largely unexplored areas in empirical social research. He trained many students who went on to shape major aspects of the field to this day. Somewhat ironically, this product of Vienna's socialist culture is now often seen as representing a "typically American" empirical approach to social thought.

Alfred Schutz, on the other hand, having found much less of an audience for his teaching during his lifetime, made creative contributions to the borderland between phenomenological philosophy and sociology that have come to be fully appreciated only since his death. In retrospect, Lazarsfeld and Schutz loom largest in terms of influence on American sociology.

This section closes with an analysis of the strange trajectory of the sinologist-sociologist Karl August Wittfogel, who moved during his years in America from orthodox Marxist thought to a no less orthodox neo-conservative position. He was, and still is, an odd man out who enriched not only sinological but also sociological and anthropological studies, yet remained without a stable audience or dependable disciples, plowing a lonely furrow in an academic no-man's-land.

The Institute for Social Research and "Critical Theory" in America

When a number of young, mostly unaffiliated, German Marxists resolved in the early 1920s to transform an informal discussion group into a permanent institute with university affiliation, they approached a prosperous Argentinian grain merchant, Hermann Weil. Weil consented to provide the financial foundation for this undertaking and set up an initial endowment providing a yearly income of 120,000 marks. Since in those years it took about 200 marks per month to support an unmarried research assistant, this was a considerable sum of money. Never before had a radical institute been able to flourish under such favorable financial conditions. Moreover, the grant was later supplemented by additional capital gifts. I shall not deal here with the early years of the Institute, when it was led by the labor historian Carl Gruenberg, but only with the period after 1930, when the critical theorists under Max Horkheimer (1895–1973) assumed command.[1]

When the Institute sought affiliation with the University of Frankfurt, a relatively new and liberal institution, it at first resolved to call itself the Institute for Marxism, but then decided that this name would be too provocative and chose instead the more neutral title of The Institute for Social Research.

The relative affluence of the Institute, and the tendency of its directing members to hew to an independent course of action while being circumspect about its relations with a wider public inside and outside the university, continued to characterize the activities of the Institute after its key members came to the United States. Even within their native Germany they seem to have seen themselves as internal exiles in a world that threatened to engulf them. This tendency was reinforced once they became refugees in America. They were acutely aware, both in Germany and in America, of the twin dangers of being absorbed by the dominant culture or being crushed by the dominant social powers. Yet, far from regretting their perilous condition, they accepted and even gloried in their marginal status. Even so, as will be seen, many of them ultimately came to be largely absorbed by American culture.

Some of the early members of the Institute were Gentiles, but the majority were sons of prosperous Jewish businessmen and professionals. Although they had broken with the world of their fathers at an early age, most of them retained the life-style of the *grande bourgeoisie*. Even though most of them in the days of the Weimar Republic and after professed identification with the working class, they knew little about workers through direct experience. They were much closer to the cultural style of affluent German professionals than to that of the lower classes. When, once in the 1940s in New York, I timidly queried their intellectual leader, Max Horkheimer, about the seeming discrepancy between their radical ideas and their bourgeois way of living, he answered brusquely, "When in Rome, do as the Romans do."[2] Whether in Germany or in this country, they saw themselves as living spiritually in Babylonian exile, but they refused the option of living in material self-denial or abnegation. Resolutely opposed to what they perceived to be the decadence of bourgeois society, they still managed to find a relatively satisfying niche within it.

A great number of social scientists and humanist scholars worked at the Institute over the long period of its existence, first in Germany, then in America, and then again in Germany. I shall concentrate here on only a few of its core members: Max Horkheimer, Herbert Marcuse, Leo Lowenthal, Friedrich Pollock, and Theodor Adorno. (Three other collaborators of the Institute, Franz Neumann, Erich Fromm, and Karl August Wittfogel, are dealt with in separate chapters.)

Horkheimer was born in 1895, the son of a Jewish textile manufacturer; Marcuse, born three years later, was the son of a Jewish businessman; Lowenthal, the son of a Jewish physician, was born in 1900; Pollock, born in 1894, was also the son of a Jewish businessman; Adorno, born in 1903, came from a family of Jewish wine merchants. All of them had similar social backgrounds and belonged to roughly the same generation. Some of them served as very young men in World War I, others did not; but all of them were crucially influenced by the war and its revolutionary aftermath. All of them revolted against the bourgeois complacency of their parents and turned with youthful enthusiasm to the postwar Socialist and Communist movements. They all came to call themselves Marxists, but most of them never joined either the Communist or the Social Democratic party. Marcuse was a short-lived SDP member as a youth. The two prominent members of the Institute who joined the Communist party, Franz Borkenau and Karl August Wittfogel, were Gentiles. Most of the key members wished to maintain their autonomy as unaffiliated left radicals and felt repelled by the unexciting routinized

politics of the Social Democrats as well as by the brutal orthodoxies of
Stalinist Communists. Standing between the fronts, they hoped to be
above the fratricidal battles of the Left so as to have the occasion to
elaborate a Marxist cultural critique of capitalist society which they came
to call "critical theory."

Horkheimer was from the beginning the undisputed intellectual leader
of the group that elaborated "critical theory," even though he was probably not its most eminent thinker. While some of the others were un-
worldly intellectuals, Horkheimer was a superb academic entrepreneur
who had the ability to formulate and define the group's common intellectual perspective.[3] Marcuse, who had originally been influenced by the
existential philosophy of his teacher Martin Heidegger and had attempted a merger between existentialist and Marxist streams of thought,
joined the staff of the Frankfurt Institute shortly before the group's emigration and was hence not involved in the initial formulation of "critical
theory." Adorno, a student of Alban Berg and Arnold Schoenberg, concentrated mostly on the study of music in the 1920s and became closely
associated with the work of the Institute only after an extended stay in
Vienna. Pollock, an economist, and Lowenthal, a student of literature,
were closely tied to Horkheimer from the beginning and assumed many
of the burdens of administration and editing that Horkheimer dele-
gated to them.

All of these men had university educations and received the Ph.D. in
their respective fields of study. Some also successfully passed *Habilitation,*
the examination that allowed them to teach at the university, but only
Horkheimer held a chair. He became a professor of social philosophy at
Frankfurt in January 1931. A few months earlier, at the age of only
thirty-five, he had become director of the Institute.

Although the Institute had published a number of important monographs in the 1920s, Horkheimer, who disliked the mammoth tomes so
characteristic of German scholarship and preferred an aphoristic style,
resolved soon after taking command that the group he had gathered
round him would best present its ideas through essays rather than through
large-scale treatises. A new publication, the *Zeitschrift fuer Sozialforschung,* was to diffuse the thought of the Institute. The bland title, *Journal for Social Research,* seems typical of Horkheimer's cautious intellectual strategy. Most of the major articles were written by the core group,
although more peripheral members as well as congenial outsiders also
collaborated. The principal programmatic articles in the *Zeitschrift* did
not concern themselves with social research, as the title suggested, but
rather dealt largely with macrosociological questions, with cultural analysis and criticism, and with the history of ideas. The *Journal* was infused
by a Hegelianized Marxism derived in large part from an earlier gen-

eration of Marxist thinkers, especially Georg Lukács and Karl Korsch. But it also attempted to work toward an integration of Marxism and psychoanalysis, both of which, so the core members believed, offered the best chances of formulating a radical critique of bourgeois culture. The early issues still gave testimony to the editors' belief that only the working class and a proletarian revolution could be expected to save European culture and society. These beliefs receded into the background after their emigration. Later issues were limited largely to cultural and social criticism without providing much hope of redemption for a fallen bourgeois world.

When the core group of the Institute became convinced in 1932 that the victory of the Hitler movement was imminent, they arranged to transfer all funds, as well as part of the library, to Geneva. This is why, when Hitler came to power the next year, the Institute found it easy to transfer its activities abroad. In March 1933 the Institute was closed down by the Nazis, and a month later Horkheimer was formally dismissed from his Frankfurt chair, together with Karl Mannheim and Paul Tillich. For the next year, Geneva was the headquarters of the Institute, with smaller branches operating in Paris and London, and the *Zeitschrift* was published in Paris under the prestigious imprint of the Librairie Felix Alcan. Even though the Nazis prohibited the selling of copies in Germany, the *Zeitschrift* continued to be published in the German language. Its editors wished to make it clear that they considered themselves German exiles who would continue their critical analyses of modern culture and society within a largely German intellectual tradition. Adorno once graphically described their position as that of men who sent messages to their homeland as if in a sealed bottle entrusted to the sea.[4]

The upholders of critical theory maintained a similar stance when they transferred the headquarters of the Institute to New York in 1934. One gathers that Horkheimer and his associates were somewhat surprised when the archconservative president of Columbia University, Nicholas Murray Butler, offered to house the Institute in a university-owned building and to facilitate its loose affiliation with Columbia. Morningside Drive, at the edge of the Columbia campus, became the main locus of the Institute for the next decade, even though some members of the core group, as well as more peripheral scholars, worked there for only relatively short periods.

It was in the New York years that Horkheimer's leadership and entrepreneurial capacities came to full flowering. He managed to maintain the Institute's autonomy even while he built several bridges to Columbia and other universities as well as to sources of research funds. He invited a number of American scholars to contribute to the *Zeitschrift*, while making sure that the core group remained fully in command. He made

it clear that the key members of the Institute did not wish to seek positions within the academic establishment but considered themselves exiles by continuing to publish the *Zeitschrift* in German, thus excluding
most potential American readers. Yet, even while wholly determined to
maintain the *Zeitschrift* as an outpost of critical German thought abroad,
Horkheimer was also acutely concerned about not offending the powers-that-be in America. The Institute made an effort to downplay its still
basically Marxist orientation. It cultivated the use of certain code words
that were designed to camouflage its real orientation. Marxism had already become "critical theory." Bourgeois culture became "affirmative
culture." A reference to communism in a piece by Walter Benjamin sent
from Paris was replaced by "the constructive forces of mankind" in the
edited version. Where Benjamin referred to "imperialistic warfare," the
edited version read "modern warfare." The *Zeitschrift* thus consciously
cultivated its use of Aesopian language to protect itself from possible
political harassment. It tended to refer to Hegel when it really meant
Marx. Shortly before the end of the war, Horkheimer told me with a
twinkle in his eye that he had just received a postcard sent from Trier,
the birthplace of Karl Marx, by a former student who was with the
American forces in Germany. It read: "With best regards from the birthplace of Hegel."

Ambivalence and an adversary stance continued to characterize the
orientation of the Institute toward American culture and society until
the outbreak of World War II. Its members continued to see themselves
as exiles rather than refugees, and they took a great deal of pride in
their largely self-willed marginality. Things changed, however, with the
outbreak of the war in Europe. To begin with, the *Zeitschrift* could no
longer be published in France. I take it to be highly significant that
Horkheimer then decided to publish it in America, and in English. Its
reappearance as *Studies in Philosophy and Social Science* in 1941, marked
a change of orientation in the Institute. In February 1940, Horkheimer,
Pollock, Marcuse, and Lowenthal had taken out naturalization papers.
From that time on, all the publications of the Institute appeared in English. The major collective work of the Institute in the years before the
war, *Autoritaet und Familie,* was written in German and hence was hardly
noticed by more than a handful of American specialized readers. In
contrast, the monumental series *Studies in Prejudice,* particularly its key
work, *The Authoritarian Personality* (1950),[5] although it picked up ideas
already adumbrated in *Autoritaet und Familie,* found a wide audience in
the American social science community.

Perhaps even more significant is that a number of the members of the
Institute took government-service positions after America entered the
war. Herbert Marcuse joined the Office of Strategic Services, a precursor

of the CIA, as did two other members of the Institute, Otto Kirchheimer and Franz Neumann. Leo Lowenthal served with the Office of War Information both in Washington and in New York. Pollock served as a consultant on the Board of Economic Warfare and for the Department of Justice.

The reasons for this move of erstwhile revolutionary Marxists to the seats of power in Washington are complex. To begin with, the capital endowment of the Institute had shrunk considerably in the late 1930s, partly because it had spent considerable sums of money to help fellow refugees, and partly as a result of disastrous real-estate transactions in Upstate New York. (Marxist economics proved by no means superior to the bourgeois variety when it came to real estate.) The unaccustomed financial stringency forced the Institute to discontinue publishing *Studies in Philosophy and Social Science* after only a few issues. More important, the Institute was forced to reduce its staff. While this reduction affected only the more peripheral members, the core members may also have felt that it was opportune to look for alternative sources of employment.[6] But apart from these material considerations, it stands to reason that, despite all their reservations, the key members of the Institute felt that it behooved them to participate in the anti-Fascist war effort. Many of them still harbored hopes that Hitler's reign would be followed by a socialist regime, so that they were justified in contributing to a war effort which would topple the Nazis.

Most of those who had moved to Washington in the war years left it soon after the war's end, but it is interesting to note that the most prominent among them, Marcuse, continued in government service at the State Department for a number of years. He returned to lecture at Columbia only in 1951, soon afterward to move to the Russian Research Center at Harvard and then to Brandeis University. Otto Kirchheimer also continued to work for the State Department even during the McCarthy years, leaving only in 1955, first for the New School and then for a Columbia professorship. Lowenthal continued to work for the Office of War Information after the end of the war. As these cases make clear, as their years in America lengthened and their hopes for a postwar socialist Germany receded, a number of the members of the Institute gradually mellowed in their attitudes toward things American.

The Institute's adversary stance toward the American academic and intellectual establishment also became gradually toned down in the war years and after. As their existential situation changed, as they moved from the protective cocoon of Morningside Drive into a variety of government and, increasingly, academic positions, most of the members subtly changed their orientations. When Adorno and his collaborators contrasted the authoritarian personality to the "democratic personality" in their American study, instead of contrasting it, as they had done in the earlier German version, to the "revolutionary personality," this might be considered a half-conscious effort to camouflage their radical stance. But after the war, many others began self-consciously to reject, or at least to modify, their previous Marxist convictions. Most of them continued to react in a critical manner to many aspects of American culture, but they no longer condemned it entirely. Marcuse and Adorno, to be sure, maintained their rigidly critical position toward bourgeois civilization to the end of their lives, but most of the others mellowed. Leo Lowenthal, for example, surveying his career in America just before his eightieth birthday, wrote: "I have become [an] integral member of the American educational system and of the American intelligentsia, without giving up my German traits. . . . I no longer feel an exile. I would not return [to Germany]. . . . I am largely an American; to be sure, I am also a German Jew, but I am also an American. And there is much in America that is good."[7]

While many members of the Institute moved to Washington during the war, others went to California. Largely because of the somewhat precarious state of his health, Horkheimer went to Santa Monica in early 1941 and Adorno, probably mainly out of personal loyalty, soon followed him. Both of them, however, spent much time in New York even after moving to California. The gradual dispersal of its key members slowly undermined the common outlook the Institute had displayed when they all shared offices at Morningside Drive. While the Washington group mainly engaged in work directly or indirectly tied to the war effort, Horkheimer and Adorno now turned their attention to specifically American subject matters. Adorno continued his analysis of popular culture; Horkheimer was instrumental in securing institutional backing for studies of authoritarianism and prejudice largely directed by Adorno. Horkheimer managed to obtain the financial support of the American Jewish Committee and the Jewish Labor Committee for large-scale studies that explored the American setting and thus helped to bring about a reorientation of the focus of the Institute from Europe to America. Not that Institute studies now neglected Europe entirely; yet, as compared to the earlier period, European data served mostly comparative purposes and were no longer the center of attention.

This shift of focus is most noticeable when one looks at *The Authoritarian Personality*, a large and highly influential piece of social research that Adorno produced with the collaboration of a number of social psychologists—most, but not all, of them native Americans. While its predecessor, *Autoritaet und Familie*, had relied mostly on structural factors, particularly class factors, to explain authoritarian traits, *The Authoritarian Personality* concentrated mainly on the analysis of subjective dispositions and attitudes. Whereas earlier the irrationality of decadent bourgeois society was seen as the root of authoritarianism, *The Authoritarian Personality* concentrated on the irrationality of individuals. To be sure, the earlier work, in tune with the psychoanalytical explanatory categories of Erich Fromm, dealt with character deformations of the personality, but it always explained them as being rooted in the irrationality of the social order. Such an emphasis almost completely disappeared from *The Authoritarian Personality*. Moreover, while revolutionary change was the ostensible goal of the earlier research, education for tolerance was the avowed aim of the new study. Even though some remnants of the old orientation could still be discerned in the new work, they were not likely to strike the ordinary reader. By and large, the work was impregnated with impeccable New Dealish and liberal values. Though the merger was not fully successful, as many critics pointed out, *The Authoritarian Personality* accomplished a turning away from "critical theory" to traditional American social and psychological explanatory schemes and the latest techniques of American social psychology. If it had a critical edge, that edge was largely blunted. Even though Adorno's later work, after his return to Germany in 1950, indicates that he had not permanently abandoned his intensely critical attitude toward mass culture, popular culture, and the American scheme of things in particular, it remains true that during and immediately after the war years both he and Horkheimer, from their secure niche overlooking the Pacific, had come to take a more benign and reformist outlook on American cultural phenomena. The impeccably bourgeois sponsorship of their studies in prejudice was surely in part responsible for their change in emphasis, but it would be an insult to their memory to suggest that they simply trimmed their sails to accommodate the prevailing winds.

After the war's end, some core members of the Institute gradually drifted to positions in the American academy. Lowenthal taught for many years at the University of California at Berkeley and continues to reside there after his retirement, still lecturing occasionally at the university. Marcuse spent over a decade at Brandeis University and then taught for several years at the University of California at San Diego, where he retired. Franz Neumann and Otto Kirchheimer taught at Columbia. Most of those who stayed in America after the war, with the major exception of Marcuse, tended after a while to shed some of the more sharply honed weapons of critical theory and to speak in an idiom that was, even though their own, not far removed from that of their academic colleagues. This is why it is hardly justified to speak of a "Frankfurt School" approach when it comes to the postwar years in America. To be sure, after Horkheimer and Adorno returned to Germany, they created such a school there, but this is not part of my story. Insofar as those former critical theorists who stayed in America are concerned, they diverged to some degree from their previous orientations. Such a change was, to be sure, explainable in part by their disillusionment with the Soviet Union, their abandonment of the belief in the working class as the universal class that would save mankind, and a host of other ideological factors. But one need hardly be a rigid believer in the social determination of forms of knowledge to realize that their changed social positions in the structure of American society during and after the war was related to their changed attitudes toward things American. While they had fiercely resisted absorption into American society during the first ten years or so of their stay, they were at least partly absorbed afterward, except, of course, for those of them who chose to return to their native land[8]

The major exception to what I have just said is Herbert Marcuse. He, too, somewhat softened in his attitude toward America in his position as a tenured and highly respected professor. His winning personality, as well as his contacts with leading native-born intellectuals in Washington during the war years, had brought him many friends in the academy, most of whom did not fully share his critical views. Moreover, he was not one to deny himself the pleasures that his newly found secure financial circumstances made possible. This principled adversary of the capitalist system was not even averse to playing the stock market from time to time. I remember a conversation with him, after he had delivered a fiercely "critical" lecture on American society at Brandeis, where he suddenly asked me after a few drinks, "Lew, you know more about these matters than I do, should I sell my General Motors shares and buy some General Electric?" But when all is said and done, the fact remains that Marcuse remained much truer to his original stance than all the other members of the Institute who stayed in America. This largely explains why, at an advanced age, he became the guru of the New Left of the 1960s, which otherwise tended to distrust anyone over thirty.

Adorno's criticism of mass culture found some echo among American radical and liberal thinkers, and the studies on authoritarian personality directed by him exercised a considerable influence on the development of American social psychology; but it is undoubtedly Marcuse's work that had the most general impact on a wide public, especially in the 1960s. Marcuse first became known to a wider intellectual audience in America with his *Reason and Revolution: Hegel and the Rise of Social Thought* (1941).[9] In this book, Marcuse attempted to rescue Hegel from what he considered a distortion of his message that made him appear to have been a prophet of unreason and a precursor of Nazi thought. In tune with other Hegelianizing Marxists, such as Lukács and Korsch, Marcuse argued that Hegel's thought was basically progressive and that Marx's dialectical method and critical humanism had been able to utilize many of Hegel's premises precisely because Hegel was far from being a reactionary. Marcuse then provided a reading of Marx, based largely on the recently discovered so-called Paris Manuscripts, that stressed the humanist dimensions of Marx's thought and slighted his occasional positivist tendencies. Hegel's and Marx's critical orientations were then counterposed to prevailing empiricist and positivist features in the social sciences in both the nineteenth and twentieth centuries.

Reason and Revolution was a *succès d'estime*. Marcuse's next major book, *Eros and Civilization* (1955),[10] enjoyed considerably wider popularity. In this book, he attempted to do for Freud what he had earlier done for Hegel—that is, rescue him from the accusation of having been a conservative, if not a reactionary. He attempted to historicize Freud's contentions by arguing that repression and the reality principle, which had been basic to Freud's thought, could be made relative if it was understood that psychic forces that had to be repressed in bourgeois society might well be given free rein in a good society. In the world of abundance which now loomed on the horizon, "surplus repression" would become obsolete, and "the performance principle" embodied in the demands of a rigid work ethic would no longer be functionally required. One could look forward to an age in which the body, so long denied, would come into its own. Sexuality would no longer be restricted to the genital area but "polymorphous sexuality," the general eroticization of life, would allow people for the first time to live unalienated and pleasure-oriented lives. What the German Romantics had called the "play drive" would become the new reality principle of liberated men and women.

Readers of Marcuse's first two major books might well have been surprised by his *One-Dimensional Man* (1964).[11] While the earlier books clung to an optimistic and utopian vision of a good society, Marcuse now turned to a vision of doom. Having been disappointed in the generous hopes of his youth and middle years, Marcuse now argued that the road to a better future was irremediably blocked. In contemporary mass society, manipulation had won a decisive victory over reason; the working class, along with all other classes, was securely integrated into this mass society. False consciousness had swallowed up rational and critical thought. In the social sciences positivism had carried the field, and technological rationality had displaced substantive rationality in the world at large. All that was still possible, Marcuse argued, was to exhort minorities to continue in their adversary stance and to practice what he called "the great refusal."

It is a historical irony that Marcuse's highly pessimistic and despairing vision in *One-Dimensional Man* had a major impact on a social movement, while his earlier optimistic call to arms had not led to any kind of praxis. The book came just in time to provide ideological ammunition to the New Left movement of the 1960s. One may doubt that many of its members fully grasped Marcuse's thought. They borrowed from him not his pessimistic conclusions but his merciless dissection of the irremedial decay of Western culture in an age of false consciousness.

Just when Marcuse was arguing that the American political scene was closed to radical challenges, such a challenge had in fact appeared; and, moreover, irony of ironies, the new movement claimed that Marcuse's work had inspired it to take up the challenge.

Marcuse was perplexed about this course of events, as were some of his earlier readers. He did not quite know at first how to react to the enthusiasm of New Left admirers. But he soon attempted in a series of less important works to justify and glorify the New Left and all it stood for. He even wrote an unfortunate essay in which he argued that tolerance was an antiquated and regressive idea and that the intolerance of the New Left was justified when it served the battle against oppression. In these later writings, buoyed by his new followers, he returned to the more optimistic vision of *Eros and Civilization* and called for a combination of erotic and esthetic elements to be joined to the political militancy of students and minorities. He occasionally warned against anti-intellectual and antirational trends of thought within the New Left, and even defended the university as one of the last abodes of rationality against its New Left critics, but by and large he had become a prisoner of New Left rhetoric. He was slightly uncomfortable about having become a totem of not only the American but also the European New Left, but he enjoyed his exalted standing among the young. (When the English poet Stephen Spender, who had some physical resemblance with Marcuse, visited the French student militants milling around the Sorbonne in May 1968, he was astonished to find that they received him with enthusiasm and devotion—until he realized that they had mistaken him for Marcuse.)

So, while many of his former colleagues who had remained in America had been absorbed by the broad liberal American academic culture, Marcuse, who had resisted this tendency throughout his career, came at the end of it to be largely absorbed in the adversary culture of the New Left. His work became a permanent feature of the American scene, even though it entered through the back door, as it were. When Marcuse died in 1979, it had become clear that this former refugee would leave a permanent mark on American culture, along with such men as Thorstein Veblen and C. Wright Mills, as an exemplar of the great American tradition of dissent.

Only those members of the Institute who returned to their homeland after the war managed to resist the enormous absorptive capacities of America. All the others, to varying degrees, became at least marginal natives.

The New School for Social Research:
A Collective Portrait

Most refugee scholars who came to America in the 1930s were widely dispersed in colleges and universities throughout the country. Yet institutions also arose in which a number of refugees formed a cluster and managed to gain a measure of collective identity. Among these were Black Mountain College in North Carolina, Roosevelt University in Chicago, and the Institute for Advanced Study at Princeton. The most important cluster was the "University in Exile," soon to be renamed the Graduate Faculty of Political and Social Science of the New School for Social Research.

The birth of the "University in Exile" is so intimately bound up with the personality of its founder and long-time president, Alvin Johnson, that a brief sketch of this remarkable man is in order. Johnson was born of Danish immigrant parents in 1874, was trained as an economist, and was imbued with the populist and progressive traditions of the Middle West. His teaching was largely influenced by the institutional economics of Thorstein Veblen and Wesley Mitchell. Johnson maintained that economics should be cultivated with an eye to its practical uses and that it might be developed best in close cooperation with other social sciences, especially sociology and political science.[1]

Johnson held academic positions from 1901 to 1918 at Bryn Mawr College and at Columbia, the University of Nebraska, the University of Texas, the University of Chicago, Cornell University, and Stanford. He also served in editorial positions at Columbia's *Political Science Quarterly* and at the *New International Encyclopedia*. In 1917 he became an editor of the *New Republic*. Two years later, in conjunction with such figures as the *New Republic* editor Herbert Croly and the historians Charles Beard and James Harvey Robinson, he founded The New School for Social Research.

The New School mainly engaged in adult education and was meant to be an institution that gave shelter to a variety of liberal and radical thinkers. One of these was Thorstein Veblen, who, like others who had unconventional views, found it rough going in the major universities during the war and after. Johnson became director of the New School in 1922 and served in this capacity for eighteen years. When the economist Edwin Seligman, whom Johnson had known while teaching at Columbia, embarked on the ambitious project to publish the *Encyclopedia of the Social Sciences,* he asked Johnson to join its staff as associate editor in 1927. Both Seligman and Johnson were impressed with the high caliber of German scholarship in the social sciences and hence made a deliberate effort to recruit German scholars to write for the *Encyclopedia.* In consequence, Johnson made a number of trips to Germany to talk to German social scientists in an effort to solicit their contributions.

When Hitler came to power in early 1933 and a number of the German scholars who had contributed to the *Encyclopedia* lost their positions, Johnson immediately started thinking of ways to help them come to America. Initially, he seems to have been concerned only about the Marxist economist Emil Lederer, but soon he broadened his scope and conceived of the idea of creating a "University in Exile" as an adjunct to the New School.[2] He sent out a letter to some two hundred influential philanthropists and social scientists asking them to sponsor his plan. Edwin Seligman wrote a supporting covering letter. All but four of the recipients agreed to help.

Within a month after his letter went out, Johnson had received some $17,000. But the real turning point came when a well-known industrialist, Hiram J. Halle, promised Johnson $120,000, which was all Johnson needed to start the school. In later years Johnson succeeded in gaining financial support for faculty salaries from a number of foundations. The Rockefeller Foundation provided a total of $54,000 from 1933 to 1940; the Rosenwald Family Association provided $110,000; and a number of other foundations gave lesser but still significant grants.

While working at the *Encyclopedia of the Social Sciences,* Johnson had accumulated a body of information on left-leaning German academics. He was especially impressed by a number of sociologists and political scientists who worked in the tradition of Max Weber, by psychologists in the Gestalt orientation, and by economists who, like Lederer, worked in a broadly Marxist vein. Johnson sent a representative to Germany to approach a number of social scientists, and himself went to London to work closely with Lederer, who was already there, on the selection of suitable candidates for positions at the "University in Exile." A list of twelve names was agreed upon: Eduard Heimann, the economist and Christian socialist; Arthur Feiler, economist and journalist; Max Wertheimer, Gestalt psychologist; Arnold Brecht, lawyer and civil servant; Frieda Wunderlich, labor economist; Albert Salomon, sociologist; Karl

Brandt, agricultural economist; Hans Neisser, economist; Gerhard Colm, economist and specialist in public finance; Herman Kantorowicz, jurist and historian; Hans Speier, sociologist; and Lederer himself.

Speier, who was only twenty-eight years old at the time and not yet burdened with the family responsibilities of his older colleagues, agreed to come to London to meet with Lederer and Johnson and to return to Germany to deliver letters of invitation to the others chosen to teach at the "University in Exile." Nine of the twelve scholars came in 1933, in time to start teaching in October of that year. The other three came somewhat later. As the years went by, other scholars were attracted to the roster of what soon became the Graduate Faculty of Political and Social Science of the New School.

The twelve-member faculty of 1933 had grown to twenty-six by 1941 and continued to grow after that time. In the fall of 1934, 153 students registered with the Graduate Faculty; by the fall of 1940 the student body numbered 520. While the first group of faculty was weighted in favor of economists and other social scientists, later such distinguished philosophers as Felix Kaufmann, Leo Strauss, Alfred Schutz, Hans Jonas, and Aron Gurwitch joined the staff.

The term "University in Exile" had been appealing as a fund-raising device during the formative period, but a number of the new faculty members resented the term *exile* and pressed for a name that would clearly indicate that the new institution was an integral branch of the New School and a permanent part of the American educational system. Yet, despite its status as a branch of the New School, the Graduate Faculty preserved a high degree of autonomy, elected its own officers, determined its own curriculum, and had authority for hiring, firing, and promotions. It had its own dean, first Emil Lederer and then for many years Hans Staudinger, formerly a distinguished German civil servant and Secretary of State in the Prussian Ministry of Commerce. The first governing committee of the Graduate Faculty included John Dewey, Felix Frankfurter, Oliver Wendell Holmes, Robert M. Hutchins, and the Columbia sociologist Robert MacIver.

Organizational arrangements between the New School and the Graduate Faculty, which granted much autonomy to the latter while yet tieing it firmly to the New School, mirrored the intellectual climate at the Graduate Faculty. The faculty consisted largely of refugee scholars who attempted, at least in the early years, to build a kind of European scholarly enclave in the American academic scene while also wishing to be fully recognized as part of an American institution. Some of the European scholars had an intensely "local" orientation and cared relatively little about what went on in the outside academic world; others, with a more "cosmopolitan" cast of mind, looked to the wider academic vista and wished to receive recognition and esteem from native-born colleagues at other centers of learning. Thus, while Johnson would always rejoice when a member of the faculty received an offer to move to a prestigeful institution elsewhere (that is what he wanted in the long run), some "local" members regarded those who accepted such offers as "traitors" to the cause of the New School.

Soon after its inception, the Graduate Faculty, under the prodding of Johnson, resolved to start its own publication, the journal *Social Research.* Johnson stressed the duty of faculty members to contribute to *Social Research* because he conceived of it as a valuable means of bringing the Graduate Faculty to the attention of the wider academic community. The journal was, of course, published in English and sought an audience among native Americans, whereas the *Zeitschrift fuer Sozialwissenschaft* continued to be published in German until the outbreak of World War II, thus signifying, as has been noted, that the editors did not wish to build strong bridges to their American colleagues but chose to continue in splendid isolation. From its inception the contributions to *Social Research* were of unusually high quality, and this was soon recognized by American native academics. Yet many of the contributions still read very much like translations from the German—as many of them were.

As the years went by, one could notice an interesting bifurcation in the publication record of members of the faculty. Some of them published almost exclusively in *Social Research,* while others, not ceasing to publish in the house organ, began to publish frequently in the specialized journals of their respective disciplines. There was a correlation between the publication record of members of the faculty and their subsequent careers. Those who published mostly in *Social Research* stayed at The New School, while those who frequently published elsewhere tended to leave for other academic positions. Publication in journals other than *Social Research* contributed to their anticipatory socialization. Thus the economist Emil Lederer, who stayed at the New School until the end of his career in 1939, published largely though not exclusively in *Social Research,* as was true of the sociologist Albert Salomon, who also stayed at the New School throughout his American career. Jacob Marschak, the mathematical economist, on the other hand, published in *Social Research* only at the beginning of his academic career in America—and moved to the University of Chicago after teaching at the New School for only three years. Almost all the journal articles of the philosopher Kurt Riezler and the sociologist of religion Carl Mayer appeared in *Social Research.* Mayer taught at the New School to the end of his career and Riezler moved to the University of Chicago only toward the end of his career. Hans Speier, who left the Graduate Faculty in 1942, had begun to publish elsewhere soon after his arrival in America.

All indicators point to the fact that the Graduate Faculty, even though functioning as an accredited American academic institution, was nevertheless not fully part of American cultural and intellectual life. This was an asset as well as a liability. On the one hand, it did a great deal to deprovincialize the New York academic world. Johnson had insisted from the beginning that all members of the faculty must participate in a general seminar in which professors would present papers before the faculty, students, and invited guests. This imposed a heavy burden on the new faculty members, whose command of the English language in most cases still left much to be desired. But it had the distinct advantage of contributing to interdisciplinary contacts within the faculty as well as serving as a kind of advertising to other academics of the New School scholars' contributions to intellectual life in New York. Topics discussed ranged from "The City" to "Peace and War" to "Labor in the United States and Abroad." These general seminars, the likes of which did not exist at Columbia or elsewhere in New York, were successful for many years and served to establish and sustain contacts between refugee scholars and their native American counterparts. At times, eminent refugee figures not on the faculty, such as theologian Paul Tillich and philosopher Ernst Bloch, also participated.

In addition to general seminars, the Graduate Faculty offered interdisciplinary seminars. Thus the Gestalt psychologist Max Wertheimer, the psychoanalyst Karen Horney, and the sociologist Hans Speier, might offer a joint seminar on some common topic; the philosopher Leo Strauss participated in a seminar with the psychologist Solomon Asch. The topics discussed at these seminars included "Methodology of the Social Sciences" and "The Forerunners of Modern Psychology." The general seminars as well as the special seminars helped acquaint younger members of the New York academic community with the contributions of the refugee scholars. Such diverse figures as political scientist Gabriel Almond[3] and the psychologist Abraham Maslow have told me how deeply impressed they were as young students by the privilege of participating in these seminars, and how their subsequent intellectual development was fostered by the seminars as much as, or perhaps more than, by their formal academic studies. Students at Brooklyn College and at the College of the City of New York looked with awe and admiration at the academic giants, as they saw them, of the New School.

While a number of moves to break down the isolation of the European scholars at the New School were crowned with success, there were other factors that made for the insulation of the refugee academics from their surrounding milieu. To begin with, in the early years of the school the refugee scholars were a rather homogeneous lot in terms of background characteristics. Almost all of them came from Germany or Austria, even

though somewhat later a few scholars from other countries were added
to the Graduate Faculty roster. Most of them had held prestigeful academic positions in their native country; some of them had been academic Marxists, more of them had been fairly close to German social
democracy, and several had been highly placed civil servants in the Social Democratic administrations of Prussia. Their homogeneity of background and of age as well fostered a tendency among the refugees to
seek out the companionship of like-minded men and women and to create what I have called a gilded ghetto in New York City. Hans Speier,
whom I asked about this,[4] did not think that many of the men, at least,
were homesick, but he thought most of them nevertheless felt closer to
the mores and culture of pre-Nazi Germany than to American culture.
All of them were forced to lecture in English, but one of them, Henry
Pachter, who taught at the New School but not in the Graduate Faculty,
has written that "a correct English pronunciation would be conspicuous
or improper."[5] When he first entered his lecture room, unknown to the
students, Pachter heard a woman ask, "Does the teacher speak English?"

A high proportion of the early New School faculty lived on Manhattan's Upper West Side or in Riverdale, and this residential proximity
reinforced their tendency to restrict their social contacts mainly to other
refugee scholars living in this area. Those who, like Hans Speier, soon
established relations with native American scholars—Speier reports that
almost from the beginning he spent about 50 percent of his social life
with native Americans—were those who tended to leave the New School
for other academic or extra-academic settings.

Despite these tendencies toward encapsulation—Pachter suggested in
jest that the Graduate Faculty should really have been extraterritorial in
New York—it was eminently successful in the 1940s and 1950s. "No-
where else," Pachter has written, "could one get genuine Max Weber,
genuine Gestalt, genuine phenomenology, or as close a reading of Plato
as Leo Strauss taught his admiring followers."[6] In an age when many
American graduate departments were stressing methodology, statistics,
techniques of gathering factual information, most members of the New
School upheld the supreme dignity of theoretical inquiry. For many years,
for example, the sociology department considered it degrading to offer
courses in statistics. Among the twelve first Ph.D. degrees in sociology
conferred by the graduate school, four dealt with the thought of eminent theorists—George Herbert Mead, Thorstein Veblen, Max Weber,
and Carl Jung, respectively—and a number of other dissertations, while
presenting empirical findings, were still more theoretically oriented than
the dissertations produced in most other sociology departments in the
country.[7] In a number of fields, such as phenomenology, econometrics,
and Gestalt psychology, the Graduate Faculty offered early and pioneer-

ing instruction at a time when such fields were largely ignored by most university departments.

In the early years, most members of the faculty offered courses that they had previously taught in their native land. But gradually the course offerings became "Americanized." Yet even then they still tended to differ to some degree from the routine teaching in other universities. Where else could a student take a sociology course on the social structure of France based on the novels of Balzac?

On the other hand, the Graduate Faculty never attempted to develop a unified and coherent structure of thought, as did the Horkheimer group. In fact there was a great deal of diversity in faculty opinion and in course offerings. What most members of the faculty had in common was a leftist-liberal outlook, even though there were also a few conservative members, such as Leo Strauss, Kurt Riezler, E. Hula, and Karl Brandt.

With the outbreak of World War II, a number of the members of the faculty, such as Hans Speier, who served in the Federal Communications Commission, the Office of War Information, and the State Department, and the economist Gerhard Colm, who served in the Commerce Department and the Bureau of the Budget and was largely responsible for conceiving the postwar German currency reform, worked for the federal government. Colm also served as a member of the President's Committee of Economic Advisers. Some of them later returned to the New School, others stayed on in high Washington positions. Such government service came easier to them than to the Marxists of the Frankfurt Institute.

The success of the Graduate Faculty can partly be measured by the quality of its graduate students. In all the fields taught by the faculty, a significant number of students later achieved considerable eminence on the American academic scene. In sociology, for example, Peter Berger, Maurice Natanson, Bernard Rosenberg, Ephraim Fischoff, Helmut Wagner, and Thomas Luckmann received their Ph.D. degrees in the early years of the faculty. In psychology, Mary Hendle and Solomon Asch were largely guided by Max Wertheimer's teaching. Robert Heilbroner, Alexander Erlich, and Franco Modigliani, all leading economists today, were trained at the New School.[8] The academic success of Graduate Faculty "products" is especially remarkable given the fact that New School graduates were often treated with a measure of suspicion by department chairpersons who considered training there to be somewhat inadequate and more or less deviant. Most of the younger American scholars trained at the Graduate Faculty continued the New School tradition of interdisciplinary learning, sensitivity to the philosophical underpinnings of the research they conducted, and emphasis on theoretical as distinct from purely empirical scholarship. They continued to contribute to the deprovincialization of the American mind that their teachers had begun.

Just as in the personal lives of immigrants, where the first generation usually did not manage full integration into American culture and only the second became "Americanized," so in academia the first generation of the Graduate Faculty remained largely marginal to major trends in American culture, whereas their students, spreading their teachers' messages to a number of college and university campuses, became a vital part of American scholarship. The first generation lived a partly encapsulated existence while their students went out into the wider academic world. The Graduate Faculty phenomenologists, for example, had little influence on sociology and philosophy during their lifetimes, but their students made phenomenological research in both sociology and philosophy a vital movement that is now widely represented on many campuses. The chapters on Schutz and Gurwich provide convenient examples.

A list of the works published by the members of the Graduate Faculty would fill several pages; so I shall not attempt to enumerate them here. In addition to the works of the scholars dealt with separately in these pages, such a list would range from Emil Lederer's seminal *State of the Masses* (1940), one of the first original interpretations of the Nazi phenomenon, to Hans Jonas's *The Gnostic Religion (1963)*, Felix Kaufmann's book on *The Methodology of the Social Sciences* (1958), and Arnold Brecht's monumental study of public administration and political structures.[9] The New School also sponsored for a number of years workshops in the performing arts and supported the Ecole des Hautes Etudes for French and Belgian scholars during World War II. I do not deal with these projects here because this book excludes the arts from its concern and limits itself to academics who spent many years in the United States. (The French and Belgian scholars returned to their home countries soon after the end of the war.) Several historical studies of the Graduate Faculty are now in progress, so that in a few years it will be possible to assess its highly significant contribution to American thought and scholarship more fully.

Paul F. Lazarsfeld (1901–1976): From Austro-Marxist to Founding Father of American Social Research

The career of Paul Lazarsfeld contained a number of paradoxes: he largely initiated systematic sociological survey research in America; yet he had practically no training in sociology, having received his university degree in applied mathematics. In his native Vienna he had been an ardent socialist youth leader and organizer; yet he proved very adept, after coming here, in harnessing the resources of American business to the task of developing social research. He is renowned as the father of sophisticated studies of mass communications and of the factors that lead people to make choices between political candidates or between competing products; yet he was not really interested in these substantive areas but was concerned with developing appropriate methodologies for the social sciences. An overview of the course of his life both in Austria and in this country will help to explain some, though perhaps not all, of these paradoxes[1]

Lazarsfeld was born in Vienna in 1901 to a Jewish family of intellectuals. His father was a lawyer and his mother, Sofie Lazarsfeld, became in due course a prominent Adlerian psychotherapist. His parents were often apart when Paul Lazarsfeld was young, so his mother, to whom he remained deeply attached to his dying day, was his only effective parent. It is through her, an ardent socialist with many ties to the intelligentsia of Vienna, that Lazarsfeld was attracted to the socialist movement. First as a member of the youth organization, *Rote Falke*, later as an organizer of groups in his high school and at the University of Vienna, Lazarsfeld lived in his early years almost completely within the confines of Vienna's socialist movement.

Friedrich Adler, the socialist leader who had assassinated the Austrian prime minister in protest against the war, was a close friend and probably a lover of Lazarsfeld's mother during most of the war and became a revered mentor of her adolescent son. Adler had been trained as a theoretical physicist but had later chosen a career as a socialist political leader instead. He instilled in the young Lazarsfeld a love for the natural sciences and mathematics, as well as for politics, and it is largely owing to Adler's influence that Lazarsfeld decided to study mathematics at the University of Vienna simultaneously with courses in economics and political theory. There can be no doubt that the two diverse passions which dominated the intellectual orientation of the young Lazarsfeld were the politics of socialism and the logical force of mathematical reasoning as applied to empirical inquiries.

Austrian social democracy never developed the doctrinaire rigidity that characterized, for example, the Communist movement of the 1920s. The Viennese socialist intelligentsia perceived no opposition between Marxism and empiricism. Lazarsfeld's thinking was in the Austro-Marxist tradition of combining millenarian hopes with pragmatic concern for concrete social improvements that could be facilitated through disciplined empirical study. Given this outlook, it was by no means surprising that Lazarsfeld organized an interdisciplinary social science seminar in which scholars of divergent political orientations participated. Here the philosopher Rudolf Carnap, the psychoanalyst Heinz Hartmann, the economist Oskar Morgenstern, and the political theorist Erich Voegelin worked side by side. All of them are dealt with in this book, since they all came to settle in America.

Lazarsfeld's empirical orientation was powerfully reinforced when he made the acquaintance of Karl and Charlotte Buehler, who came from Germany to the University of Vienna in 1932 to build a new department of psychology (see pp. 37–39). Lazarsfeld participated in their early seminars at the university, and was soon asked to give a course in statistics at their newly established Psychological Institute. Shortly before that he had received his degree in applied mathematics and had begun teaching mathematics and physics in a Viennese gymnasium. A man of astounding energies, Lazarsfeld found time to become an assistant of the Buehlers, a high-school teacher, and an active socialist organizer, although his political activity took pride of place.

The Buehlers' theoretical orientation, as has been noted, was rooted in the concern of the so-called Wuerzburg school of psychology with the springs of human actions. In contrast to most behavioral or associationist psychology, this approach attempted to account for human goal-striving and rejected attempts to explain human activities in terms of external stimuli or instinctual predispositions. In their work in Vienna, the Buehlers applied this general approach mainly to the study of infants, children, and adolescents. Given his strong political bent, Lazarsfeld was much more interested in older children, adolescents, and adults, whose motivations had relevance in the political sphere. Even though political concerns lost much of their salience for Lazarsfeld when he came to America, explanations in terms of action schemes largely derived from the Buehlers remained the focus of his work in this country, as it had been in Vienna.

Although Lazarsfeld continued to be active in the socialist student movement, he could not ignore the fact that, as the 1920s proceeded, the chances of building a socialist society steadily decreased. As various kinds of nationalist movements grew, the socialists were forced to engage in defensive strategy. Attempting to account for the lack of success of their propaganda, young socialists now began to turn to psychological studies. As Lazarsfeld put it at the time: "A fighting revolution requires economics (Marx); a victorious revolution requires engineers (Russia); a defeated revolution calls for psychology (Vienna)."[2]

It was partly the wish to understand the lack of success socialism had in Austria which gave Lazarsfeld the idea of creating within the Buehlers' institute a social-psychological research center that would be devoted to the application of psychology to social and economic problems. The center was created in 1925, and Lazarsfeld assumed its leadership. Its most enduring piece of research, Die Arbeitslosen von Marienthal (The Unemployed of Marienthal),[3] first published in 1932, became a widely praised study of a total community of unemployed. Its frame of reference was Buehlerian action theory, but it was infused with the compassionate socialist convictions of its authors.

Realizing that the work of his center would not be subsidized by the university, Lazarsfeld set out to do market research for commercial clients who wished to explore the motivations of potential customers for buying their products. This anticipated his pattern when he came to America of financing disinterested inquiries with funds from market research. He was often attacked for this practice by those who did not know that the funds derived from private clients were used for public benefit by developing research methods that could be applied to other than privately sponsored projects. Lazarsfeld's Vienna Research Center struggled along precariously for a number of years. Practically the whole staff, all underpaid, consisted of Lazarsfeld's friends and companions in the socialist movement. Even if it accomplished nothing else—as was not the case—it certainly served to keep these young political radicals afloat.

The Marienthal study brought Lazarsfeld to the attention of the Rockefeller Foundation, and as a consequence he was awarded a traveling fellowship to America. He arrived here in September 1933. When news of the putsch of the Conservative party of Austria and the outlawing of the Socialist party reached him in February 1934, Lazarsfeld had his fellowship extended for another year and then decided to stay in this country. His first and second wives, Marie Jahoda and Herta Herzog, and most of the others who had been active in the Vienna Research Center, also reached America, some of them after a period of imprisonment.

Lazarsfeld used his Rockefeller fellowship for a series of extensive travels throughout the country. The log of these travels shows that he did not visit all the prestigious departments in the social sciences but paid particular attention to those centers in which active social research, whether under academic auspices or not, was being carried on.[4] These initial contacts paid considerable dividends after Lazarsfeld had decided to stay in America and start a new career here. He also profited greatly from the fact that he acquired a patron and academic broker soon after his arrival here. Robert Lynd, the author (with Helen Lynd) of *Middletown*, then a well-established social scientist with many connections in academia and especially its reform-oriented outskirts, took great interest in Lazarsfeld. Lynd saw some parallels between his own community study and that of the authors of *Marienthal* and felt that Lazarsfeld would help him undertake similar studies on the American scene.

Lynd recommended Lazarsfeld for his first job in America. The New Jersey Relief Administration had collected a large number of questionnaires from youngsters aged fourteen to twenty-five and needed someone to analyze them. The president of a small, struggling institution, the University of Newark, agreed that a research position at the university, created with the help of the National Youth Administration, could undertake the job. Lazarsfeld seemed eminently qualified, as he had written a book on *Youth and Occupation* (1931) while still in Austria.

The Research Center of the University of Newark was set up under Lazarsfeld's direction and patterned after his former Vienna Research Center. Only part of his salary was paid by the university; the rest was to come from "other sources." To supplement his inadequate university salary, as well as to supply stipends for student assistants and research expenses, Lazarsfeld followed the Vienna precedent of soliciting outside funds. Various federal and local government agencies commissioned studies of unemployment in New Jersey. Horkheimer's Institute, recently come to America, located some of its research in Newark, and cultivation of market-research contacts resulted in some commissioned work for commercial sponsors.

The Newark Research Center soon made a name for itself through numerous publications, some academic and some devoted to market research. (One of Lazarsfeld's most famous programmatic articles, "The Art of Asking Why" [1935], for example, first appeared in *The National Marketing Research Review*.) The fact that, as Lazarsfeld put it, he had "a foot in both the commercial and academic camps made for a certain amount of maneuverability."[5] In the days before grants were available from the National Science Foundation and other government agencies, and at a time when university grants for research hardly existed, this proved to be crucial.

A list of the academic and nonacademic committees on which Lazarsfeld served over the years would fill several pages. His network of associates in the world of commercial research and in the mass communications industry was widespread. Much of his work in radio research, for example, was made possible by the sponsorship of an up-and-coming executive at CBS holding a Ph.D. in psychology, Frank Stanton, who later become president of the network. Later work in voting studies was considerably facilitated by Lazarsfeld's close connection with the heads of various commercial survey-research firms. Relations with market-research firms allowed him to place some of his students and associates in these firms (at a time when academic positions in social research were few indeed), as well as to secure funds for some of his projects.

Lazarsfeld's standing in the research community grew so quickly that when the Rockefeller Foundation decided to sponsor a large-scale study of the effects of radio on American society they turned to Lazarsfeld. The main academic proponent of the idea of studying radio's impact was the Princeton social psychologist Hadley Cantril, whom Lazarsfeld had met during an earlier visit to Harvard. Lynd recommended Lazarsfeld to Cantril, who, after some initial hesitation, offered him the job as director of the Office of Radio Research at Princeton, with Frank Stanton as the indispensable codirector. The office stayed in Princeton for only two years (from 1936 to 1939). Some strains having developed between Cantril and Lazarsfeld, the latter prevailed upon the Rockefeller Foundation to have it transferred to Columbia University, where Lazarsfeld was appointed a lecturer. A year later, largely because of Robert Lynd's backing, he became a permanent member of the Columbia University Department of Sociology, where he continued to teach until his retirement in 1969. The Office of Radio Research became the now-famous Bureau of Applied Social Research in 1944. Lazarsfeld served as its director until the 1950s, when he relinquished the official position, but he continued to act as the gray eminence who led it in fact, though not in title.

Lazarsfeld directed the Office of Radio Research and its successor in the same unorthodox manner he had used in directing his Vienna office. He always wanted his research organizations to be much more than a place for work—namely, collaborative *Gemeinschaften* rather than tightly organized bureaucratic machines. They were to be a kind of kibbutz, although he always insisted that the director be firmly in command, a true "coach of the team." Detailed organizational blueprints did not appeal to Lazarsfeld, and administrative efficiency was not his strong suit. Nor was his handling of financial details likely to appeal to a C.P.A. In all these respects the bureau operated in a somewhat chaotic manner. Columbia University contributed little to its upkeep, so funds were always scarce, and government funds were even scarcer in the early years. The radio industry provided research funds at first, various government contracts did so in a later period. Throughout, Lazarsfeld's method of creative financing allowed him to borrow from Peter to satisfy Paul, to pay the overdue bills of one project from newly acquired funds for a prospective enterprise. Those who worked in this organized chaos did not always find it the happy gemeinschaft that Lazarsfeld dreamed of. Some graduate students complained that they were not really being trained by learning through doing but were in fact being exploited as drudges. Others grumbled that the bureau was in fact an adjunct of the business interests that provided much of the funds. Some study directors felt uncomfortable with Lazarsfeld's restless habit of turning from one area of inquiry to another as his fancy dictated. But somehow, despite all this, the bureau institutionalized a new mode of doing research in the social sciences in America and provided a sense of identity for generations of students.

Lazarsfeld came to America at a time when interest in survey research had just started. His own success in developing it is largely due to the fact that his focus on the springs of human action reached the receptive ears of younger sociologists who were dissatisfied with the fairly crude behavioral views that still dominated the field. It is worthy of note that, even though he had considered himself a psychologist in Austria, his audience in America was composed of sociologists rather than psychologists. In this country, psychologists were mainly oriented toward experimentation on individual behavioral consequences of various stimuli and neglected the assessment of the attitudes and behavior of large groups of people. At the time Lazarsfeld arrived in America, it was only sociologists—not psychologists—who were concerned with aggregate behavior. The Lynds' *Middletown* had appeared in 1929 and was soon to be followed by *Middletown in Transition* (1937). The research for what was to become Lloyd Warner's *Yankee City* series had been started, and so had the research on the attitudes and behavior of factory workers that culminated in F. J. Roethlisberger's and W. J. Dickson's *Management and the Worker* (1939). Systematic interviewing to determine some concomitants of the social behavior of aggregates of people was increasingly recognized as an important method of social research.

In his native country Lazarsfeld's concern with the growth of the conservative movement and the decline of the socialists must have loomed large in his interest in election results. Sensitized by Buehlerian action theory, he wished to find out how people made up their minds in the political realm, how internal dispositions were translated into voting behavior. This is largely why, when he came to work in America, he tried not just to ascertain the opinions of individuals but to discover the underlying dynamics of the social behavior of aggregates of people. He wanted to know whether people who express certain opinions, or who state that they behave or would behave in a certain manner under certain conditions, also had something in common, whether they knew it or not, in their relations to other people in the society in which they were embedded.

Lazarsfeld was not so much interested in predicting the outcome of elections when he undertook his voting studies; he wanted to know what the relation was between predisposing factors and intentions or actual behavior. He also wanted to show how multiple allegiances and the resulting cross-pressures would often lead people to refrain from voting, even when they were unaware that this was the reason. Cumulative consistent pressures would lead to strong voting preferences; cross-pressures would motivate people to stay away from the polls.

This emphasis on the behavior of aggregates of people is also present in most other Lazarsfeld studies. In studying the answers to a survey on what brands of coffee people preferred, Lazarsfeld found that there were people in each local community who acted as "opinion leaders." Surely his interpretation came not from the individual answers themselves but from finding out that people who gave similar answers had something in common in their relationships to others in the community.

Or take Lazarsfeld's study of the impact of the McCarthy threats and persecutions on the behavior of university teachers. It would seem on the surface that he was interested in the responses and opinions of individuals. But what his research showed was that reactions to McCarthy's threats depended on the differential social climates in various types of colleges and universities, and the relation between the academic and community settings.

Thus Lazarsfeld was always intent upon relating the behavior of people, whether as individuals or as aggregates, to the latent social structure. The structure was latent because the individuals living in it usually failed to recognize the factors that prompted their behavior—be it voting, buying coffee, or refraining from teaching controversial subjects. Moreover, Lazarsfeld always distinguished between predispositions and actual behavior, emphasizing that predispositions could be transformed into action only under specified social conditions. This overall orientation should make it clear why Lazarsfeld, trained as a psychologist, became a sociologist *malgré lui*.

Undoubtedly, survey research would in due time have overcome its initial phase of more or less sophisticated head-counting. But surely Lazarsfeld's methodological approach greatly enhanced its success in moving to a new phase in which theoretical and methodological refinements advanced its progress from a research technique for the study of individual opinions to a mature mode of analysis of the latent springs of action among aggregates of people.

Lazarsfeld's impact on American social science came not only through his published papers and books but also through the great number of students he trained in the Bureau of Social Research as well as in his courses and seminars at Columbia. His former students and associates—James Coleman, Peter Rossi, Hanan Selvin, Charles Kadushin, David Sills, Charles Glock, Elihu Katz, Patricia Kendall, Marjorie Fiske, Bernard Berelson, Allen Barton, Edward Suchman, Morris Rosenberg, to mention just a few of them—spread the distinctive bureau approach to other campuses and research institutes. Even those Columbia students who did not choose to work within the tradition (even though the bureau was a house of several mansions)—largely because they preferred to do more theoretical work under the guidance of Lazarsfeld's close friend and associate, Robert K. Merton, or were attracted to Robert Lynd's style of work—were nevertheless to some degree influenced by Lazarsfeld's way of thinking. It takes no ingenuity to discern his influence in, for example, the work of Seymour Martin Lipset, formally a student of Robert Lynd, or of Peter Blau, Alvin Gouldner, Alice Rossi, and Rose Laub Coser, who were mainly trained by Robert K. Merton.

The intimate collaboration of Lazarsfeld and Merton over several decades, though it cannot be discussed in detail here, nevertheless deserves some comment. Merton's orientation was derived mostly from the mode of functional analysis developed by Talcott Parsons at Harvard. This orientation would appear at first blush to be very much at variance with Lazarsfeld's empiricist social psychology. In fact, both traditions put the analysis of social action in the forefront of social inquiry. In both traditions the interplay between motivated predispositions to achieve particular goals and environmental constraints imposed by social structures were the center of attention. Lazarsfeld tended to focus on the character of motivations, Merton on the character of the structural context. And so it was that Merton and Lazarsfeld, despite their pronounced dissimilarities in background and academic tradition, worked in tandem through decades. Although the first tended to concentrate on theoretical work and the second on empirical research, they constantly interchanged ideas and conceptualizations, so that between the 1940s and the 1960s the Columbia department became a model pointing the way toward the integration of sociological theory and empirical research.

What accounted for Lazarsfeld's impact, in addition to his oustanding gifts, was his creative entrepreneurial spirit, his ability to bridge the gap between academic and commercial research, his unflagging energy and ebullient enthusiasm for new ideas. But even more important was his firm belief that what was needed in social research was not so much the accumulation of substantive findings as the development of a refined methodology that could lead the research enterprise from the gathering of data to attaining results of theoretical significance.

The Bureau of Applied Social Research gave annual Christmas parties where students produced skits in which they impersonated the director and study directors. One year a student disguised as Lazarsfeld appeared on the scene happily announcing that his wife had just had a baby. "Is it a boy or a girl?" he was asked. His answer was: "I don't really know, all I care about is the method." This skit fully captured the spirit of Lazarsfeld and also pointed to his major contribution to the social sciences.

What Lazarsfeld intended in his methodological approach to survey research was to construct causal explanations that could account for the actions, decisions, or intentions of aggregates of individuals. Even though he pursued seemingly different types of research, ranging from decisions to buy a product, to vote for a specific candidate or party, to choose an occupation, or to listen to a specific radio program, he was basically less interested in the substantive findings, as such, than in the development of a method that would allow the assessment of causes for the action or decision. This same method can be used, so Lazarsfeld argued, whenever one intends to study the subjective determinants of individual action. To proceed in such an attempt, Lazarsfeld argued further, one must establish an "accounting scheme" made up of a list of all the factors that can be assumed to produce or inhibit a particular action for the specific case at hand. Such accounting schemes necessarily rest on the interplay between the subjective views and desires of the actors, on the one hand, and the restraints, requirements, and incentives of the environment in which the actor moves, on the other.[6]

This approach was consistently applied in all of Lazarsfeld's now classic studies. Whether it was in a series of books on *Radio Research* published by the Bureau collaborators in the early 1940s,[7] the numerous contributions to such publications as the *Public Opinion Quarterly,* or his studies on voting behavior, from *The People's Choice* (1944)[8] to *Voting* (1954), or his study of the impact of McCarthyism on the academy, *The Academic Mind* (1955), or his accounting for *Personal Influence* (1955),[8] a continuously refined action scheme always underlay Lazarsfeld's work.

Lazarsfeld's love affair with America can be explained, at least in large part, by the circumstances of the time. When he arrived here, the New Deal was at its zenith, and Roosevelt's pragmatic reformism strongly appealed to a young radical who had grown up in a socialist movement for which activist meliorism had ranked as high as revolutionary zeal. Under these circumstances, Lazarsfeld, who considered himself "a Marxist on leave," and who was a reform-oriented social scientist with highly developed research skills, could, as he said, serve as "a connecting cog" between European and American social research. There was a kind of "structural fit," as he put it,[9] between Lazarsfeld's personal orientation and political and intellectual conditions in America at the time.

Yet, there was also a major difference between his positions in Vienna and in America. In Austria, Lazarsfeld had been able to address a double, yet largely overlapping, audience. He could attempt to help his socialist comrades advance their cause through social-political research. At the same time he could speak to his academic associates in a language strongly imbued with his underlying socialist convictions. The research he did was governed by scientific criteria; yet the questions he asked (except for his market research) were suggested to him by the socialist milieu in which he moved. But in America there existed no socialist movement of consequence, and so Lazarsfeld lost the socialist audience he had taken for granted in Vienna. He was left with only one audience for his work: his academic peers, his students, and his fellow researchers in and out of academia. This situation may well have contributed to his inability ever to feel fully at home in America. But other reasons also came into play.

As all who knew him well will testify, and as is amply documented in the many interviews with him and with his closest associates,[10] Lazarsfeld never felt entirely at ease in America. In most cases, career success tends to allay insecurity and a sense of marginality. But this was not so for Lazarsfeld. Even continuing success could never completely eradicate his sense of not fully belonging, of being an outsider and a marginal man. His self-deprecatory remarks about his life in America may in part have been a calculated pose; yet surely they were not only that. He often remarked in his later years, for example, that he had twice missed being elected to the presidency of the American Sociological Association, gaining the position only on the third try, when he ran against an especially weak candidate. He was self-conscious about his pronounced "Jewish appearance" and pointed out that being categorized as a foreigner saved him from being categorized as a Jew.

Much of this may be summed up in a reply he gave to a question by Morrison about anti-Semitism and its effect on Lazarsfeld's career:

> You know, when I first came here there was still a certain amount of genteel anti-Semitism. And my accent. As a matter of fact I was less affected because my being a foreigner overshadowed my being Jewish. I think I would have had more difficulty as an American Jew at that time than as a Austrian Jew. I

think I could not have been appointed at Columbia at that time—not really—
not if I had been an American Jew. No one thought of me as a Jew because of
my foreignness—the accent saved my life.[11]

Indeed, Lazarsfeld never shed his pronounced central European accent
and once advised me, when I came to study at Columbia, that one should
lose most but not all of one's accent because a touch of an accent gives
one some exotic appeal. Around Columbia he is said to have replied to
someone who asked him what life was about, "most of the time people
stick needles in you, and then you take a great deal of time to pull them
out again."

It is irrelevant here to decide how much of Lazarsfeld's lack of security
was grounded in reality and how much was due to what his former wife,
Marie Jahoda, called his "most idiotic, but persistent, inferiority feeling."[12] He was, in any case, never a full member of the wedding, even
after he was elected to both the National Academy of Sciences and the
National Academy of Education. Yet it seems plausible that precisely this
feeling of being apart may have stood Lazarsfeld in good stead. It allowed him a distance that he could turn to his advantage when dealing
with his environment in a way so as to further his larger purposes, or
when looking at the passing scene with the clarity that comes from a lack
of full involvement.

The "Marxist on leave" from socialist Vienna became a major force in
institutionalizing social research in capitalist America. He became a
founding father of social research and a pioneer in the analysis of the
complex web of reasons and motives that determines the goal strivings
of human actors. His was a brilliant and fruitful career, even though he
paid a considerable price in his efforts to come to terms with America.
The many social scientists who follow in his tradition in contemporary
America and the continuing number of annual citations of his work in
current publications (over one hundred in 1982, according to the Social
Science Citation Index) indicate that his influence on American social
science will endure.

Alfred Schutz (1899–1959): Fountainhead of Phenomenological Sociology

During his career in the United States, Alfred Schutz was a successful teacher who trained a number of gifted students in both philosophy and sociology. In addition, he wrote a considerable number of scholarly papers, but he was not widely known among his American peers and colleagues during his lifetime. Now, however, he has moved into the front rank of sociologists and, to a lesser extent, philosophers, as one of that small company who are widely read, commented upon, and critically evaluated. A short sketch of his career in Europe and America helps to explain why his fame has been largely posthumous.

Schutz was born in Vienna in 1899 to an upper-class Jewish family. As befitted his status, Schutz went to a gymnasium in Vienna. After a year of service in the Austrian army during World War I, he entered the University of Vienna, from which he received a doctorate in law after only two-and-a-half years of study. Unlike many other brilliant Jewish students in this period, Schutz did not embark on an academic career but decided to become a legal adviser to an association of banks and later a member of a private banking firm with international interests. He was mainly involved in drawing up contracts and agreements and advising on tax matters.[1]

But while engaged in a business career, Schutz pursued his interests in the social sciences and their philosophical underpinnings. He had studied under such positivists as the great legal scholar Hans Kelsen and the classical liberal economist Ludwig von Mises (see pp. 139–42) and also took a course with the organicist sociologist Othmar Spann. None of these scholars, it appears, had much effect on Schutz's subsequent thinking. Instead, he turned to the work of Max Weber in sociology and to the philosophical approaches, first of Henri Bergson, and later of the founder of phenomenology, Edmund Husserl. His main work from this period, *Der sinnhafte Aufbau der sozialen Welt: Eine Einleitung in die verstehende Soziologie* (1932), which he published after twelve years of re-

search, attempted explicitly to ground Weber's *verstehende Soziologie*—i.e.
a sociology that is concerned with tracing the motives and grounds of
action of human actors—in the phenomenological approach of Husserl.
Schutz had never met Husserl when he was writing his book, but Husserl reacted to the finished copy Schutz sent him with exuberant enthusiasm. He called Schutz "one of the very few who have penetrated to the
deepest and relatively inaccessible meaning of my life work." Soon after,
Husserl invited Schutz to become his assistant at the University of Freiburg, but Schutz declined the invitation, apparently because of his business ties.

In 1938, the Nazi occupation of Vienna compelled Schutz to leave the
country. After a year's stay in Paris, he decided to come to the United
States and arrived in New York in 1939. Like many of his fellow refugees, Schutz soon joined the faculty of the New School for Social Research, serving first as a lecturer and later as a professor in the Graduate
Faculty of Political and Social Science. But unlike almost all of the others, he decided to continue the unusual life-style that he had established
in Vienna. Until shortly before his death he continued to work full time
as a businessman and legal expert on Wall Street while confining his
lectures and research to afternoons and evenings. As one of his students, Maurice Natanson, notes, "His philosophical academic career was
an additional labor, carried on at the expense of an enormous and pre-
cious effort."[2] Husserl once called him "a banker by day and a phenomenologist by night," and this was indeed what Schutz was, both in Europe
and in America. Just as Wallace Stevens apparently thought that the
combination of insurance and poetry was a natural thing, so Schutz seems
never to have felt that the combination of business and social philosophy,
apart from being time-consuming, was in any way unusual.

Despite this double occupational involvement, Schutz managed to write
a considerable number of important papers, nearly forty in all, during
his stay in the United States. Most of them now have been collected in
three large volumes, and there are still other papers and projects for
full-length books that have been published or are about to be published
by his disciples.[3] Schutz is now considered one of the most creative and
original of writers in the phenomenological tradition.

Most of Schutz's work in America was not, however, widely known
during his lifetime. To be sure, his students at the New School were
familiar with it. Two native-born phenomenologists, Marvin Farber and
Dorion Cairns, and a fellow refugee, Aron Gurwitch, all of whom had
been students of Husserl, provided essential sounding boards for Schutz's
ideas. The New School house organ, *Social Research,* and the journal
Philosophy and Phenomenological Research, on whose editorial board he

served, published most of his work, but the readers of the major general journals of philosophy and the social sciences were probably hardly aware of him during his lifetime.

Schutz's relative obscurity in America can be accounted for largely by his isolation from his native-born peers in sociology and philosophy—a common characteristic of the New School faculty, most of whom lived in a world populated by fellow refugees. Schutz's efforts to initiate a dialogue with the dean of American sociological theory, Talcott Parsons, soon ended in failure. Despite Schutz's valiant attempts to build bridges of understanding to Parsons, who was, like himself, deeply influenced by Max Weber, the dialogue soon ceased. It was in fact, as I have said elsewhere, largely a dialogue of the deaf.[4] I know of no other attempt on Schutz's part to engage native-born American social scientists or philosophers of his generation in sustained intellectual interchange. Most of Schutz's intellectual exchanges were limited to fellow refugees such as the economist Fritz Machlup and the political philosopher Eric Voegelin.

Schutz's relative isolation and consequent lack of resonance in American academia are all the more remarkable since, in contrast to many of his fellow exiles, he made a sustained effort to acquaint himself with the American philosophical tradition and to utilize it creatively. He had already profited from William James's work while in Europe. In his years in America, he drew a great deal of inspiration from a thorough study of the other main thinkers in the American pragmatic tradition. His work contains many references to John Dewey and George Herbert Mead, to Charles H. Cooley and William I. Thomas. Yet, despite this resolute effort to "Americanize" his fund of knowledge, Schutz remained during his lifetime a marginal stranger in the American academy.

This situation changed drastically soon after Schutz's death. Not only did some of the brilliant students he had managed to attract during his years at the New School—Peter and Brigitte Berger and Helmut Wagner in sociology, Maurice Natanson in philosophy, to mention just a few—draw attention to his work as they themselves began productive scholarly careers, but others who had not been formal students of his began to depend on him for inspiration in their work.

Among the latter, Harold Garfinkel, who teaches sociology at UCLA, probably deserves pride of place. Garfinkel did his doctoral work at Harvard, where he studied under Talcott Parsons. But much like Schutz in relation to Weber, so Garfinkel in relation to Parsons felt that *verstehende Soziologie* and an emphasis on a "voluntaristic theory of action" needed to be built on more secure philosophical foundations than Weber or Parsons was willing to supply. Garfinkel hence turned to Schutz, just as Schutz had turned to Husserl a few decades earlier. It seems that Garfinkel spent many hours of conversation with Schutz in New York while completing his formal doctoral work with Parsons at Harvard.

During Schutz's American years, American sociological theory was dominated by the functionalist approach of Parsons and his many disciples and fellow thinkers, such as Robert K. Merton, Kingsley Davis, Wilbert Moore, and Robin Williams. Theirs was the dominant explanatory scheme, even though other approaches, such as the symbolic-interactionist school based on George Herbert Mead, continued to find exponents and defenders. Yet in the early and mid-1960s, for reasons that would lead us too far astray to explain here, the functional type of explanation lost much favor among younger sociologists. Some turned to neo-Marxism; others searched in a number of directions; but many turned to phenomenology, or what they believed phenomenology to be. This latter group contended that in its prepotent concern with objective structures of society and the constraining influence of normative injunctions and objective determinants of action, current sociological theorizing had paid insufficient attention to the subjective dimension of human experience and to human agency, that it was neglecting the point of view of the human actor. In their attempts to get closer to the subjectively experienced world of social actors, a number of younger sociologists in the 1960s turned not so much to Husserl, whose work they generally found too hermetic and demanding, but to Schutz and his students, and to Garfinkel.

Husserl had struggled throughout his career to develop a transcendental phenomenology so as to discover what he called "the ultimate structure of consciousness." This facet of Husserl's search did not interest Schutz. What he intended was to build a phenomenological social psychology that, as distinct from the drift of much of Husserl's writings, was concerned with intersubjectivity as much as with subjectivity. To this purpose, Schutz developed a key notion that appears only in a fleeting manner in Husserl's last writings: the notion of *Lebenswelt,* or "life-world." Building on his previous work on Weber, Schutz attempted in most of his American writings to explore the world of everyday life in which all actors are involved. He was concerned not only to uncover the roots of everyday experience in daily life, in the routines of quotidian living, but also to explore the cognitive settings and social relationships that underlie intersubjective processes and structure the realm of individual experience. People, he taught, do not simply accept given objective realities, they construct realities, in their intercourse with others. What the social scientist has to be attentive to is not some dead reality as it may be given in statistical studies that rely on preestablished categories, but the living reality that is intentionally brought to life in the experience of the actor in his life-world.

Harold Garfinkel, while acknowledging his great debt to Schutz, nevertheless, perhaps because of the structurally induced need for marginal differentiation in the world of academia, insists that his theory, which he has termed "ethnomethodology," departs in significant ways from the work of the earlier phenomenological approaches. In particular, as two ethnomethodologists have expressed it, "Schutz spoke of the everyday world as constituted by mental acts of consciousness. Garfinkel transformed the phenomenologist's mental acts into public, scenic, interactional activities, and ethnomethodology was born."[5] Be this as it may, phenomenological sociology, as well as ethnomethodology, became major currents in sociology in the late 1960s and 1970s, the former largely on the Eastern seaboard, the latter on the West Coast. Both tendencies assumed certain sectarian characteristics and attempted to erect impermeable boundaries between the core of "true believers" and the exoteric mass of the as yet unenlightened. Yet there can hardly be any doubt that at this time an approach to the data of sociology which was initiated by a relatively obscure refugee from Europe has come to assume an important position among the trends and currents of contemporary sociology.

Alfred Schutz, refugee scholar, businessman cum social philosopher, ensconced on Wall Street and at the New School and largely isolated from the usual hustle and bustle of the two academic disciplines, philosophy and sociology, to which he wished to contribute, became after his life's work was done a potent influence on American sociology and, to a lesser extent, on social philosophy. It is hard to conceive of these disciplines today without considering Schutz's impact on them.

Karl August Wittfogel (1896–): Asian Scholar and Odd Man Out

Karl August Wittfogel, the refugee author of one of the most influential, but also controversial, books in the recent history of the social sciences, *Oriental Despotism: A Comparative Study of Total Power* (1957),[1] was trained as a sinologist in Germany and had published widely in that field before his arrival in this country. His masterpiece of historical and sociological research built upon intellectual foundations already established in Germany. Yet Wittfogel's ideological stance and political orientation changed drastically a few years after coming to America. Having been a committed Marxist and a member of the Communist movement in his native land, he became a violent anti-Communist in America and can now be located on the far right of the political spectrum. Since Wittfogel has insisted throughout his long career on the close interrelations between political engagement and scholarly concerns, the following pages will have to deal in some detail with his ideological and political commitments. In fact, his career in America can be understood in large part in terms of the reaction of the American scholarly community to his ideological position.

Wittfogel was born in 1896 in a small North German village, the son of the village schoolteacher. His father retired when he was seven years old, and the family moved first to a small market town and then to the district capital of the province of Hanover, where Wittfogel attended the local gymnasium. His lifelong concern with the peasantry and rural life seems to have had its source in his boyhood spent in rural areas on the periphery of the Lueneburg Heath.[2]

Like so many young people of his generation, Wittfogel was influenced by the romantic and rebellious German youth movement, which he joined in 1912. Essentially a middle-class movement in revolt against middle-class values, it preached a return to nature in reaction against what it conceived to be the artificiality, deceit, and hypocrisy of bourgeois culture. Originally unpolitical in character, it provided a kind of safety valve for idealistic youth in their revulsion from urban culture and the world of bourgeois modernity.

While for most of its members the *Wandervoegel* movement provided a moratorium in which young people could evolve an acceptable identity while in transition between romantic revolt and middle-class respectability, Wittfogel and the friends he gradually gathered around himself maintained their rebelliousness into adulthood. When World War I broke out in August 1914, all of Wittfogel's classmates volunteered for the army, but he did not follow their example and developed instead a strong antimilitaristic orientation. At the University of Leipzig, where he studied under the psychologist and ethnographer Wilhelm Wundt and the historian Karl Lamprecht, he was soon attracted to the socialist movement. The *Leipziger Volkszeitung,* a socialist antiwar newspaper, seems to have provided much of the fuel that gradually impelled Wittfogel from his previously apolitical rebelliousness to a socialist political position.

During the early war years, Wittfogel, disaffected, searching for secure moorings in a left-wing weltanschauung, restlessly moved from one university and one field of study to another. He briefly attended the universities of Berlin, Munich, and Rostock, taking courses in ancient history, philosophy, geology, geography, and art history. In addition, while in Munich, he involved himself in the Bohemian life of the Schwabing artistic community, writing plays, poetry, and literary essays, all strongly imbued with youthful rebelliousness and ardent striving for a new socialist world to emerge from the bloodbath of the war.

In the spring of 1917 Wittfogel was drafted. He was assigned to light duty in Berlin and hence could continue his studies there. He concentrated in geology and geography, but also worked under Eduard Meyer in ancient history and under Alfred Vierkandt in sociology. Berlin also afforded him an occasion to establish closer contacts with left-wing academics such as Gestalt psychologist Max Wertheimer and the philosophy students Hans Reichenbach and Rudolf Carnap—all of whom, incidentally, later became his fellow refugees in the United States.

When the German revolution broke out in November 1918 and soldiers' and workers' councils sprang up all over Germany, Wittfogel enthusiastically joined the forces of the extreme Left. He soon became one of the leaders of the German Socialist student movement. When the Independent Social Democrats, the left wing of the socialist movement to which Wittfogel belonged, split off from the majority Social Democratic party in the fall of 1920, he joined the German Communist party, to which he remained faithful until he became a refugee from Nazi persecution. From the beginning of his career as a Communist, Wittfogel, largely because of his rural background, immersed himself in the problems of the peasantry and agrarian societies, problems which most of his city-bred peers tended to ignore. This prepotent interest also accounted for the fact that Wittfogel now concentrated his studies in Leipzig, Berlin, and Frankfurt on Asian societies in general and Chinese history in particular.

In these years, Wittfogel, with his many-sided interests and his total political engagement, moved in the various intellectual Communist circles and in the milieu of the artistic vanguard. The young firebrand, who fascinated his audiences when he lectured learnedly on the Marxist interpretation of Chinese history, also wrote revolutionary plays and published essays on socialist esthetics. In 1922, he published his first book in the social sciences, *The Science of Bourgeois Society, a Marxist Inquiry*,[3] a polemical attack on "bourgeois science" and on some of his teachers. In this book, and in other publications that followed in its wake, Wittfogel defended orthodox Marxism of the Leninist variety; yet, in contrast to many of his fellow thinkers, he also showed considerable respect for positivism. He wished to establish a science of society based on the Marxian categories of the different modes of production, pursued in terms of a rigorous methodology derived at least partly from positivism. Wittfogel held fast to his overall orientation even though many of his intellectual peers, Karl Korsch and Georg Lukács in particular, sharply criticized his positivistic tendencies from the vantage point of Hegelianized Marxism.

The year 1925 was as crucial for Wittfogel's later development as it was for the international Communist movement. Stalin realized that for the time being the hope of revolution in the West had to be abandoned and concentrated his attention on revolutionary movements in the East. This shift in emphasis was most welcome to Wittfogel, who had already decided to devote most of his work to the analysis of Eastern peasant societies. In the summer of 1926, Wittfogel published his first Marxist survey of Chinese society and history, entitled *Awakening China*,[4] under the auspices of the Frankfurt Institute for Social Research. This book contains in embryonic form the gist of Wittfogel's later major thesis on oriental despotism. Combining Marx's observation that a peculiar "Asiatic mode of production" had developed in those areas of Asia that depended on irrigation and Max Weber's conclusion that the bureaucracies, in controlling the irrigation networks, had accumulated social power, he now proposed that Asiatic societies such as China had developed a centralized ruling class that controlled the major means of production.

Wittfogel's key thesis, more fully elaborated in his *Economy and Society in China* (1931),[5] caused a number of complications in his relations with those who directed Communist policy from the Kremlin. There being very few experts on China within the ranks of the Communist International, it stands to reason that Wittfogel's services were at times eagerly sought by the Russian heads of international communism. However, certain of his theses, particularly his point that the Asiatic mode of production in general and centralized hydraulic agriculture in particular were crucial to the understanding of Chinese history, found a chilly reception in Russia. The Russian decision-makers felt that, even if Wittfogel had not intended to do so, it would be easy to establish an uncomfortable parallel between the emergence of despotism in China and current developments in the Soviet Union. If the Chinese ruling class had, as Wittfogel claimed, established its domination without resting it on private ownership of the means of production, would it then not become possible to argue that the Bolsheviks had, in their turn, become a ruling class even in the absence of private property? A debate on the Asiatic mode of production was carried on in Russia for a number of years, but it was finally and authoritatively concluded that this notion "perverted the methodology of Marxism," that it was "politically harmful," and that the history of China was marked by the long dominance of feudalism rather than by any special Asiatic type of social formation.[6]

After the mid-1920s, Wittfogel's scholarly work was carried on under the auspices of the Marxist-oriented Frankfurt Institute for Social Research, first directed by the economic and labor historian Carl Gruenberg and later by the philosopher Max Horkheimer (see pp. 315–16). Wittfogel had become a protégé of Gruenberg in the mid-1920s. When Horkheimer took over in 1931, after Gruenberg's death, Wittfogel's relations with the Institute became somewhat attenuated, as his own concerns were much closer to the emphasis on social and economic history that Gruenberg had favored than to the stress on philosophy and ideology that came to prevail under Horkheimer. He nevertheless continued to collaborate with the Institute until the Nazi takeover and after. It is to be presumed that this connection afforded him a scholarly and financial basis that made it easier for him to maintain relative independence from the Communist bureaucracy than was the case with many of his comrades-in-arms who were wholly dependent on the Communist party.

After the considerable success of Wittfogel's *Economy and Society in China,* published under the auspices of the Frankfurt Institute, the heads of the institute suggested that Wittfogel spend some time in China before completing a projected sequel to the work. Wittfogel decided, however, that the Nazi movement had become so menacing that he should direct all his energies toward combatting it. He laid his scholarly tasks aside and devoted himself entirely to the writing of pamphlets and articles dealing with the Nazi threat. Wittfogel was one of the few non-Jewish members of the Institute, yet he wrote extensively on the dangers of anti-Semitism in Germany, while the other members, most of them Jewish, remained silent on that topic.

Wittfogel's relations to the German Communist party became complicated in the last two years before Hitler's victory. He seems to have been convinced that the strategy of the party, according to which the Social Democrats, now called "social fascists," were the main enemies, whereas the Nazis were seen as only a passing phenomenon, was suicidal. A scholar who had made it one of his main tasks to study total systems of power could only be highly skeptical of the Communist thesis that Nazi domination would prove short-lived so that "after them come we." Wittfogel nevertheless continued, despite his misgivings, to militate within the ranks of the party.

Soon after Hitler gained power early in 1933, Wittfogel attempted to flee across the Swiss border but was recognized and arrested by the border police. He spent most of the rest of the year in various Nazi prisons and concentration camps. Largely owing to pressures from international scholarly quarters, he was released as the year 1933 drew to a close. He went into exile, first to London in January 1934, and then to New York in September of that year. In New York he soon established a connection with the Institute of Pacific Relations, many of whose directing members shared his leftist views, and the institute agreed to finance an extensive study trip for Wittfogel and his wife. They left for China in the spring of 1935 and returned to America in the middle of 1937, when the war between China and Japan broke out.

During the years in China, Wittfogel, despite his growing misgivings about Russia's policies and the strategies of the Communist movement, still associated mostly with American scholars who belonged to the left of the political spectrum. Upon his return to America, he reestablished his ties with the members of the Frankfurt Institute, now resettled in New York, and also with former German associates, most of them on the left, who now lived as refugees in and around New York City. One has the impression that, even though he enjoyed considerable reputation among sinologists with no political involvements, his major American supporters in the 1930s were scholars who, to one degree or another, can be said to have been fellow travelers of, or sympathetic to, the Communist party. Despite his expressed misgivings about many aspects of Communist policy, especially in Germany, they saw in Wittfogel a man who shared their cast of mind. All this changed on August 23, 1939, when it became known that Molotov and Ribbentrop had concluded a Nazi–Soviet pact. Many fellow travelers continued on their previous course, but Wittfogel did not. He now severed all his relations with the party. Communism had provided the guidelines for his political thinking for almost twenty years and had given meaning to his life as a person and as an author. All this ideological baggage now had to be jettisoned. Wittfogel still clung to many strands of Marxist doctrine, and he continued to associate with many non-Communist Marxist scholars and writers, but he no longer considered himself a Marxist, and he became a principled anti-Communist.

During the war years, Wittfogel immersed himself in scholarly work. The Chinese History Project which he had established at Columbia University after his return from China, financed by the Rockefeller Foundation, allowed him to gather a staff of collaborators. Despite some political tensions within its ranks, together they attempted the monumental task of writing a full institutional history of China. The only major part of that project, *The History of Chinese Society, Liao (907–1125)*,[7] which Wittfogel wrote with a Chinese collaborator, Feng Chia-Shong, was published in 1949. It was well received by leading sinologists.

During the war years and after, Wittfogel began to elaborate his notions about the special place of hydraulic societies in social and political history. He now proceeded to apply this notion to areas other than Asia, particularly to various regions in Latin America. As a result, some leading anthropologists, among them one of the deans of American anthropology, Julian Stewart, came under Wittfogel's influence. A number of other anthropologists found the notion fruitful, and many a thesis and monograph written in the 1940s and later testifies to Wittfogel's strong influence on American anthropology, especially among Latin American specialists.

Yet Wittfogel did not seem able for very long to limit himself to scholarly work. Soon after the war he began to publish articles on, for example, "How to Checkmate Stalin in Asia" in magazines such as the strongly anti-Communist *Commentary* and *New Leader*. More important, Wittfogel, who had maintained as late as 1946 that there was no connection between Oriental hydraulic societies and the history of Russia, soon after proceeded to argue that Russian society since the Mongol invasions was essentially Asiatic in character, even though hydraulic agriculture did not exist there. Basing his views in part on the warnings of such Russian prewar Marxists as George Plekhanov, he now argued that Russia had experienced after the Revolution what Lenin once called an "Asiatic Revolution," and that she was now a part of the unfree world of total power in the hands of despotic rulers. How far these new developments in Wittfogel's thought can be explained by his studies of Russian history or by his growing anti-Communist ideological involvement is hard to tell; probably both factors were operative.

Wittfogel's new anti-Communist militancy, his pronounced hostility not only to the Russian but also to the Chinese Revolution, alienated many of his former friends. Owen Lattimore, a leading expert on Soviet Asia who had been a close friend in both China and the United States, parted company with Wittfogel in 1947 when Wittfogel came to the conclusion that Lattimore believed in, and probably welcomed, the inevitability of a Communist victory in China. Gradually, other friendships and associations between Wittfogel and his sinologist colleagues came to an end. He began to be seen by many of them as a man obsessed with the Communist issue and no longer capable of looking at the passing scene in Russia and China with scholarly detachment. On his part, Wittfogel seems to have felt that many of his early associates wittingly or unwittingly played into the hands of totalitarian power holders. The history of estrangement between Wittfogel and his erstwhile colleagues and friends came to a climax in 1951, when he testified, under subpoena, before Senator McCarran's Internal Security Subcommittee, which was charged to investigate the extent to which the State Department and the Institute of Pacific Relations had been infiltrated by subversive forces "trying to influence the formulation and execution of U.S. Far Eastern policy in favor of Communism." The hearing largely concerned Owen Lattimore. Wittfogel testified that he did not know whether Lattimore was a member of the Communist party, but he nevertheless incriminated his former friends in a most virulent manner, stating, for example, that Lattimore had told him in October 1944 that a Russian takeover of Korea would be the best solution for that country. (Lattimore violently denied ever having said such a thing.) Following his testimony, Wittfogel wrote a letter to the McCarran Committee in which he stated, inter alia: "Realizing how Lattimore's special and unusual talents were increasingly furthering the aims of total power, we should examine more than this single man, who without doubt did great harm to the free world. We should study the entire political nexus that encourages the Lattimores."[8]

After his McCarran Committee testimony, Wittfogel was a marked man, not only among his former political associates but among students and members of the scholarly community. He had held a position as a professor of Chinese history at the University of Washington since 1947. Though this was primarily a research professorship entailing a very light teaching load, he attracted many eager students to his seminars and lectures during the first few years of his stay at Seattle. He had some fifty students in 1950. But hostility against him on the campus after his McCarran testimony in 1951 was such that his Washington associates suggested that he stay away from the university in 1951 and 1952. When he returned in 1953, only two students had registered for his class, and none for his seminar.

The more isolated he became, the more dogmatically Wittfogel hewed to his anti-Communist line. His tendency to discover secret Communist sympathies among a variety of scholars who disagreed with him now assumed somewhat paranoid features. On the issue of feudalism in China's past history, for example, Wittfogel argued that the Stalinist interpretation insisted that China had been feudal in character so as to divert attention from the bureaucratic monster state that had in fact dominated Chinese society for many centuries. It followed, according to Wittfogel's peculiar logic, that any scholar who insisted on China's feudal heritage was wittingly or unwittingly playing into Stalin's hands.

Given the charged atmosphere in the academic community whenever the name of Wittfogel was mentioned, it is understandable that when *Oriental Despotism* was published in 1957, it soon became the fulcrum of impassioned debates. In this book Wittfogel presented his general thesis on the hydraulic society as the basis of Oriental despotism in the most elaborately developed form so far, but he also endeavored to link his writings on the history of China with a detailed discussion of Russia's "Asiatic Restoration." Many scholars who found the Chinese part of the book illuminating failed to be convinced by the tortuous logic involved in claiming that, even though waterworks had played no part in its development, Russian society since the period of Mongol rule had nevertheless absorbed the major characteristics of despotic hydraulic society by, as it were, cultural diffusion or osmosis.

Within a few months after its publication, *Oriental Despotism* had been reviewed in over one hundred publications, not only by orientalists but by political scientists, historians, anthropologists, sociologists, and geographers. While many reviewers, such as the Yale anthropologist George Peter Murdock, the Oxford historian Max Beloff, the Harvard Far Eastern specialist Edwin Reischauer, and the Harvard anthropologist Clyde Kluckhohn, pronounced the book a breakthrough in the social sciences, many others—among them Arnold Toynbee, the Berkeley Chinese historian Wolfram Eberhard, and the great Marxist historian of China, Joseph Needham—remained skeptical. It is not for a nonspecialist to evaluate this debate, which continues to this day.

It is conceivable that the storm of criticism that swirled around Wittfogel would gradually have abated had it not been for the fact that soon after the book was published a dramatic event brought him again into the political limelight. On the morning of April 4, 1957, a few days after *Oriental Despotism* was published, the press announced that the Canadian ambassador to Egypt, Herbert Norman, had committed suicide in Cairo. The news reached the Boston meetings of the Association for Asian Studies, which Wittfogel attended, just before the sessions were to end. Norman was well known among Far Eastern experts, and he had been prominent in the Institute of Pacific Relations. Wittfogel had testified against him in the McCarran hearings. When the counsel of the Mc-

Carran Committee, Robert Morris, asked Wittfogel, "Was it obvious . . . that [Norman] was a Communist?" Wittfogel had answered unequivo- cally, "Yes." Subsequent Canadian investigations had cleared Norman of the charge of being a member of the Communist party, even though he seemed to have had associates in the party. Wittfogel's unsupported charge had meanwhile hampered Norman's career, and it was assumed by many that his suicide was caused by despondency over repeated investigations and accusations. Wittfogel was held responsible for his death by many of Norman's friends. In fact, when Wittfogel returned to his Columbia office after the Boston meetings, a reporter telephoned to ask whether he intended to leave the country.

Wittfogel continued to write and publish after 1957, but he now wrote, as it were, in a vacuum. To be sure, he was supported by a variety of rabid anti-Communists as well as by defenders of his interpretation of despotism in Asia and similar phenomena in Central and South Amer- ica in terms of the hydraulic mode of production, but he became in- creasingly isolated, an embittered doctrinaire unwilling to accept criti- cism and stubbornly clinging to his contentions, be they scholarly or political. When I listened to him lecture on China in 1977, I had the impression that he had not changed his interpretation at all since I had first heard him speak thirty years earlier.

Wittfogel's writings on Chinese history and the social structure of Ori- ental despotism have had considerable impact on sinological scholarship in the past and are likely to continue to be of consequence in the future.[9] He has fructified anthropological research. His writings on Russia are likely to be less influential. But Wittfogel the man, one-time dedicated social idealist and great scholar, will continue to be considered a flawed figure whose ideological zeal led to the betrayal of some of his formerly intimate friends. Academicians are known to be most tolerant of per- sonal failings, but they are not likely to forgive those who break the solidarity of the scholarly community, against whom it employs the po- tent sanction of ostracism.

IV
Economics and Economic History

Introduction

The interplay between the success of refugee intellectuals and the conditions they encountered in America upon their arrival is especially salient in the field of economics. The Austrian economists managed to find high-ranking positions in this country soon after their arrival, whereas German economists by and large were much less successful. This puzzling situation can be explained by the fact that the Austrians were largely educated in neoclassical liberal theory while their German colleagues were mainly the products of the historical school of economics. The Austrians were quickly accepted here because they spoke the same mathematical language as their American colleagues and usually worked in the same tradition. Hence they soon moved to prestigious departments of economics, while most of their German colleagues remained at the New School or had to be content with more marginal academic positions. All four Austrian economists dealt with in this section came to be seen as major figures in their profession, while none of their German historically oriented colleagues had comparable careers in their new country. The apparent exception—the Russian-born but German-educated Jacob Marschak, who became a pioneer in econometrics in America—in fact proves my point; his success came, at least in part, because he was not beholden to the historical school despite his German education.

During the interwar years, Vienna not only boasted a strong neoclassical school but was also the home of Austro-Marxism. Two prominent refugee students of economics were greatly influenced by this approach, but Alexander Gerschenkron and Karl Polanyi, both highly influential through their work even though only Gerschenkron had a secure academic position here, made their contributions and gained renown as economic historians rather than as theoretical economists. Russian-born but German-educated Paul Baran, the only Marxist economist dealt with in this section, was considered a maverick by his colleagues not only because he held unconventional political views but perhaps mainly because he had no use for the dominant neoclassical tenets. That he managed to secure a position at a major institution was to some extent a freak event. Finally, Albert O. Hirschman, whose background was somewhat atypical because he was German-born but West European in his education, worked first in the area of economic development, where neoclassical doctrine never attained the dominance it achieved in other branches of economics, and later became a widely acclaimed student of the interplay of the economic, political, and social factors in the history as well as the current operation of economic and social affairs. He managed creatively to combine the contributions of several traditions in economic thought.

By and large, those refugee economists who were neoclassicists, mainly of the Austrian school, were best equipped for a successful career in America. Most of their colleagues who came to economics through Austro-Marxism and related schools of thought either worked as historians of economics or had somewhat deviant and atypical careers.

Ludwig von Mises (1881–1973), Oskar Morgenstern (1902–1977), Fritz Machlup (1902–1983), and Gottfried von Haberler (1900–) :The Austrian School of Economics in America

The Austrian school of economics, founded by Carl Menger and best known for explaining economic behavior in terms of utility, developed in the course of the teaching of three generations of scholars. In its first generation, during the 1870s, 1880s, and 1890s, in addition to Menger, Eugen von Boehm-Bawerk and Frederick von Wieser played leading roles. In its second, beginning around the turn of the century, Ludwig von Mises and Joseph Schumpeter, and in its third, after World War I, Gottfried von Haberler, Friedrich Hayek, Fritz Machlup, and Oskar Morgenstern assumed prominence. Mises, Haberler, Machlup, and Morgenstern eventually settled in America. Schumpeter and Hayek, although they stayed in America, did not come as refugees and will hence not be considered here.

The founding members of the Austrian school, as well as most of their prominent disciples, had enjoyed high social standing in their native Austria. Menger, Boehm-Bawerk, and Wieser were all Excellencies and Life Members of the Upper House during the Austrian-Hungarian monarchy. Wieser, Boehm-Bawerk, and Schumpeter were cabinet ministers either during the monarchy or the republic. Other members of the group also held high office, and Menger, though he did not, was one of the tutors of the Crown Prince.[1] The younger members of the group, who achieved their eminence at home during the Austrian Republic and later abroad, did not have such illustrious standing but moved largely in the circles of the high-and-mighty in commerce and industry. Their high rank in their native society, which distinguished them from most of the other refugee scholars considered in this book, may help account for the conservative ideological stance they assumed in America. Haberler is a resident scholar at the neoconservative American Enterprise Institute, and Machlup belonged to that institution until his recent death.

The eminent position of the Austrian utility theorists in their native land seems to have facilitated their movement into similarly elevated positions in this country. But in addition, the transferability of their skills and the international character of much of economic thought in the 1930s contributed to their rapid acceptance. In contrast to many of the German-born economists, rooted in a tradition of history-oriented economic theory, the members of the Austrian school, with the exception of Mises, developed a science of economics that was founded on mathematical reasoning. They built a tradition of economic theory closely related, though not identical, to the roughly contemporary school of mathematical analysis led by Pareto, Walras, and Jevons. The Austrian economists, despite the characteristics of their native tradition, spoke a professional language that was easily understood.

When Ludwig von Mises, a member of the second generation of the Austrian school, came to this country in 1940, he already had achieved great eminence at home. Much of his life's work was done. That work, moreover, was well known to his American colleagues. He, nevertheless, did not immediately secure a teaching position. He was a guest of the National Bureau of Economic Research in New York from 1940 to 1944 and financed his research during those years by various grants. He became a visiting professor at the Graduate School of Business Administration of New York University in 1945 and served in this position until 1969. A large number of professional economists, as well as people from other walks of life, attended his seminars and were attracted by Mises's ideas. Some became his disciples. Among the economists who were prominent at the time or became prominent later were Laurence S. Moss, William H. Peterson, Mary Lemholz, Murray N. Rothbard, and Israel M. Kirzner. Mises was named a Distinguished Fellow of the American Economic Association shortly before his retirement in 1969. The citation accompanying the award noted that he had published nineteen volumes during his career—forty-six, if all revised editions and translations were included. It also remarked that "The stream of students that has come out of his seminars is no less remarkable than his literary output."

Born in 1881 in Lemberg, Austria, the son of a railroad engineer, Mises graduated from the University of Vienna in 1906. His principal teacher was Boehm-Bawerk. Mises served as economic adviser to the Austrian Chamber of Commerce from 1909 to 1934; taught economics at the University of Vienna from 1913 to 1938; was a founder and acting vice-president of the Austrian Institute for Business Cycle Research from 1926 to 1938; and was Professor of International Economic Relations at the Graduate Institute of International Studies at Geneva, Switzerland, from 1934 to 1940. His position at New York University was, to be sure, not quite so eminent as those he had occupied previously, but it ought to be kept in mind that he was no longer a young man when he came to America. Most refugee scholars of his age found it considerably more difficult than Mises did to secure a position and to hold it for as long a time, many years beyond the usual retirement age.[2]

In his first major book, *The Theory of Money and Credit* (1912),[3] and in a subsequent work, *The Origins of the Economic Crisis* (1931),[4] Mises adumbrated the themes in economic doctrine that he was to develop over a lifetime. He argued for strict laissez-faire, reductions in government expenditures, and hard money. Excessive booms, he held, result from inflated money supplies and artificially low rates of interest. Downturns in economic cycles can best be overcome by reliance on market forces and are unnecessarily prolonged by artificial propping up of wages and attempts of governments to stimulate demand. Interventionism leads to distortion of market forces.

Socialism relies on the planned direction of the economy, Mises argued in his well-known *Socialism: An Economic and Sociological Analysis* (1922),[5] but such planning, lacking a true price system, cannot calculate economically and hence leads to chaos. This is why laissez-faire liberalism was to Mises the only viable economic system. Mises was philosophically committed to methodological as well as to substantive individualism. He claimed that explanations must proceed from the analysis of individual behaviors and must not be based on structural characteristics or collective properties. Similarly, in matters of policy he was opposed to collectively oriented economic measures that presumed to restrain the choice of individual actors.[6]

Unlike the other members of the Austrian school, Mises rejected the mathematical approach in economics and in the social sciences generally. He attempted instead to develop a science of human conduct— *praxeology*, as he called it—that was to be built on the unchangeable structures of the human mind. He felt that in these structures it was possible to discover the a priori basis for understanding the principles of logical choice. Human choices can be accounted for by general and formal characteristics and are not affected by historical and contextual circumstances. In this view, economics is conceived as that part of praxeology in which calculation in regard to choices is possible. Denying that mathematics can be used even probabilistically to predict future events, Mises argued in *Human Action* (1940)[7] and elsewhere that economics has to limit itself to the analysis of current economic behavior by individual actors. Mathematical models, Mises believed, divert the mind from the necessary search for aprioristic knowledge.

Although Mises's message was not heeded during the years of ascendancy of Keynesian theory, from the 1930s to the 1960s, his work gained a new hearing during the 1970s. The major representatives of the Chicago monetarist school in particular, although they differ from Mises in important respects and reject his antimathematical bent, agree with him in their philosophical and policy orientations. It is largely because of Milton Friedman and his associates that Mises, together with other representatives of the Austrian laissez-faire approach such as Hayek, have again found a hearing in American economics and are to be reckoned among the fountainheads of contemporary neoconservatism.

There are at present few economists who would call themselves "pure Misians," yet Mises had some influence on his contemporaries and on a younger generation. Some of this influence can be traced to his seminars at New York University, some of it came through his books, whether written here or abroad; but no matter what the mode of transmission, Mises's imprint on American thought, though by no means as pronounced as that of Hayek, will probably continue to be felt, especially if present-day conservative trends come to be strengthened in the future.

Oskar Morgenstern did not come from an "impeccable" social background, as did most of the members of the Austrian school. He was born in Goerlitz, Germany, in 1902, the son of a small businessman and an illegitimate daughter of Emperor Frederick III of Germany. When he was young the family moved to Vienna, where he attended high school and the university. His major teachers at the university were Karl Menger (the economist son of Carl Menger) and Boehm-Bawerk. After receiving his doctorate in 1925, Morgenstern obtained a Rockefeller Fellowship that enabled him to study in London, Paris, and Rome, as well as at Harvard and Columbia, for three years.

After his return to Vienna in 1929, Morgenstern became a Privatdozent at the University of Vienna. By then he had completed his first major work, *Wirtschaftsprognose* (1928),[8] on the difficulties and paradoxes involved in economic predictions. He was promoted to professor in 1935.

During his years in Vienna, Morgenstern devoted himself not only to theoretical research but also to applied economics. He was the editor of the leading Austrian journal in economics, *Zeitschrift fuer Nationaloekonomie*, and an adviser to the National Bank of Austria. For seven years he was a director of the Austrian Institute for Business Cycle Research. He also served as an adviser to the Ministry of Commerce. As is true of most of his colleagues in the Austrian school of economics, Morgenstern's interests transcended the field of economics. It is not surprising to find that he was a regular participant in the philosophical discussions of the Vienna Circle, led by Moritz Schlick and later by Rudolf Carnap.[9]

Morgenstern was on a lecture tour in the United States in 1938 when he learned that Hitler had occupied Austria. He decided to stay in this country and was offered posts at several leading American universities. He chose Princeton, partly because his fellow refugee, the mathematician John von Neumann, originally from Hungary, was a Permanent Fellow of Princeton's Institute for Advanced Study. Morgenstern remained at Princeton until his retirement in 1970. He died there seven years later.

The pathbreaking *Theory of Games and Economic Behavior* (1944),[10] jointly written by von Neumann and Morgenstern, attempted a merger of Austrian utility theory and von Neumann's previous work in the theory of games but extended game theory into then virgin territory. All subsequent work in this general area takes its point of departure from this book. Much of Morgenstern's subsequent writings consists in attempts further to refine game theory, although he also continued to contribute to more traditional economic inquiry.

In view of the subsequent success of game theory on the American academic scene, it is interesting to note that, when Morgenstern first presented its guiding ideas to graduate students in economics at Princeton University in the early 1950s, he met with indifference, even hostility. He was perceived as an eccentric and, as Martin Shubik puts it, "an essentially 'high risk' member of the faculty to be involved with." "He was an outsider," Shubik continues; "no one in economics really understood what he did."[11] In addition, graduate students were intimidated by the formality that Morgenstern had brought from Vienna to Princeton. By and large both colleagues and students seem to have felt that the best way to cope with their unease in the presence of Morgenstern was to treat him patronizingly and with some derision. They may have felt that he had something important to say, but for the time being he had better be kept at a distance. Many graduate students in economics seem also to have believed that to study with more traditional professors would offer a safer route to future appointments. For all these reasons, most students interested in game theory were initially to be found in mathematics, not in the economics department.

Although game theory was at first looked upon with little favor among his students and colleagues in Princeton's economics department, Morgerstern nevertheless trained a number of students there, among them Martin Shubik and Herbert Scarf, both now teaching at Yale, who continued game-theoretical inquiries in various academic settings and brought this type of theorizing to major university campuses. By 1977, more than six thousand contributions to game theory had been published.

Like most of his Austrian colleagues, Morgenstern had a strong concern with public policy and applied economics. Not only did he write several books on questions of national defense and on political, economic, and military forecasting, he was also an accomplished middleman and entrepreneur in linking academic to governmental interests. He was a consultant to the Rand Corporation, the Atomic Energy Commission, and the White House. He was closely linked to the Office of Naval Research, which financed many of his investigations and those of his students, and he was an editor of the *Naval Logistics Research Quarterly.* He founded *Mathematica,* a highly successful consulting firm employed by both private industry and the federal government, and he remained chairman of its board until his death. He was also a director of the Market Research Corporation of America. In the last few years of his life—from 1970 to 1973—Morgenstern taught at New York University, where he founded the Center for Applied Economics.

The theory of games may best be characterized in Morgenstern's own words. "It is a mathematical discipline designed to treat rigorously the question of optimal behavior of participants in games of strategy and to determine the resulting equilibria. In such games each participant is striving for his greatest advantage in situations where the outcome depends not only on his actions alone, nor solely on those of nature, but also on those of other participants whose interests are sometimes opposed, sometimes parallel, to his own. Thus, in games of strategy there is conflict of interest as well as possible collaboration between participants. There may be uncertainty for each participant because the actions of others may not be known with certainty. Such situations . . . are found not only in games but also in business, politics, war, and other social activities. . . . In their *Theory of Games and Economic Behavior,* von Neumann and Morgenstern extended [von Neumann's previous theory] especially to games involving more than two players, and gave application of the theory in economics."[12] The major applications of game theory in economics can be found in theories of oligopoly—that is, in a market where there are only a few sellers—in bilateral monopoly, or one seller and one buyer; and in bargaining theory. The overall objective is to specify a theory in which interest, the availability of information, and rational choice determine courses of action.

Central to game theory are the processes by which individual players attempt to maximize their expected utilities. This theory, just like the utility theories of the Austrian school in which Morgenstern had been trained, rests on methodological as well as substantive individualism and shares with utility theory a pronounced distaste for structural and collectivist explanations of economic phenomena.

Despite initial resistance, game theory has been accepted as a major tool of research not only in economics but also in other social sciences, wherever the strategies of individual actors rather than structural conditions and constraints are in the forefront of analytical attention. The theory of games has now been developed and applied in a variety of spheres, from contingency planning in strategies of war to computerized chess playing. Now it is often seen as a peculiarly American contribution, even though it was originally developed by two refugees, one from Austria, the other from Hungary.

Fritz Machlup, a major figure in the third generation of the Austrian school, was born into a prosperous manufacturer's family in 1902 and was reared and schooled in Vienna. Later he went to the University of Vienna, where he studied under Mises and Wieser and completed his dissertation, which was supervised by Mises, in 1923. While still a graduate student, Machlup became a partner in a cardboard-manufacturing firm in Austria. Soon after receiving his doctoral degree, he acquired an interest in a Hungarian paperboard corporation. A few years later, he became the lawyer to a cartel of Austrian cardboard mills. While engaged in these widespread business activities, Machlup also continued research in economics and, together with Mises and Hayek, assumed high office in the Austrian Economic Society. He also formed a discussion circle with Hayek, Haberler, Morgenstern, and the philosophers Felix Kaufman and Alfred Schuetz, all of whom later came to America. They met regularly to debate interdisciplinary issues in social science methodology. In addition to several books and articles on economic problems, Machlup also wrote some 150 articles for the liberal journal *Neues Wiener Tageblatt* on current economic issues, as well as on the need for the liberalization of international trade relations. A Rockefeller Fellowship from 1933 to 1935 allowed him to get acquainted with many of the major economists of America at Columbia, Harvard, Chicago, and Stanford. During a subsequent sojourn in England, he visited Maynard Keynes, Joan Robinson, Piero Sraffa, and John Hicks.

Machlup received an appointment as a professor of economics at the University of Buffalo in 1936 and stayed there, except for wartime service, until 1947, making major contributions to price theory and to the study of international finance. He continued work in these areas after moving to Johns Hopkins University in 1947. In 1960, he accepted an appointment at Princeton University, succeeding the eminent Jacob Viner in the Walker Chair of International Economics. Machlup's major preoccupation during the Princeton years was international monetary reform. He made sustained efforts to influence American monetary policy. He also was instrumental in setting up a series of conferences between government officials and academic economists in his endeavor to establish a new program for international monetary reform under a system of floating exchange rates. Upon retiring from Princeton in 1971,

Machlup accepted a professorship at New York University and subsequently became a Resident Fellow at the American Enterprise Institute in Washington, where he remained until his death.[13]

A number of honors came to Machlup. He was president of the American Economic Association in 1966 and president of the International Economic Association from 1971 to 1974. In addition, having long been active in the American Association of University Professors, he served as its president from 1962 to 1964.

In tune with his philosophical interests, which had developed in Vienna, Machlup is the author of a pathbreaking study on *The Production and Distribution of Knowledge in the United States* (1962),[14] a major contribution to the sociology of knowledge. Machlup intended to expand this work into a new edition of no less than eight volumes. An incredibly prolific writer, Fritz Machlup wrote more than two dozen books, was coauthor of another eleven volumes, and published about two hundred and fifty articles in various journals and collective works. Despite this vast written output, Machlup took his teaching and supervision of dissertations most seriously, as many of his graduate students have testified. Machlup loved teaching, and he taught with enthusiasm and vitality. His facility with the English language and his lucid expository style were legendary.

His students, in addition to stressing Machlup's excellence as a teacher, often remark about the ways in which his strong belief in liberal values permeated his teachings. Like his companions in the Austrian school, Machlup was devoted to individual freedom and the removal of most governmental restraints on the free market, but he also devoted a good part of his energies to the defense of academic freedom.

Machlup's stance differed from that of other opponents to McCarthyism. Most of those who spoke up against the infringements of academic freedom in the McCarthy years and after argued against "unsupported accusations" and urged that professors not be dismissed without a hearing when charges of Communist affiliation had been made. For most academics of liberal persuasion the major sin of McCarthyism was its infliction of punishment on the innocent. This was not Fritz Machlup's view of the matter. For him it was not a question of whether charges could be supported or not, or whether due process was observed, that should stand in the center of discussions of academic freedom. He saw academic freedom as an integral part of what it means to be a teacher. He rejected any infringements on the freedoms of academicians, no matter whether they came "from the ouside" or emanated from more tactful encroachments "from the inside." When it was argued by some, the philosopher Sidney Hook for example, that freedom should not be granted to those who abuse it, Machlup countered that "so-called abuses of academic freedom, far from being incompatible with the existence of academic freedom, are the only proofs of its existence."[15] Machlup scoffed at the notion that academic freedom is "only for loyal citizens." "Thoughts," he stated, "know no nation." To Machlup, "a university that forbids certain subjects, books, or speakers violates freedom." He upheld this basic conviction during the McCarthy days and during the struggles that punctuated academic life in the 1960s. Far from shaking his convictions, the dire consequences of the rise of fascism in central Europe only reinforced his belief that infringements on free teaching and research must be opposed under any circumstances by those who are committed to the life of the mind.

Machlup served as visiting professor at some ten major universities, both here and abroad. For many years he was a consultant to the Department of the Treasury and the Department of Labor. He held honorary degrees from a number of colleges and universities. His maximum impact in economics came from his writing in international finance and monetary theory and *The Political Economy of Monopoly* (1952),[16] but his writings in the methodology of the social sciences[17] and on the distribution of knowledge have made his name familiar to many social scientists outside economics. His ability to move from academic contexts to an audience of government officials or business leaders was largely due to his capacity to operate with equal effectiveness in a variety of networks, inside and outside economics, in which he became involved over the years. His total commitment to liberal values endeared him to many, even if their political ideas were at variance with his own. Like his companions from the Austrian school, he has had a shaping impact on traditional liberal economics and on the general theory of laissez faire liberalism.

Gottfried Haberler's career in this country has been smooth and uneventful. His basic ideas in economics overlap with those of his colleagues of the Austrian school of economics, which have already been discussed. Even more than his fellow Austrians, Haberler found it easy to adjust to the requirements of academic and public life in America, and he was made welcome by his native-born colleagues. In particular, Haberler was spared the many academic peregrinations that are the usual lot of university teachers, whether native-born or refugee. He joined the Harvard faculty soon after his arrival in America, in 1936, and taught there until his retirement thirty-five years later.[18]

Haberler's academic career in his native Austria seems also to have been fairly untroubled. Born in provincial Pukersdorf in 1900, he grew up in Innsbruck. He then went to study economics at the University of Vienna under Friedrich von Wieser and Ludwig von Mises. Hayek,

Machlup, and Morgenstern were his contemporaries and colleagues. He received the doctorate in political science (*Staatswissenschaften*) in 1923 and a doctorate in law two years later. In 1928 he passed the habilitation examinations enabling him to teach economics and economic policy. Soon thereafter, he became a professor of economics at his alma mater, where he taught, with some interruptions, from 1930 to 1936.

Perhaps most important in the shaping of Haberler's subsequent career was the happenstance that he had established major ties to Harvard University very early in his life. A Rockefeller Fellowship for the years 1927 to 1929 allowed him to visit a number of British and American universities, among them Harvard. Contacts made at that time, as well as his close friendship with the great Austrian-American economist Joseph Schumpeter, who had taught there in the 1920s and become a regular member of the Harvard faculty in 1932, led to an invitation to become a visiting professor at Harvard during the academic year 1931–32. When Haberler decided to settle in America permanently in 1936, he was appointed, largely through the efforts of Schumpeter, to a professorship in economics at Harvard, and later became the Galen L. Stone Professor of International Trade there. His ties to Harvard were so enduring that he apparently never felt the need to leave Harvard Yard for any length of time. Only after his retirement in 1971 did Haberler break his ties to the Cambridge area to move to Washington, where he became a resident scholar at the American Enterprise Institute. There he was reunited with his old Vienna comrade-in-arms Fritz Machlup.

Haberler's principal contributions to economics are largely in the area of international monetary relations. His first major book, *Theory of International Trade* (1936),[19] was a pathbreaking work in its day and is still considered among the classic treatments of the subject. While most writing in this area was at the time largely descriptive and atheoretical, Haberler succeeded in working out an analytical apparatus that utilized the most highly developed modern economic theory. In this treatise, as well as in all his subsequent work, Haberler, in tune with his Vienna colleagues and friends, stood for a policy of international free trade and against any attempts of governments to influence the flow of international trade relations. By the time of the publication of the book, all major governments had abandoned free trade policy in efforts to protect their home markets from the general deterioration of international trade relations during the Great Depression. Haberler argued that the general abandonment of free trade in no way invalidated its correctness. As he said in his introduction, "Nobody will ask the medical sciences to change their judgment as to the health hazards of certain practices under the pretext that most everybody engages in them."

Haberler's second major book, which he completed while temporarily working for the League of Nations from 1934 to 1936, *Prosperity and Depression: A Theoretical Analysis of Cyclical Movements* (1937, 2d ed. 1939),[20] again attempted to join empirical inquiry with theoretical analysis. The second edition, in particular, contains one of the first major critical attacks on Lord Keynes's *General Theory* from the standpoint of Austrian utility theory. Its impact may be judged by the fact that Schumpeter, in his *History of Economic Analysis* (1954),[21] wrote that he did not feel the need to deal with this work at great length since he was confident that every economist was familiar with Haberler's "magisterial treatment."

Over his lifetime Haberler has published twenty-one books and large treatises as well as over a hundred articles. Most of them further develop arguments adumbrated in his first two major works. They argue with persistency and passion for the major tenets of Austrian utility theory, free international trade, and free markets. When it comes to internal economic developments, Haberler stands in the broad camp of monetarist theory, even though he seems less dogmatic in this respect than the Chicago School. He is aware, for example, that stagflation is not only due to budget deficits and extraordinary increases in monetary supplies but also has its roots in the various monopolies that characterize modern capitalist societies and hamper attempts to reestablish market adjustments. Inflation results if various vested interests resist attempts to reduce their claims and if there exists no mechanism leading to an adjustment of these incompatible claims. Haberler, as distinct from the strict monetarists, is aware of the political and social causes of stagflation, but in essence he remains a stout defender of laissez-faire economics.

Throughout his career, Haberler has tried to combine theoretical work with practical advice to the makers of economic policy. During World War II he served as an expert adviser to the Board of Governors of the Federal Reserve Board. For many years he has been a valued consultant to the Treasury and other Washington agencies. In particular, the abandonment by Washington policymakers of fixed exchange rates in favor of the present system of flexible exchange rates was largely due to the advice of Haberler and Machlup and to the influence of their many students in the Washington corridors of financial power.

While Haberler's career in America has perhaps been not quite so spectacular as those of some of his Austrian friends and colleagues, he has surely made an impact on that branch of American economics that is in the vanguard of the advocacy of international free trade. Given the lineaments of internal economic policy that marked the first term of President Reagan, it seems not too fanciful to suggest that the work of Haberler and his colleagues will have considerable influence in the federal government during the 1980s. Whether the present eclipse of Keynesian modes of thought will turn out to be permanent or not we do not know. But as long as this eclipse lasts, Austrian economic theory, whether strictly monetarist or not, is likely to have significant impact both in the field of economics and among policymakers. In any case, the Austrian economists who came to these shores in the 1930s are likely to continue to leave their mark on economic thought and affairs. More so than almost any other group of refugees discussed in these pages, they managed a smooth transition from their high-status positions in their native land to similar positions here. Given their valued skills, their social standing, and their congenial liberal values, they found a ready hearing both in the American academy and in the federal house of economic power.

Jacob Marschak (1898–1977), Pioneer of Econometrics

Russian-born Jacob Marschak came to this country as a refugee in 1938, after a distinguished career in both Germany and Britain. Not only through his own work, but also because he helped to institutionalize econometric research as the first director of the well-known Cowles Commission for Research in Economics, he achieved considerable eminence in America. He was instrumental in developing econometrics, a form of economic measurement based on formal statistical methods and economic theory, from a small sect into a major force in the field of economics. Working in conjunction with such scholars as Wasily Leontief and Tjalling Koopmans, both winners of the Nobel Prize, and later with another Nobel Prize winner, Kenneth Arrow, Marschak came to be known as a founding father of econometrics and one of the moving spirits in mathematical economics. His later contributions to information theory also proved influential.[1]

Marschak was born in 1898 in Kiev, the capital of the Ukraine. His parents were well-to-do assimilated Russian Jews who gave him an excellent private education during his early years. He learned German and French from governesses. His parents' wealth did not, however, shelter Marschak from the prevailing anti-Semitism. At the age of nine he was refused admittance to the local gymnasium, which opened its doors to only a small proportion of Jews, and was hence forced to attend the academically inferior School of Commerce. His parents sympathized with the first Russian Revolution of 1905, but Marschak later remembered only the pogrom that followed it. Marschak was never religious, but his Jewish identity was forcefully impressed on him by the anti-Semitism from which he had to suffer.

Like many other youngsters of liberal Russian-Jewish background, Marschak was drawn early to revolutionary movements that opposed the hated czarist regime. He became a Marxist in 1915, the year in which he entered the Kiev School of Technology. As a militant in the Menshevik Internationalist (antiwar) faction led by Julius Martov, he was arrested in December 1916 and released only after the fall of the czar in February of the following year. Having joined the municipal government of Kiev, he was soon forced to leave because Ukrainian nationalists expelled the representatives of the various socialist factions. Fearing persecution, Marschak and his family moved to a small town in the northern Caucasus.

In the Caucasus, political infighting was as pronounced as it had been in Kiev. Bolsheviks were pitted against Mensheviks, and all the parties of the Left were, in their turn, caught between reactionary Cossacks and Moslem mountaineers who had no love for any socialist measures. For a while Marschak was Secretary of Labor of a provisional government of the northern Caucasus, led by Mensheviks and Social Revolutionaries in an uneasy alliance with the Cossacks and opposed to the Bolshevik government which had come to power in Petrograd. When this government gradually fell under the control of a local dictator, a much disillusioned Marschak returned to Kiev, which was still under the control of Ukrainian nationalists. Like many of his Menshevik friends and associates, he now felt that further involvement in politics would be useless. He later called the Caucasian government of which he had been a part a *paedocracy*, a government of children.

After some brief studies of statistics at Kiev, Marschak decided in 1919 to emigrate and to take up economics in Germany. He worked at the University of Berlin with the leading economist and statistician Ladislaus von Bortkiewicz, who influenced him a great deal, and then moved to the University of Heidelberg, from which he received his Ph.D. in 1922. As was the custom in Germany, Marschak not only took courses in economics with the socialist economist Emil Lederer, among others, but also studied with the philosopher Karl Jaspers and the sociologist Alfred Weber.

Like other Menshevik emigrés in Germany, Marschak was helped to start on his career by recommendations and introductions from his co-thinkers in the German Social Democratic party. After a stint as an economic reporter for the *Frankfurter Zeitung*, he joined the staff of the Research Center for Economic Policy in Berlin, which was sponsored by the labor unions and the Social Democratic party. Subsequently, having gradually overcome his Russian accent (a useful achievement, since Germans tended to be sensitive in this regard), Marschak moved into the world of academic research. He joined the staff of the well-known Institute for World Economics at the University of Kiel. This was largely due to the initiative of the institute's director, Bernhard Harms, a skillful academic entrepreneur with a good eye for talented men who had difficulty finding regular academic appointments. In 1930 Marschak was appointed privatdozent at his alma mater, the University of Heidelberg.

His first papers indicate that, although he now was removed from direct political involvements, Marschak still held fast to his socialist convictions. He refuted the antisocialist theory of the leading Austrian economist Ludwig von Mises (see pp. 139–42) as expressed in Mises's *Socialism* (1922), which argued that a socialist economy was doomed to failure because it would lack the regulative constraints of the market. Marschak replied to this theory the following year, in a paper showing that under socialism the market system not only could be used but was likely to be more efficient since it would be free from the distortions that monopolistic corporations create under capitalism. His other major paper of this period was a pioneering empirical study of "the new middle class,"[2] written under the inspiration of his former teacher, Emil Lederer, in which Marschak argued, in tune with much Social Democratic thinking, that white-collar workers were workers economically but sociologically middle class.

In the late 1920s and early 1930s, Marschak began to work in the field that was later to be named econometrics. His early paper on the elasticity of demand (1931), together with the contemporary works of Jan Tinbergen, Wasily Leontief, and Ragnar Frisch, provided the foundation for the development of this new field. His subsequent work, except for the final period of his life, was almost entirely within the tradition of econometrics. His youthful political and practical interests subsided, and he became increasingly aloof from socialist thinking and even from concern with specific economic policy.

Marschak left Germany soon after Hitler came to power and went to Oxford, where, through the offices of the economist Revers Opie, he was appointed a Chichele lecturer at All Souls, a position specially created for refugees. Two years later, he was appointed the first director of the newly created Oxford Institute of Statistics upon the recommendation of Opie and the famous economist Roy F. Harrod. Most of the Oxford economic community treated the Institute with reserve, partly because of its emphasis on econometrics and partly because it had largely been created with the support of American funds, mainly from the Rockefeller Foundation. Despite its initially cool reception by Oxford economists, the institute soon established itself as a major center of statistical and empirical analysis in economics. In addition to inspiring the work of many of his associates at the institute, Marschak himself wrote a series of seminal papers during his stay in Britain, on labor mobility, monetary theory, and demand and capital formation.

Marschak spent the period from December 1938 to August 1939 in America as a Rockefeller Foundation Traveling Fellow. Anticipating the outbreak of World War II, he brought his family over, and in 1940 he was appointed professor of economics in the Graduate Faculty of the

New School for Social Research, largely on the recommendation of Emil Lederer, who was one of the leading figures there.

It turned out that the New School was only a way-station on Marschak's academic road. Yet in the four years he served there he took an initiative that was to be consequential for the development of econometrics in the United States. Having well-developed entrepreneurial abilities, Marschak persuaded the National Bureau of Economic Research to organize a seminar on mathematical economics and econometrics. This seminar brought together senior economists and many of the younger econometricians who were later to form the econometrics establishment in America. It was attended by such European-born economists as Tjalling Koopmans, Joseph Schumpeter, Wasily Leontief, Abraham Wald, Trygve Haavelmo, and Franco Modigliani, but also included some of the most promising younger American economists, such as Carl Kaysen, Paul Samuelson (a later Nobel Prize winner), and Sidney Alexander. The papers that grew out of this seminar laid much of the foundation for subsequent work in econometrics. Most of the participants seemed to have felt that a turning point in its development had been reached under Marschak's leadership.

The opportunity to extend the work of the New York seminar and to find an institutional home for it presented itself in 1943, when the Cowles Commission for Research in Economics moved from the University of Colorado to more prestigious surroundings at the University of Chicago. Mainly upon the suggestion of the well-known Polish economist Oskar Lange, who was then teaching at the University of Chicago, Marschak was offered the directorship of the commission. Even though his budget was modest, Marschak, having learned from Harms's policies at the University of Kiel, took advantage of the depressed academic market: he seized the opportunity to attract a remarkable group of young economists to the commission at bargain prices. Koopmans secured a tenured faculty position; the others were hired as research associates. Many of them were foreign-born, but a number of native-born economists also joined the Cowles Commission staff. Kenneth Arrow, Evsey Domar, Herman Rubin, Leonard Hurvica, Lawrence Klein, Trygve Haavelmo, Theodore Anderson, among many others, began their brilliant careers at the Cowles Commission. Still another group from the Chicago area, including Abba Lerner of Roosevelt College, Marschak's former student Franco Modigliani, now at the University of Illinois, and Herbert Simon (who subsequently won a Nobel Prize) of the Illinois Institute of Technology, participated in much of the work of the Cowles Commission.

In Chicago, Marschak was mainly the academic entrepreneur and published relatively little. But such entrepreneurship should not be underestimated. His associates have testified that without his leadership, the Cowles Commission research might never have reached the success it attained in fact. Koopmans states that Marschak's terse opening chapters to the two methodological volumes that illustrated the novel approach of the Cowles Commission "supplied a framework and direction for the interrelated efforts of the team."[3]

In 1948, Marschak decided to hand over the directorship of the commission to Tjalling Koopmans and return to scholarly pursuits. So, at age fifty, he turned his attention to sets of problems that were only peripherally related to his previous work. Partly stimulated by the theory of games of von Neumann and Morgenstern, he began to work on information theory and the analysis of decision-making, particularly in groups or teams. It is likely that his leadership of the Cowles Commission team had sensitized him to issues arising from teamwork and group processes. As Kenneth Arrow puts it, "He sought to formalize the idea of a number of individuals each having to make decisions which affect every other, and each having access to different information."[4] This work ultimately gave rise to a formal theory of organization based on modern statistical decision theory. Arrow wonders whether Marschak's openness to influences of various sorts made him especially sensitive to problems of uncertainty and the importance of communication. Marschak was the first to develop a systematic theory of the economic value of information.[5]

Ever eager to learn from scholars in other disciplines, and impatient with departmental parochialism, Marschak, at Chicago and later, formed an extensive network of intellectual contacts in a variety of academic areas. He was a close personal friend of Leo Szilard, the atomic physicist, and through him met other European scientists who had earlier participated in the Manhattan Project, which created the atom bomb. He took an active part in an interdisciplinary seminar on the behavioral sciences which included, among others, the psychologist James G. Miller and the biostatistician and game theorist Anatol Rapoport. It is worth recalling in this connection that Marschak's theoretical models of choice behavior and information transfers were at first more fully appreciated by psychologists than by economists. But by now studies of the economics of information, of its value or demand price and the benefits of its optimal uses, have become a major research area in economics. Marschak's student Roy Radner and his Chicago associate Jack Hirshleifer have been most productively engaged in this area of inquiry.

In 1960 Marschak left the Cowles Commission (which had moved to Yale five years earlier) and accepted a professorship in economics and business administration at the University of California at Los Angeles, where he stayed until his death. His interdisciplinary concerns were as much in the forefront of his work in Los Angeles as they had been earlier at Chicago and Yale. For over fifteen years he was the leader of the Interdisciplinary Colloquium on Mathematics in the Behavioral Sciences at UCLA. He died in 1977, while working on his presidential address to the forthcoming meetings of the American Economic Association.

Roy Radner has said of Marschak that "Throughout his work ran the important message that economists must come to grips with problems of uncertainty."[6] If this is so, it seems plausible to suggest a direct connection between the course of Marschak's life and the main problematics of his work. When he was young, he was twice marginal, as a Jew and as a Ukrainian in Russia. Though born into a wealthy family, he refused the comforts of a bourgeois existence and became a socialist militant instead. Exiled from Russia and then again from Germany, he moved to England and finally to America. Marschak was surely aware of the problems of uncertainty. It stands to reason that his own existential condition should have provided the focus for his lifework.

When Kenneth Arrow served as chairperson of the nominating committee of the American Economic Association in 1976, he at first believed that Marschak should be its president "but that his age and the remoteness of his interests from those of the general membership would surely serve as a barrier. When the committee met, it turned out that everyone there had been either an associate or a student of Marschak's and all felt the same way [i.e., that he should be president]."[7] This story may serve as an indication of Marschak's influence in America. There are few American scholars outside of the natural sciences who have taught or been otherwise closely associated with five Nobel Prize winners. There are also few who have been instrumental in institutionalizing a whole new field of inquiry and lived to see it flourish. Nor are there many who, at a time when most people begin to think of retirement, start a new research career in an area fairly remote from their earlier work. Marschak did all this, and more. The former militant socialist from Kiev became a creative force in American scholarship.

Alexander Gerschenkron (1904–1978) and Albert O. Hirschman (1915–): Two Students of Economic Backwardness and Development

Theories of economic development became a special focus of economic research after World War II. Ever since Adam Smith, of course, the major classical economists had concerned themselves with the causes of economic backwardness and progress, and dissident economists such as Marx and Veblen were also attempting to uncover the causes of what are now called the stages of economic development. After World War II, however, the rise of the economies of the Soviet bloc and the apparent failure of the countries of the Third World to follow the lead of the West moved such questions into the foreground of attention of American economists and economic historians. In the ensuing debates, two refugee scholars played central roles: Alexander Gerschenkron mainly through exploring the historical record of European countries; and Albert Hirschman largely through the analysis of the present predicaments of countries of the Third World generally and of Latin America in particular. Neither of these men created a "school," but both had numerous followers and left a mark on all future studies of modernization.

Alexander Gerschenkron was born in 1904 in Odessa, in the south of Russia, and received his primary and secondary schooling there. He later described the Russian gymnasium he attended as "atrociously bad," a place where one wasted time in "dull and resentful coma." In 1920 his father, who had been manager of a cigarette factory in Odessa, succeeded in sending his wife and daughter to England and, with his son, set out on foot for Rumania. At the border, a soldier threatened to shoot them to save the trouble of taking them back to the Russian military post. They persuaded the soldier to let them pass over into Rumania by giving him Gerschenkron's father's coat and a gold cigarette case. From Rumania they made their way through Hungary and then to Vienna, where they settled and where Gerschenkron completed his secondary education and attended the university.

The economics taught at the University of Vienna was largely based on the liberal, laissez-faire model developed by Austrian utility theory (see pp. 139–50). The young Gerschenkron acquired much of his subsequent sophistication in economic analysis from his teachers there, but he probably was influenced even more by an extra-academic tradition, that of Austro-Marxism, which flourished in Vienna during most of the interwar years. Austro-Marxism, though adhering to the main tenets of Marx's message, was less rigid and doctrinaire than the Marxism of neighboring Germany. In particular, although men like Rudolf Hilferding, Max Adler, Karl Renner, and Otto Bauer did not deny the importance of economic determinants in politics and ideologies, they did not hold a strictly deterministic view of the relations between infrastructure and superstructure. They argued instead that ideas and politics possess a large degree of autonomy. They held, moreover, that such factors as ethnic competition, nationalism, the clash of world views, and contests between moral visions have to be taken into account in order to assess the course of social and economic development.

Gerschenkron became a convinced Austro-Marxist socialist during his years in Vienna, but he never became a rigidly orthodox Marxist. After he came to America in 1938, he seems to have abandoned any political involvements, but he continued to be inspired by a moral vision acquired from his involvement with Austro-Marxism. His economic analyses were always guided by the notion that backwardness and development cannot be understood in terms of economics alone but must be informed by concern with political, ideological, and moral factors.

After receiving his doctoral degree from the University of Vienna in 1928, Gerschenkron had considerable difficulty in gaining a position. Russian emigré scholars were hardly received with open arms in the Depression years, and socialist convictions did not recommend one to Austrian academic economists, who were for the most part Catholic traditionalists or old-fashioned liberals. This is why Gerschenkron held a number of marginal positions, largely in socialist-dominated institutions. From 1928 to 1938 he served as a manager of the Vienna branch of a Belgian motorcycle factory while teaching courses at the People's University from 1928 to 1931; from 1931 to 1935 he was a research analyst with the Austrian Wholesale Cooperative Society; finally, from 1937 to 1938 he was associated with the liberal Austrian Business Cycle Research Institute, directed by Oskar Morgenstern (see pp. 142–45). The institute's excellent international connections enabled Gerschenkron to establish contacts with American scholars that were to be most helpful to him in his later career in America. In particular, he met Charles A. Gulick, professor of economics at Berkeley. The two struck up a lasting friendship at first sight. It was Gulick who later enabled Gerschenkron to obtain an immigration visa to the United States by signing an affidavit of support.

When Hitler invaded Austria in March 1938, Gerschenkron managed to escape over the mountains into Switzerland and to reach America soon after. Having held no previous academic position, and not having a publication record, he spent his first ten years in this country mainly in research, first at the University of California at Berkeley, and later on the research staff of the Board of Governors of the Federal Reserve System in Washington. At Berkeley, Gerschenkron was the guest of Charles Gulick for over a year and helped him write his two-volume study of the history of Austria from the Hapsburgs to Hitler.[1] From 1938 to 1942 he was a research associate and member of the Trade Regulation Project conducted by J. B. Condliffe and Howard S. Ellis. From 1942 to 1944 he was a lecturer in the Department of Economics at Berkeley, giving courses on European economic history and the theory of international trade. For a while he moonlighted as a steelworker in a Kaiser shipyard, where he hugely enjoyed the close contact with his fellow workers. He confessed later: "I seriously considered staying in the shipyard. The work did not follow you home at night into your leisure and dreams."[2]

In Berkeley, Gerschenkron wrote his first book, *Bread and Democracy in Germany* (1943),[3] a detailed analysis of agricultural protectionism in the German Empire and the Weimar Republic with special emphasis on the large landowners in East Germany and their role in bringing Hitler to power. The book is considered a pioneering study among political scientists. It was one of the first studies on the political influence that interest groups wield in modern societies. Gerschenkron also collaborated with Howard S. Ellis in the writing of Ellis's work on exchange control in Central Europe.[4] When Ellis joined the staff of the Federal Reserve Board in 1943, he arranged for Gerschenkron to join him there in 1944 as an "economic specialist." Two years later, Gerschenkron became chief of the Foreign Area Section in the research and statistics division of the Federal Reserve System. He held that position until 1948.

Gerschenkron's truly consequential career began only in 1948, when, at the suggestion of Gottfried Haberler, he was appointed to the faculty of Harvard. He taught European economic history and Soviet economics and was director of the economic division of Harvard's Russian Research Center. In 1956, Gerschenkron decided to leave the field of Soviet economics to devote himself entirely to the study of European economic development. When he retired in 1974, he was director of Harvard's Economic History Workshop and Barker Professor of Economics.

Lest it be thought that Gerschenkron's "Americanization" was limited exclusively to the academic scene, it should be noted that he became an avid baseball fan and was a Red Sox fanatic while at Harvard. His fascination with index numbers stood him in good stead: he developed an extensive historical knowledge of baseball scores. It is also interesting to note that this urban Jew became in his Harvard years an avid hunter, stalking along the unpaved roads of his country retreat in New Hampshire, always with a shotgun or rifle in the crook of his arm.

Gerschenkron first came to the attention of economists by devising an ingenious method of assessing the growth of the Soviet economy. Russian economic specialists had been aware for some years that the official Russian statistics presented an exaggerated picture of economic growth but had found it impossible to correct the distortions of Soviet statistics, given the absence of more reliable measurements. In several publications beginning in 1947, Gerschenkron was able to show that, by using a dollar index and by taking American prices as a control, it was possible to correct the exaggerations of the official Russian statistics. There is no such thing as a "true" index number, but Gerschenkron demonstrated that in periods of drastic change, an index based on early-period prices is bound to reflect a higher rate of growth than an index based on late-year prices. In particular, he was able to show that while the official Soviet index indicated a fourteenfold increase in machinery output during the years 1927/1928 and 1937, the actual increase was only slightly more than fivefold. The "Gerschenkron effect" was later found in a variety of other Soviet industries. It is still the foundation stone of most analyses of Russian trends, and it also has been used in the analysis of other nations, such as the People's Republic of China.

While Gerschenkron's work on the statistics of economic development in the Soviet sphere revolutionized the study of Soviet economics, it mainly interested area specialists and foreign-policy officials. His subsequent work found a wider audience. The centerpiece of his work in economic history consists of a series of powerful hypotheses, eventually crystallized in a model, of the pathways through which latecomers in the process of industrialization attempt to catch up with countries that have enjoyed an early start. Following Thorstein Veblen's brilliant suggestions about the advantage latecomers have and "the penalty of taking the lead," Gerschenkron argued in a number of essays[5] that there could be advantages in relative backwardness and that, in any case, late industrializers have different industrializing experiences than the early ones. The pioneers have already made the necessary organizational and technological innovations, so latecomers do not have to invent but need only to borrow, imitate, or import skills. Hence they can skip stages in economic development while the pioneers have to proceed step by step. The new members of the industrial club had still other advantages. The capital stock of their advancing modern sector was, by and large, newer and more up to date. Moreover, contrary to what had been conventionally assumed before, skilled labor was scarce in developing nations so that there existed a powerful incentive to develop capital-intensive industrial plants. Finally, competition from the pioneers forced the newcomers to emphasize those industries in which technological progress was the most rapid.

Gerschenkron's contributions to the understanding of backwardness and modernization were not exhausted by his stress on the advantages of backwardness. He also emphasized that potential advantages could come into actual play only if facilitating factors emerged on the historical scene. In Germany the unification of the Reich played this part. In Russia the abolition of serfdom, and especially the state-supported building of railroads, proved a decisive turning point. In France the ideology of the Saint-Simonians was a major catalyst that sparked industrial developments. Where adequate private investment funds and ample domestic markets were absent, investment banks, as in France, Germany, and Austria, or state intervention, as in Russia and Hungary, provided the needed capital. In the case of the English industrial revolution, the initial impetus had come from what Marx had called the primitive or original accumulation of capital through the enclosure movements and the commercialization of agricultural production, but in other countries different factors provided the spur.

Even this cursory enumeration of the factors that Gerschenkron specified as facilitators of industrial development shows that he synthesized what he had learned from Marx and Veblen with the heritage of Austro-Marxism that he had come to appreciate in his youth. Though focusing his analysis on economic factors, he was eager to show that ideological and moral factors, as in the case of the Saint-Simonians, or political factors, as in the case of state intervention in Russia and political unification in Germany, provided powerful spurs to the industrialization process. Gerschenkron eschewed monistic schemes in favor of pluralistic explanations.

As one of his former students Henry Rosovsky, the former dean of Harvard's Faculty of Arts and Sciences, has testified, Gerschenkron was a highly effective teacher. His course on the economic history of Europe was one of the great Harvard courses for some twenty-five years. No fewer than a thousand economists were introduced to economic history through these lectures. Gerschenkron's was practically the only course in post-Schumpeterian Harvard that opened comparative vistas to students who were previously provincial in their outlooks on economics. The small seminars Gerschenkron offered and the doctoral dissertations he supervised brought him students and disciples who subsequently made major contributions to the study, not only of the economic developments of Central Europe and the Soviet Union, but of the growth of other industrial latecomers as well. Rosovsky's studies of Japanese economic developments, Alexander Eckstein's pioneering work on the economics of the People's Republic of China, Alexander Erlich's writings on the early stages in Soviet economic development, Joseph Berliner's work on later stages in Russia's drive for industrialization—all owe an enduring debt to Gerschenkron's work.[6]

Even a short sketch such as this would be incomplete were it not to mention that Gerschenkron, a true polyhistor, wrote on many other subjects in addition to economic history. He wrote a superb analysis of *Doctor Zhivago;* he contributed an erudite critical commentary on Nabokov's translation of Pushkin's *Eugene Onegin;* and he commented perceptively on problems of translation and other linguistic issues. His knowledge of languages was legendary. Apart from his native Russian and the German he learned to speak with barely an accent in his Vienna days, he had a working knowledge of French, Italian, Swedish, Dutch, and Bulgarian, among others. Toward the end of his life, Gerschenkron's interest in problems of translation led him to check the Russian translation of Paul Samuelson's famous text *Economics: An Introductory Analysis.*[7] Discovering numerous errors, he was especially delighted to notice the following: Samuelson was fond of brief quotes from Lewis Carroll's *Alice in Wonderland.* One of these was the well-known line, "The time has come, the Walrus said, to speak of many things." The Russian translator, not understanding what a walrus had to do with economics, decided that the word must be a misprint of Léon Walras, the famous nineteenth-century economist, who taught for many years at the University of Lausanne, and wrote, "The time has come, Walras said, to speak of many things."

Gerschenkron, a Russian refugee schooled in the economics of Austro-Marxism, grew, over a quarter-century, into a kind of institution at Harvard, begot a brilliant group of younger students who renovated American economic history, and powerfully influenced research on economic backwardness and development. More generally, he succeeded in becoming the leader of what is often called the modern quantitative school of economic history. Gerschenkron was honored by economists and economic historians alike—he was a Distinguished Fellow of the American Economic Association as well as president of the Economic History Association. He was instrumental in leading American scholars in both disciplines out of their previous parochialism. The man who started by selling Belgian motorcycles in Vienna became an institutionalized innovator in the shade of the Harvard Yard.

Albert O. Hirschman was born in Berlin, the son of a well-known Jewish surgeon. He was educated at the French gymnasium in Berlin, from which he graduated in 1932. An active member and section head in the Socialist Youth Movement, and therefore in some danger, he decided to leave Germany soon after Hitler's accession to power. He studied economics in Paris from 1933 to 1935, where he gave German lessons to earn some money, assisted by his mother, who had remained in Germany. Hirschman moved to England to study at the London School of Economics in 1935, but left in the following year for Italy, where he continued his studies in economics. He received his doctorate from the University of Trieste in 1938; but in that year, the racial laws adopted by Mussolini forced him to leave Italy and return to France. During his stay in Italy, Hirschman had actively supported the Italian underground opposition to the Fascist regime. In Paris, he worked as a freelance economic journalist and as a research economist. When the war broke out, Hirschman, having previously served as a volunteer in the Spanish Republican army in the summer of 1936, volunteered for the French army and served from September 1939 until the French defeat in June 1940.

After his discharge and until the end of 1940, Hirschman worked in Marseilles as the principal assistant of Varian Fry of the Emergency Rescue Committee, an American organization for rescuing European political and intellectual refugees from Nazi-occupied Europe. Fry's work was instrumental in saving the lives of many European intellectuals. As Fry's main European assistant, Hirschman engaged in the many more or less clandestine operations that were necessary to save refugees from the Nazis and the Vichy police. Asked in a questionnaire of which achievements in his life he was most proud, Hirschman listed his work with the Italian anti-Fascists and with Varian Fry first, before his academic work on development in Latin America and his books and articles.[8] When his arrest in Vichy France seemed imminent, Hirschman left for the United States in January 1941 on a Rockefeller Fellowship to do research at the University of California in Berkeley.

In 1938/39, after Hirschman's return from Italy to Paris, he had established a small reputation as an expert on the Italian economy under the Fascist regime. Because of this he was contacted by John B. Condliffe, a New Zealander and former League of Nations economist who was then in the process of moving to Berkeley, where he was to be a professor of international economics and was to organize a large research project on the new exchange-control regimes of Europe. Condliffe commissioned Hirschman to write the Italian section of that study, which Hirschman completed before the war broke out. It was Condliffe, then already in Berkeley, who obtained a Rockefeller Fellowship for Hirschman on the basis of which Hirschman was granted an American visa.

Soon after arriving at Berkeley, Hirschman met Gerschenkron, who was also working on Condliffe's project, and struck up an intellectual friendship with him. In 1946 Gerschenkron invited Hirschman to join him at the Federal Reserve Board, and it is likely that he was also influential in obtaining Hirschman's appointment to Harvard, in 1964. Later on, however, their paths diverged and their friendship suffered as a result. Hirschman continued to draw a great deal on Gerschenkron's work and to esteem him highly, but the two scholars developed quite different political outlooks on the basis of their differing experiences. During his long stay in Latin America (see below), Hirschman had become intensively exposed to economic injustices and mass poverty, which gave renewed impetus to his youthful zeal for social change. Gerschenkron, on the other hand, was relatively insulated from such experiences at Harvard, where he attained the highest academic success and developed a fairly conservative outlook.

During his stay at Berkeley, Hirschman wrote his first book, *National Power and the Structure of Foreign Trade* (1945).[9] Publication of the book was delayed by Hirschman's service in the United States Army from March 1943 to December 1945. It received little notice when it was first published but slowly won considerable recognition as an early analysis of relationships of dependency and asymmetry in international economic affairs. It established Hirschman's reputation as a technical economist.

While at the Federal Reserve Board in Washington, Hirschman worked primarily on problems of European postwar recovery. When it seemed to him that these problems were receding in importance, largely because of the success of the Marshall Plan, he became eager for a change and made a move that was to be consequential for his subsequent career: in 1952 he accepted the offer of the Colombian government to become an adviser to its newly founded National Planning Council. When his contract expired two years later, Hirschman decided to stay on in Bogotá as a private consultant to Colombian officials and to private firms.

Working on the Marshall Plan in Washington in the postwar years, Hirschman had met many fellow economists who did similar work and who were soon to move into the universities. Among them were Thomas Schelling, Henry Wallich, and Robert Triffin, all of whom joined the thriving economics department at Yale University. These men were probably responsible for bringing Hirschman to Yale as a visiting research professor in 1956. During his two years' stay at Yale, Hirschman

wrote his first major book, *The Strategy of Economic Development* (1958).[10]
This book had its origin in its author's conviction that the economic development he had observed in Latin America bore little resemblance to
what authorities in that field had said about it. Beginning with this book,
Hirschman wrote a number of works that departed in significant ways
from the received wisdom in the field of modernization and developed
a distinctive style of economic analysis that owed at least as much to his
powers of observation and his practice-oriented analytical skills as to
previous theorizing.

To have lived in six countries, fought in three armies, and participated
in three anti-Fascist and socialist movements is an unusual preparation
for an American academic career. But it evidently served Hirschman
well. Having been involved in various political situations in which practical coping with concrete tasks and an it-can-be-done orientation were
valued, Hirschman approached problems of Latin American development with the same pragmatic, problem-solving cast of mind that had
stood him in good stead in his earlier career. The impact of his teaching
and writing and the success of his general academic career seem to indicate that this approach found an echo among his American colleagues.

After his stay at Yale University, Hirschman embarked on a highly
successful academic course. He served as a professor of international
economic relations at Columbia University from 1958 to 1964 and then
as professor of political economy at Harvard, where he taught until 1974.
Since then he has been a professor of social science at the Princeton
Institute for Advanced Study.

The gist of Hirschman's approach to problems of development can
best be understood in contrast to previous theorizing against which he
reacted. In the first pages of his *Strategy of Economic Development,* Hirschman deals with his predecessors under the suggestive title "The Search
for the Primum Mobile." He argues that successive generations of theorists of development had dealt with explanation in terms of a single
overriding factor. For a long time, natural resources held center stage;
later, capital came to be considered the principal agent of development.
This was challenged by a view that considered entrepreneurship and
managerial ability to be the necessary sparkplugs of modernization. Still
later, supportive attitudes, value systems, and climates of opinion were
seen as decisive elements. Finally, the role of creative minorities and of
deviant behavior became the pivot of many explanatory schemes. As
each new explanation was proposed, the previous ones were rejected.
Hirschman suggests that the time has come to give up attempts at a
monocausal explanation. He proposes instead that "development depends not so much on finding optimal combinations for given resources

and factors of production as on calling forth and enlisting for developmental purposes resources and abilities that are hidden, scattered, or
badly utilized."[11]

Just as he considers the search for the one primum mobile to be a vain
and fruitless undertaking, so Hirschman also warns, especially in his
Journeys toward Progress (1963),[12] against the search for the one ultimate
solution to problems of modernization. Borrowing the term "la rage de
vouloir conclure," the mania for wanting to conclude, from Flaubert,
Hirschman holds that the quest for *the* all-encompassing solution to
problems of development is apt to be an obstacle to any realistic strategy.
He argues for emphasizing incremental gains and a problem-solving
strategy instead of pursuing the will o' the wisp of Unique Comprehensive Reform. Pervasive backwardness will be overcome, in Hirschman's
view, through active "reform-mongering" rather than through grandi-
ose overall strategies.

Excessive expectations of success from "tomorrow's" ventures only hold
back action on today's projects. In the same way, the "ego-focused image
of growth," where the maximization of individual benefits is pursued at
the expense of the rest of society, and excessively "group-focused" orientations, where change is conceived as essentially profiting the group
while conditions for individuals remain the same, have to be resisted
equally. Instead, strategies of development need to steer a middle course
that rewards individual initiative while still keeping in mind that the
cooperative component must be strengthened.

If the major task of development consists in mobilizing hitherto un-
used economic resources and human abilities that were previously
hidden or badly utilized, a strategy that is alert to the balancing of individual aspirations and group commitments is of the essence. Development consists largely in creating institutional means to bring potential
resources to life. How this is to be done depends on concrete circumstances and conditions; there is no predetermined royal road. Beneficent spirals of development consist in the creation of disequilibria that
can be overcome through benefits that outweigh economic as well as
psychic costs and hence induce further innovation, as well as further
disequilibria.

In recent years, Hirschman has turned from problems of economic
development to a series of other themes which, while related to his earlier preoccupations, transcend their scope and deal with the impact of
political and ideological factors on economic behavior. His *Exit, Voice,
and Loyalty: Responses to Decline in Firms, Organizations and States* (1970),[13]
a book which almost immediately after publication was widely hailed
both here and abroad, discusses variant strategies open to groups or

individuals who are dissatisfied with the activity of a given political or economic organization. There are basically two courses open to them, Hirschman says. They may raise their voices in criticism and disagreement, or they may leave altogether. Customers of a firm, for example, may stop buying its product, the exit option, or they may voice their dissatisfaction directly to management. In the political sphere, members of an organization may raise their voice in opposition and try to throw the rascals out, or they may leave the organization and join another. The major point is that whether the exit or the voice option is taken depends not so much on the organization in question as on the environment in which it operates. If, for example, alternative means of transportation are readily available, a badly run railroad will further decay because many of its previous customers will take the exit option. If few alternatives are available, dissatisfied individuals or groups are more likely to resort to the expression of their grievances within the organization. Yet, when few alternatives are available, voices are likely to be ineffective because members cannot threaten to "vote with their feet." On the other hand, too many easily available alternatives make for situations where initial deterioration continues unabated precisely because the remaining faithful will fail to raise their voices.

Loyalty, finally, by keeping the most quality-conscious from being the first to leave, in the hope of fighting "from within," may help to stabilize the situation. Excessive loyalty, on the other hand, may prevent needed reforms and lead to petrification. Hirschman's scheme is fruitful in elucidating many issues in the marketplace but also on the political scene, from the economics of competition to the strategies of presidential elections. His is one of the few books in the social sciences that speak to all social scientists rather than only to the members of a single discipline.

Hirschman's next book, *The Passions and the Interests: Political Arguments for Capitalism before Its Triumph* (1977),[14] is an elegant and lucid discussion of the justifications advanced for capitalist development from the Renaissance to Adam Smith. He develops the idea that when, after the Renaissance, traditional arguments relying on the efficacy of moral and religious exhortations against the predominance of self-serving passions lost their hold, there developed instead the idea that one passion could be opposed by another, and, more particularly, the idea that avarice, later transmuted into interest, could countervail the wilder passions for power and glory. Rather than following the traditional path of attributing these ideas mainly to Adam Smith, Hirschman argues that the contributions of such scholars as Montesquieu and James Stewart were even more consequential. He shows that Adam Smith forgot all, or virtually all, about the *political* benefits of capitalism and stressed only its economic benefits for the general welfare, whereas several of his predecessors centered their attention on the political effects of capitalist economies.

It should be apparent that the themes of his later books were suggested to Hirschman by his earlier work on problems of modernization, but it is also evident that he has now broadened his frame of reference so as to attack central issues in social and political decision-making, on the one hand, and in the ideological justifications of social and economic action, on the other—issues that have preoccupied not only classical thinkers but modern analysts from Weber to Parsons. With *Exit* and *Passions*, which have already been translated into seven languages, Hirschman moved into the front ranks of today's social science. He is a recipient of the prestigious Frank Seidman Distinguished Award in Political Economy. He is among the most cited contemporary social scientists. (The Social Science Citation Index lists 140 citations of his work in 1978 and 113 in 1979.) He is still actively at work, and it would be premature to assess his overall influence, but it is not too early to say that this refugee scholar, former socialist militant and volunteer in the Spanish and French armies in the fight against fascism, has become an intellectual force to be reckoned with on the American academic scene. It should also be noted that his appreciative audience is by no means limited to the United States. Younger political economists in Latin America consider him an intellectual hero. His paper on when and how to divest a foreign company of its holdings has become a classic both here and in Latin America. The relationship of trust he has been able to build up with many Latin American social scientists continues to be a very important aspect of his professional life. Particularly during the establishment of authoritarian regimes in Brazil, Argentina, and Chile, he has maintained close contacts with and extended what help he could to many of those who were fired from their positions or otherwise persecuted for their views. After raising his voice in many an adversary context, after leaving intolerable situations through the exit door open for refugees, he has become a loyal member of the American academy who has made his voice heard.

His latest book, *Private and Public Happiness: Pursuits and Disappointments* (1982),[15] in which he advances a highly original theory to explain period swings in modern societies between the maximization of private or public benefits, has further served to enhance Hirschman's stature as a social thinker who, by following unusual pathways of analysis, has moved into the forefront of contemporary social commentators and theorists.

Karl Polanyi (1886–1964) and Paul Baran (1909–1964): Maverick Economic Historian and Maverick Economist

Karl Polanyi and Paul Baran were two refugee students of economic phenomena who differed from most of their colleagues by taking a radical stance. Polanyi never managed to find a secure position within the American academy; Baran became a professor of economics at Stanford University. Yet despite this difference both remained marginal to the academic world throughout their lives in America.

Karl Polanyi was born in Vienna in 1886 and grew up in Budapest.[1] His father was a wealthy Jewish engineer and contractor who built several Hungarian railways and collaborated in building a major railroad in Switzerland. When his enterprises collapsed, he insisted that the shareholders be paid, so that thereafter his family lived in poverty.

The young Polanyi studied law and philosophy in Budapest. He was expelled from the university for fighting with reactionary and clerical students and consequently had to complete his studies at a minor provincial university. During his student days Polanyi became the first president of the Galilei Circle, the breeding ground of the liberal, rationalist, and radical young intelligentsia of Budapest, to which such figures as Georg Lukács and Karl Mannheim also belonged. The members of the Galilei Circle, though most of them were classical liberals, also provided much of the intellectual leadership for the postwar Hungarian Revolution in both its Social-Democratic and its Communist phases. Many of its members later became major figures in the intellectual life of Europe and America.

Although Polanyi served for a time as general secretary of the Radical Citizens party of Hungary, and although he was a convinced radical, he was not much of a political activist in Hungary or later. After having done his military service as an officer on the Russian front and been imprisoned by the Russians, Polanyi moved to Vienna, where he was to reside until 1933. There he met and married Ilona Duczynska, a brilliant woman who had played a distinguished role in the Hungarian Revolution and had fled to Vienna after its failure. From 1924 to 1933, Polanyi was on the staff of the *Osterreichische Volkswirt,* the leading Central European economic weekly, comparable in prestige to the London *Economist.* When the Austrian clerical-authoritarian regime assumed dictatorial powers in Austria, Polanyi, a lifelong radical and socialist, was dismissed and soon decided to make his way to England.

During his stay in Great Britain, Polanyi earned a precarious living lecturing for the Workers' Educational Association and holding tutorial classes for the extramural branches of Oxford University and the University of London. He also toured the United States in the 1930s, lecturing on the world situation and the menace of fascism. After another lecture tour in 1940, Polanyi decided to stay in this country and accepted a post as a resident scholar at Bennington College. He stayed there for three years and, with the help of a fellowship from the Rockefeller Foundation, wrote his most important work, *The Great Transformation* (1944).[2]

Polanyi was pleased when Columbia University, on the initiative of the chairman of the sociology department, Robert McIver, who had been impressed by *The Great Transformation,* invited him in 1947 to become a visiting professor, but he was dismayed when Mrs. Polanyi was denied an entry visa into the United States because she had been a member of the Hungarian Communist party twenty-five years earlier. Polanyi nevertheless accepted the appointment and taught as a visiting professor at Columbia until his retirement in 1953. His wife settled in Canada, so that her husband was forced to shuttle between New York City and their home in Pickering, outside Toronto, during the years he taught at Columbia. He continued to do so later when, together with the anthropologist Conrad Arensberg, he worked at Columbia on an Interdisciplinary Project on the Economic Aspects of Institutional Growth. This seminar led in 1957 to the publication of *Trade and Markets in the Early Empires* by Polyani et al.[3] This work has greatly influenced economic anthropology and economic history and, next to *The Great Transformation,* is Polanyi's most important publication.

America did not treat Polanyi kindly.[4] Although he received some foundation support, and although he had academic affiliations, he remained marginal to the academic establishment. He was not a regular member of the permanent faculty either at Bennington or at Columbia, despite the fact that his name was widely known after the publication of *The Great Transformation* in 1944 and a seminal paper on "Our Obsolete Market Mentality" three years later.[5] Polanyi's pronounced anticapitalist stand and his critique of free enterprise and the market economy did not stand him in good stead among many economists committed to the received wisdom of their discipline. Polanyi was a free spirit who, as distinct from Baran, cared little for position or money and hence probably did not suffer much from his marginality. But marginal he was nevertheless.

It was not only his lack of a permanent position that limited Polanyi's impact in America. As has been seen, the witch-hunting atmosphere during the Cold War had led to the exclusion of his wife from America, obliging her devoted husband to travel back and forth between New York City and Canada. As he was perpetually in transit, Polanyi understandably put down no roots in New York, either social or academic. Although he was an active participant in Columbia's interdisciplinary seminars and warmly supported by Conrad Arensberg, who served as his academic sponsor, McIver, and other members of the sociology department such as Robert K. Merton and Robert S. Lynd, one gains the impression that Polanyi largely remained a stranger to New York's intellectual life and to the meetings of professional associations in economics, economic history, and anthropology. Although he was physically present in New York at least several days each week during his Columbia appointment, his was, so to speak, a false presence. Given the peculiar circumstances of his life in America, he was largely unable or unwilling to participate in the networks of associates and peers that normally characterize the lives of academicians. Moreover, since he was not a regular professor, he had no occasion to direct dissertations of graduate students, even though he inspired a good number of students who considered themselves his followers. Even at Columbia, and more pronouncedly in regard to overall academic and intellectual life, Polanyi remained a stranger who stood largely outside the gate.

Even a short summary will suffice to indicate the power of Polyani's heretical ideas in economic history and economic anthropology. The core of his work can be found in his effort to demonstrate that market-guided economies, far from being "normal," are in fact exceptions in the course of human history. In past times, the economy was embedded in society; in capitalism the reverse occurred—society became embedded in the economy. In most stages of human development and in most non-Western societies until recently, the production and distribution of goods were not guided by autonomous economic systems but were, instead, intertwined with the institutions of kinship, religion, and residence. To be sure, all societies must have structural arrangements to insure the provision of livelihood for their members, Polanyi argued, but only in very special, modern circumstances do such arrangements acquire a large degree of autonomy. Polanyi warned against the analytical mistake of confounding the notion of formal economics, as taught in Western de-

partments of economics, with substantive economics, the study of the
ways in which various societies arrange for production and distribution
of the means of livelihood. To quote Hans Zeisel, "By confining itself to
market phenomena, Polanyi felt, economic theory has become inadequate in two ways: it has removed from its ambit the social organization
which links the economy to the cultural, psychological, and political
structure of society; and by its exclusive concern with industrial capitalism, it has forced the analysis of other societies into a conceptual framework . . . that does not fit them."[6]

The market economy, far from being the ideal and prototype of all
economic arrangements, was to Polanyi only one of the three major patterns of integration of economy and society. Arrangements based on
reciprocity and redistribution are more frequent and more widespread
if the whole spectrum of substantive economies is considered. Polanyi
used this overall scheme in his study of the English Industrial Revolution in *The Great Transformation*. This study illustrates its author's instinct
for the jugular insofar as it was precisely the Industrial Revolution that
served as the major test case for the classical economists against whom
he argued. That revolution, said Polanyi, had hugely increased productivity. But the autonomy of the market mechanisms it had brought in its
wake had helped to atomize society, had loosened or destroyed communal bonds and obligations, and had led to the pervasive loneliness of
acquisitive individuals. The possessive individualism of the modern capitalist world destroyed the human fabric. As Polanyi showed with great
effect in his study of late eighteenth-century and early nineteenth-century
Poor Laws, when the cash nexus became the most important bond between human beings, communal solidarities atrophied.

Polanyi's work in economic anthropology, in which he largely built on
the writings of Weber, Thurnwald, Malinowski, and Durkheim, was intended to paint the main lines of a non–market-directed model of society by demonstrating the "embeddedness" of economic arrangements in
kinship and political institutions. Such a model made it possible to disas-
sociate the study of the economic structures of other societies, past and
present, from the special theory appropriate for the analysis of market-
dominated economies.

Polanyi's writings always state, implicitly or explicitly, his preference
for systems based on redistribution and reciprocity and his dislike of the
workings of the market system. He saw in the New Deal the first progressive reaction against market dominance in the United States; but he
wished to go beyond the New Deal and toward a democratic, humane,
and socialist planned society based on communitarian concerns instead
of on acquisitive individualism.

Polanyi's later work was of a more specialized nature and was read largely by academics and professionals. *The Great Transformation,* in contrast, found a wide lay audience for a decade or two, was used extensively in college courses, and went through many printings. It no longer enjoys that much attention, but, together with his more technical work, it assures Polanyi a major place among that small band of heretical economic thinkers, from Veblen to Galbraith, who have been perturbers of the intellectual peace in traditional economics departments. Furthermore, and perhaps even more important, Polanyi's work has become a foundation stone of modern economic anthropology and of the study of the economic and social consequences of the Industrial Revolution.

To call Paul Baran—the radical economist who came here as a refugee in 1939—a marginal man is an understatement. The notion of marginality implies the idea of a stable core on the periphery of which marginal persons can be located. Baran moved through his life in many orbits, and in the most diverse social and cultural situations, but was at home in none of them. Georg Simmel defines a stranger as a potential wanderer, a person who comes today and may leave tomorrow. Baran found it hard to stay anywhere.[7]

Paul Baran was born in 1909 in Nikolaev in the southern Ukraine on the Black Sea. His father was a Jewish physician who had been active in the socialist movement as a Menshevik prior to the Revolution of 1905, but had then withdrawn from political involvements to practice medicine. His continuing lively interest in politics left its mark on his young son. Baran's father welcomed the overthrow of the czar in 1917 but, repelled by the October revolution, left Russia in 1921, first for Poland and then for Germany. Baran's parents assumed Polish citizenship, so their son was later able to use a Polish passport, which gave him a measure of independence in his movements between Russia and Germany.

When the older Baran moved to Dresden, he hoped to open an office there but found to his disappointment that foreigners were not allowed to practice medicine in Germany. His precarious position as a medical researcher there motivated him in 1925 to return to the Soviet Union, where he was offered an attractive position in his medical speciality. Paul Baran was left behind in Germany to continue his studies at the Dresden gymnasium and later in Berlin. (Up to his eleventh year he had been tutored by his father rather than attending a formal school, and his parents now felt that a gymnasium education was essential for him.) Baran's formative adolescent years were hence spent in Germany, and he has said that he came to feel more at home in German than in either Russian or English. During his gymnasium years, from 1921 to 1926, Baran plunged enthusiastically into radical student activities and joined the Communist youth and student organizations.

After his graduation in the fall of 1926, Baran rejoined his parents in Moscow and enrolled in the local university's Institute of Economics. These were the years in which the epic battle between Stalin and Trotsky was being fought within the Communist movement, and the young Baran soon discovered his sympathies for the Trotskyist opposition. Dispirited and oppressed by the Stalinist offensive against that opposition, he welcomed an invitation in 1928 to move back to Germany to work as a research associate at an agrarian institute and to continue his studies at the University of Berlin.

In Germany Baran was appalled by the escalating Stalinist police methods being used against the Russian opposition and by the German Communist line of rejecting an alliance with the Socialists. When the German Communists began their so-called Third Period course in 1928, proclaiming that the Social Democrats were in reality Social Fascists and constituted the main enemy, Baran severed his connections with the Communist movement and joined the Social Democratic party. After his research assignment expired, he decided not to return to the Soviet Union but instead to accept an offer from the Institute for Social Research in Frankfurt to help its associate director, Friedrich Pollock, to complete a work on the Soviet economy. In 1933 Baran simultaneously completed a dissertation on economic planning at the University of Berlin under Emil Lederer.[8] While in Berlin, Baran also made the acquaintance of the leading socialist economist Rudolf Hilferding, who arranged for him to write frequently for the Social Democratic periodical *Die Gesellschaft*, which Hilferding edited.

Soon after Hitler came to power in 1933, Baran fled to Paris. Finding no regular employment there, he returned to Moscow in 1934. This time conditions in Stalinist Russia horrified him. A wave of terror culminating in mast arrests and deportations started that year. Many of Baran's professors and student friends were deported and later shot. Under the circumstances, and given that Baran was an ex-Communist, the fact that the Russian authorities did not extend his permission to stay beyond January 1935 probably saved his life. With no apparent prospects anywhere in the West, Baran went to his father's birthplace, Vilna, now part of Poland, to work there for his uncles, who were in the timber business. He turned out to be an excellent businessman, and for two years he worked for the Vilna Chamber of Commerce as well as in Vilna and Warsaw for his uncles. From early 1938 to the spring of 1939, he lived in London as the sales representative of Vilna timber firms. Although his income was much higher than he could hope to attain in an academic career, Baran was dissatisfied with business and longed to return to academic life. Perceiving that he had no chance for an academic job in England, and also sensing the approach of World War II,

Baran took his savings of several thousand dollars and moved to the United States.

Baran enrolled at Harvard soon after his arrival. By early 1941 he had passed his general Ph.D. examinations. He then accepted a fellowship at the Brookings Institution in Washington and soon after, when America entered the war, entered government service, first with the Office of Price Administration, later with the Office of Strategic Services, and still later with the United States Strategic Bombing Survey. After working for the Department of Commerce through most of 1946, Baran accepted a position at the Federal Reserve Bank in New York, where he was in charge of the British desk. He held that position until he came to Stanford University in 1949. This appointment was made possible largely through the sponsorship of an old friend, Tibor Scitovsky. Baran served as an associate professor for two years and was promoted to full professor in 1951. His peregrinations were now over. He remained a member of the Stanford University faculty until his death in 1964.

From 1945 on, Baran's government services were continuously in jeopardy owing to the smears and innuendoes of the *Washington Times Herald,* who pictured him as a probable Soviet agent on the basis of his Communist affiliations in the 1920s. Even after he joined the faculty of Stanford, Baran was hounded by unfounded accusations, refused the extension of his passport, and harassed in other ways. Only in 1955, after the worst days of McCarthyism were over, was he finally cleared of all charges.

Baran was a very successful teacher and attracted large numbers of students to his courses. His more conservative colleagues looked upon him with some suspicion but tolerated him because he brought many students to the department. They also may have come to see him as a kind of court jester, especially since he was much more flexible in his conversations than in his publications. Baran, in his turn, fumed in a letter to his friend Paul Sweezy, "I do feel bitter about the superficiality, smugness, opportunism, cowardice, and outward stupidity of the so-called profession. And what you call 'the hostile intellectual surrounding' is contributing undoubtedly its large share to [my] pent-up aggression by continually kindling it." He also complained about "being treated like a dog" and being given a "teaching load twice as large as his peers, and at a pay about 60% of theirs."[9] But he nevertheless stuck it out at Stanford, where he spent a much larger span of time than in any of his multiple previous positions.

It is true that Baran was not paid as much as some other members of his department and that he often had to carry more courses. But it is also a fact that at Stanford, as at other universities, salary raises were usually granted in response to other universities making competing offers—and Baran received no such offers. Course loads were reduced when faculty members received grants that allowed them to buy back time—and there were years when Baran received no grants. Hence Baran seemed to have been treated according to standard operating procedure. There is, however, one notable exception. The president's office froze his salary after it learned of Baran's study trip to Cuba in the early period of Castro's coming to power. The freeze lasted for about eighteen months. It was finally lifted as a result of pressure from the Department of Economics, and Baran received salary increases thereafter.

Salary discriminations, whether imagined or real, hurt Baran a great deal, in part because, despite his radicalism, he was also a man who valued the good life. He delighted in good food, fine furnishings, rare books, and travel, and generally wanted to live in style. So an appropriate income was very important to him.[10]

What is curious is that, despite his bewildering number of positions in the business world and in various governmental departments, Baran never changed his basic socialist ideas and allegiances. He seems to have been a fine commercial agent and an excellent government economist and yet to have withheld any inner allegiance to the various organizations in which he worked. He seems always to have considered himself a free radical intellectual who simply happened for a while to work in various "bourgeois" contexts.

This ability to remove himself psychologically from the institutional context in which he happened to work seems also to have come into play at Stanford. Moses Abramovitz, chairman of the Department of Economics during part of Baran's tenure there, put the matter well when he wrote: "Baran's views and [those of his colleagues] diverged, sometimes moderately, often radically. I think it would be too much to say that for most of his years here he was isolated. On many issues he found intellectual allies and intellectual support. But on the deepest issues, he usually stood alone. He debated with his friends, he felt the weight of their negative judgments and had to sustain his position by himself." Abramovitz adds, "In his last years there was a period of at least partial withdrawal. Whether we withdrew from him, or, as many of us think, he withdrew from us, I cannot say."[11]

Not only his stance in regard to his Stanford colleagues but also his relation to the wider professional world of American economics testify to Baran's tendency to withdraw. He contributed only five articles to professional economic journals, and these were mainly written in the early years of his time in America. He also wrote some fifteen book reviews for professional journals, and there is a record of a few talks and discussions in the *Papers and Proceedings of the American Economic Association*. He also made a few contributions to collaborative works.[12] But apart from these, all of Baran's writings appeared in the radical *Monthly Review*, edited by his friend Paul Sweezy, and in a few other radical publications. His major book, *The Political Economy of Growth* (1957), was likewise not published by a regular commercial or university house but by the Monthly Review Press. Much of this can, of course, be accounted for by the fact that the market for socialist and Marxist writings in economics was severely restricted during Baran's lifetime and differed considerably from the present situation in both journal and book publications. Yet Baran's intentions and orientations seem to have been more decisive in the matter than was objective circumstance. He was not much interested in an audience of fellow economists, for most of whom he felt contempt. He preferred to address himself to fellow radicals. The considerable radical audience that developed in the late 1960s and 1970s did not exist during Baran's lifetime. As a consequence, he looked for an audience abroad, particularly in Asia and Latin America. And this is indeed where he found it. *The Political Economy of Growth* was translated into nine languages and has become a kind of Bible among the radical intelligentsia of Latin America, Japan, and less developed nations. Sweezy was correct when he wrote: "He is the *maestro*, the revered teacher, of the younger generation of Latin American economists, compared to whom no other American economist is capable of arousing nearly the same degree of intellectual response and personal loyalty. And I can well believe that the same condition prevails in most other parts of the 'third world.'"[13]

Rejected by many of his colleagues in America, and in his turn rejecting most of them, Baran was forced to find another audience for his writings. But he paid a high price for this strategy. Lacking sustained critical intercourse with others who did not share his views, limited to intimate contact with only the handful of Marxist economists surrounding the *Monthly Review*, adored and adulated by enthusiastic followers abroad, he wrote in a manner that seems rigid, dogmatic, without subtlety and flexibility. His Marxism seems to compare poorly with more recent writings in that tradition. While Marxists of the present generation are involved in a fruitful dialogue with their more conservative colleagues and profit from that dialogue, Baran's work appears to suffer from a hardening of the Marxist categories. It does not seem to be in the same league as, say, the work of Otto Lange or Joan Robinson. Nor is it as original as the work of Polanyi.

Baran's writings largely involve an extension of classical Marxist thought to the analysis of economic growth in the underdeveloped countries of the world and polemics against those "bourgeois" thinkers who believe that economic growth can be attained in these areas without large-scale revolutionary change. The crucial hurdle obstructing the development of underdeveloped countries, Baran argued, is that the economic surplus that can be attained there is small and is "usually frittered away on unproductive purposes." A small upper-class elite, much of it composed of large landowners leading a "feudal" style of life, consumes most of the surplus, so that there is little room left for savings. Furthermore, even if some surplus that could serve investment purposes were available, no suitable investment opportunities are in fact present because of the lack of an infrastructure of roads, electric power stations, railroads, and so on. Finally, the lack of internal markets and the domination of existing facilities by large supernational corporations condemn the underdeveloped countries to what the Marxist economist Gunner Frank has called "the development of underdevelopment." Baran concludes from this diagnosis that only a revolutionary breakup of the pattern of landownership, destruction of the parasitic upper class, and replacement of market economies by national economic planning are likely to bring economic growth to the underdeveloped nations. He called his major work *The Political Economy of Growth* in order to emphasize the interdependence of political and economic factors in such growth. He believed that the weakness of liberal economic theory in relation to issues of modernization lay in its inability to see that economic advancement is predicated on drastic and revolutionary change in the political sphere. Baran's analysis of the morphology of backwardness was based on his unwavering belief that only the Chinese or the Cuban ways, despite their shortcomings, pointed in this direction of a rational, less wasteful, and more humane future for the Third World.

Baran was a sparkling conversationalist and a brilliant lecturer who could at times be something of a showman; but he found it difficult to write. An extended psychoanalytic treatment undertaken to remove his writing block seems to have been only partly successful. This being the case, one might well wonder whether this condition may not have been caused by the lack of an audience for his work in America at least as much as by his personal psychological problems. An unseen audience abroad may not have provided the same incentive for sustained intellectual work that a more immediate audience would have stimulated. In any case, Baran produced only one major book, on which his reputation largely rests. *Monopoly Capital,*[14] nominally coauthored by Baran and Sweezy and published in 1966, two years after Baran's death, was largely written by Sweezy. Baran also wrote a number of incisive essays, most of them geared to the radical audience of Sweezy's *Monthly Review,* which have now been collected in one volume.[15]

Baran's influence on radical economists in the Third World has been enduring and powerful, even though a number of them have now pushed well beyond his somewhat rigid categories. In America, a younger generation of Marxist economists still read him, but it is my impression that they quote him today not nearly so much as they did in the past, when other contributions to radical economics were still quite rare. Given his restless life-style, his double or triple marginality, it is perhaps altogether fitting that Baran is at present finding eager disciples and readers in Buenos Aires, Rio de Janeiro, and Tokyo rather than in the United States.

George Katona (1901–1981), Peter Drucker (1909–   ), and Fritz Redlich (1892–1978): Three Innovating Students of Economic Behavior

I have attempted in the preceding pages to sketch the careers of a number of refugee economists and economic historians who had major impacts on their discipline after coming to America. Some of them followed in the mainstream; others chose to pursue a more independent path. At least three other refugee scholars in economics and economic history, even though perhaps not as prominent in scholarly eyes as those I have singled out above, are judged by a number of experts as having played a pioneering part in American economic studies. All three men whose careers I shall outline briefly have enriched their fields in a double way, through the merging of European and American approaches to the subject, and through the bridging of disciplinary boundaries.

The Hungarian-born but German-educated George Katona developed a novel theory of consumer behavior—a field that had not been studied in a sustained manner since Thorstein Veblen. Katona was trained as a psychologist in the Gestalt tradition and was a close associate of Max Wertheimer, one of the founders of that school. Historians of psychology state that his work on memory, *Organizing and Memorizing* (1940),[1] is among the important contributions to Gestalt psychology. But after working, upon his arrival in America, with Wertheimer at the New School for Social Research, and after a stay at the University of Chicago, Katona moved his interest to the borderline between psychology and economics.

Most classical and neoclassical economists had up to then neglected consumer behavior as a variable in economic decision-making and forecasting because they assumed that recent disposable income would provide the best indicator of future purchasing decisions. Katona showed, on the basis of a series of consumer surveys conducted for many years at the University of Michigan, that a combination of disposable income and consumer *attitudes* will predict future durable-goods expenditures more accurately than estimates based on disposable income alone. Putting his previous training in psychology to creative use, he was able to show that consumer demand was at least as much a function of the willingness to buy as of the ability to buy. By undermining the traditional rationalistic assumptions of most economics and introducing psychological variables into economic forecasting, Katona breached the barrier that had heretofore prevented a fruitful cross-fertilization of psychology and economics. He utilized the European tradition of Gestalt psychology to revitalize the American art of economic forecasting.[2]

While Katona's name is likely to be familiar mainly to specialists, the Vienna-born Peter F. Drucker is known to a wider public through a series of popular books, such as *The End of Economic Man* (1939), *The Future of Industrial Man* (1941), *The Concept of the Corporation* (1946), *The New Society* (1949), and, more recently, *Management: Tasks, Responsibilities, Practices* (1974),[3] and through many articles in the popular media. Although he taught at Bennington College in the 1940s and was for many years a professor of management at New York University, he considers himself, and is considered by others, mainly a management consultant and a publicist rather than an academic economist. His principal argument in most of his work is a stress on the need to distinguish modern industrial modes of operation from nineteenth-century entrepreneurial modes. Drucker not only described and analyzed managerial behavior, he glorified it. Drawing on the classical liberal tradition of his native Vienna and combining it, at least in part, with American trends in organizational sociology, he became in the public eye a kind of Max Weber for managers. However, he attempted to substitute for Weber's gloomy vision of the future a rosy picture of the benevolent features of manager-dominated society.

Fritz Redlich's lifework, by contrast, was devoted to the study of entrepreneurial history. While Drucker throughout most of his career has bathed in the glory of public acclaim, Redlich, except for a short period of his life in America, lived in comparative obscurity and lacked academic, or any other, recognition.

Fritz Redlich was born in Berlin in 1892, where he also studied and received his Ph.D. in economics.[4] But instead of continuing in an academic career, he resolved, after serving in World War I, to join his father's chemical business. Only shortly before Hitler's coming to power did Redlich return to academic study. His *Habilitationsschrift* (the additional thesis required for qualification to university teaching), on advertising and the role of the entrepreneur in that industry, was published in 1935. A year later Redlich landed in New York, penniless, without many American contacts, but armed with the idea that the study of entrepreneurship was the field to which he should devote his abundant energies. It is this study that he pursued despite a great many personal difficulties throughout his life in America.

Even though the two leading Harvard economists of the time, F. W. Taussig and Joseph Schumpeter, encouraged Redlich to turn to the study of American entrepreneurship and attempted to smooth his academic path, Redlich for many years managed to gain employment only in various second-rate university departments in different parts of the country. At times, mainly through support from Taussig, the New School for Social Research, and the Social Science Research Council, he succeeded in interspersing his teaching with periods of research. The major fruit was the first volume of a projected multivolume series on American business leaders.[5] After moving to Cambridge in the early 1940s, Redlich first held positions of a minor kind with the Federal Public Housing Authority and the Massachusetts State Housing Board. Despite this daily and distracting work, Redlich managed in 1947 to publish the first volume of his magnum opus, *The Molding of American Banking, Men and Ideas, 1781–1840*.[6] Only when he was already sixty years old, in 1952, did he receive an academic appointment commensurate with his stature. He then became a senior research associate, and clearly the major intellectual force, in the newly organized Research Center in Entrepreneurial History of Harvard University. For the first time in his life he could devote his full time and energy to the subject that almost obsessed him. The second volume of his history of American banking had been published a year before, and a stream of further contributions to entrepreneurial history followed. All in all, Redlich published over 150 books and articles, as well as two volumes of collected articles.

When, after a few years, the Research Center for Entrepreneurial History ended its existence, largely because of lack of funds, Redlich was again reduced to the status of a *Privatgelehrter* (private scholar) living an isolated and fairly lonely life in a one-room apartment in a rather shabby building near Harvard Square. He died there at the age of eighty-six.

Redlich attempted to merge entrepreneurial and business history in the tradition of the great German scholars he had known—Max Weber, Werner Sombart, Otto Hintze, Ernst Troeltsch, and Wilhelm Dilthey—with streams of thought coming from American sociology and organizational studies. He drew attention away from the study of motives and personalities to the study of process and structure in the history of entrepreneurship. In this he was successful, and he influenced, among others, the present dean of American organizational studies, Alfred D.

Chandler, Jr. But even while he was publishing his major works, a new school of economic historians who rejected his organizational and institutional approach in favor of detailed quantitative study of economic phenomena began to preempt the academic scene. Redlich's work continues to be consulted and has inspired many monographic studies of entrepreneurial and business history. Yet, all in all, his impact on American scholarly life was not so powerful as he might well have hoped. His life and work stood in the shadow of adversity. It is almost miraculous that despite this he managed to gather the rich harvest of his studies.

V
Political Science and Political Theory

Introduction

When European political scientists arrived in America, they soon realized that their discipline was beginning to experience a serious identity crisis in this country. The subject had been taught for many years at American universities and colleges, but it had little internal unity since its practitioners were mainly concerned either with commentary on the great political theorists of the past or with teaching the principles of public administration. In both these areas, providing guidelines to what was considered desirable and appropriate conduct tended to take precedence over concern with actual political behavior.

Beginning in the late 1930s and coming to fruition in the 1940s and 1950s there occurred what is usually called the behaviorist revolution in political science. Taking a leaf from the more positivistic orientations of other social sciences, in particular sociology, Young Turks in political science proclaimed that they wished to ban moralistic and normative considerations from their field of study and to concentrate on the actual behavior of political actors, whether they be voters, politicians, or officials.

Among major refugee scholars, reactions to the behaviorist dispensation differed markedly. Three of them—Hannah Arendt, Leo Strauss, and Eric Voegelin—rejected it out of hand and asserted that neutrality of values in political science opened the floodgates to nihilism and the loss of all standards. All three of them, even though they differed significantly in other respects, argued that only recourse to the great Greek classical thinkers would allow political science to return to its central humanistic concerns. The impact of these antibehaviorist refugees on American political thinking was highly consequential, but their adverse stance in regard to the dominant orientation in political science nevertheless barred them from the major university communities in which the behaviorists rule. Arendt, whether from choice or from necessity, never occupied a permanent position in academia. Strauss taught for many years at a peripheral institution, the New School, and moved to a teaching position at the University of Chicago only during the last twenty years of his academic career. Voegelin taught at a second-rate Southern university.

On the other hand, those who wholeheartedly endorsed and contributed to the behaviorists' orientation, Karl Deutsch in particular, swiftly gained prestigious positions in the political science establishment.

Hans Morgenthau and Franz Neumann cannot be so neatly categorized. The former shared with the behaviorists a rejection of moralistic and normative criteria in the analysis of international relations. Much of what he had to say in this respect followed from the tradition of German political thought, with its emphasis on "reason of state" and national interests. Yet Morgenthau was also beholden to a humanistic philosophical tradition which led him, especially in the last period of his life, to advocate an almost prophetic role for students of the international scene. The moral considerations which he had thrown out the front door returned through the back, which accounts for the ambivalence of some of his teachings. He nevertheless reached a position of great eminence, especially in the late 1940s and the 1950s, and was the teacher not only of a high proportion of all scholars studying international relations but also of many key Washington decision-makers.

Neumann started out as a Marxist, closely allied with, though never fully a part of, the Horkheimer group but, after wartime experiences in Washington bureaucracies and with the waning of his hopes for a German revolution after the war, was on his way to a relatively undogmatic position. He stressed the need to revive an interest in the classical texts of political theory, yet remained more in sympathy with American liberal values and orientations than thinkers like Strauss and Voegelin. He died prematurely, and hence it is hard to say where he would have found a new moral and political resting point. But most of the students he trained in the few years that were granted him at Columbia University, many of them historians of ideas rather than political scientists, developed a democratic and liberal stance, rooted in humanistic scholarship but far removed from dogmatic behaviorism as well as from the neoconservative thrust of the teaching of Strauss or Voegelin.

In sum, refugee scholars in political science shared no unified outlook or orientation and had an impact as diverse as their philosophies. Those who reinforced the tide of the behaviorist revolution prospered, but even those who opposed it made a significant impact in their field of study by continuing to uphold classical standards which, so they felt, would be swept aside were political science to abandon its roots in humanistic and normative thought.

Hannah Arendt (1906–1975):
Self-Proclaimed Pariah

Throughout her life, Hannah Arendt considered herself a marginal person. Like Rahel Varnhagen, the German-Jewish early nineteenth-century salon hostess and friend and sponsor of Goethe and the Romantics, to whom Arendt devoted a biographical study, she saw herself in her native Germany as well as in the New York of her exile years as a "self-conscious *pariah*."[1] She believed that modern Jews like herself had only two basic ways in which to come to terms with the surrounding gentile society. They could turn into parvenus, or they could choose to become what in fact they were, pariahs. To Hannah Arendt, only the second choice was an authentic and existentially justified decision. Yet it is the paradox of her life in America that this self-chosen marginal woman became a strong influence on the culture she felt the need to reject as alien.

Hannah Arendt grew up in East Germany's central city, Koenigsberg. Her grandparents were assimilated Jews, prominent and wealthy members of the Jewish community but also deeply attached to German culture. They sought, as one of Arendt's biographers has put it, "a reconciliation in their lives between the claims of *Judentum* and the claims of *Deutschtum*."[2] They were never troubled by their Jewishness and would have felt it undignified to deny their Jewish identity. Hannah Arendt's parents, in contrast, had left the claims of *Judentum* behind and replaced it by active involvement in German politics. They were members of the German Social Democratic party and supported its reformist right wing. Her mother also greatly admired the left wing's leading figure, Rosa Luxemburg.

Hannah Arendt's father died in 1913 when she was only seven years old, so her mother became the main familial authority for the young Hannah. Though she rejected some of the world views of her own parents, the mother made it a point to instill in her daughter the sense that to deny one's Jewish identity was despicable and that to fight anti-Semitism was an essential requirement for every Jew.

189

At the outbreak of World War I, the Arendt family, for fear of a Russian advance on East Prussia, moved to Berlin, where they lived in straitened circumstances. In 1920, the widowed Martha Arendt married Martin Beerwald, a small manufacturer, in whose household mother and daughter temporarily found domestic peace and financial security. But Beerwald's firm went bankrupt in the 1920s. At that time, Hannah had already left home to pursue her studies. When her stepfather was unable to sustain her financially, an uncle assumed the burden.

Arendt, as was the wont of German students, attended several universities: Marburg, Freiburg, and Heidelberg. What was not so common was that she studied with all three of the major philosophers of the twenties—Martin Heidegger, Edmund Husserl, and Karl Jaspers. All three influenced her profoundly; but Jaspers, who supervised her dissertation on Saint Augustine's concept of Love, was closest to her intellectually, even though Heidegger had been her first lover. The dissertation was finished in 1929, and soon after she embarked on her study of Rahel Varnhagen, subtitled *The Life of a Jewish Woman*. The book was not just a biography but an essay in self-definition, which may account for the fact that it took Arendt some nine years to finish it, when she was already living as an exile in Paris. She published it only in 1958, when she was living as a "self-conscious pariah" in New York.[3]

During the first few years of preparatory work on the Varnhagen book, Hannah Arendt, who up to this point had had very little interest in things political, began to be preoccupied with the rising tide of anti-Semitism in Germany. In the late 1920s and early 1930s she increasingly moved into the orbit of Zionist circles and became a full-fledged Zionist in 1933. As shall be seen, her Zionist allegiance was always qualified, and she renounced it ten years later. Among the Zionists it seems she did not lose the feeling that she was a pariah among pariahs.

After the Nazis came to power, Arendt sheltered a number of German Communists in her apartment despite her previous unconcern with political affairs, perhaps as a symbolic gesture of defiance. She was arrested as a result but was released after a few days. Soon afterward, she left for exile. In the succeeding years she lived as a refugee in Paris. Her first marriage in Germany to Guenther Stern, the son of the famous German psychologist William Stern, ended in divorce after a relatively short time. She then married a German Communist exile, Heinrich Bluecher, a man of working-class origin with practically no formal education but prodigious self-taught knowledge. Bluecher was not a Jew, nor a trained intellectual, but the marriage endured until Bluecher's death in New York many years later.

In Paris, Hannah Arendt moved in the circle of Jewish refugee intellectuals, among them the great critic Walter Benjamin and the philosopher Eric Weil, but also that of political refugees, both Communist and Socialist—some Jewish, some not. She never shared the political beliefs of these groups, but, as a "social pariah," she admired their nonconformist stance.

In the spring of 1940, as Hitler's army began to approach Paris, Arendt was interned by the French as an "enemy alien," first in Paris and then in the women's concentration camp of Gurs in southern France. After the collapse of France, Hannah Arendt managed to escape from her camp and rejoined her husband, who had also escaped from his own internment. Six months later, the Bluechers left for New York, where they made their home until their respective deaths.

During the war years in New York, the Bluechers lived largely among German Jewish refugees, whose language, if nothing else, provided some kind of anchorage. But as she gradually mastered the English language, Hannah Arendt began to extend her network of contacts and friendships, although most of her closest associates continued to be refugees. During the first years in America, still a convinced Zionist, Hannah Arendt looked for the audience of her writing mainly to German or American Jews. She began to write profusely on such themes as Jewish identity and the dilemmas of the refugees. She passionately counseled her fellow exiles to eschew the assimilationist route, which seemed so much more open than it had been in Germany, and instead consciously to assume the burden of continued marginality.[4] She also urged the formation of a Jewish army to fight the Nazis and advocated the creation in Palestine of a binational Jewish-Arab federation. When, instead, the State of Israel was proclaimed after the war, Arendt left the Zionist movement, claiming that a Jewish state would only create new nationalist passions. The Jews, she believed, could never rest secure in Zion; they would have to continue to be pariahs if they rejected the assimilationist route of becoming parvenus.

During the war years and after, Arendt lived as an unattached intellectual in New York. She worked from time to time for Jewish educational and welfare institutions, and she served as an editor at Schocken, a Jewish publishing house. But she did not secure, nor did she desire to secure, as so many of her refugee friends did, a permanent niche in the academic world. Arendt, in tune with her general stance as an outsider, may have felt that a position in the academy, with all the regularized work and time schedules that this required, would make it more difficult for her to engage in the autonomous life-style she so highly valued. It is also probable that no academic department during her early years in America made an effort to attract a philosopher who was also a woman, a refugee, and a Jewess.

As an outsider in New York living in straitened circumstances, Arendt nevertheless managed, and more so after the language barrier was successfully overcome, to establish enduring contacts with many American intellectuals, whether they were Jewish or not. She gravitated to the group around *Partisan Review*, that small band of highly sophisticated writers who themselves, though native-born, felt they did not really belong, that they were, if not pariahs, at best marginal to the mainstream of genteel American culture. Editors like Philip Rahv and William Phillips of the *Partisan Review*, writers like Dwight Macdonald and Mary McCarthy, who became a lifelong close friend, began to follow Arendt's writings, which had now moved from purely Jewish themes to the examination of the totalitarian phenomenon, with passionate intensity. Soon after the war, Hannah Arendt became a figure to be reckoned with in the New York intellectual milieu.

In 1951 Arendt published *The Origins of Totalitarianism,* a book that suddenly propelled her into the general cultural limelight. The book was probably her greatest achievement. Not only did it reach a wide audience, but it was one of those rare and seminal works that profoundly influenced many of its readers. It was widely praised and also widely criticized, but it is not excessive to say that it changed the thoughtways of a whole generation. The book is too well known to require summary. It will suffice to recall its major thesis: namely, that even though nazism and Stalinism had vastly different ideological pretensions, even though one was conventionally associated with the political Right and the other with the political Left, they bore essentially similar structural features. The ruling elite in both societies, Arendt argued, dominated an atomized society in which the variegated social formations, from voluntary association to social classes, that had given security and protection to individuals in the past had been destroyed. The underlying population was now a privatized mass of manipulated individuals who resembled an ant heap rather than a human community.

Critics of the book often have remarked that it appeared at the beginning of the Cold War and seemed to provide ammunition for those who wished to show that because there was no essential difference between Stalin's Russia and Hitler's Germany, both had to be destroyed. The very term *totalitarianism*, which Arendt popularized if she did not invent it, lent itself to these political uses. But it seems clear that such political calculations were far from the mind of the author. We need to recall that the book also provided ammunition to those who feared for the fate of American liberties under the assault of McCarthyism. The picture of what a totalitarian society was really like strengthened the determination of McCarthy's adversaries, who became convinced after reading Arendt that it could also happen here.

After the phenomenal success of her book on totalitarianism, Hannah

Arendt became a major political-literary personage in America. She may still have seen herself as a pariah, but now she was a pariah in a golden cage. Many universities vied with each other in inviting her to lecture. Leading publications, from the *Partisan Review* to *The New Yorker,* and, many years later, *The New York Review of Books,* competed for her collaboration.

It is noteworthy that only in the last two decades of her life did Arendt teach regularly within a university environment. She was a visiting professor at Princeton, Berkeley, and Columbia, and subsequently joined the staff, first of the University of Chicago's Committee on Social Thought, and later of the New School. None of these was a regular professorial appointment, however. Even granted that Arendt was attracted to the free-wheeling milieu of New York intellectuals and may have hesitated to leave the city permanently for "the provinces," it is still likely that none of the prestigious philosophy departments of the Eastern seaboard made her an attractive offer in her earlier years in America.

Although she never abandoned the idea that she was a pariah on the American scene as she had been in her native Germany, Hannah Arendt nevertheless became progressively more immersed in public activities in America. She was a regular participant in the annual meetings of the American Political Science Association, contributed to various academic symposia all over the country, and was a consultant to the National Endowment for the Humanities and the National Book Awards Committee. She was awarded a dozen honorary degrees by American universities and was elected a member of both the National Institute for Arts and Letters and the American Academy of Arts and Sciences. The latter awarded her its Emerson-Thoreau Medal in 1969. Even though she was in many respects a very private person who often felt, as she wrote in a letter, *"ein bisschen allein"* (a little lonely), Hannah Arendt seems to have relished her public roles. Her theoretical work extolled the virtues of action on the public scene, and she tried as much as possible to leave an impression on the public intellectual life of America. There was hardly a political controversy, from the civil rights movement to the Vietnam War and Watergate, on which she did not take a passionate stand.

Immersed as she was in the public issues of the day, Hannah Arendt saw them, as it were, as an outsider. She and her husband were formed by the catastrophic events they had witnessed in their native land, and they never quite overcame the tendency to look at things American through glasses ground by their German experience. They were, as one of their friends once put it, "catastrophe-minded." At one point they even feared that Joseph McCarthy might become the next president.

Their ambivalence about the American scene can be partially explained by their complex set of relations at the intersection between their circle of European friends and associates, whom they often called "the tribe," and their American friends. It also seems worthy of note that Hannah Arendt, despite the empathetic assertion of her Jewish identity and her close association with the Jewish intellectual milieu during the first phase of her stay in America, also managed as time went on to build close friendships with non-Jewish American intellectuals. The poets Randall Jarrell and W. H. Auden were close to her, and Mary McCarthy became her most intimate personal friend. Auden even made her an offer of marriage after her husband died. Her closest intellectual companion in the last few years of her life was the existentialist philosopher J. Glenn Gray.

Situated at the intersection of a variety of social networks, linked to diverse intellectual circles, speaking to a variety of audiences both academic and nonacademic, Hannah Arendt maintained her intellectual and moral autonomy not, as so many of her fellow emigrés chose or were forced to choose, through withdrawal from the American cultural scene, but through immersion in it. Never relinquishing her fierce desire to speak in her own voice to the public issues of the day, she drew her strength from her involvement with many, often divergent, currents of thought and networks of associates. She was the prototypical intellectual who, in Carl Becker's phrase, "thought otherwise," and she could do this because she was at the same time both an insider and an outsider.

In the last two decades of her life Arendt produced an astonishing number of books, articles, and lectures. Her fertile mind secreted ideas as naturally as a bee secretes honey. The range of her concerns seemed to be ever widening. She wrote on political theory, on revolution, on violence; on Eichmann in Jerusalem, on Walter Benjamin, Bertolt Brecht, Rosa Luxemburg, and Hermann Broch; on education, on civil disobedience, and on truth and lying in politics.[5] It is impossible in these pages to follow all the main roads and byways of her thought. Instead, an evaluation of only a few general directions her mind took will have to do.

Hannah Arendt's political thinking was largely shaped by her existential condition as an exile—a person, so she believed, excluded from political involvement and participation, yet craving above all freedom and autonomy. True freedom, she suggested time and again, could be attained only within the public sphere. Freedom restricted to the realm of privacy was a sham. This is why in Arendt's writings the private sphere is devalued in favor of the public, much as in Hegel, civil society, the sphere of private involvements and entanglements, is devalued in favor of the public life of the state. This deep attachment to the public sphere explains Arendt's lifelong fascination with, and admiration for, the life of the polis in ancient Greece, as it also explains her love for the participatory democracy of the various revolutionary councils that sprang up during the twentieth-century revolutions, especially during the Hungarian Revolution of 1956. Her horror of totalitarianism was mainly based on her conviction that it utterly destroys the public sphere of action.

Socioeconomic programs and activities left Hannah Arendt relatively cold, as did the realm of labor. These spheres were for her mainly a matter of administration and organization. Truly worthwhile activities were limited to the political sphere. As George Kateb has said, "Freedom and worldliness can serve as the terms that stand for what Arendt prizes most. She regularly connects them; she sees them as dependent on each other. Freedom exists only when men engage in political action."[6] In her view, all other activities—except, of course, thinking and contemplation, which can only be private—occur in bondage to some other persons and never allow the attainment of autonomy and freedom.

This overall commitment to public action and contempt for the sphere of labor explains Arendt's ambivalent relation to Marx and the Marxist tradition. She valued the Marxian commitment to participatory democracy, at the same time considering its glorification of productive processes and the central place it assigned labor a grievous mistake. This stance also helps to explain why Arendt ranked the American Revolution well above the French. The former remained concerned with the reconstruction of public and political realms, while the latter pursued the chimera of wishing to transform private lives and socioeconomic arrangements. Arendt excluded the whole sphere of social welfare and socioeconomic inequalities from the realm of the political. This gives her cast of thought a decidedly conservative bent. She was an elitist thinker, and she explicitly rejected liberal theories of politics. Yet her conservative elitism, building on the Greek model, is far removed from the vulgar neoconservatism that presently pervades political thought.[7]

The idea of the supremacy of political action was coupled in Arendt's writings with a defense of the mind's sphere as the privileged locus of thought and contemplation. At a time when people were unable to act in common, only an ongoing dialogue between men and women still capable of evoking in thought the preeminent value of free political action allowed any hope for the future. She wanted to contribute to that dialogue. Hannah Arendt, who never joined a political party, who rarely engaged in any political activities, nevertheless became one of the foremost exponents on the American scene of the idea of political freedom through involved participation in the arena of politics. She measured current political events by these austere standards and found them wanting. Her impact on American culture—and it was profound—probably rests on the twin pillars of her anatomy of totalitarian unfreedom and her ideal picture of participatory freedom as a measuring stick to be applied to the passing political scene. Current cant still too often connects her exclusively with such notions as that of the "banality of evil," the idea that in an administered and bureaucratized world the classical standards of good and evil and of public morality have become obsolete. A person such as Eichmann should no longer be judged, she contended, in terms of older standards of sin or guilt; he was simply a banal link in a bureaucratic chain of command. This is an interesting though flawed observation, but the enduring significance of her thought surely lies elsewhere, despite the fact that her book on Eichmann made her name a household word. Her ferocious independence may often have led her into some questionable byways of thought, but her enduring significance as a political philosopher is not to be sought in occasional misjudgments. It lies in her self-chosen role as a defender of freedom through political action.

Hannah Arendt, the exile, surely ranks among the most significant thinkers in political theory in these barren times. Six years after her death, no fewer than nineteen editions of her work were listed in *Books in Print*. The *Social Science Citation Index* for the first four months of 1979 includes sixty different citations to her work; many more appeared in the literature of the humanities. It is amusing to note that Thomas Hobbes has only twenty-six entries in the *Index* for this period, and a major contemporary of Arendt, her fellow refugee and political philosopher Leo Strauss, only thirteen. Arendt left no disciples, though political theorists such as Sheldon Wolin, George Kateb, and John Schaar have testified to the impact of her thought on their own. She did not wish to found a "school" or a sect, but she intended to reopen the dialogue, inside and outside the academy, on the virtue and glory of political commitment through participatory democratic action. And in this she succeeded.[8]

Franz Neumann (1900–1954): Marxist on the Way to Liberalism

Franz Neumann is less well known to contemporary American students of the social sciences, as the historian H. Stuart Hughes has noted, than he was to their predecessors in the late 1940s and early 1950s.[1] Yet his impact on American thought is such that he needs to be dealt with, even if briefly. This impact came in the main through his masterful and, though flawed, yet in many respects still unsurpassed anatomy of Nazi Germany, to which he gave the Hobbesian title *Behemoth* (1942).[2] But it also came through his students and associates at Columbia University who have, in their turn, made major contributions to American scholarship.

Franz Neumann was born in eastern Germany in 1900 of Jewish parents. As was characteristic of German Jews from the border areas of the east, Neumann's parents found no difficulty in reconciling their allegiance to Germany with a self-assured identification with Judaism. Neumann himself, while not religiously observant, never felt a need to deny his Jewish identity, even though he was also a self-conscious German before he became a refugee.

Neumann served in the German army toward the end of World War I and became a committed socialist while working within the revolutionary Soldier's Councils that sprung up all over Germany after the defeat of 1918. In tune with his convictions, he resolved to study labor law and then settled in Berlin in 1927 as a labor lawyer. During the next five years, he served as a legal adviser to various unions and also to the executive of the Social Democratic party. It is likely that, had the Nazis not come to power, he would have had a major political career. As it was, he was forced to emigrate. Though he first believed, like so many of the refugees in the early years, that Hitler's regime would not last long, Neumann went to London after friends had warned him of his imminent arrest by the Nazis. In the meantime, however, as he combined political idealism with a pronounced practical bent, he realized that a German law degree was of no use whatever abroad and took a degree in political science with Harold Laski at the London School of Economics. When it became clear to him that the Nazi regime would not be as short-lived as he had once believed, he left for the United States in 1936.

When Neumann arrived in America, the New Deal was at its zenith, and this warmed his Social Democratic heart. The fact that he came to America in the Roosevelt years greatly facilitated Neumann's adjustment to his new homeland; it smoothed his transition from the world of European socialism to that of American liberalism. Soon after his arrival in New York, he resolved to put his legal training and newly acquired skills in political science to use by writing an anatomy of nazism. He conceived of the book as a scholarly work, but also as a contribution to the education of the American public and American policymakers concerning the true nature of the Nazi monster. Even though Neumann appeared in this work as a detached observer, he nevertheless remained *engagé*. With support from the Institute for Social Research, directed by his fellow emigrés Theodor Adorno and Max Horkheimer and loosely attached to Columbia University, he set to work on his *Behemoth*. It is for this major study of the Nazi regime that he is chiefly remembered.

When the war broke out, Neumann left his scholar's study for Washington, where he served as a chief expert on German affairs, first for the Office of Strategic Services and then for the Department of State. After the war ended, Neumann, realizing that the new Germany that was slowly emerging hardly bore the socialist features he had hoped for, resolved on a university career. When he was offered a professorship in political science at Columbia, he eagerly accepted. He taught there until his untimely death in an automobile accident in 1954.

Neumann carved a large niche for himself at Columbia. Although he had never taught before on a regular basis, he attracted first-rate students and won a great deal of attention and respect from his colleagues. One of my own teachers, Robert Lynd, author of *Middletown*, almost invariably used to start his seminar by saying, "As Franz Neumann said at lunch. . . . " Neumann's students at Columbia formed a brilliant galaxy. Many of them were sons of fellow emigrés, for whom his thought seemed to build bridges between European and American cultural traditions. Native Americans, as well, were fiercely loyal to him and attempted to meet his high scholarly demands and his political commitment to the ideas of the Left. Most of his students, such as Yale historian Peter Gay and Columbia historian Fritz Stern, both sons of refugees, did not follow him into political science; but others, such as David Kettler, attempted to walk in his footsteps as political scientists *engagés*, and the native-born Herbert Deane later came to be a professor of political science at Columbia.

When discussing Neumann's ideas and their impact, it seems advisable to distinguish *Behemoth* from his later writing. In the former work Neumann still wrote in a broadly Marxian perspective, though he rejected vulgar Marxist explanatory schemes that saw the Nazis as simple "agents of monopoly capital." The Marxist bent is clearly evident in the overall plan for the work. Here Neumann specified that exclusive concern with purely legal or administrative forms amounted to not seeing below the tip of the iceberg. Even though he analyzed these forms with his finely honed lawyer's mind, he nevertheless considered them secondary. The basic clue to the Nazi regime had to be sought, so Neumann contended, in the economic realm. Rejecting the then fashionable explanation of the Nazi phenomenon in terms of the dominance of a new "managerial class," Neumann showed in exhaustive detail the multiple ties that linked the Nazis to the old business elite. Yet, at the same time, Neumann rejected the Marxist notion of a single capitalist ruling class. Nazi Germany, he argued, was ruled by four distinctive elites: big industry, the army, the state bureaucracy, and the Nazi party. Even though these were seen as separate elites, Neumann also showed that they were in the process of amalgamation, partly through marital alliances. In the course of time, Neumann argued, practitioners of violence would become businessmen and businessmen, practitioners of violence.

While Neumann's structural analysis of the Nazi society influenced not only scholars but also Washington policymakers, such was not the case with another theme developed in the book. Perhaps because of his legal training, Neumann argued that Nazi Germany could no longer be described as a state at all, since the notion of statehood implies adherence to sets of legal and moral norms. Only those who tend to identify the state with a privileged sphere of higher morality, in the Hegelian tradition, were able to follow Neumann on this point; and there were few Hegelians in America. Without the guidance of Neumann's structural analysis of the power elites of Germany, the work of C. Wright Mills, who deeply admired Neumann, is hardly conceivable. His other train of thought found, to my knowledge, no echo.

After the war's end, and after realizing that his hopes for a socialist and democratic Germany were not to be realized, Neumann gradually changed not only certain of his socialist ideas but also his interests. Partly because of the exigencies of his teaching, he turned to a new analysis of classical political theory in general and the liberal tradition in particular. In this last period, Neumann increasingly focused on the kind of political thought that he felt had an impact on the political climate of America. Appreciative and shrewdly analytical essays on Montesquieu and John Stuart Mill, for example, were written in that period. Others dealt with "The Concept of Political Freedom" and related topics. Still another set of ideas attempted, even if only in a tentative way, to supplement the previous structural analysis of Nazi Germany with notions such as "anx-iety," derived from psychoanalytical thought, to which Neumann in-creasingly turned in the last period of his life.[3] In all these essays, Neu-mann was searching for new moorings for his political credo. By now he was being influenced by the American climate of ideas; yet he was also still critical of many facets of it. McCarthyism and the Cold War caused him a great deal of pain and worry; he now attached crucial importance to the notions of political freedom and democracy that he found institutionalized in America. It is hard to say in what specific po-litical direction he would have moved had he not died so early.

Neumann, who managed with comparative ease to move between high-level positions in Washington and the scholarly milieu of Columbia Uni-versity, was able to influence intellectual trends in his adopted country partly because much of his thought, in addition to having German bases, bore the indelible traces of his close immersion in American styles of thought.

In the Washington years as well as at Columbia, Neumann had the opportunity to move with facility between refugee milieux and estab-lished networks of association of scholars, administrators, and policy-makers. Though he was responsive to the climate of opinion in all circles, he seems to have avoided full identification with any one of them. He had one foot in the world of Horkheimer's Institute for Social Research and another in the world of Washington policymakers. This seems at times to have created a good deal of tension for Neumann, but perhaps it was just that tension that led him to his fruitful trains of thought.

As mentioned earlier, Neumann once remarked that three possible paths may be chosen by exiled scholars in America. They may abandon previous intellectual positions and accept the new orientation without qualification. They may retain their old thought structure in its entirety and either attempt to revamp the American pattern or withdraw to an island of their own. And finally, they may "attempt an integration of new experience with old tradition."[4] Neumann believed the last path to be the most rewarding but also the most difficult to follow. It was the path he chose.

Behemoth appeared soon after America entered the war with Germany. The book helped to shape American images of the bases of the Nazi regime both in scholarly circles and among policymakers. Neumann's influence on policy and policymakers was further reinforced when he moved to Washington. It would be fascinating to trace in detail just how much Neumann and his associates helped to shape American policy to-ward Germany during the war years and after. This task cannot be undertaken here, but it seems safe to say that their impact was conse-quential. In any case, for almost a decade, until the appearance of Hannah Arendt's *The Origins of Totalitarianism* in 1951, *Behemoth* was the major guide to the Nazi phenomenon. Even now it remains an indispensable book.[5] Neumann's later essays are not likely to resist the tooth of time as successfully. But as the teacher of such eminent scholars as Peter Gay and Fritz Stern, as well as of less eminent but more publicly visible persons as Jeanne Kirkpatrick, Neumann exerted influence on American culture that remains to be reckoned with.

Leo Strauss (1899–1973): Political Philosopher and Guide to the Modern Perplexed

It would be an understatement to say that the conservative political philosopher Leo Strauss had many students in America. The fact is that he alone among eminent refugee intellectuals succeeded in attracting a brilliant galaxy of disciples who created an academic cult around his teaching. They formed a little band of people in the know, a company of elect, who saw themselves as having access to esoteric knowledge denied to the *vulgus*. This cult has proved its capacity to survive the death of its charismatic founder. Even if its practices may have become somewhat routinized with time, it has not lost its vigor. At present, in addition to scholars taught by Strauss, a second and even a third generation of Straussians dominates the teaching of political theory in universities and colleges as diverse as the universities of Michigan, Toronto, and Michigan State; Boston and Kenyon colleges; St. John's, Claremont, and Middlebury colleges; and many others. Prominent Straussians hold leading positions at Harvard and the University of Chicago. Neoconservative journals like *The Public Interest* and *Commentary* have been influenced by Straussian thought, and neoconservative intellectuals such as Irving Kristol and James Q. Wilson, though they were not technically students of Strauss, have figuratively "gone to school" with him. One of his students, Robert Goldwin, was President Ford's "intellectual in residence" at the White House.[1] To explain this amazing success, a brief consideration of Strauss's career, as well as a sketch of the substance of his teaching, are in order.

Strauss was born in 1899 in Kirchhain, a small town in southern Germany. In contrast to the parents of most German-Jewish intellectuals of his generation, Strauss's parents were provincial Jews, unassimilated and orthodox in their religious beliefs. Strauss had a traditional gymnasium education. After serving in the German army, he went on to study philosophy at the universities of Frankfurt, Marburg, Berlin, and Hamburg. He received his Ph.D. at Hamburg in 1921 for a dissertation sponsored by Ernst Cassirer. He also spent a postdoctoral year at the University of Freiburg, where Husserl held the chair of philosophy and Heidegger served as Husserl's assistant. After the termination of his studies, Strauss went to Berlin to assume a position as a research assistant at the Academy of Jewish Research, where he concentrated on biblical criticism and the thought of Spinoza. In 1932, he received a Rockefeller grant and left Germany forever. After living in Paris and Cambridge, Strauss came to the United States in 1938. For the next ten years he taught at the New School for Social Research. He then moved to the University of Chicago, where he taught political theory for twenty years, until his retirement in 1969. Although he had already trained a number of eminent political theorists at the New School, most of his disciples came under his spell in the years he spent at the University of Chicago.

Strauss must have been a most outstanding teacher. Although unprepossessing in appearance, and disdaining the histrionics and deliberate stage manners of many successful university lecturers, Strauss left an indelible impression on his students despite—or because of—his simple, almost naive, presentation of self. "[Pristine] simplicity," writes Werner J. Dannhauser, one of his students, "is one of the first and most lasting impressions I have of the man."[2] While many Continental scholars after they came to America still insisted on the professorial prerogatives and deference to which they had been accustomed in the past, Strauss demanded that he simply be addressed as "Mr. Strauss." But what impressed students as well as occasional listeners when attending Strauss's lectures and seminars was his unalloyed devotion to the life of the mind. Although he had stopped going to synagogue, it is likely that Strauss saw himself as a successor to a long line of rabbis for whom the search for knowledge of the true and good dominated their life career. Though his quest for certainty was largely not religious but philosophical, it still resembled that of Maimonides.

Strauss's thought was marked by his revulsion from the preponderant tendencies of the modern age. His conservatism rested on his conviction that modern trends of thought, be they positivistic or historicist, were inimical to—nay, destructive of—what he cherished as being the perennial values. The fact that he was born a Jew in a country that had seemed for a century to be in the vanguard of enlightenment and modernism and yet had experienced descent into a barbarism unthinkable to nineteenth-century German Jewry[3] may explain some of Strauss's motivations when he embarked on his intellectual journey. If Germany, for long the chief seat of humane learning, had succumbed to the inhuman mass movement of Hitler, so Strauss seems to have reasoned, and if most of its leading intellectuals had either gone over to the victorious Nazi cohorts or stood passively on the sidelines, then a searching examination of the intellectual roots of this disaster was essential. The main currents that dominated the German mind, Strauss reasoned, were historicism and the various schools of thought, from positivism to neo-Kantianism, that had their origin in the Enlightenment. It was these currents of thought that needed reexamination if the intellectual roots of the German disaster were to be uncovered.

Both positivism and historicism, Strauss argued, are based "on the assumption that the conflict between different values or value-systems is essentially insoluble for human reason."[4] By undermining the notion of timeless values that was the characteristic achievement of classical Greek thought, these systems of ideas opened the floodgates to a nihilism of values of which the Nazi movement was the most extreme outcome. When Max Weber argued for a value-free social science, Strauss contended, the reason was not "his belief in the fundamental opposition of the Is and the Ought but his belief that there cannot be any genuine knowledge of the Ought." Weber thus denied the possibility of any rational or philosophic knowledge of "the true value system." Ethical neutrality in the social sciences for Strauss necessarily leads "to the view that every preference, however evil, base, or insane, has to be judged before the tribunal of reason to be as legitimate as any other preference."[5] In a similar vein, contemporary American political science, in its exclusive concern with political behavior and its refusal to judge values and to pay attention to the ethical dimension of human activities, posits "in effect the equality of literally all desires; it teaches in effect that there is nothing of which man ought to be ashamed; by destroying the possibility of self-contempt, it destroys with the best of intentions the possibility of self-respect. By teaching the equality of all values, by denying that there are things which are intrinsically high and others which are intrinsically low . . . it unwittingly contributes to the victory of the gutter."[6]

If positivism, neo-Kantianism, and modern behavioral social sciences, those heirs of the Enlightenment, contribute to nihilism on the contemporary scene, historicism, though largely stemming from counter-Enlightenment sources, also leads to the same conclusions. It contends that the values embodied in a given philosophical or ethical system depend on social and historical contexts. This relativization of all values, this rejection of the notion of timeless values, leads, according to Strauss, to the defenselessness of historicist scholars in the face of the brutal onslaught on all civilized values of modern totalitarian movements.[7] "Historicism rejects the question of the good society, that is to say, of *the* good society, because of the essentially historical character of society and human thought." But political action no longer guided by a positive image of the good and the true must succumb to the forces of unreason.

What is striking in the many polemical pronouncements against relativism, positivism, and historicism that have come from Strauss's pen are his self-assurance and dogmatic certainty. He is not only a man who knows, he knows that he knows. Many commentators have contended, for example, that Strauss completely misunderstood Max Weber; but this seems never to have disturbed him or his followers.

This imperturbable certainty is even more recognizable in Strauss's interpretations of the thought of, among others, Maimonides, Machiavelli, Hobbes, and a number of Greek thinkers.[8] In his exegetical work on these figures, Strauss refuses to lend credence to any previous interpretations and argues that truly to understand them it is necessary to search for hidden meanings. In all such cases, Strauss argues, we must uncover the author's true intentions, even though the author himself, mainly for prudential reasons, took pains to hide these from all but the most attentive readers. Whenever one of these authors uses inconsistent arguments, whenever he employs examples that seem not to prove what they were really intended to prove, this indicates to Strauss that the author really intended to say something other than what appears on the surface of the text. Some of the cryptographic methods that Strauss utilized in these exegetical works have brought forth interesting results, but the fact seems to be that many of his interpretations are nonfalsifiable. As an unsympathetic critic of Strauss's method, J. G. A. Pocock has said about Strauss's interpretation of Machiavelli, "Everything he finds in Machiavelli must have been intended by Machiavelli; the whole book is a guide to Machiavelli's true intentions; and he seems utterly indifferent to the question of whether anyone has ever detected them before. . . . The gorgeous landscape [Strauss] reveals to us may never before have been seen by human eye—not even Machiavelli's."[9]

Strauss's dogmatic critical exegeses neatly parallel his dogmatic rejection of all modern or modernistic trends of thought. In all these cases, Strauss seems to proceed from an unperturbable certainty that he has privileged access to certain perennial truths that are hidden from the noninitiated. To Strauss, modern political philosophers, from Spinoza and Machiavelli to Hobbes, Hegel, Nietzsche, and Heidegger, were engaged in a "conspiracy" to subvert the perennial philosophy that had its roots in the Greek polis. For example, one of Strauss's followers, Allan Bloom, says of Spinoza: "[he] was a member of a conspiracy the project of which was the alteration of what were previously considered to be the necessary conditions of human life. This project required a totally different view of human nature, and it is the essence of modernity."[10] The modern age, so Strauss argues, is sunk in a morass of relativized values where even the best lack all convictions because they have no access to the eternal wisdom of the ancient philosophers.

Strauss's onslaught against the very idea of modernity and all those thinkers who uphold modern values, combined with his self-confident sense that it was granted to him to discern the essence, the truth, of phenomena hidden from the eyes of the vulgar, goes a long way toward accounting for his amazing success in attracting disciples and followers. Many of these appear to have come to him vaguely dissatisfied with modern trends of thought yet unable to cut themselves loose from the guiding assumptions they had acquired in their exposure to the modern world. Strauss provided a secure foundation for what had previously been only a lingering sense of dissatisfaction with the present. In a world of relative values, in which they found it difficult to find their way un- aided, Strauss provided a guide for the modern perplexed. His adver- saries called Strauss arrogant, self-righteous, dogmatic; but in the eyes of his devoted followers these vices, through a peculiar alchemy, came to be transmuted into virtues. To them he was a true "lion" in a world mainly inhabited by indecisive, doubting, scheming "foxes." He had the courage of his convictions on a scene in which most intellectual spokes- men had shown a failure of nerve. To his followers, Strauss was more fully devoted to the life of the mind than most of the intellectual Ham- lets of the dominating establishment. But they also felt that throughout his life he was devoted to what John Dewey called "the quest for cer- tainty." What is more, he attained certainty, if not in all its aspects, at least in certain crucial ones. Committed to the few (who do know) against the many (who do not), devoted to intellectual aristocracy and to an elite that must keep in check the vulgar thought of the demos and of those who abet its base desires, the Straussian knows that the road to the re- generation of the fallen world of modernity is marked by signposts to be found in the work of Leo Strauss.

Strauss is a difficult writer. His argumentation is complex and many- stranded, and the involutions of his thought are often difficult to disen- tangle. It is hence hardly astonishing that he never found a wide audi- ence. But it is likely that he cared very little about that. He addressed himself largely to an elite; the reception of his thought among circles of initiates was what really mattered to him.

Although all Straussians are devoted to the general message of the founding father, they have worked in various fields and have done spe- cialized work in a number of areas. Allan Bloom, together with Harvey Mansfield, Jr., of Harvard the chief Straussian apostle who taught at Yale, Cornell, Toronto, and is now at the Committee on Social Thought at the University of Chicago, is best known for a new translation of Pla- to's *Republic*. Bloom has, in his turn, already inspired students who have published books on Epicurus, Rousseau, and Montesquieu. The late Howard White, a former dean of the New School's graduate faculty, has written on Bacon and Shakespeare. Joseph Cropsey, now at the University of Chicago, has written on Adam Smith and coauthored a *History of Political Philosophy* with his master. Harry Jaffa, now of Claremont College, has authored a noteworthy book on Lincoln. Ralph Lerner and Muhsin Mahdi have written on medieval political theory. Walter Berns and Harry Clor have done distinguished work in constitutional law. Many other Straussian scholars could be listed. Enough has been said to indicate the truly remarkable success of Leo Strauss in influencing American political philosophy, albeit in a profoundly conservative direction.

It has often been argued that in the past few decades the American scholarly establishment has become rigidified, routinized, and unable to make way for new winds of doctrine. Strauss's career goes a long way to disprove such contention. If a newcomer with ideas that are much at variance with the dominant trends in the scholarly community can manage to create a cult of followers who successfully invade the academic establishment, the American scholarly community is clearly much more open than its critics allege. If Strauss's strategy of rigid and uncompromising opposition to prevailing patterns of thought has proved successful, the widely shared opinion that only accommodation will bring rewards is placed in doubt. It should be obvious that I do not share many ideas with the Straussians. But this does not prevent me from documenting their success. If this is value neutrality, so be it.

Karl W. Deutsch (1912–): An Academic Success Story

Only some twenty-five years after arriving in America as a refugee from Central Europe with only a degree in law to his credit, Karl Deutsch had achieved an eminent position in American political science and was ranked at the top of his discipline. His is indeed a true academic success story.

A study of citation references by prominent scholars in the field of international relations in the late 1960s reveals that Karl Deutsch led the field by a wide margin. He was cited 437 times, while the next highest on the list received only 281 citations.[1] This is an amazing record considering that Deutsch, who arrived in this country from Czechoslovakia in 1939, was in his mid-forties when he began teaching American graduate students on a regular basis. His impact not only on the field of international relations but also, more generally, on the development of behaviorally oriented political science has been consequential. His students can now be found in high positions in many leading university departments of political science.

Deutsch was born in Prague in 1912 to a German-Jewish family. His father was an optician; his mother, a left-wing political activist, became one of Czechoslovakia's first women members of the Czech parliament. After graduating with high honors from the German *Staatsrealgymnasium* in Prague, Deutsch went to study at the German University in that city in 1934. His leadership of various anti-Nazi groups on campus soon led to clashes with the pro-Nazi majority of the faculty, and he was forced to interrupt his studies. He went to England to study mathematics and optics and, on returning to Prague, gained admission to the Czech national Charles University, an honor only rarely granted to students not ethnically Czech. Soon after he received his doctorate of law in 1938, Deutsch and his new bride left for the United States. They had intended only a brief stay, but decided to make their home in America when the Munich pact and the Nazi takeover of the Sudentenland signaled that the end of an independent Czech nation was near.

Having received a scholarship for refugees from nazism, Deutsch entered Harvard University for graduate training in political science. After America's entry into the war, he worked for the government as chief of research sections in the Office of Strategic Services and the Department of State and then became a member of the International Secretariat of the San Francisco Conference of 1945, which created the United Nations.[2]

Returning to his doctoral studies at Harvard at the end of the war, Deutsch also accepted a teaching position at MIT. He now began to publish widely in the field of international affairs. In 1952 he was promoted to the rank of professor of history and political science at MIT. A year later his first major book was published. It was largely based on his Harvard dissertation and was entitled *Nationalism and Social Communication*.[3] From then on Deutsch was much in demand in the community of political scientists. In 1953–54 he headed an interdisciplinary group of scholars who produced a much-cited work, *Political Community and the North-Atlantic Area*,[4] under his leadership. In 1956–57 Deutsch was a Fellow at the Center for Advanced Study in the Behavioral Sciences at Palo Alto and laid the groundwork for what is perhaps his most influential book, *The Nerves of Government* (1963).[5] Other appointments and honors followed in rapid succession. Deutsch was a visiting professor at the University of Chicago in 1954 and received his first Guggenheim Fellowship in 1955 (a second followed in 1971). In 1957 he went to Yale University as a visiting professor, and a year later he accepted a permanent appointment there as professor of political science. During the next ten years spent at Yale, Deutsch not only continued to publish widely (his *Germany Rejoins the Powers* [1959],[6] with Lewis J. Edinger, dates from this period) but also started a number of influential research projects. Among them, the Yale Political Data Program to develop quantitative indicators for the testing of various social science theories and propositions and the Yale Arms Control Project are the best known.

After holding visiting professorships at the universities of Oxford and Heidelberg in the 1960s, Deutsch moved to Harvard University in 1967. Although active as a teacher and researcher at Harvard, Deutsch also taught as a guest professor in no less than six major European universities during his Harvard tenure. In addition, he lectured throughout the world and served as a consultant to various government agencies. Deutsch was president of the New England Political Science Association in 1964–65; president of the American Political Science Association in 1969–70; and president of the International Political Science Association in 1976–79. He holds honorary degrees from a number of European and American universities.

This bare enumeration of Deutsch's positions and honors indicates that this refugee intellectual spent little time as an outsider after coming to America. Soon after his arrival he became an almost prototypical insider. Rapidly gaining membership in various partially overlapping networks of academics and nonacademics, equally at home in the common rooms of universities, among foundation officials, in the classroom, on the lecture platform, and in the reception rooms of the high and mighty, he seems to have the ability to play several roles without showing any undue strain. Ebullient as a speaker in the lecture hall, shooting off ideas in rapid fire in graduate seminars, always willing to engage all comers, be they peers or students, in an exciting dialogue, Deutsch has left a deep impression on almost all he has encountered. Surely part of his enormous success in America can be laid at the doorstep of his personality, his talents, and his highly developed social skills. Yet there have been others with similar gifts who have not had the success that Deutsch has enjoyed. Why this is so requires a short overview of the state of affairs in political science and the study of international affairs when Deutsch, shortly after the war, began to carve out a niche for himself in these disciplines.

Deutsch made his entry on the scene of American political science at a time when, owing to the so-called behavioral revolution that took place soon after World War II, the field took a direction highly congenial to his orientation. Soon after the war, the Young Turks of behaviorism became dominant figures in the political science establishment, partially building on a tradition first developed during the interwar years at the University of Chicago by such scholars as Charles Merriam and Harold Lasswell. Rejecting the concern with classical political theory, normative theorizing, and historical approaches that had prevailed until then, they stressed the need to make political science a true social science devoted to the discovery and analysis of empirically derived data. The methodological standards of the older political science, so the behaviorists argued, were loose. In contrast, the new behavioral dispensation had to become methodologically self-conscious. The new behavioralists wished to replace unsystematic data collection by precise criteria and techniques. They wanted to collect data on the behavior of individuals or groups through survey research aimed at uncovering the underlying motivations for the political choices of voters, through questionnaires, interviews, or tests. They wished to establish scientifically valid generalizations about political behavior and contrast these to what seemed to them the unsystematic, untested, and unscientific propositions that had dominated political science in the past.

While in the hands of lesser scholars the prepotent concern with data collection, methodological sophistication, and scientific criteria often degenerated into a tedious, dustbowl (i.e. totally atheoretical) empiricism, the major behavioralists, and above all Deutsch, never lost sight of general theoretical ideas even when they immersed themselves in empirical data. This is quite apparent in Deutsch's major works.

Deutsch had grown up in a country of diverse and warring ethnic groups. The tragic consequences of ethnic rivalries were deeply impressed on his mind when he attempted to understand the collapse of the Czech Republic, and of the Austrian-Hungarian Empire before that. Accordingly, a major part of Deutsch's work in America concerned problems of ethnicity and nationalism, as well as the conditions under which wider consensually based national and international communities could be built in the face of ethnic diversity. His *Nationalism and Social Communication* presented a novel model of nationalism, tested by the application of quantitative data and based on the idea that nation-building largely rests upon the possibility of opening channels of communication between people. Shared habits and outlooks can emerge only when channels of communication are open. Barriers to communication, on the other hand, lead to a parochial closure between groups and hence to the breakdown of common standards and beliefs. This stress on the crucial importance of communication is further extended in *Political Communication and the North Atlantic Area,* where Deutsch argues that the enlargement of political communities depends less on a common language or a common enemy than on complementaries of values and expectations and high levels of mutual responsiveness. Just as the development of nationalism largely hinges on two-way channels of communication between elites and masses, so the establishment of transnational communities, Deutsch argues, depends on developing networks of communication between elites and non-elites in component national entities.

Deutsch's *The Nerves of Government,* like its predecessors, focuses on processes of communication, but it utilizes a new approach, that of cybernetics. Deutsch tries here to specify and to put into operational terms the variables (and their interactions) that help steer such systems as national and supranational decision-making units. In this work and in succeeding publications, Deutsch examines, inter alia, such aspects of political communication as the ratio between external and internal messages and transactions within a nation. The flow of messages helps account for the degree of closure or openness of a system. Other aspects considered here concern governmental facilities for monitoring and controlling the flow of information, the problem of communication overloads, and the consequences of decentralization in governmental decision-making.

In these works, as well as in many subsequent publications, the trademark of Deutsch's approach is always the merging of creative theoretical ideas with the search for quantitative data to buttress his argumentation. He gathered impressive arrays of data on population movements, language assimilation, and the flow of national and international transactions through trade or mail. What is more, he helped establish cross-national data banks, such as the *World Handbook of Political and Social Indicators*,[7] which can be used to test various theoretical approaches with empirical data. To Deutsch, quantitative data and data banks are necessary tools for the creative development of theories, but he is aware that the data never speak for themselves but must be addressed by a "theory-soaked" inquiry.

Even this short discussion should make it apparent that Karl Deutsch's work exhibits to a superlative degree the virtues that the behavioralists have been striving for. This being the case, it becomes apparent that his success is due not only to his gifts but to the fact that he came to America and to American political science at precisely the right moment.

The behavioral revolution was brought to dominance by large-scale support from foundations, such as the Ford Foundation, and Deutsch soon developed the ability to enlist foundation support for his various projects. The success of the approach depended heavily on its proponents' ability to convince political decision-makers that the new political science, as distinct from its predecessors, could provide valuable theories and data for their use, and Deutsch managed to establish significant channels of communication between Washington officials and academics in major universities. Using and manipulating various communication networks, Deutsch's praxis flowed from his theories in ways that no Marxist ever dreamed of.

The development of large-scale research projects allowed Deutsch to train a great number of students in the new techniques he had helped to develop. While the esoteric knowledge of the humanist scholar is often hard to transmit, theoretical approaches based on empirical techniques can be taught with somewhat more ease. In addition, Deutsch's enthusiasm about novel empirical inquiries served him in attracting students. In any case, though he never developed a "school" around himself, scores of his students now carry on his message. Deutsch was kind enough to send me a list "of about the upper half of those students [of his] who have ended up as university professors."[8] The list includes twenty-four names, most of them occupants of prestigious positions at Yale, Harvard, Berkeley, Stanford, Cornell, Columbia, the University of Michigan, and the University of Illinois, as well as at foreign universities. It includes such names as J. David Singer, Bruce Russett, Richard Merritt, Nelson Polsby, and Arend Lijphart.

If Deutsch had arrived in America at a less propitious moment in the history of political science, his impact would probably not have been as great as it has proved in fact to be. But it can also be argued, and I am inclined to do so, that the development of the behavioral revolution in American political science would have been significantly slower had it not benefited from the vigorous intellectual leadership of Karl Deutsch and his many students and disciples. Deutsch's success story in America is intimately linked to the success story of American behavioralism in political science during the 1940s, 1950s, and 1960s.

Eric Voegelin (1901–): Conservative Gadfly of the Political Science Establishment

The prominent conservative political theorist Eric Voegelin, who came to America in 1938, had a marked impact on American political thought even though he was entirely at variance with its major orientation. He largely wrote in opposition to prevailing trends and assumptions. Voegelin's political theory is rooted in the idea that only transcendental truth, discovered through faith and reason, can serve as a foundation of political thought. As a consequence, he relentlessly attacks most modern thought in general and the Enlightenment and positivism in particular. These are antitranscendental doctrines that must lead, he argues, to the destruction of the social order. Yet Voegelin started his career in a very different intellectual climate, not far removed from positivism.[1]

Born in 1901 in Cologne, Germany, Voegelin lived for many years in Austria. He took his doctorate in law at the University of Vienna in 1922. In his apprenticeship years in Vienna, he served as assistant to Hans Kelsen, the great positivist legal scholar. A few years later, Voegelin published a highly laudatory article on Kelsen's work in the *Political Science Quarterly* in which he praised Kelsen for destroying "any undue respect for existing legal institutions."[2] Following Kelsen, Voegelin at this stage in his thinking argued that the content of law is not tied to an eternal sacred and transcendent order but is the result of compromises between opposing social forces. In a subsequent study of Max Weber's work, Voegelin had begun to question the rigid separation between the world of fact and the world of value which is one of the hallmarks of the positivist tradition, but he still treated Weber with respectful admiration.

Voegelin's initial disposition in favor of positivistic social science was reinforced by a stay in America from 1924 to 1927 as a Rockefeller Fellow. During this period, he came under the influence of the pragmatically oriented labor economist John R. Commons, although attendance at lectures by Alfred North Whitehead at Harvard and the perusal of the work of George Santayana had already begun to awaken his interest in metaphysics and to arouse doubts about a purely immanentist position (i.e. one not dependent on transcendental values) in the social sciences. But the real change in Voegelin's fundamental outlook came not through books and lectures but through lived experience.

In the late 1930s the shadow of Hitler's march to power darkened the political scene in Austria. The Austrian constitution of 1920, written principally by Voegelin's former mentor, Hans Kelsen, seemed no longer adequate to contain within its bounds the fierce ideological contests between Nazis, Christian conservatives, and Social Democrats. No compromise between the contending ideological forces seemed attainable. As a result, Voegelin made his peace with the Catholic-corporatist state of the Dolfuss regime and even accepted a position as a civil-service examiner in the new order.

In 1938 the Nazis invaded Austria and overthrew the corporatist state. Voegelin was fired from his position as an Extraordinary Professor at Vienna University, and he was sure that the Nazi regime would not tolerate him as a member of the civil service. He fled across the border to Switzerland and soon thereafter emigrated to the United States. When I asked him why he had decided to come to the United States, Voegelin answered that he noticed soon after Hitler's victory that many of the Viennese scholars he knew, most of them Jewish, as he was not, had left for the United States, so he went where they went.

After a short instructorship at Harvard and a little later at Bennington, Voegelin went to the University of Alabama in 1939 and then moved to Louisiana State University in 1942, where he taught for sixteen years. When asked why he chose to go to the South, a fairly atypical move for refugee intellectuals, Voegelin answered that he had already been "Americanized" during his first stay in the United States and that he wished to avoid the refugee milieu of the East. He seems to have made a self-conscious decision to reject identification as a refugee and to build networks of colleagues among native Americans.

The choice of Louisiana State University proved to be an eminently favorable one as far as Voegelin was concerned. Even though it was not among the major American universities, and even though it did not enable him to teach advanced graduate students, since the political science department conferred only M.A. degrees, the university provided a haven for Voegelin. It had attracted in these years an unusually brilliant company of artists and scholars, most of them very much in tune with Voegelin's increasingly conservative inclinations. Prominent literary figures such as Cleanth Brooks, Robert Penn Warren, Katherine Anne Porter, and Robert Heilman taught there at the time. Many of them participants in so-called Southern fugitive, agrarian opposition to the life-styles of modern and Northern industrial civilization, they provided a circle of friends and associates in which Voegelin could test and clarify his newfound conservative philosophical and political ideas.

Voegelin stands for a new political theory that is mostly anchored in a return to Plato and Aristotle and the tradition of Christian thought. His is a theocentric humanism, a strongly elitist and Platonic view of the central necessity for social order, which self-consciously opposes all those modernistic trends of thought that reject the search for transcendental truth based on faith and reason in favor of what he calls the "gnostic heresy." Gnosticism, to Voegelin, stands for all vain attempts to cut people loose from their existential moorings in a transcendentally validated order. The gnostic stream of thought, Voegelin contends, has pre-Christian roots, and the messianic and chiliastic creeds based on antinomian gnosticism appeared periodically in the medieval world and after, but these trends make their most destructive appearance in the totalitarian movements of the present.

Attempts to shore up social order against the onslaughts of masses that refuse any longer to accept the guidance of political elites, and against the gnostic assault against the very idea of social order, can be considered to lie at the inner core of Voegelin's philosophical and political message.

Given this orientation, it is hardly surprising that Voegelin found incomprehension, even outright hostility, in the American political science establishment when he proclaimed the need for a new science of politics[3] based on his key philosophical ideas. In fact, it is astonishing that a scholar so sharply at variance with current doctrine within and without the academic community nevertheless managed to attain a considerable succès d'estime. Since he aims his sharpest polemical shafts against the Enlightenment and the positivist tradition, which he sees as rooted in gnosticism, it is remarkable that his colleagues, who are largely the self-conscious heirs of that tradition, gave him a considerable hearing, even when they characterized him as an inveterate ideologist. The American Political Science Association, for example, dominated by behavioralists though it was throughout the period of Voegelin's ascendancy, over the years organized three different panels on his thought at its annual meetings.

His first major book in America, *The New Science of Politics* (1952), originated as a series of presentations in the prestigious Walgreen Lectures at the University of Chicago. The book itself was widely reviewed and called forth sharply polarized reactions. Voegelin says that he received a good deal of hate mail after its publication, and some of the reviews were harshly antagonistic, but he also received a good deal of appreciative comment. The book sold some twenty thousand copies, a high sale given its rather difficult subject matter and the fact that Voegelin's writing, at least during that period, was still studded with German grammatical constructions and liberal use of neologisms.

Voegelin's subsequent work, especially the first four volumes of his monumental *Order and History*,[4] is devoted largely to a close analysis of Greek philosophical thought, preeminently that of Plato and Aristotle, the world of the Old Testament, and the growth of human consciousness throughout the ages. These volumes did not sell as well as the earlier book but still seem to have achieved respectable sales figures of seven or eight thousand copies each. Conservative thinkers praised the work extravagantly. Russell Kirk, for example, considers it "the most important historical work of our century." Even Crane Brinton, who was not in the explicitly conservative camp, has said that "This whole work seems to me clearly to take rank with the works of Toynbee, Spengler, Sorokin, Collingwood."[5] There was, however, no dearth of sharp polemical attacks accusing Voegelin of elitist, if not proto-Fascist, thought.

Between the appearance of *The New Science of Politics* in 1952 and volume 4 of *Order and History* in 1975, more than eighty reviews and review essays have been devoted to the critical evaluation of Voegelin's work. A collection of essays on him as well as a full evaluation of his work by Eugene Webb have recently been published.[6] He has been awarded a number of honors and prizes. He received a Guggenheim Fellowship fairly early in his American career and a number of years later was awarded the Lippincott Prize of the American Political Science Association. (This prize for political theory, by the way, has been given to three other refugee political thinkers—Hannah Arendt, Sir Karl Popper, and Leo Strauss.)

Despite the fact that he could not train Ph.D. students at Louisiana State University, Voegelin has attracted a number of disciples, such as Dante Germino at the University of Virginia, William Havard at Vanderbilt, and Ellis Sandoz at Louisiana State University. Nor is his influence limited to political scientists; his work has found an echo in divinity schools and faculties of theology in both the South and the North. Even though Voegelin has not reached as wide an academic audience in America as his fellow political philosopher and refugee scholar Leo Strauss, and even though his name is much less likely to be known to a general cultivated public than that of Hannah Arendt, his career in America testifies to his continued impact on a significant segment of mainly conservative political scientists, as well as on theologians concerned with the borderland between the political and the divine order. His polemical warfare against "gnosticism" and the whole idea of modernity, while surely not victorious, has nevertheless been significant. Although he may not have convinced most of his adversaries, he has forced them to define their positions more clearly than they otherwise might have done.

By serving as a critical gadfly to the established community of political science and political philosophy, Voegelin has contributed, whether intentionally or not, to the continued vitality of American political thought.

He was able to do so, it would seem, because, although an intellectual outsider, he found from the beginning of his career in America an audience and a sustaining company of like-minded thinkers who were open to his message.

Voegelin went to his native Germany to teach in 1958, returning to America in 1964. He is today associated with the Hoover Institution at Stanford, where he lives in semiretirement. When I had the privilege of talking with him, I had the distinct impression that, despite all his combative and dogmatic stances, Voegelin is a man much at ease with himself. He seems to know that his impact on American thought, though perhaps not as consequential as he might once have hoped, has been far from negligible. Surrounded by a network of admirers who give sustenance to his continuing intellectual labors, he seems to feel that he made no mistake when he left Europe at the time of the Nazi plague to bring his conservative message to "positivistic" and "gnostic" America.

Hans Morgenthau (1904–1980): Advocate and Critic of Power Politics

Many refugee scholars pursued lines of inquiry in America that they had already initiated before coming to this country. This was not the case for Hans Morgenthau. Little in his career in Germany indicated that he would become one of America's foremost theorists of international relations.

Morgenthau was born in Coburg, Germany, in 1904 to a well-to-do German-Jewish family. He was initially drawn to the study of philosophy and literature. When his father objected to the latter as an "unprofitable occupation," and when he found that the kind of philosophy he was taught at Frankfurt University was arid and largely irrelevant to his moral and emotional concerns, he turned to the study of law at the University of Munich. There he also continued to take a number of courses of broader scope. Among the teachers who impressed him were art historian Heinrich Woelfflin and historian Hermann Oncken. The latter, a gifted academic exponent of Bismarckian Realpolitik, made a deep impression on Morgenthau and seems to have had some formative impact on his later thought about international affairs. It was also at Munich that Morgenthau attended Rothenbuecher's seminar on Max Weber's political and social philosophy. Weber's hard-headed realistic approach to the domain of power politics, and his concomitant conviction that power is a diabolical force in human affairs, were to become a leitmotiv of Morgenthau's later work.

After passing his first law examination in Munich, Morgenthau went back to Frankfurt to obtain his doctorate. While working on his thesis, he prepared for his second legal examination by clerking in various legal offices, both public and private. In particular, he was employed in drafting briefs for the Supreme Court in both labor and criminal law. In this period Morgenthau became convinced that it was not, as he puts it, "the merits of different legal interpretations but the distribution of political power"[1] that was decisive in judicial decision-making. His immersion in judicial practice, as well as the joint influences of Oncken and Weber, were probably decisive in shaping Morgenthau's overall orientation in the spheres of law and politics.

Toward the end of 1931, Morgenthau, still a young man, was appointed acting president of the Labor Law Court in Frankfurt. He served in this capacity for the next two years while also publishing several books and articles on labor law. He left Germany soon after the Nazis came to power and, after teaching for a while in Geneva and Madrid, arrived in New York in 1937.

At first Morgenthau had no sponsors in America. Soon after his arrival, he discovered that the one scholar who might have helped him had died less than a year before.[2] The social worker who interviewed the newly arrived Morgenthau at an agency for assistance to refugee scholars was so unimpressed by his past achievements and so convinced that specialists in continental law had no academic future in America that she suggested he take a job as an elevator man. Despite this discouraging advice, Morgenthau remained undaunted and managed to secure a part-time job at Brooklyn College. He taught nights and was paid by the hour. When such part-time employment became intolerable, he moved to Kansas City in 1939, where he attained an appointment at the university through an employment agency. Realizing that the practice of law in the United States differed vastly from that in Germany, Morgenthau resolved to study American law in order to be admitted to the American bar. In teaching courses in American law at the University of Kansas City, Morgenthau kept one step ahead of his students, prepared himself for the bar examinations, and was admitted to the bar in 1943. He prepared only a few briefs, since in the same year he was called to the University of Chicago as a visiting professor of political science. Two years later he became a member of the faculty.[3] He served there until 1968. After his retirement from the University of Chicago, Morgenthau taught at the City University of New York until 1974. He was professor of political science at the New School for Social Research until shortly before his death.

When Morgenthau came to the University of Chicago, the political science department was dominated by Charles Merriam and Harold Lasswell, both committed to a positivistic and "scientific" study of political phenomena and disinclined to look with favor on Morgenthau's philosophical approach to law and politics. They had expected him to lecture on comparative law and seem to have been taken aback when he decided to include Aristotle, the philosophy of the social sciences, and the philosophy of international relations. Nor was his colleague Leonard White, who taught public administration as a study of "the practical and concrete," very appreciative of Morgenthau's "continental ways." Quincy

Wright, however, who dominated the teaching on international law and international organizations when Morgenthau came to the University of Chicago, seems to have been more tolerant of Morgenthau's "realistic" yet philosophical approach, even though his own orientation, with its strong normative commitment to international understanding and transnational collaboration, differed in crucial ways from Morgenthau's.

Despite such obstacles, and some basic disagreements with his fellow refugee Leo Strauss, who had come to Chicago largely upon Morgenthau's initiative, Morgenthau soon made a major name for himself at the University of Chicago. President Maynard Hutchins supported him from the beginning, as did other top administrators. What was more important, however, was that Morgenthau soon found a growing audience among younger colleagues in his own department and elsewhere, and attracted increasing numbers of gifted graduate students.[4] It is no exaggeration to say that in the 1940s and 1950s Morgenthau's "realistic" approach to political affairs became a dominant influence not only in the academy but also in Washington. In these years, together with a few others—Reinold Niebuhr and George Kennan in particular—Morgenthau dominated thinking in international affairs and helped define its character and emphasis. Morgenthau has contributed many lucid and highly perceptive analyses of specific international constellations and issues in foreign affairs, past and present, but his major importance as a scholar lies elsewhere. While most American political science previous to his writings was largely rooted in either moralistic rhetoric or legalistic considerations, Morgenthau succeeded, in a series of influential books, of which *Scientific Man vs. Power Politics* (1946), *In Defense of the National Interest* (1951), and *Politics among the Nations* (1948)[5] are perhaps the most important, in developing a coherent philosophical basis for the understanding of international affairs.

The code of behavior which, according to Morgenthau, is to guide the statesman engaged in the world arena must take cognizance of the root fact that the international field of forces is largely shaped by the quest for power and for the eventual realization of national interests. Power and interest are to Morgenthau the key terms for understanding the motives of international actors. The moralizing approach to international politics, so he argues, glosses over and obfuscates the irreducible fact that international affairs involve, above all, the struggle for power among actors committed to striving for what they conceive to be the national interest. Morgenthau's "realism" is premised upon this recognition.

If the pursuit of power and interest is the foremost determinant of the behavior of international actors, it follows that the behavior of the statesman must be guided by realpolitik, a realism untainted by the moral considerations appropriate in the world of private citizens. If need be, the statesman must be ruthless in the pursuit of national ends. Personal moral qualms that would be most appropriate in the world of private morality can lead only to muddle and weakness. Statesmen cannot afford to be squeamish.

Yet, while Morgenthau seems to pursue a Machiavellian path here, he counterbalances this by stressing that international politics also involve a strong ethical dimension. Just like Weber's insistence that the display of power is the *ultimo ratio* in the international arena, but that power itself belongs to the realm of the devil, so Morgenthau has argued over and over again that "Political ethics is indeed the ethics of doing evil. . . . Neither science nor ethics nor politics can resolve the conflict between politics and ethics into harmony. . . . To know with despair that the political act is inevitably evil, and to act nevertheless, is moral courage. To choose among several expedient actions the least evil one is moral judgment."[6]

Morgenthau's vision is hence a tragic one; nations must act in their own interest, but in so acting they necessarily become embroiled in evil actions. The best that can be hoped for is a course which, while recognizing the Machiavellian imperative, still attempts to temper action by the moderating virtues of prudence and self-restraint. The drive for power cannot be exorcized from the world of international politics, but prudent limitations and minimizations of its uses are the marks of statesmanship. It is impossible to rise above power politics, but it is desirable and possible to surround it with barriers of moral checks and restraints. The great statesman, while accepting the brute facts of power struggles, is not a bully, and the international arena, though it bears some resemblance to a Hobbesian state of nature, is not an arena where, to modify Hobbes's telling phrase, club alone is king.

Given this complex view of international affairs, it stands to reason that Morgenthau's message was often received selectively by his various audiences at different periods of time. During the Cold War years, Morgenthau was the darling of the foreign-policy establishment, and Washington policy-makers gladly availed themselves of his "realistic" approach when attempting to justify their policy in regard to the Soviet Union. But in more recent years, when Morgenthau tended to stress more pronouncedly the notions of ethical and prudential restraint on realpolitik, and when he was moved in the name of ethical principles as well as realistic considerations to oppose the war in Vietnam, Washington turned a deaf ear to his warnings while he gained a wide new audience among the dissenting groups of the young.

Morgenthau surely enjoyed the popularity in which he basked in the 1940s and 1950s, but he seemed to be unaffected by his lack of popularity among the high and the mighty in later years, even though he seems to have been a rather lonely and somewhat embittered man in his last years. "A political science," he has written, "that is true to its moral commitment ought at the very least to face the risk of unpopularity. At its very best, it cannot help being a subversive and revolutionary force with regard to certain vested interests—intellectual, political, economic, and social in general; for it must sit in continuous judgment upon political man and political society, measuring their truth . . . by its own."[7]

Morgenthau had a lofty conception of the role of the political scientist, to be sure, but he would have no part of the hubris of certain of his colleagues who believed that political theory can become a predictive science. His expectations were more modest. Here again, largely reasoning in the wake of Max Weber, Morgenthau argued that theorizing in international affairs can only "develop different alternatives and clarify their necessary preconditions and likely consequences. It can point to the conditions which render one alternative more likely to materialize than the other. But it cannot say with any degree of certainty which of the alternatives is the correct one and will actually occur."[8]

Morgenthau had a high opinion of the calling of the political scientist, yet he also had an acute sense of the existential limits of a science of politics. Throughout his writings, idealism and realism continue to be engaged in a fruitful dialectical tension. Though recording and analyzing the work of the devil in the interplay of power and interest among nations, he still continued to be guided in his work by a moral vision that refused to concede to diabolic forces total dominance in the affairs of nations.

When conducting a series of informal interviews among political scientists,[9] I found that, even though they differed considerably in their concrete appraisals of Morgenthau's work, they all seemed to agree that the modern study of international affairs in America is hardly conceivable without Morgenthau's stimulus. He helped make it intellectually respectable. He provided it with philosophical underpinnings that allowed it to emerge from the morass of legalistic or moralistic argumentation to claim equal rank with other branches of the study of human affairs.[10] The former labor lawyer from Frankfurt thus became in his maturity a founding father of one major branch of American political science.

VI
Writers

Introduction

The section that follows is not meant to be an overview of European writers who took refuge in this country. The purpose of including a discussion of refugee writers in America is to provide a cursory typology of their reactions to the alien environment of American cultural life and its reflection in their literary work. Some of these writers, such as Alfred Doeblin and Leonard Frank, who by an accident of fate found themselves employed in the Hollywood dream factory, felt like stranded whales in their new environment. As a result, they never managed to build links to the American scene. Others, like Hermann Broch, deliberately insulated themselves from American cultural influences and pursued their writing careers untouched by anything that happened in America: they might as well have lived in Tahiti. Neither of these two types had any contact with American influences. In contrast, writers like Thomas Mann responded to cultural events in America and cast out lines to many significant figures on the political and social landscape, while yet restricting their intimate contacts largely to fellow emigrés.

Finally, writers like Vladimir Nabokov set out from the beginning to make a major place for themselves in the world of American letters and built a variety of bridges to fellow writers and critics in America. As a result, Nabokov came to occupy a prominent and probably enduring place in the history of American literature, while the work of Broch gained him hardly any American audience. The Hollywood writers by and large experienced America as a nightmare with which they were unable to come to grips in their literary work. For Mann, America was a beloved country of refuge for many years, but he never dealt with American themes or topics in his work. America still remained largely alien territory even though this Olympian German writer was treated here with almost as much reverence as Albert Einstein. This crude typology of the relation between European writers and the alien cultural territory they were constrained to inhabit may eventually have to be refined, but it seems to be a serviceable approach to understanding the complex relation of European refugee writers to the world of American letters and culture.

Exiled Writers in New York and Hollywood

All refugee writers in America shared one predicament: the loss of their previous audience. For most of them it proved extremely difficult, if not impossible, to write in a language other than their native tongue. Although a number among the better known managed to have some or all of their previous work translated into English, few found the American public they thus acquired to be an adequate substitute for the audience they had once had. The prominent German novelist Leonard Frank put it well when he said of himself, "In the emigration he played a stone fiddle."[1] Even those refugee writers who clung to their native language, as most did, felt that as a result of being excluded from the living linguistic universe of which they had once been a part they tended to use their own language as if it were a dead tongue. The emigrant, wrote the Bulgarian-Austrian refugee author Elias Canetti, "is the custodian of a dead treasure."[2] The loss of an audience, the petrification of language, and the general uprootedness of the exiled writer go a long way toward explaining why, with a few exceptions, the work that refugee writers produced in exile tended to be markedly inferior to their previous literary production. The most notable exceptions are Vladimir Nabokov, Thomas Mann, and Bertolt Brecht.

While practically all writers experienced the loss of their former audience, the conditions in which they pursued their work in America and the various niches they found for themselves in the American social and literary world differed considerably. This accounted for their differing adjustment, or lack of adjustment, to American life and letters. In a later chapter I will attempt, through a few examples, to show the effects on the refugee writer of inclusion in or exclusion from networks of native-born colleagues and peers. Here I shall attempt to show, at least in broad strokes, the consequences that followed from a relatively high concentration of refugee writers in a given setting as compared to the effects of relatively high dispersal. I shall describe the lives of German and

229

Austrian writers in Hollywood in contrast to those of their fellow writers who settled on the East Coast, particularly in New York City.

Thanks to the variety of cultural institutions in New York, exiled writers could follow many pathways in their attempts to put down some cultural roots and to gain a livelihood in America. Some managed to make academic connections—for example, at the New School for Social Research. Others, especially during the war, secured government employment in the Office of War Information, the Office of Strategic Services, and elsewhere. Others still found jobs in publishing houses or on the staffs of magazines. Writing for emigré publications or for the foreign press allowed some to eke out a meager existence. Translating, editing, research, occasional lecture tours, and book reviewing provided a livelihood for others. Many writers found employment in occupations and professions unrelated to their previous craft, so that they wrote, if they wrote at all, only in their spare time. A few, renouncing allegiance to their native language, were able to write in the American idiom.

The wide variety of their occupations in New York City accounts in large part for the fact that New York refugee writers tended to live in relative isolation from each other. There were, of course, many small cliques of friends and associates, some of them centered in coffeehouses and restaurants, largely on Manhattan's West Side. There also were various literary clubs where writers of a particular nationality might gather from time to time. But by and large New York refugee writers lived relatively private lives, isolated from their fellow refugees as well as from native American colleagues and their networks.

The fate of the prominent German playwright and author Ernst Toller, though extreme, highlights the isolation and loneliness of many exiled authors. Toller committed suicide by hanging himself in the bathroom of his New York hotel in May 1939. Earlier he had complained to friends that he wrote for and spoke only to an audience composed of fellow refugees. A few days before his suicide he had attended a White House reception for exiled writers, but he remarked privately that his isolation left him spiritually exhausted. This isolation was dramatically revealed at his cremation. Only three people attended: Toller's only close personal friend in America, the refugee author Ludwig Marcuse; a distant cousin who hoped for a legacy; and an American woman journalist with whom he had had an affair.[3]

Whereas writers in New York saw little of each other, writers in Hollywood, living among their fellows in what might be called a gilded ghetto, probably saw too much of one another. That so many prominent or once prominent refugee authors came to live in and around Hollywood was largely due to historical accident. Well-wishers in Hollywood and elsewhere were able, after the fall of France, to convince the directors of

major Hollywood film companies, Warner Brothers and Metro-Goldwyn-
Mayer in particular, that many prominent European authors could be
saved if they were given one-year contracts as scriptwriters.[4] Such contracts would convince the American consular authorities abroad that these
men and women would not become public charges when they came to
America and would hence facilitate the obtaining of visas. In addition,
the contracts would allow the writers to make a decent living during the
first period of adjustment to America. Several dozen such contracts were
indeed issued, enabling such prominent writers as novelists Heinrich
Mann, Alfred Doeblin, and Leonard Frank; short-story writer Alfred
Polgar; playwright Carl Zuckmayer; and poet Walter Mehring to come
to America and to settle in the vicinity of Hollywood. Most of these contracts lapsed after a year, but a few were extended beyond that time.
Those writers who did not manage to find regular employment after
their initial contracts had run out usually managed to secure some financial aid from various refugee assistance organizations. By and large
these men and women were able to have a material existence superior
to their colleagues in the East, yet with few exceptions they seem to have
been utterly miserable.

It was probably not the general Hollywood atmosphere alone that made
for the pervasive unhappiness and isolation among these exiled writers.
Long before Hitler came to power, a number of Central European directors, actors, musicians, and composers had come to Hollywood, and
it seems that most of them managed to adjust to Hollywood conditions
without undue difficulties. It also seems that most actors, producers, and
musicians who came as refugees did not express a sense of alienation
and cultural malaise in any way comparable to that of the writers. What,
then, accounted for this widely shared despair among writers?

Part of it can surely be attributed to the general sense of alienation
that arises when serious writers, used to following their literary imagination no matter where it leads, are forced to accommodate themselves
to unaccustomed labor in a factorylike atmosphere where scripts are
treated as "products" to be shaped and reshaped for sales appeal and
profit. William Faulkner and F. Scott Fitzgerald complained about Hollywood in terms not very different from those of their foreign-born colleagues. They experienced the degradation of status comparable to becoming hired hands. But most native-born writers knew something about
Hollywood mores before they went to California; they came to refurbish
their fortunes and replenish their pocketbooks, and few had any illusions about the artistic possibilities that Hollywood offered. Refugee authors, on the other hand, had little knowledge about the demands they
would face in their new employment. To them Hollywood was a strange
new world for which they were not prepared. They experienced a pro-

nounced culture shock. Most of them knew only a little English, and they knew even less about what was expected of writers in the film business.

When a writer arrived in the studio that had agreed to employ him, he was assigned to an office in the Writers' Building, where he was supposed to work from 9 A.M. to 5 P.M. producing, or more often rewriting, film scripts. Most refugees had only the vaguest idea what was expected of them, and even if they fully understood their assigned tasks, they felt utterly unable to comply with the wishes of their employer. It is not surprising that hardly any of the projects on which these writers labored ever came to fruition. For men and women whose sense of self had largely been nurtured by their literary productivity, their new existence as producers on an assembly line was a shocking ordeal. Asked to write in a language they had mastered only imperfectly, required to deal with ideas, situations, and plots that were generally completely remote from their own experiences, they felt shattered.

Although the $100 a week that most of them were paid sufficed to insure them a decent style of life, these writers lived in a milieu where such salaries were considered picayune. A native scriptwriter who made $3,500 a week once told Leonard Frank that one could hardly expect anybody being paid as little as Frank to contribute anything worthwhile. So, although the exiled writers did not suffer from absolute deprivation, their relative deprivation was acute in a world where everybody who was anybody was paid five, ten, or twenty times as much as they. In addition, the enormous earning gap between the native and the refugee writer also meant that the exiles could hardly share the social life of their American colleagues. They were virtually excluded from the glittering world of posh restaurants and bars in which the native writers thrived. Given the relatively straitened circumstances in which the refugees were forced to live, few of them were invited to the elegant and sumptuous private parties that punctuated the daily routines. By and large, they were seen as charity cases, as strangers outside the gate of Hollywood society.

There were a few exiled authors, some connected with the film industry and some not, who earned excellent royalties on their work, found an American audience, and did not share the alienation of their colleagues. Franz Werfel, Lion Feuchtwanger, and Thomas Mann were the most prominent. Most of them did their best to help their less fortunate colleagues. Yet it is hardly surprising that the few fortunate ones were often envied, even slandered, by the same men and women who benefited from their assistance. When the ordinary exiled writer looked at the bourgeois life-style of the Manns or the luxurious existence of the Werfels, he suffered a sense of relative deprivation even more pronounced than when he compared himself to his native-born counter-parts. Emigré Hollywood consisted of the haves and the have-nots, with the latter in the great majority. Even though they most honorably kept themselves accessible to the have-nots and helped wherever they could, the refugee haves evoked a great deal of envy and resentment. What was even more galling was that the native-born haves had practically no contact with the refugee have-nots.

The autobiographical accounts and especially the letters of refugee writers make depressing reading. "One does nothing, absolutely noth-ing," writes the novelist Alfred Doeblin about his work in the studios. "Supposedly we are collaborating on something, but up to now that is only a rumor. We take care of our correspondence, telephone, read newspapers, write on our own—whatever one can do in a sitting posi-tion."[5] In another letter he writes, "There are only two categories of authors who live here on the West Coast . . . those who live in the fat, and those who live in the dirt."[6]

The hopelessness of their social and cultural condition was trans-muted at least by many of the emigré authors, into a pronounced hos-tility toward American society and culture in general and West Coast life-styles in particular. Bertolt Brecht, even though his personal life in the war years he spent in the Hollywood atmosphere was in no way as impoverished as that of most of his colleagues, expressed what many of them felt in his poem On Thinking about Hell:

> On thinking about Hell, I gather
> my brother Shelley found it was a place
> Much like the City of London. I
> Who live in Los Angeles and not in London
> Find, on thinking about Hell, that it must be
> Still more like Los Angeles.[7]

The same Brecht, in an essay entitled "Letter to a Mature American," had this to say about his land of refuge: "It is no wonder that the rela-tions between people [in America] are marked by something undigni-fied, infame, lacking of dignity. This has been transmitted to all things, to apartments, to workshops, even to the landscape itself."[8] In Brecht's diaries one finds entries such as this: "In hardly any place did I find life more difficult than in this showplace of easy going." He also noted, "One feels here like Francis of Assisi in an aquarium, Lenin in the Prater, or a chrysanthemum in a mine."[9]

In the minds of many, though not all, exiled writers, revulsion toward all things American encouraged and was fed by a nostalgic view of the ways things used to be in Europe. European culture, in this view, had been refined; American culture was nasty, brutish, and crude. Even the mild Hollywood climate was compared unfavorably with their own. Leonard Frank complained that there was "no air in the air." He noted that in "the eternally sunkist, lifeless hell of Hollywood" one lost all sense of the rhythms of the seasons.[10] Frank also recounts that he often found himself gazing at the ocean, imagining that he was looking toward his beloved Europe; only after several weeks had gone by did he realize that in fact he was looking toward Asia.

The frustrations of life in Hollywood were compounded by the fact that the great majority of exiled writers were almost exclusively dependent on one another for their social life and even in their quest for status and recognition. They lived not only in a ghetto but also on a ship of fools. Erna M. Moore, in a fine study of these Hollywood exiles, writes perceptively: "[Their life histories] convey the picture of a miniature society living in a voluntary ghetto which consciously closes itself against the natives and attempts as far as circumstances allow to continue to adhere to traditional forms of life and customs." If and when the purely material requirements of the refugees were met, social needs came to the foreground. People were highly conscious of their literary rank, and they reinforced in their mutual dependency the sense that they represented German culture. Max Reinhardt had provided an auditorium in his theater in Los Angeles where these men and women who had been excluded from other social gatherings, from social display, and from belonging to an elite could find compensation for their lost social rank. As the literary critic and historian Ludwig Marcuse put it, "We played 'society'—and imitated what was denied us."[11]

This mutual dependence in sustaining and validating their claims to status made the refugee writers into a little ghetto society that seethed with hostility. As in Jean-Paul Sartre's play *No Exit,* many of the company of writers in Hollywood felt that *L'enfer c'est les autres*— that they were in hell precisely because they were bound to others of their kind. To be sure, camaraderie and in-group solidarity also existed, but, as Ludwig Marcuse has said, "If one was not linked by friendship, one was at least linked by enmity."[12] Backbiting, mutual recriminations, hypercritical remarks about fellow writers and their wives too often punctuated the intercourse of refugees who nevertheless knew that it was mainly the company of their fellows that saved them from total isolation and loss of status. The others represented Sartre's hell—but without them there would only be hell twice compounded.

No wonder that most of these refugee writers left Hollywood whenever an occasion presented itself. Having sunk no roots in the West Coast soil, they fled to the East or to Europe as soon as they could manage. The gilded ghetto in which they spent the Hollywood years was perceived by them as a cage from which one escaped as soon as some bars could be removed. Whereas others—actors, musicians, composers, producers, partly because they did not depend on the resources of language—stayed on and made lasting contributions to American cultural life, the Hollywood writers, with very few exceptions, left hardly a mark on it. Their social situation condemned them to artistic sterility.[13]

Hermann Broch (1886–1951): The Complete Outsider

Hermann Broch, a writer of world stature whose work has often been compared to that of Joyce, Mann, and Proust, lived in the United States from 1939 until his death in 1951. Throughout these years, Broch had only minimal contacts with American intellectual life and with his American peers.[1] Precariously supported by grants from several foundations, he made no effort to gain a livelihood from publishing in America. During his stay in the United States, he published only one book, his masterpiece, *The Death of Virgil*, which he had begun in Vienna, and two articles in the *Saturday Review*.

It would appear that Broch's one major lifeline to American literature was established through his friend and patron, Henry Seidel Canby of the Book-of-the-Month Club, who arranged for foundation support for Broch and at whose country place in Connecticut Broch stayed for a long time while writing *The Death of Virgil*. Soon after his arrival in America, Broch was invited to spend a summer in the Yaddo artist colony, but, fearing that he had displeased its director, he never applied for another stay. The American Academy of Arts and Literature awarded him a prize for literature in 1939, and when his *Death of Virgil* was finally published in 1945, it was respectfully, even admiringly, reviewed by such critics as Waldo Frank and Aldous Huxley. But the book failed to make much impact in the world of letters. It received a front-page review in the *New York Times Book Review*, which, owing to a trucking strike, reached few readers. Largely responsible for Broch's lack of influence was his self-conscious decision to limit his relations in America almost exclusively to fellow emigrés, although his highly idiosyncratic writing style may have been a contributing factor. Broch deliberately refused to build new networks of acquaintances and peers in this country. Insofar as the American cultural landscape was concerned, Broch made hardly a dent on it.

For seven years Broch stayed in Princeton, in the home of a fellow

emigré, the writer Erich von Kahler (Erich Kahler). When he decided
to marry for a second time toward the end of his life (his previous marriage having ended in divorce many years earlier in Europe), he married
the widow of the art historian Meier-Graefe, a fellow emigré. *The Death
of Virgil* was issued in both German and English by a fellow emigré, Kurt
Wolff, then publisher of the Pantheon Press[2]. The two most important
essays about his work published in America during his lifetime were
written by Hannah Arendt, a fellow emigré, who also provided the introduction to the paperback edition of *The Death of Virgil.*

Broch was a compulsive letter writer who often complained that this
compulsion had hampered his creative output. Leafing through his collection of letters written during his American sojourn, one realizes that
very few of them are addressed to Americans, apart from business letters and exchanges with Aldous Huxley and with Waldo Frank, the latter in German. Of the several hundred letters published after his death,
only a handful are addressed to American recipients; all the rest are to
fellow emigrés and, after the end of the war, to European correspondents.

Broch's letters provide good evidence that he was well aware of his
isolation in this country. He wrote from Princeton to Mrs. Else Spitzer,
also a fellow emigré: "It is curious that you, and probably also Fritz [her
husband], are still bothered by so-called homelessness. I am much more
realistic in this respect. Given all my love for certain landscapes, I have,
through all my life, felt exclusively in a diaspora."[3] He wrote to the same
correspondent a few years later, in 1949: "How do you get the idea that
this country makes me happy? The pursuit of happiness [English in the
original]. Swabian pessimism has originated a beautiful motto, 'I am
everywhere a bit grudgingly (*ungern*)', and that applies to me too. It is
also true, however, that I am everywhere a little bit willingly (*gern*), first
because I have a thoroughly abstract relation to the here and now, and
wish no interference with my need for solitude"[4]

When Broch was asked toward the end of his life about American
influences on his writings, he replied in a lengthy letter, of which these
are the highlights: "As far as *I* can see [American influences] are to be
rated as *zero*. And that seems to me quite right. . . . And so I consider
the question as to the influence of America on immigrant authors as
very badly posed. To be sure, one can talk about literary influences, for
example of the influence of modern technique of novel writing (from
Dreiser to Hemingway to Wolfe); but to experience these one doesn't
have to come to America, just as one has not to go to Russia to come
under the influence of Dostoievski. And finally the influence of language. But here also, yes, here above all, childhood impressions are decisive. . . . The great stylists were unilingual in their childhood, and al-

most all of those who later changed to another language are easily given to a forced style"[5] Finally, when asked to evaluate America's influence on him personally, Broch allowed that he was deeply influenced by American democracy, but failed to go into particulars.

Throughout his long stay in this country, Broch refused to widen his circle of associates and to admit American newcomers to it. He lived among German exiles, shielded within a cocoon of old friends and acquaintances from contact with Americans, their cultural life, and their literary institutions. His work shows no signs of his stay in America—it might as well have been written anywhere else. Similarly, and more important for the theme of this book, his influence on American culture also seems to have been slight. To be sure, a specialist in German or comparative literature may refer to him on occasion, but while there is a profusion of criticism and scholarship on Broch in Germany and other European countries, there is almost none in this country. Although specialists may sometimes discuss him as a towering figure in modernist literature, he has made no impact on American culture comparable to that of Mann, Joyce, or Proust. His books are not much read nowadays in this country; Americans, whom he rejected as potential associates and readers, have in turn ignored him.

In the last years of his life, even though he had been offered a publishing contract for a new novel by Alfred Knopf, Hermann Broch decided to lay literature aside and to devote himself to systematic philosophy and ethical commitment to the plight of his fellow exiles.

Thomas Mann (1875–1955): Insider Yet Outsider

At first blush, the American period in the life of Thomas Mann, who lived in America from 1939 until a few years before his death, seems wholly at variance with that of Hermann Broch (see pp. 236–38). Mann had already achieved a towering reputation by the time he came to this country, and he was received accordingly. Not only did men of letters and leaders of the arts vie for his attention, but so did the high and mighty world of politics. He spoke at the Library of Congress and a great number of universities, from which he received many honorary degrees. He was enthusiastically acclaimed wherever he made an appearance. President Roosevelt and his wife, Eleanor, invited him to the White House and to Hyde Park. Leading magazine and book publishers time and again asked him for contributions. Translations of his earlier work as well as of the books he wrote in America, particularly the last volume of the Joseph cycle, *Joseph the Provider* (1944; 1st Eng. ed.), and his great *Doctor Faustus* (1948), were eagerly read and exhaustively evaluated by reviewers and literary critics. His great political speeches on "The Problem of Freedom," on "War and Democracy," and many other subjects were beamed by the Voice of America to Germany and the rest of Europe. Thomas Mann became, in a way, an American institution. He seemed to be firmly ensconced in the inner core of American cultural affairs.

Mann was proud of the impact he made on Americans; again and again he mentioned his encounters with American political or literary personages. Whether it was poet Archibald MacLeish, actors Charles Laughton or Charlie Chaplin, publicist Walter Lippman, or politicians like Francis Biddle, Mann gratefully records having met such people and profiting from his conversations with them. Moreover, whereas Hermann Broch wrote his letters almost exclusively to refugees and other Europeans, Mann's correspondence with Agnes E. Meyer, the wife of the powerful publisher of the *Washington Post* and herself a well-known

journalist and writer, continued for a great number of years. And yet, a
closer perusal of his autobiographical writings and letters, as well as the
testimony of his wife, paints a somewhat different picture.[1]

Soon after his arrival in the United States, Mann moved to Princeton
to lecture at the university. Though he had pleasant relations with Dean
Christian Gauss and others of the Princeton faculty, his more intimate
associates were largely fellow refugees. As one of his biographers, Roman Karst, puts it, "The Manns' house in Princeton became from the
first day on a kind of spiritual center of the German immigration in the
United States."[2] Eric Kahler, Hermann Broch, and Albert Einstein lived
in the immediate vicinity and engaged in sustained intellectual intercourse with Mann. Other close friends such as Franz Werfel, Bruno Walter, and Max Reinhardt were frequent guests. It was in the circle of these
men and women that Mann was able to exchange ideas, test out new
projects, and find intellectual companionship. It is to them that he would
from time to time read chapters from works in progress. One gains the
strong impression that in the Princeton years Mann, though highly appreciative of his enthusiastic reception in America, was still very dependent on his audience of fellow exiles.

This pattern continued after the Manns moved to the West Coast, to
the house they built in Pacific Palisades. Some of their Princeton friends
followed them there, but now their circle of refugee associates was considerably enlarged by a number of exiled artists and writers who had
moved to southern California. Such well-known German writers as Alfred
Doeblin, Alfred Polgar, and Walter Mehring were among those who had
found temporary employment in the movie industry, more often as the
result of an act of charity than because of their productive contributions.
Others, such as Lion Feuchtwanger and Franz Werfel, had succeeded in
reaching a large audience in America and lived in comparative luxury
in the Hollywood area. In these years, Los Angeles was rapidly becoming a center of musical culture; Arnold Schoenberg resided there permanently, while his great rival, Igor Stravinsky, established temporary
residence. Major refugee conductors such as Bruno Walter and Otto
Klemperer also made the Hollywood area their headquarters. All these
artists and writers, as well as others, such as the German novelists Bruno
and Leonard Frank and Alfred Neumann and the sociologist-philosopher
Max Horkheimer, became frequent guests in the Manns' home. They
clearly formed a fairly close-knit intellectual community; they were linked
to each other by a common cultural background, but also by multiple
common interests and cultural assumptions.

As is to be expected in such relatively closely bound intellectual communities, in addition to mutual support and admiration, there was a
great deal of tension, backbiting, and jealous competition. Some people

whom Mann had supported in the beginning—Alfred Doeblin, for example—later turned against him for reasons that Mann apparently never understood. Just as in the Paris emigration of the nineteenth century so movingly described by Alexander Herzen in his *Memoirs,* the coming together of so many strong egos, some of them suffering from lack of recognition and others conspicuously successful, generated a good deal of friction and even of subjacent paranoia. Yet common bonds were also established and strengthened in the forge of common fate. It would appear, for example, that Thomas Mann and his brother Heinrich (who had also moved to the Los Angeles area) grew closer to each other during these years than they had ever been before. The tensions between the politically engaged Heinrich and his loftily detached brother, which had separated them ever since World War I, were resolved in shared exile.[3]

The circle of refugees surrounding Thomas Mann provided social and intellectual support. It is to these men and women that he turned when he needed advice and counsel. More particularly, when he embarked on his last great work, *Doctor Faustus,* the story of a diabolical German musician, he consulted the members of his circle who had musical knowledge superior to his own. The key role in regard to the musical parts of the book was assumed by the musician-philosopher Theodor Adorno, a neighbor of the Manns, to whose intimate involvement with the musical aspects of the work Mann repeatedly testified. Arnold Schoenberg and other musicians were also frequently consulted. Mann, of course, read assiduously, as was his custom in such cases, in the history of German music, but it seems that most of the time it was Adorno and others of his circle who guided him to the relevant literature.

Mann's dependence on his circle is poignantly revealed in a letter dated November 27, 1945. There he wrote: "[Bruno Frank] is now dead, and Werfel is dead, the widows left for the East, also Leonard Frank, a most interesting human being, went there, and it is becoming lonely. There is enough sociability, but there is hardly anybody with whom one can talk," and he adds as an afterthought, "at least in German."[4]

One has the strong impression that Mann used his Princeton and California circles as a kind of oasis from which he would occasionally venture out into, not hostile, but basically alien territory. He lived, so he must have felt, among friendly strangers—but strangers nevertheless. He repeatedly expressed his admiration for America. He loved Franklin D. Roosevelt, and it appears that Roosevelt provided major characteristics for his portrait of Joseph the Provider. America was to him the exemplar of a democratic nation. When, in the McCarthy era, the country turned toward the politics of reaction, Mann left for Switzerland, deeply disappointed, like a spurned lover.

In assessing Mann's impact on American culture during his stay here, one faces a major stumbling block. He was, of course, already well known before he came. The big American sales of his books (they usually sold between 20,000 and 40,000 copies; *The Buddenbrooks* sold many more), as well as the profusion of critical attention he had received before his arrival, testify to this fact. One might thus argue that he would have left a major imprint on American literature and cultural life even if he had never come here. Yet it would seem that the many years of personal exposure to American audiences, as well as the adulatory attention paid him by the mass media and by cultural and political leaders, contributed to Mann's growing reputation. I vividly remember one of his lectures at the University of Chicago where, despite the Germanic stiffness of his presentation, a large student audience was enthralled by his lecture. It would be hard to believe that many of them did not go to the library afterward to take out some of his books, which they otherwise might never have read.

Though he commented on things American in his lectures, Mann never dealt with American themes in his fictional work. This seems evidence of his feeling that, being only inorganically linked to the American landscape, he could not deal with things American in an authentic manner. He read very few modern American authors and had only few and fleeting contacts with them.[5] What Alfred Kazin has said about the creation of *Joseph and His Brothers* may also apply to Mann's other work written in this country: "Mann's unweaving the Bible into a modern novel somehow depended on his ability to live in Princeton and Hollywood without quite taking in the sounds around him."[6]

Living in Olympian detachment within a protective circle of refugee friends and associates, which helped to keep alive his profound ties to European and especially German culture, Mann, though he became a public institution in America, remained a European artist, albeit an artist who had the gift of appealing to a variety of American audiences when he evoked perennial human problems over and above national cultural traditions.

Vladimir Nabokov (1899–1977):
Reluctant Insider

When Vladimir Nabokov arrived in America in 1940, he had an asset that most other European refugees did not: full command of the English language.[1] Born of high-status Russian parents (his father was a leading Russian liberal who fled Russia and its revolution in 1919), the young Nabokov was able to attend Trinity College, Cambridge, where he studied French and German literature, before establishing residence in Germany and later in Paris. When he came to this country, even though he was by then a recognized master of Russian literature, he immediately made the decision to become a writer in English. In fact, even before coming here, while still in Paris, he had written his first novel in English, *The Real Life of Sebastian Knight* (1959). Nabokov later testified to "the intensity of pain which he experienced at the loss of his native language." He told his biographer that "it equalled in many respects and was a logical continuation of the pain he had experienced at the loss of Russia."[2] Be that as it may, his command of idiomatic English was a substantial advantage to this newcomer. He resolved to become an English writer because, as distinct from the writers discussed so far, he did not wish to live and work in a subcultural enclave in America. He wanted to immerse himself in the mainstream of American intellectual and artistic life. In this he succeeded superbly, and in a very short time.

The happenstance that very soon after his arrival in this country Nabokov met Edmund Wilson, then the literary editor of *The New Republic*, gave strength to his resolve. Wilson was to become his major guide and mentor in regard to the ways and byways of literary life in America.

Here is how he met Wilson. Soon after his arrival, Nabokov had tried to interest literary agents in translations of his Russian novels, but to no avail. However, his first novel in English was accepted by *New Directions* on the recommendation of the literary critic Harry Levin, who had been alerted to it by Nabokov's Russian refugee friend, the historian Michael Karpovich, Levin's colleague at Harvard. Delmore Schwartz, then a rising star in poetry, had also recommended the novel to James Laughlin, the publisher of *New Directions*. Laughlin in his turn brought the book to Wilson's attention. Wilson soon invited Nabokov to do a number of critical pieces for *The New Republic* and also smoothed the way for him to do another series for the *New York Sun*. As a result of these reviews, Nabokov was asked to do a review for *The New York Times Book Review,* and soon afterward two of his Russian short stories were accepted by *The Atlantic Monthly*. After this auspicious beginning, Nabokov's name never disappeared from the pages of major American publications. *The New Yorker* in particular, again mainly because Wilson smoothed the way, printed a host of Nabokov's stories and other writings over the years.

Again largely through Wilson, Nabokov was quickly introduced to some of the central figures in American literary life. Sometimes staying in Wilson's flat in New York, Nabokov there met Allen Tate, poet and literary critic, as well as a then rising star, poet Robert Lowell. Meeting Wilson in Cambridge or staying with him on Cape Cod, he was able to reinforce his friendship with Harry Levin, who tried unsuccessfully to secure a permanent appointment for him at Harvard, and with William James's son Billy. Mary McCarthy, who was married to Wilson during the years Wilson and Nabokov established their ties, liked Nabokov a great deal and was later moved to devote some fine critical commentaries to his work.[3]

Still in his first year in America, Nabokov was placed on the lecture-circuit roster of the Institute of International Education. He delivered a series of lectures at Stanford on creative writing, drama, and Russian literature and also lectured at Wellesley College, where he was soon to accept a position as a resident lecturer. No wonder that Nabokov could write to a friend in Europe roughly a year after his arrival: "I am convinced that you will find work here without difficulty. This is a cultured and exceedingly diverse country. The only thing you must do is deal with genuine Americans and don't get involved with the local Russian emigration."[4]

Not that Nabokov strictly followed his own advice in his own life and in regard to his own interests. He spent a good deal of his time with Russian exiles, and he depicted their lives in some of his work, above all in his wonderful tragicomic portrait of a fellow Russian emigré in *Pnin* (1957). (The circle of Russian exiles depicted there is closely modeled on the social life at the Vermont summer retreat of his friend Karpovich.) Yet Nabokov, after his existential break with his native language when he came here, wished to be considered "an American writer, born in Russia and educated in England." When a French journalist hinted to him that *Lolita* was an attack on America, Nabokov answered: "mais j'adore l'Amérique, c'est mon pays." And to another French journalist he said, "Quant à l'Amérique, elle m'a offert tout ce que la Russie n'a pas pu me donner."[5]

None of this implies that Nabokov was especially close to many American writers and critics. Wilson was probably his most intimate friend, and even that friendship came to an end over a literary quarrel. But even so, as his biographer Andrew Field puts it, "He was quite friendly (much more than he ever had been with West Europeans during his first period of exile) with many people during his twenty-year residence."

As a lecturer at Wellesley, and also doing research on his beloved butterflies as a Fellow of the Museum of Comparative Zoology at Harvard in the 1940s, the holder of a chair in literature at Cornell from 1948–58, the recipient of two Guggenheim Fellowships and an American Academy of Arts and Letters award, contributor to all the major literary reviews, author of many books—some of them translated, some written in English—Vladimir Nabokov had already made a considerable mark in American letters when he published *Lolita*, but the book suddenly propelled him into the forefront of literary attention and made him for the first time the author of a best-seller.

Lolita draws our attention because it is the only novel by a refugee so far discussed that has an American setting. What is more, the closely observed reporting of American life-styles, and the exquisite attention to the language of American teenagers that one finds in this work, make it as "typically American" a book as *The Great Gatsby*. As John Updike has put it, "*Lolita* brims with a formidable density of observed detail."[6] Nabokov had made detailed notes on the world of American motels and fast-food joints on his trip to Stanford and after, and he took a long series of bus rides during his stay in Ithaca in order to observe the peculiarities of American teenage jargon. This is why *Lolita*, as his biographer Andrew Field puts it, "speaks in an American idiom whose purity has seldom been equalled in modern American literature."[7] *Lolita* may possibly become as emblematic of American culture as that other novel about a teenager, *Catcher in the Rye*.

Nabokov left America in 1959 to establish permanent residence in Switzerland, returning here only on occasional visits. Most of his novels deal with the milieu of the Russian emigration or with events in a European setting. Much of his writing in later years consists of commentaries on or translations of Russian classics. Nevertheless, Nabokov has never ceased to be in the forefront of attention of American literary life. Most major literary critics, from Stanley Hyman to John Updike, Fred Dupee to Frank Kermode, have commented on his work with close attention. Nabokov has permanently enriched American culture.

In Nabokov's case it is much easier than in the case of Thomas Mann to arrive at the conclusion that his stay in America enabled him to make a major contribution to American cultural life. His concern with things American, even though it always remained what Robert K. Merton has called "detached concern," enabled him to probe dimensions of American culture that other emigré writers never fathomed. This is why he became a genuinely American writer despite his deep and enduring involvement with Russian culture. His ability to capture American experience on the wing, just as he captured rare American specimens of his beloved butterflies, stood him in very good stead in transmuting his impressions into artistic creations. Having multiple links to American artistic and intellectual life, even though many of them may have been rather weak, allowed Nabokov to shed the parochial disdain for America that many of his fellow exiles harbored. It would be foolish to assert that he became a hundred percent American, but it is, I believe, correct to say that he contributed almost as much to American culture and letters as his fellow Slav, Joseph Conrad, contributed to the British.

What another exiled writer, the Polish poet Czeslav Milosz, wrote about the Russian exile poet Joseph Brodsky also applies to Nabokov. "He accomplished," Milosz wrote, "what previous generations of Russian emigré writers were unable to do: to make the lands of exile, however reluctantly, their own, to take possession through the poetic word."[8]

VII
The Humanities

Introduction

The many spheres of humanistic scholarship in America were unevenly developed when the refugee scholars arrived, and this uneven development also helped to determine the impact of the Europeans in various fields of inquiry. Art history, though it had entered a phase of rapid expansion in the immediate post–World War I period, was still under-developed in America and profited hugely from the fresh streams of thought, largely rooted in German historicism and *Geisteswissenschaft,* which were brought to the attention of their native-born American colleagues by a distinguished group of Continental scholars. As a result, European-style art history found for itself an enduring place in the American cultural landscape. In a similar way, structural linguistics as represented by European scholars managed to replace to a large extent an earlier American tradition of historical philology, though profiting from an empirically oriented approach to structural linguistics that had developed in America prior to the coming of refugee scholars.

In literary studies, by contrast, even though refugee scholars attained positions of influence in America, and even though their scholarship and teaching bore fruits here, one gains the impression that they helped to enrich previous approaches without developing new lines of inquiry, except in comparative literature. In historical scholarship as well as in the classics, one likewise perceives that refugee scholars significantly enriched teaching and research in America, especially by stressing the German habit of looking at cultural phenomena through spectacles ground in the tradition of *Geisteswissenschaft,* but that they proved less innovative in their approach than their contemporaries in art history or linguistics.

It would seem, then, that in all these cases the impact of refugee scholars was largely conditioned by the previously existing state of affairs in America in their respective field of study. They helped innovate and reinvigorate fields in which new seeds of thought had already begun to sprout. In fields that had already developed vigorously before their coming, their impact was less significant.

Roman Jakobson (1896–1982): Elder Statesman of Linguistics

Roman Jakobson, who has been described by Noam Chomsky as "the elder statesman of linguistics" and who is among the handful of scholars who have shaped American linguistics during this century, came to America as a refugee in 1941. Despite initial difficulties in finding an academic position, he achieved eminence as a scholar teaching linguistics as well as Slavic languages and literatures, first at Columbia and later at Harvard and MIT. By his own count, about 100 of his former students are now teaching in various American universities.[1] His influence has been pervasive.

Jakobson was born of Jewish parents in Moscow in 1896. His father was a chemist with wide intellectual interests and his son was brought up speaking both French and Russian. The youth was taken to attend many poetry recitals, and he began to write poetry at a very early age. In 1914 he enrolled in the philological faculty of Moscow University, where he joined a number of fellow students in founding the Moscow Linguistic Circle, over which he presided from 1915 to 1920. The circle had members with backgrounds in philosophy and linguistics as well as students of literature and poets. It was concerned with practical and poetical language but also with folklore and ethnology. In the 1920s, together with a comparable circle in Leningrad, it helped to establish an important school of literary criticism known as Russian Formalism. Later in the decade, the Soviet authorities looked upon the development of Formalism with increasingly jaundiced eyes and eventually suppressed it. Foreseeing what was to come, Jakobson left Russia in the late 1920s and moved to Prague.

During his years in Czechoslovakia, Jakobson developed a distinctive style of structural analysis of linguistic phenomena and also published studies in folklore, sociolinguistics, poetics, medieval Slavic culture and literature, and the historical phonology of various Slavic languages, as well as literary criticism and essays on painting, theater, and films. In

1926 he was one of the founders of the famous Prague Linguistic Circle and served as its vice-president. The Prague Circle soon achieved a great deal of attention in the international linguistic community, and Jakobson himself, given his widespread contributions and interests, was recognized not only as an innovator in linguistics but also as a Slavic scholar of international eminence. Nevertheless, he had to wait until 1937 to receive a tenured appointment at the Masaryk University in Brno. Older professional colleagues, still largely preoccupied with historical philology, apparently looked askance at the young innovator, whose structural linguistic and synchronic studies of linguistic phenomena threatened their established position. The story was to repeat itself a few years later, when Jakobson moved to the United States.[2]

When the Nazis took over Czechoslovakia, Jakobson fled to Scandinavia in the spring of 1939. He first lived in Denmark and Norway, but when Norway was invaded in April 1940, he escaped by walking across the border to Sweden. He finally came to the United States in June 1941.

Structural linguistics, largely owing to the work of Edward Sapir and Leonard Bloomfield, already enjoyed a firm position in America. Jakobson's reception here was nevertheless decidedly cool. This can be accounted for by both theoretical and practical factors. Jakobson's approach differed from that of most of his American colleagues in that he rejected their pronounced empiricism in favor of a more general and theoretical perspective. Historically oriented philologists, in their turn, totally rejected synchronic and structural approaches. But more practical considerations also played their part. These were years in which positions in university departments were scarce, and many younger American linguists felt, as one of Jakobson's colleagues has put it, that "positions were snatched from under their noses and given to European refugees." Jakobson himself later wrote that these "chauvinistic protectionists . . . launched quasi-ideological arguments in order to repress competition."[3]

Jakobson's first appointment in America was at the "University in Exile," the Graduate Faculty of the New School. Here Jakobson met a fellow-refugee member of the faculty, the young anthropologist Claude Lévi-Strauss, whose subsequent work came to be profoundly influenced by Jakobson's structural linguistics. Jakobson's influence on American students, however, had to wait until he moved to a less marginal teaching environment.

The rapid expansion of Slavic studies and the lessening of competition for jobs in the postwar years enabled Jakobson to obtain a professorship at a leading university. In the fall of 1946 he became a professor of Czechoslovakian studies at Columbia University. Three years later he moved to Harvard, where he taught until his retirement in 1967. From 1957 on he held a concurrent appointment at MIT. Jakobson's move to

Cambridge made Harvard the leading center of Slavic studies in the country. A large percentage of American Slavic scholars were trained by him, and a fair number of important linguists were also his students there. Many leading linguists, who were not Jakobson's students, such as Noam Chomsky and Charles Hockett, attended his lectures. Jakobson has said that wherever he went to lecture at American universities he was surrounded by former students in general linguistics and in Slavic studies.[4]

Jakobson's erudition was legendary. He could lecture in Russian, French, Polish, Czech, German, or English, although it has been said that he spoke "fluent Russian in six languages." He read about twenty-five Western European languages. His knowledge of modern literature and art may have been almost as extensive as his knowledge of medieval Slavonic. Indeed, he said that he was drawn to linguistics not so much by the teaching of linguists as by "the great artists of my youth—Picasso, Braque, Le Corbusier, Joyce, and Stravinsky, and the great Russian poet Khlebnikov." The wit and wisdom of Jakobson as a conversationalist and lecturer have likewise become legendary. When it was once suggested that Vladimir Nabokov be offered an appointment in the Slavic department at Harvard, Jakobson is reputed to have said that he didn't have anything against elephants but he wouldn't appoint one a professor of zoology.[5]

Jakobson's obituary in the *New York Times* for July 23, 1982, so well captures his personal style that I shall reproduce a part of it here:

> Harvard, which treasures its eccentrics, found a gem in Dr. Jakobson. His flat looked as disheveled as his hair. There was a huge desk littered with papers. Books were scattered everywhere and were piled up even under the windows. All the local Slavic students (and many who weren't) trickled in at night for little chats, which were, in truth, private theatricals, with Dr. Jakobson talking in several languages, gesticulating with both hands and then running a hand through his unkempt hair.
>
> Once when his small green lovebird escaped, Dr. Jakobson spent the night scouring the neighborhood and trying to coax it back to its cage. When it did return, the story goes, the scholar censured the bird in language he thought appropriate and then locked it up in its webbed cage.

Despite the rocky start of his career in America, Jakobson became a leading figure in both linguistics and Slavic studies after he moved to Columbia and then to Harvard. Never averse to polemical exchanges or reticent about expressing sharply critical views on ideas he disapproved of, he continued to flourish, as he once put it, "now and then in hostile, and often in amicable contexts."[6]

It is impossible to describe the many specialized studies Jakobson produced over his years in America in Slavic languages and literature and in related subjects; I shall hence limit myself here to indicating briefly his key contribution to structural linguistics.

Jakobson's point of departure in linguistic analysis, first developed by him and his associates in the Prague Circle and then extended in this country, involved a means-end model of language. Language is seen first of all as a tool or instrument of communication. As a goal-directed activity, it has to be described and analyzed in terms of the functions it performs. Yet such functional analysis of language cannot be done without concomitant attention to its structure.[7] Each language forms a structural system, or rather a system of subsystems which may be only imperfectly adjusted to one another. While the goals of the language user may be referential, expressive, or directive, these goals can be reached only with the structural resources that a language offers.

Jakobson's major contribution to linguistics was in his study of the sounds of speech. Each language, Jakobson found, has its own system of distinctive sounds, its own system of *phonemes*. These phonemes in their turn, are not just arbitrary aggregates but form distinctive patterns that can be analyzed as binary features. The elements of this view were elaborated by Jakobson in close collaboration with another member of the Prague Circle, Nikolaj Trubetzkoy, and profited a good deal from the work of de Saussure and the American linguist Edward Sapir. Jakobson's elaboration of these views, especially his central idea (which deeply influenced Lévi-Strauss) that phonemes consist of bundles of distinctive features in binary patterns, seems peculiarly his own. The crucial idea that functional contrasts characterize the relationships of the entities comprising phonological systems was later extended by Jakobson to many other areas of linguistic studies. This emphasis on binary analyses, while not shared by all linguists, has been accepted by many.

Although by no means all American linguists have been convinced by Jakobson's version of structuralism in linguistics, he has been instrumental in changing attitudes in linguistics in such a way that structural and synchronic studies have now largely replaced historically oriented philology and diachronic analyses of language change.

Jakobson's pioneering analyses of the pattern of sounds in the language of children has opened up a whole new area of investigation. Chomsky's distinction between surface and underlying forms can be said to derive in large part from Jakobson's work. While American contributions tended to be cast in a strongly empiricist and positivist tradition that was concerned with the analysis and description of observable features of a language, Jakobson's work drew attention to the need to examine relations beneath surface manifestations and stressed the importance of underlying, implied, unobservable features. This mode of approach enhanced opportunities for abstract generalizations and the investigation of universals. Jakobson's work is dominated by the search for invariance in the underlying structures of semiotic systems which seem on the surface to be characterized by a great deal of variability. Finally, Jakobson helped to lead linguistics out of its previous isolation from other disciplines because he took a more general perspective, placing it in the framework of communication and information theory. He himself is the best person to indicate the synthesizing breadth of his theoretical mind:

> One cannot but follow Lévi-Strauss's triadic conception that in a society communication operates on three different levels: exchange of messages, exchange of commodities (namely, goods and services), and exchange of women (or, perhaps a more generalizing formulation, exchange of mates). Therefore, linguistics (jointly with other semiotic disciplines), economics, and finally kinship and marriage studies approach the same kinds of problems on different strategic levels and really pertain to the same field.[10]

Jakobson's papers totaled more than six hundred, fifteen of which were published in the last year of his life, 1981–82. *Dialogues,* published by the MIT Press in September 1982, a few months after his death at age eighty-six, consists of conversations between Jakobson and his wife, Krystyna Pomorska, professor of Russian literature at MIT.

Erwin Panofsky (1892–1968) and the Influence of Refugee Art Historians in America

Contrary to what is often believed, the field of art history was not introduced to America by refugees from central Europe. To be sure, the subject originated in German scholarship, and "its native tongue," as an American scholar expressed it to Panofsky, "was German."[1] A full professorship in the subject was established in Goettingen as early as 1813, and the Germans and Austrians were international leaders in the field for a century after that. Yet when central European refugee scholars began to arrive on these shores in the 1930s they found a flourishing field of scholarship.[2]

Having originated before the turn of the century as the private hobby of such men of letters as Henry Adams and Charles Eliot Norton, American art history, slowly differentiating itself from connoisseurship, art criticism, and related subjects, evolved into an autonomous discipline early in the twentieth century and especially after World War I. Its early practitioners, having as yet no native tradition to draw upon, had come from classical philology, philosophy, literature, even theology, and they had slowly to disentangle their field from practical art instruction and art appreciation. Some of them were private collectors; others were men of means for whom art history was an avocation rather than a full-time vocation. But, in spite of all initial difficulties and impediments, the work of such native American scholars as A. Kingsley Porter, Charles Rufus Morey, and others had so impressed the international fellowship of art historians that by the 1920s American art history had become securely institutionalized, especially at such centers as Harvard and Princeton. The decade from 1923 to 1933, as Erwin Panofsky has written, "looked like a Golden Age."[3] It was at the height of these developments that the refugee scholars arrived on the American scene.

Refugee art historians, like refugee physicists, came at the right time.

Not only did they have the benefit of a flowering native scholarship, but this was also a period when new resources from collectors and sponsors became available. The Museum of Modern Art, the Institute of Fine Arts of New York University, the Princeton Institute for Advanced Study, all endowed by generous donations from wealthy families, had just opened their doors, and a number of important private collections had become available for scholarly research. Soon after the refugees' arrival, New York City came to be recognized as the capital of modern art in the world. It is not likely that American art history would have developed as quickly and powerfully in the succeeding decades had the refugee scholars not left their mark on it, but it is also true that they could not have made such a mark were it not for the fact that they found a milieu which powerfully enhanced their various individual efforts. After their arrival, the residual influences of rich and well-born connoisseurs largely disappeared from the American scene, and philosophical and historicist *Geisteswissenschaft* assumed prominence. But some of these developments, though powerfully supported by the new arrivals, also grew organically out of previous American trends.

On balance, the judgment of a prominent American art historian seems to hit the mark: "By the early 1930s, after a decade of brilliant contributions, art history in America remained sporadic and provincial. It was the task of the refugees from Germany to establish it as a unified discipline and to bring it abreast of continental practice."[4]

The flowering of art history prior to the arrival of the refugee scholars seems to have been largely responsible for the fact that at least the more prominent among them found it relatively easy to gain positions in university departments and research institutions. This is especially remarkable in view of the fact that the early generation of American art historians tended all too frequently to be genteel—or even not so genteel—anti-Semites who previously had made efforts to limit the art historical fraternity to a private domain of well-born Christian gentlemen. These barriers to entry seem to have broken down under the influx of many internationally famous Europeans and persons of worldwide reputation who simply could not be refused positions without making discrimination blatantly obvious.

Although there was some residual resentment among native-born scholars toward the refugee art historians, there were also some notably generous efforts by them to find positions for their exiled colleagues. For example, the Princeton medievalist Charles Rufus Morey invited a refugee fellow medievalist, Kurt Weitzman, to Princeton even though his approach differed in major respects from Weitzman's. Walter W. S. Cook, who was largely responsible for establishing the New York University Institute of Fine Arts, found permanent chairs there for, among others, Walter Friedlaender, Karl Lehmann, and, initially, Erwin Panofsky. Panofsky recalled that Cook used to say, "Hitler is my best friend; he shakes the tree and I collect the apples."[5]

The career of Erwin Panofsky, the acknowledged dean of refugee art historians, illustrates these developments. Panofsky knew the American scene before he arrived here as a refugee. He first came to America to teach at the new Institute of Fine Arts of New York University in the fall of 1931, on leave from his position as professor of art history at the University of Hamburg, and then spent three years teaching alternate terms in Hamburg and New York. When the Nazis came to power, Panofsky resolved to stay in America, and after a short period of teaching at Princeton and New York University, he joined the newly constituted Institute for Advanced Study in Princeton, where he stayed until his retirement. He continued to teach at the Institute of Fine Arts of New York University until his death.[6]

At Hamburg, Panofsky had been one of the most prominent members of the Warburg Institute, that extraordinary center of art studies founded by Aby Warburg, a member of a prominent Jewish banking family who had resolved early in the century to devote his share of the family fortune to creating the institute and library that bore his name. An enormously gifted art historian himself, Warburg was instrumental in attracting to his institute a galaxy of highly productive and talented art historians and historians of culture who shared his passion to bring art history into the mainstream of *Geisteswissenschaft*.

The Warburg approach, perpetuated in America largely through Panofsky, his former coworkers, and later disciples, was relatively unconcerned with the formal characteristics of works of art and even less concerned with the connoisseurship best represented in association with an American point of view by Bernard Berenson. It focused instead on the links between artistic productions, symbolic representation, and underlying philosophical trends. Thus Panofsky in his early work in Germany attempted to trace the variegated ways in which the classical heritage was received and refracted in Renaissance art. Panofsky called this type of study iconology, as distinct from iconography. Iconography, so he held, was primarily concerned with the identification of the persons and objects, and particularly the motives, that were contained in given artistic representations. It focused on the conventional symbolic meanings attributed by the artist to a given work. Thus, a depiction of thirteen men seated at a dinner table may be identified as The Last Supper of Christ and his disciples. Iconology, in contradistinction, while based on iconographic analysis, deals with the work of art as a symptom of underlying philosophical trends of which the artist may or may not be aware. It attempts to uncover links to the historical, political, scientific, religious, and economic tendencies of the age in which the work was produced. Attempting to unravel the connection between image and thought, it sees the work of art not only as an expression of the artist's personality but also as a manifestation of the prevailing intellectual atmosphere, the weltanschauung, at the time of its creation.

The Warburg approach, as it was brought to full fruition by Panofsky in this country, through its stress on both iconographic and iconological studies, brought the history of art out of its previous isolation and preponderant interest in such matters as authenticity, dating, and provenance and propelled it into the mainstream of cultural history. By shifting focus from purely formal elements and stressing concern with the historically and philosophically conditioned content of works of art, it linked art history to inquiry into all aspects of the history of the human mind. This is not to say that approaches of this type had been wholly absent from American art history prior to the coming of refugee art historians in general and proponents of the Warburg approach in particular; but they were systematized and given secure foundations by a group of refugee scholars who had been brought up in the German tradition of *Historismus* and *Geisteswissenschaft* as it had been developed in central Europe since the late eighteenth century. It continued the broad intellectual currents that ran from Winckelmann, Herder, Kant, and Hegel to Wilhelm Dilthey's work and Benedetto Croce's systematization of the logic of the *Geisteswissenschaften*.

It hardly behooves an outsider to the history of art to speculate on why Panofsky is generally considered the dean of the great scholars who brought the iconological and iconographic appraoches to America. Specialists have argued that Panofsky's unusually wide learning in a number of areas only loosely connected with art history, his amazing productivity, his wide-ranging curiosity, and his ability to immerse himself in a variety of cultural areas and historic periods account for his preeminence. Yet one feels that while all this is surely the case, there was also something about Panofsky's personality that contributed to his eminence and standing. He seems to have been an unusually generous man, able and willing to provide counsel and encouragement to younger scholars.[7] References to Panofsky's advice stud an unusually large number of works by younger scholars, both native-born and fellow refugees.

Panofsky's secure position throughout most of his American career at the Princeton Institute may also have contributed to his eminence. Over the years he succeeded in attracting an unusually gifted group of art historians to that institute. Hence to a certain extent he controlled the sluice of recruitment of younger scholars, both at Princeton and at the New York University Institute, with which he maintained close ties until the end of his life.

One other characteristic that may have helped to propel Panofsky into his eminent position needs to be mentioned briefly. Many of his contemporaries among refugee art historians maintained a somewhat aloof attitude toward things American. Though they were living and writing in the American cultural milieu, they were never fully part of the American cultural scene. This was not true of Panofsky. He made a determined effort to penetrate the mysteries of the American cultural tradition at the same time he was exploring the iconology of Italian, Dutch, or German art. Not that his writings on films or on the novelist Booth Tarkington match the profundity of his major work, but they testify, as do his many quotations from such native American writers as Henry James, to his effort to be part of the American scene.

Panofsky taught only sporadically as a guest professor in a number of American universities. His position at the Princeton Institute did not entail teaching duties. In an autobiography he pointed out that he never taught undergraduates in America. His influence was exerted mainly through his books, some of which, like his *Life and Art of Albrecht Dürer*,[8] went through several editions during his lifetime, and through his continued stream of intellectual exchanges in the form of both private letters and printed reviews.

Other refugee art historians did assume major teaching positions, not only at the New York University Institute, where for a time no fewer than five professorships were held by refugee scholars, but also in a variety of other colleges and universities. New York, Harvard, Columbia, and Princeton seem to have been most willing to turn to refugee scholars in an effort to revitalize American art history, but many other institutions followed in their footsteps. Campuses in the South, the Midwest, and the Far West for the first time began to offer art history courses, most of them taught by refugee scholars. What is more, European scholars who worked in the major universities of the Eastern seaboard trained many students who, in their turn, began to teach in the 1940s and 1950s in established or newly created departments of art history. The art history department of the new postwar Brandeis University, for example, consisted for a time almost entirely of scholars trained at New York University. In addition, many of the curators of leading museums throughout the country owe their training to the refugee scholars who taught in Eastern institutions.

Most, but not all, German and Austrian refugee scholars, whether formerly connected with the Warburg Institute or not, focused attention on the tradition inherited from *Geisteswissenschaft*. Max J. Friedlaender (1867–1958), for example, in his study of Early Dutch painting,[9] worked mainly in the older tradition of connoisseurship and was unconcerned with linking the works or art he analyzed, described, and classified to general intellectual or cultural conditions. His approach was nearer to Berenson's than to Panofsky's. Ernst Kris (1900–57), a Viennese art historian turned psychoanalyst under the direct guidance of Freud, published a widely discussed collection of essays entitled *Psychoanalytical Explorations in Art*,[10] in which he attempted to unravel the relationship between the artists' inner lives and their works, between unconscious processes and creative achievements.

While Kris attempted to put the insights of psychoanalysis at the service of art history, Rudolf Arnheim (1904–   ) relied on guidelines provided by Gestalt psychology, with its emphasis on patterns of perception and the uses of the notion of configuration in the appreciation of works of art.[11] It is interesting to note, if only as an aside, that a Marxist interpretation of art history never seems to have made much headway among refugee scholars in the U.S.A., whereas it produced important scholarly work by such men as the Hungarian-born Arnold Hauser and Frederick Antal in the apparently more congenial climate of Britain.

The native-born Princeton art historian and medievalist Charles Rufus Morey, who did yeoman's work in bringing refugee scholars into the mainstream of American academic life, once told one of them: "Your task is to train the men who will take your place."[12] Had he lived long enough, he would have been pleased to see to what extent they lived up to this injunction.

Somewhere between eighty and a hundred European art historians came to this country in the 1930s and later. Among them were many eminent men and women who had already established enviable reputations in their native lands, but there were also younger scholars who made their major contrbutions while in America. It is not the case, as I have argued, that they encountered virgin territory when they came here, but it remains true that their influence was such that one cannot write of the history of American scholarship in the visual arts without recognizing it. Over half of the contributions to W. Eugene Kleinbauer's widely used anthology, *Modern Perspectives in Western Art History* (1971), turn out to be by refugee scholars.

Erich Auerbach (1892–1957), Leo Spitzer (1887–1960), and René Wellek (1903–): Comparative Literature

Literary scholarship of course had a long and honorable history in American universities before European scholars arrived here as refugees. Yet it seems hardly open to doubt that such scholarship, and especially the comparative study of literature, made major strides in America after the arrival of European refugees in the 1930s and 1940s. I shall deal here only with three of them, although it would be possible to lengthen that list considerably.

The first American periodical devoted to comparative literature, *The Journal of Comparative Literature*, appeared as early as 1903, but it did not survive the year. Its successor, *Comparative Literature*, came only decades later, in 1949. American interest in comparative literature developed only after we slowly awakened from the slumber of political and cultural isolationism in the 1930s. *Comparative Literature* has been appearing regularly since the first issue and is today recognized internationally as a leading journal in its field. From its inception it thrived on the close collaboration of refugee scholars with their native American counterparts. Leo Spitzer, for example, contributed articles to five of the first six volumes of the journal.

Until René Wellek was appointed Professor of Slavic and Comparative Literatures at Yale in 1946, Yale had had no program and no department in comparative literature. At first Wellek was the only person with a full-time appointment; much later, one of his former students, Lowry Nelson, Jr., was added to the staff. A full-fledged department was not established until 1959; but Wellek directed some fifty dissertations there before his retirement in 1972.

When Harvard decided in 1945 to resuscitate a dormant program in comparative literature and entrusted Harry Levin with that task, Levin, perhaps the most renowned native-born scholar in that field, immediately brought in an Italian refugee, the Slavist Renato Poggioli, to help him revitalize the department's program of study.

All in all, the European literary scholars who arrived in America in the 1930s and 1940s helped to broaden and revitalize a field of study that until then had possessed a somewhat provincial and antiquarian character and had attracted few gifted students. Crocean idealism, German *Geisteswissenschaft,* Hegelianism or romanticism, psychoanalytical approaches to or close textual studies of, among many others, Dante and Vico—all these and many more ideas developed from the European refugees' leavening of American studies in comparative literature and related areas.

Erich Auerbach (1892–1957)

Although Auerbach spent only the last ten years of his life in America, he exerted considerable influence on American scholarship, not only through his papers and books written here, but perhaps even more through earlier work, especially his seminal study *Mimesis.* This book was first published in German in Switzerland shortly before its author's arrival here and was not translated into English until 1953.[1]

Erich Auerbach was born in Berlin in November 1892, the son of a distinguished Jewish merchant, and attended the French *lycée* in Berlin. He originally wanted to become a lawyer and after studying law at several German universities was granted the title of Doctor Juris by the University of Heidelberg at the unusually young age of twenty-one. But soon thereafter, perhaps because he had attended a French high school, Auerbach decided to devote himself to the study of Romance languages. In 1921 he received his doctoral degree in that subject. Although in the Weimar Republic it was somewhat easier for Jewish scholars to attain university positions than had been the case in the Kaiser's Germany, a Jewish origin was still an obstacle to obtaining academic appointments. This may account for the fact that Auerbach seems not to have sought an academic post but instead served as a librarian in the Prussian State Library in Berlin from 1923 to 1929. During these years he produced his first major book, *Dante: Poet of the Secular* (English translation, 1961). Steeped in Hegelian and neo-Hegelian Geisteswissenschaft, a tradition from which the author later largely detached himself but which was still the dominant tendency in Germany, the book received academic recognition and earned Auerbach the offer of a professorship in Romance philology at the University of Marburg in 1930. His dismissal from that position after the Nazis took power came later than it did for many of his colleagues, probably because he had fought in the war and was considered a war hero. Nevertheless, he was fired in 1936 and, there being few prospects for him in Western Europe or America, decided to accept a position at the newly created State University at Istanbul.[2]

Despite the fact that he had few students who were up to his exacting standards and the even greater handicap that Turkey did not possess the specialized libraries that would have enabled him to continue his customary scholarly work, Auerbach managed in miraculous fashion to compose his masterwork, *Mimesis*. This work, though rooted in an enormous amount of scholarly knowledge and dealing with an extraordinary range of European literary works, from the classics to the moderns, does not have a single footnote. Though he was permitted to use the library of the papal legate in Turkey, Auerbach was effectively cut off from recent journals and scholarly monographs. Like the Belgian historian Henri Pirenne, who wrote his most searching work while a prisoner of war in Germany, Auerbach made a virtue of necessity, compensating by breadth for an occasional lack of detailed depth. In *Mimesis* he managed to achieve panoramic dimensions. From Homer and the Bible to Virginia Woolf, he documented the gradual growth of "realism" in the Western literary tradition. The subtitle of *Mimesis* is "The Representation of Reality in Western Literature." Auerbach attempted to depict, in the words of Harry Levin, "the representation of reality by means of words, so that textual explanation becomes the key to a concrete understanding of the Occidental past." To Auerbach "realism" does not mean the special and narrow literary doctrine that emerged in the nineteenth century. To him, to quote Harry Levin again, "a mob scene under the Roman Empire and the stream of Mrs. Ramsay's consciousness in *To the Lighthouse* are equally real."[3]

Soon after the German publication of *Mimesis,* and perhaps because of its publication, Auerbach received his first American appointment, at Pennsylvania State University, in 1947. From then on, his scholarly work was no longer hampered by the lack of libraries and colleagues that he had experienced in Turkey. After one year at Pennsylvania State, where he would have received tenure had not a medical examination revealed a heart ailment, Auerbach spent a year at the Institute for Advanced Study in Princeton, where he met many of his fellow refugee scholars. Recognition by American scholars now came quickly. He was invited to give the prestigious Christian Gauss Seminar during his stay in Princeton. In 1950 he was called to Yale, where he not only found congenial colleagues such as the French-born Henri Peyre and the Czech refugee scholar René Wellek, but could pursue his studies in an environment that he considered "almost ideal." Some of his later work can be found in *Scenes from the Drama of European Literature,* originally published in German in 1951 but translated into English in 1959, two years after his death. Another collection of essays, *Literary Language and Its Public in*

Late Latin Antiquity and the Middle Ages, was also published after his death in the fall of 1957, just before he was scheduled to give a course on Dante at Harvard.

It is likely that had Auerbach been able to come to America immediately after his dismissal by the Nazis instead of spending so many years in the culturally barren Turkish educational establishment, he would have produced even more abundantly. Nevertheless, he made admirable use of adversity in producing his masterwork. Had he written *Mimesis* in America, it might have taken him many more years to finish because he would have felt obliged to consult many books and papers that were simply not available in Turkey.

Schooled in the tradition of German romanticism and Hegelianism, and beholden to a historicist tradition that rejected all absolutist interpretations in favor of what he called "historical perspectivism," Auerbach developed a complex interpretative scheme for the literary depiction of the self-interpretation of Western literature. This scheme, as his friend René Wellek put it with a characteristically ironic twist, provides "insights which are 'true' unhistorically. . . . In *Mimesis* he has written a book which is not only a great work of scholarship and a symptomatic pronouncement of our age, but a work of truth, insight, and art which cannot be superceded and made obsolete by mere historical change."[4] Even though he worked in America for only the last decade of his life, Auerbach left an indelible mark on American literary scholarship by reintroducing historicist approaches to criticism, which had been in danger of extinction under the flood of purely formalistic modes of interpretation.

Leo Spitzer (1887–1960)

Leo Spitzer was born in Vienna in 1887, to Jewish middle-class parents. He worked for his doctorate in his native city under the direction of the renowned professor of Romance languages, Wilhelm Meyer-Luebke, and received his degree in 1910 with a thesis on the techniques of word formation in the work of Rabelais. While his dissertation sponsor espoused a rigidly positivist philology, attempting completely to divorce linguistics from literature, the young Spitzer resolved early in his career to eschew such rigid departmentalization and to try to bridge the gulf between linguistics and literature. In his Vienna years, his studies developed under the influence of Freud into psychological stylistics. Even though he renounced psycholinguistics in his later career in America, his work was nevertheless informed by the attempt to merge esthetic, linguistic, and psychological approaches in the study of literary styles. Whereas Erich Auerbach, as has been seen, regarded himself as largely a historian of literary styles and expression, Spitzer had only a limited interest in historical research and concentrated instead on close *explication de textes*.

Spitzer became a privatdozent at the University of Vienna in 1913, but his career was soon interrupted by the outbreak of World War I. It seems characteristic of the man that, while serving for a time in the Austrian Censorship Office, he decided to do a study of Italian circumlocutions for hunger which he found in the letters of Italian prisoners of war.

At the war's end, Spitzer prepared for a professional career and was appointed to the University of Bonn in 1920. He moved to the University of Marburg as Professor Ordinarius five years later. (Auerbach succeeded him in that chair in 1930 when Spitzer accepted an appointment at the University of Cologne.)

When Hitler came to power in 1933, Spitzer was dismissed from his chair and decided to emigrate to Istanbul, where he was offered the directorship of an innovative program in modern languages. In Istanbul, just as in Marburg, Auerbach succeeded Spitzer a few years later. But unlike Auerbach, who remained in the cultural desert of Turkey until the end of World War II, Spitzer managed to come to America in 1936. He joined the Johns Hopkins faculty and stayed there for the rest of his life.

The Johns Hopkins environment proved congenial to Spitzer partly because, given that university's emphasis, he did not have to lecture to undergraduates and could devote himself to graduate instruction, and also because Johns Hopkins, under the leadership of the brilliant philosopher Arthur Lovejoy, had become a center for the study of the history of ideas. John Hopkins gave him the solid social and collegial matrix that so many of his fellow refugees never managed to attain.

Again in contrast to many other refugee literary scholars of his generation, Spitzer had considerable interest in American literature and culture. Not only did he have an impact on America but, as Harry Levin puts it, "his adopted land had an impact on him." Spitzer wrote studies on Poe and Whitman and even an essay on "American Advertising Explained as Popular Art," which analyzes pictorial advertisements for Sunkist oranges. When Levin first met him, he was amazed to hear Spitzer comment on analogies between Ernest Hemingway's metaphors and those of the Church Fathers!

Even though Spitzer made a considerable effort to speak to his new-found American audience, he never limited himself to it. He wrote and published in five languages (German, French, Italian, Spanish, and English) and his articles, polemical exchanges, and essays—over a thousand of them—are to be found across the world.

While Auerbach became known to a wider audience largely through

the paperback edition of *Mimesis,* Spitzer never produced a unified syn-
thetic work of scholarship. His extraordinary learning and painstaking
analytical abilities were revealed mainly in detailed stylistic analyses of
specific literary works. His method was that of a secular Talmudist, as
Harry Levin has called him, who involved himself in the minute dissection of specific texts rather than painting on a larger canvas. This was
why Spitzer never reached the wide audience that Auerbach had con-
quered with *Mimesis.*

Even though he did not leave a unified oeuvre, Spitzer was a prodigious worker. Shortly before his death, a German publisher brought out
a 994-page volume containing papers in the five languages in which
Spitzer wrote with ease. The topics ranged over every Romance literature, including medieval and Renaissance Latin, Provençal, and Ruma-
nian. This volume was preceded by two Italian collections of his studies.
His major publication of essays in English, *Linguistics and Literary History:
Essays in Stylistics,* was issued by Princeton University Press in 1949. The
bulk of his reviews, papers, and essays still remain uncollected in book
form.

Spitzer seems to have been a kind of stormy petrel among Romance
philologists and students of comparative literature. Even though he
changed his point of view repeatedly during his long career, he held the
opinions he had adopted at the moment as revealed truth. Anyone who
did not share them was considered not only in error but in sin: with a
sense of righteousness that perhaps stemmed from his Germanic background, he condemned those who dared disagree with him to the in-
nermost circle of hell. He mellowed in the last few years of his life, but
during his career in America Spitzer expended a great deal of his energy in protracted feuds, partisan tracts, and vitriolic book reviews.[5] He
always maintained, of course, that when he castigated his fellow scholars
it was for their own good. One example of his polemical style will have
to suffice. In a review of a book by the Spanish philologist Stephen Gilman, Spitzer wrote:

> I have often been asked why I devote so much effort to "destructive criticism."
> The answer is that I believe that, in the discipline of Philology as in the sci-
> ences, the ultimate goal, however more arduous in its attainment or approxi-
> mation, must be Truth; and that the failure to express discontentment with
> half-truths or non-truths would amount to a conspiracy of silence against that
> noble discipline.[6]

Professor Gilman may well have felt that Spitzer's belief that he had the
truth by the tail stemmed from an unduly inflated ego. After all, every
scholar seeks the truth according to his or her lights.

When all is said and done, Spitzer's polemical thrusts, while they may at times have been destructive, also helped to raise the level of scholarly work in Romance and comparative literatures. It may well be that many younger scholars paid especially close attention to what they had to say when they contemplated the possibility of becoming an object of Spitzer's wrath. By repeatedly disturbing the peace in the gentlemanly community of philological scholars, Spitzer made its standards more rigorous. His work provided vital links between Continental and American scholarship and reduced the relative insulation of American humanistic studies from the critical traditions of Europe.

René Wellek (1903–   )

Born in Vienna in 1903 and educated in Prague, familiar with a wide range of European languages, René Wellek lived in Germany as well as in England before coming to America. Here he became a cosmopolitan student of literature, who put his exposure to a variety of cultural traditions and doctrines to good use in developing a comparative approach to literature which, at least among his contemporaries, seems almost unique in its breadth.

Wellek's work in comparative literature was not only influenced by the various locales in which he pursued his studies, it was also marked by the unusually wide set of approaches to literary scholarship that had influenced him in his formative years and after. He was receptive to the insights of a number of schools in literary history and analysis while never giving his full allegiance to any one of them. The many influences on his work led him to develop an approach that might be characterized as disciplined eclecticism, a tendency to put to use a variety of doctrines without being totally beholden to any of them. He is still at work on what is likely to be considered his masterpiece, a multivolume *History of Modern Criticism*. Wellek's panoramic treatment of the subject aims to do justice to the many divergent currents in European and American criticism, from Coleridge to Virginia Woolf, from Kant and Brandes to Gundolf and Curtius. Even a cursory history of Wellek's training and apprenticeship makes it apparent that the various settings in which he pursued his studies and the influences to which he was exposed provide a biographical context for the characteristics of his work.

When Wellek came to the Czech University in Prague in 1922 to study German philology, he found that the dominant approach in that subject was still in the German tradition of historical and philological scholarship, rooted in romanticism and glorification of the Middle Ages. Yet some of the younger professors, whom Wellek found more to his liking, were turning their attention to such figures as Kleist and Nietzsche and attempting come to terms with modernistic trends. They even delved into the young discipline of psychoanalysis in their efforts to uncover the roots of modern thought.

Although the young Wellek was not uninfluenced by the latter-day romantics and the early modernist scholars to whom he listened, a more enduring influence came from Vilém Mathesius, who taught English literature and later was a founder and president of the Prague Linguistic Circle. Yet, as Wellek put it, "I must confess that I withheld full allegiance from every one of my teachers."[7] Just as he had been willing to try out classical philological as well as psychoanalytical approaches, so he was impressed by formalistic procedures. Yet, while Mathesius was mainly concerned with Shakespeare and the Romantic and Victorian poets, Wellek was fascinated by John Donne and the Metaphysical poets, who were hardly in the purview of Mathesius's concerns.

In an effort to familiarize himself with still other perspectives on literary studies not represented among the Prague faculty, Wellek visited Heidelberg in 1923, mainly to hear the lectures of Friedrich Gundolf. He was fascinated by Gundolf, especially by his work on Goethe and Hoelderlin, but at the same time he was repelled by the hero worship, the elitism, and the claims to total allegiance that characterized the circle of Stefan George, of which Gundolf was a leading member.

Upon his return to Prague, Wellek shifted his focus from German to English literature and received his Doctor of Philology with a thesis on "Carlyle and Romanticism," under the direction of a somewhat reluctant Mathesius. Wellek then planned to devote his attention to the British Metaphysical poet Andrew Marvell. When he learned that several major works on Marvell were in preparation, he reluctantly gave up this project and, somewhat at a loss for an alternative, accepted a postdoctoral fellowship at Princeton University in the fall of 1927. At Princeton, Wellek was exposed to another set of influences. He listened to the New Humanists Paul Elmer More, who lived in Princeton, and Irving Babbit, whom he heard lecture at Harvard. He also acquainted himself with the iconoclastic treatment of American literature developed by H. L. Mencken and the young Van Wyck Brooks. But Wellek was not converted to the credo of the New Humanists or to the sardonic reaction to American pieties represented by Mencken and the early Brooks.

Returning to Prague in June 1930, Wellek again took a new turn. He completed a book on *Immanuel Kant in England,* most of which he had written in America, and focused his interest on philosophy, especially British empiricism and German idealism. The book on Kant, though alien to the concerns of his academic sponsor, Mathesius, nevertheless was accepted as a *Habilitation,* which allowed Wellek to serve as a lecturer on English literature at the university. Even though his early lectures indicated his strong partiality for the idealistic tradition in English poetry, Wellek also joined the Linguistic Circle and attended a conference on phonology organized by that circle, which allowed him to become personally acquainted with most of its leading members. He evidently never felt uneasy about being a kind of free lance who could move at will between formalist and idealist camps, learning from both traditions while captive of neither.

In 1935 Wellek was again uprooted. Since the prospects for a professorship at Prague seemed remote, he accepted an appointment as lecturer in Czech language and literature at London University. While in England, Wellek met the Cambridge anti-academic critic R. R. Leavis and began to contribute to his famous quarterly *Scrutiny.* Wellek, however, was never fully persuaded of Leavis's credo that criticism of literature should be closely related to criticism of life, and that an author's moral position should be weighed as carefully as his purely literary accomplishments. Even while he was writing for *Scrutiny,* Wellek soon found himself engaged in polemical exchanges with its editor on the proper relation between philosophy and literary criticism. At the same time, Wellek contributed sharp critical assessments of such major British literary scholars as I. A. Richards, William Empson, and Leavis himself to the Czech periodical of the Prague Circle.

After having worked for several years in the British Museum on a history of literary historiography in England, and realizing when Hitler invaded Prague in early 1939 that he would not be able to return to his homeland, Wellek resolved to emigrate to the United States. Through the good offices of Thomas Marc Parrott, who had been one of his teachers at Princeton, Wellek secured a position in the English Department of the University of Iowa. His prior knowledge of the American literary scene and his familiarity with English and American literature eased his adjustment to American conditions, although he had to look up the exact location of the University of Iowa on a map in the British Museum.

Having completed his *The Rise of English Literary History* (1941), Wellek soon made a mark on his new environment, even though the faculty was sharply divided in its allegiance to old-guard New Humanists and the "New Critics." One of the leading New Critics, Austin Warren, in fact taught at the university, and through him Wellek soon met the other major New Critics—Cleanth Brooks, Robert Penn Warren, and Allen Tate. Here again, as in so many other encounters with divergent critical traditions, Wellek profited from the new vistas provided by their perspective while keeping his distance. "I was deeply impressed by the New Criticism," he writes, "but again remained an outsider who had come with different preoccupations."[8] Even so, he collaborated with Austin Warren on a book, *Theory of Literature,* which, with its combination of Warren's New Criticism and Wellek's eclectic Continental views, became a leading graduate textbook. It has as of this date been translated into twenty-one languages.

While at Iowa, Wellek put his knowledge of many European languages to good use, teaching courses in the European novel and a seminar in German-English cultural relations. He had become convinced by then that comparative literature deserved to be taught alongside courses on national literary traditions.

Wellek went to Yale University in 1946. His eminent career there has been described at the beginning of this chapter. He still has his office at Yale working on the concluding volumes of his monumental *History of Modern Criticism*. That Yale can boast of a distinguished faculty in both comparative and Slavic literatures is largely due to Wellek's influence. Erich Auerbach's coming to Yale, as well as the appointment of a major Slavic scholar, Victor Erlich, author of the first full-length study of Russian Formalism, were probably mainly due to Wellek's influence.

Looking back on his work, Wellek has written: "I am struck with my detachment from all the phases I went through: historical scholarship, symbolist criticism in the wake of . . . Gundolf, the American New Humanism, the Prague School shaped by Russian Formalism, the Leavis group, the American New Criticism . . . I hope that I have preserved my own integrity and a core of convictions."[9] By exposing his American graduate students and the wide audience for his books to so many winds of doctrine, by allowing his listeners and readers to navigate with a measure of assurance in a sea echoing with so many siren voices luring them to pay total allegiance to this or that exclusive literary approach, Wellek has had a profoundly civilizing influence on the American scene. Many other scholars in a variety of disciplines have contributed to the deprovincialization of the American mind. But hardly any of them has contributed so significantly to a broad view of the offerings of a whole array of critical literary thought as René Wellek. That his peers have recognized the great scholarly merits of his work is attested by the fact that he has received no fewer than three Guggenheim Fellowships, the prize for Distinguished Service to Humanities of the American Council of Learned Societies, and honorary doctorates from the universities of Oxford, Harvard, and Rome.

Werner Jaeger (1888–1961) and the Impact of European Refugees on American Classical Scholarship

Classical studies had comprised one of the mainstays of college education in America since the first institutions of higher learning were founded in the seventeenth century. Yet modern scholarship in the subject dates only from the early part of the nineteenth century, when such universities as Johns Hopkins, Harvard, and Yale grafted the idea of the German research-oriented university onto the stem of the English-American college and thus provided the fertile environment for the rapid growth of classical studies. The father of classical philology in America was B. L. Gildersleeve (1831–1924), of Johns Hopkins. Like almost all of his contemporaries in the classics and many in other areas as well, Gildersleeve had studied in Germany and was deeply influenced by German scholarship. A highly productive scholar and a superb teacher, he sponsored no fewer than 67 doctoral dissertations in the classics during his long career at Johns Hopkins, and his students occupied positions in the classics departments of many major universities. Gildersleeve founded the *American Journal of Philology* in 1880 and directed it for forty years. He, as well as most of his students, was deeply beholden to the German wissenschaftliche approach to classical studies and rejected with a measure of contempt most British scholarship in that subject. American classical scholarship as a whole consciously followed in the footsteps of the German tradition.[1]

The preponderant German influence on classical scholarship came to an abrupt end with America's entry into World War I. War propaganda spread anti-German feelings. High-school teaching of German was largely discontinued. The classicists of the interwar period for the most part had only an imperfect knowledge of the German language and no longer had the intellectual equipment to move with ease in the world of German scholarship. The article on "Classical Scholarship in Modern Times"

in the *Oxford Classical Dictionary* does not even mention the name of
Theodor Mommsen. In the years between the wars, the influence of
Oxford with its Rhodes scholarships and of Cambridge eclipsed the previous dominance of Berlin, Heidelberg, and Halle in the classics as well
as in many other fields of humanistic scholarship.

While textual analysis and criticism in the German mode had dominated American classical scholarship during the period of its coming of
age, the emphasis during the interwar years shifted to ancient history
and, above all, to archeology. Interest moved from the study of texts to
the study of artifacts. Participation in archeological digs came to be considered more valuable and prestigious than digging into recondite manuscripts.

Until the 1930s, classical studies had been considered a domain for
genteel—and gentile—scholars. Modern universities were the offshoot
of private colleges whose major task had been the education of Protestant clergy, and the close ties between the teaching of Protestant theology and classical scholarship persisted long after research universities
had become separate from undergraduate colleges. What is more, a
classical education was generally perceived to be a status-enhancing pre-
rogative of the rich and well born. As Thorstein Veblen put it in his
characteristically pungent way, "[The classics] serve the decorative ends
of leisure-class learning better than any other body of knowledge, and
hence they are effective means of reputability."[2] Classics were for Christian gentlemen. Compulsory attendance at chapel service and a tacit or
overt numerus clausus kept Jews out, and those few who managed to
get in did not receive tenure. Before 1930 there was not a single Jewish
tenured professor of classics in America. As late as 1930 the Chicago
classicist and Platonist Paul Shorey actually gave Jewish graduate students harder examinations so as to discourage them from entering the
field.

The classicist James Loeb graduated from Harvard magna cum laude
in 1888. He was offered a curatorship in Egyptology at the Boston Museum of Fine Arts but was given to understand that a professional career
in classics was unthinkable for an American Jew. Loeb founded and endowed the great Loeb classical library, established a variety of fellowships and lectureships at Harvard, generously helped to finance archeological excavations, and became the leading benefactor of American
classical scholarship. Yet, rebuffed by those whom he wished to consider
his peers, Loeb lived for many years in self-imposed exile in Bavaria.
The universities of Cambridge and Munich gave him honorary degrees,
but Harvard never did. Another great Jewish classicist, Charles Wald-
stein (later Sir Charles Walston), emigrated to England when he could

find no position in America and pursued an eminent career at Cambridge, which was capped by a knighthood.

In the year after Hitler's seizure of power, some twenty senior scholars of the classics arrived in America. Such a sudden influx in the relatively small and tight-knit world of classical scholarship was bound to have significant consequences. These men and women had well-established reputations in the international world of classical scholarship, and even though most of them were Jewish or had Jewish spouses, it was impossible, given their eminence, to close the doors to them as had been the custom in regard to native American Jews. Major universities on the Eastern seaboard proved most receptive. Six of the new arrivals went to teach at Columbia. Harvard gave positions to three. The rest were dispersed over several university departments on the East and West coasts and in the Middle West.

The refugees initially faced a good deal of hostility, especially from younger scholars, who claimed that their careers had been ruined by the arrival of these eminent scholars. But most of the refugees eventually found acceptance. To be sure, none of them managed to create a "school" similar to those which American scholars had founded at an earlier time. Most of them did not sponsor more than two or three doctoral degrees. The refugees were not part of "old boy" networks and knew fewer colleagues than did the native-born. Students hence feared that the newcomers would be less able to recommend them for future positions. None of the refugees ever became president of the American Philological Association or of the Archeological Institute of America, the leading professional organizations. Yet, as their previous work slowly became accessible through English translations, and as they began to publish scholarly contributions in English, they exerted a decided influence. In particular, they stimulated interest in *Geistesgeschichte*, which had never played an important part in American scholarship.

Perhaps even more important than their contributions to American scholarship was a wholly unanticipated consequence of the arrival of these eminent refugee scholars. Once these men and women, most of whom were Jewish, had been given tenured appointments in American universities, it became impossible to refuse tenure to native-born Jews. The refugees thus became the vanguard that destroyed the bastions of discrimination in their scholarly community and helped to dispel the cloud of genteel and not so genteel anti-Semitism that had previously hovered over departments of classics. Similar developments, as has been seen, occurred in departments of art history during that period.

Despite their inability to create "schools" of their own, perhaps largely because of their dispersal over the academic landscape, classicists such as Paul Friedlaender at UCLA, G. M. A. Hanfmann at Harvard, and a number of others, left an enduring mark on various fields of classic scholarship in America. Werner Jaeger, a Protestant with a Jewish wife, was clearly the most eminent among them. Even though he was often harshly criticized by some of his colleagues, he must be considered the most influential of the refugee scholars.

When Werner Jaeger came to America, in 1934, he was in his mid-forties and at the height of his scholarly career. He was considered the dean of German classical studies, the worthy successor to his former teacher, Ulrich von Wilamowitz-Moellendorff, who was probably the greatest classicist of the twentieth century. Given this eminence, it was not surprising that Jaeger immediately was offered a high position at Berkeley and that, after a few years in a no less prestigious chair at the University of Chicago, he went to Harvard, where he taught from 1939 until his retirement in 1960. Both his biography and bibliography help to explain his career in America.

Werner Jaeger was born in 1888, the son of a Lutheran businessman, in a small Rhenish town not far from the Dutch border. Even as a schoolboy at the local classical Catholic gymnasium he moved from an interest in the Greek historians to the history of ideas and especially the study of Greek poetry and philosophy. This preponderant interest remained with him throughout his life, but unlike most of his predecessors, he also endeavored to study the world of ideas in conjunction with its matrix in Greek society and its history.[3]

After graduating from the gymnasium he spent a semester at the University of Marburg, where he became familiar with the neo-Kantian philosophers who dominated philosophical instruction. Jaeger then moved to the University of Berlin, largely because Wilamowitz taught there. When Jaeger arrived in Berlin at the age of nineteen, Wilamowitz was fifty-nine, a brilliant lecturer and spectacular personality, and a man of enormous erudition, regarded as a "heroic" figure by his adoring students. Jaeger immediately fell under his spell, and it was due to Wilamowitz's influence that he decided to become a classical philologist rather than a professor of philosophy, as he had once intended. Yet Jaeger continued to join strictly philological concerns with philosophical inquiry even though Wilamowitz did not show much interest in philosophical questions.

After four years of study at Berlin, mainly with Wilamowitz but also with other great classical scholars such as Hermann Diels, Eduard Meyer, and Eduard Norden, Jaeger defended his dissertation, summa cum laude, on the history of the origins of Aristotle's metaphysics. It was published soon after its defense and laid the groundwork for a later major study of the history of Aristotle's intellectual development (1932). Wilamowitz seems to have discerned Jaeger's gifts very early and became his academic sponsor. At age twenty-six, Jaeger, having published his habilitation on some figures in Neoplatonic thought only two years after his dissertation, was called to the philological chair at the University of Basel, which had once been held by Friedrich Nietzsche. After a fairly short stay at Basel and a few years of teaching at the University of Kiel, Jaeger was called to succeed Wilamowitz at Berlin. Although he was then only thirty-two, he was appointed over the heads of a number of candidates many years his seniors, largely because of Wilamowitz's intervention in his favor.

During his years at Berlin, Jaeger rapidly moved to the forefront of classical scholarship. The first volume of his critical edition of the works of the Church Father Gregory of Nyssa began to appear in the year of his appointment, and other volumes followed at regular intervals. His three-volume history of the Greek mind, *Paideia,* was begun at Berlin, although it was completed in America.[4] This book brought him a good deal of international acclaim and eminence among a wide audience of cultured laypersons, even though it was criticized by some of his colleagues.

Jaeger was not only a scholar of high repute, he was also an academic entrepreneur of no mean talents who endeavored to recapture for the classics the preeminent position in German intellectual life which they had been losing in the Weimar period. He was untiring in his defense of classical values and of his approach to Greek and Latin thought, which he called the Third Humanism. He founded and edited the journal *Die Antike,* which addressed the educated laity rather than professional classicists. One of his students edited another journal, *Gnomon,* devoted, as was *Die Antike,* to the proposition that classical studies continued to have important bearings on contemporary culture. Jaeger also founded and edited eleven volumes of the more strictly scholarly *New Philological Research Studies,* while continuing to publish a series of scholarly monographs.

The New Humanism, expounded in *Paideia* and elsewhere, tended to present a romantic and passionately heroic view of the Greeks. It emphasized manly virtues, an elitist view, and an almost uncritical veneration of Greek civilization. As a result, it lent itself to interpretations of a strongly nationalist character, so it was not altogether surprising that a number of Jaeger's students eventually joined the Nazi movement. Jaeger, however, can hardly be blamed for this. He himself, largely because his second wife was of Jewish origin and he refused to divorce her as the Nazis insisted, decided in 1934 to emigrate to America.

During his years in America, Jaeger continued to be a highly productive scholar. The first volume of *Paideia* was followed by two others. Books on the theology of the early Greek philosophers, on early Christianity and Greek Paideia, a critical edition of Aristotle's *Metaphysics,* as well as two volumes of essays (*Scripta Minora*) followed.

During his American years Jaeger never attempted to reenact the magisterial role he had played in the Germany of the 1920s. He knew that the classical tradition, the background against which he developed his New Humanism in Germany, was no longer a living presence in America. He sadly remarked that, in America, classical scholarship had to be pursued in a culture where humanist thought did not exist, and where only a saving remnant still believed that the classics were relevant for comprehending the present.[5]

Jaeger at Harvard showed no trace of the firebrand of his Berlin days. He was quiet, withdrawn from the public arena, a serene, gentle sage. His teaching was largely devoted to elaborate textual analysis; he resisted the temptation to present large-scale general overviews. In his early years at Harvard his students saw him as a remote figure, like many German professors. In later years he slowly adopted the more personal style of professor–student relations typical in American universities. A number of his students have testified that he spent much time with both graduate students and undergraduates. Several recall long afternoons of conversation with him. Even though he was revered by his students and influenced a number of them and was apparently much at ease on the Harvard Yard, Jaeger never attempted to reenact his previous public involvements. He became a *Stubengelehrter* who rarely attended academic conventions unless they were held in Boston and was never elected to the presidency of the American Philological Association.[6]

Jaeger's influence in America, through the students he trained and through his published work, helped bring American classical scholarship into more lively contact with the traditions of European intellectual history. He succeeded in reviving interest in the German philological tradition that had culminated in his teacher Wilamowitz, but he also alerted his audience to the importance of the German philosophical tradition stemming from Hegel, Kant, Schopenhauer, and Wilhelm Dilthey, whose works he once thought of editing for an American public.

The New Humanism died on the vine in the uncongenial climate of America. The broad initial influence of *Paideia* seems to have declined in recent years, but Greek textual criticism in Jaeger's style, particularly of the Church Fathers, is being carried on by some of his students who now occupy chairs in major universities. Many a Harvard undergraduate who chose a career far removed from classical studies was nevertheless marked by Werner Jaeger's teaching and gentle intellectual guidance. He once wrote that in a land that lacked a living classical tradition it behooved the humanistic scholar to "take pike and axe in hand to labor, just like the monks of the early middle ages, in the service of an educative mission."[7] For this American culture remains in his debt.

Two weeks before Werner Jaeger died, on October 19, 1961, he received the first copy of his latest effort, *Early Christianity and Greek Paideia,* from the Belknap Press of the Harvard University Press.

Hajo Holborn (1902–1969), Felix Gilbert (1905–), Hans Rosenberg (1904–), and Paul Oskar Kristeller (1905–): Refugee Historians

At least three dozen European historians of renown emigrated to the United States after 1933. A few came from Italy, the most prominent among them the Harvard historian Gaetano Salvemini; but the great majority came from Germany or Austria. The most imposing figure among German-speaking refugee historians was Hajo Holborn, for many years the most prominent teacher in European history at Yale University and the only refugee historian to be elected president of the American Historical Association. Three other major figures were Hans Rosenberg, Felix Gilbert, and Paul Kristeller. This selection is undoubtedly arbitrary; many historians will claim that Renaissance scholar Hans Baron, medievalist Ernest Kantorowicz, student of militarism Alfred Vagts, and still others should have been included in my list. I can only plead limitation of space. There seems, at least, no doubt that the scholars I have chosen are generally considered to be among the most important, if not the most important, of the refugee historians.

The German Background

While in some fields of learning, such as the social sciences, a high proportion of German scholars chose to emigrate, this was not the case in German historical studies. Almost all the major historians remained in Germany, even though some of them kept their distance from the Nazis and not a single ordinary professor (*Ordinarius*) of history had joined the Nazi party by January 1933. Most of the important older German historians of the period had been trained by Sybel, Treitschke, and Droysen, or their students—all of them exponents of the Prussian tradition. Their thought was rooted in the nationalist spirit of the Bismarckian and Wilhelminian Reich, and they looked back with nostalgia to the happy prewar days when the professoriat had been considered an essential pillar of the Prussian and German political establishment.

The historians who came to this country were, by and large, a younger group who had not yet received permanent appointments and were not so deeply rooted in the Prussian and Bismarckian tradition. Most of them were born around the turn of the century and hence were only in their thirties when they emigrated. Many of them shared another background characteristic: they had been students of the great intellectual historian Friedrich Meinecke at the University of Berlin.

Although Meinecke shared strong conservative and traditionalist orientations with most German historians of his generation, he differed from them in that he had consciously decided to make his peace with the Weimar Republic. He said of himself that he was a monarchist at heart (*Herzensmonarchist*) but a republican by virtue of reason (*Vernuftsrepublikaner*). Meinecke defended the Weimar Republic in the 1920s and became a sturdy opponent of the Nazis during the years of their march to power. In addition, even though Meinecke personally still advocated an approach to the history of ideas that was not contaminated by the consideration of sociological or political factors, he was nevertheless willing to support students who attempted in their work to build bridges between intellectual and social history. This accounts for the fact that a high proportion of young historians who had social concerns and who were liberals became students of Meinecke. They considered themselves to one degree or another a muted left opposition to the prevailing trends in German historiography. Holborn, Gilbert, and Rosenberg were Meinecke students, as were an unusually high proportion of the other emigré historians in America. Most of them were of Jewish origin, but some others who had no "racial" reason to emigrate left Germany because they found the Nazi regime intolerable.

Most of the refugee historians in America, and particularly those I have singled out for individual discussion, made an effort—in some cases already begun in Europe, in others initiated here—to rethink the course of German history so as to answer the insistent question: How can the Nazi seizure of power be explained in the light of Germany's past? They had been trained in a tradition that stressed the virtues of "organic" German institutions and values and compared them favorably with the Enlightenment and its corrosive rationalism, which allegedly characterized the West. Many of the emigré historians were hence moved after 1933 to evaluate the intellectual baggage of German historiography and to argue in one way or another that Germany's tragedy stemmed in large part from that country's rejection of the values and orientations of the West.

This is not to say that the former students of Meinecke in America had a unified point of view. One of them, Hans Rothfels, who taught at the University of Chicago, was decidedly conservative and was also the only one among them who, before retirement, returned to Germany after the war. A very few others might also be called conservatives. It nevertheless remains important to note that among refugee historians liberalism and the Meinecke influence were much more pronounced than they were among those who elected to stay in their native country.

The Refugee Scholars in America

By and large it seems that the refugee historians managed to create a place for themselves in the American academy.[1] Some of them, to be sure, such as the historian of the German revolution of 1848, Veit Valentin, and the historian of militarism, Alfred Vagts, never attained a regular academic position here (in Vagts's case this was partly by choice, as he had independent means and was the son-in-law and heir of Charles Beard). But most of them managed to get major positions in universities, though often after a lengthy period of teaching in a variety of undergraduate colleges. Holborn was offered a visiting professorship at Yale soon after his arrival in 1934; he became an assistant professor in 1938 and a full professor in 1940. Gilbert taught for many years at Bryn Mawr and then became a member of the prestigious Institute for Advanced Study in Princeton. Hans Rosenberg taught first at Illinois College, then for twenty years at Brooklyn College, where the demands of a heavy teaching schedule drastically cut into the time available for research and publication. Only in 1960 was he appointed to the Shepard Chair at the University of California at Berkeley. Kristeller taught at Columbia ever since his arrival here in 1939 but remained an adjunct faculty member until 1948, when he was appointed associate professor of philosophy.

A number of factors seem to have been at play to bring about the relative success, though often after a fairly long period of "apprenticeship," of the refugee historians. First of all, they were fairly young, hence more adaptable than more senior academics. Second, there were many more positions for historians at the time than for, say, classicists or musicologists. To be sure, there were obstacles. As has been seen in other fields, some of their younger colleagues looked upon them with resentment, perceiving them as competitors in the dire days of the Depression. In some cases, the refugee scholars suffered from the genteel anti-Semitism still prevalent in academia before the war. If, despite these drawbacks, most of them managed in the long run to attain positions of some eminence, this was also due in part to the fact that they were much in sympathy with the New Deal and sought consciously to build relationships with like-minded native colleagues. At home they had been democrats, and in some cases Social Democrats, and hence they greeted the New Deal with enthusiasm. They surely would have found it much harder to get their bearings in Herbert Hoover's America, but they resonated to the policies of the Roosevelt administration. This also may account for the fact that when the war came, many of them, among them Holborn and Gilbert, worked for the Office of Strategic Services and other government agencies in Washington. They undoubtedly served the war effort because of their anti-Fascist convictions, but as a number of their American colleagues such as Franklin Ford and H. Stuart Hughes have testified, they also found the Washington wartime atmosphere congenial because of the elective affinity between New Deal–oriented native Americans and central European left liberals.

Hajo Holborn

Very early in his career Hajo Holborn was considered by many of his contemporaries as the wunderkind of German historical scholarship, destined to leave a major mark on it.[2] Holborn's family background stood him in good stead. His father was a renowned physicist and a director of the *Physikalisch-Techniche Reichsanstalt* in Berlin. The Holborns' home was situated in the garden of the *Reichsanstalt,* and thus the son came to know the scholarly world in his childhood. Holborn's family, in contradistinction to the majority of German academic families, was deeply committed to a democratic weltanschauung. Father and son were exceptionally close, and Holborn's deep commitment to democracy, rather than being a result of conflict between father and son, as was often the case in Germany, blossomed organically from the son's identification with the intellectual and moral stance of his father.

Being a Berliner, and having decided to devote himself to the study of history as early as his gymnasium days, Holborn seemed foreordained to become a student of Meinecke at the University of Berlin, since Meinecke was much more committed to liberal and democratic values than other Berlin University professors. Holborn's other major teacher at Berlin was not a historian but a professor of theology, Karl Holl. While Meinecke stimulated Holborn's lifelong concern with the history of ideas and with diplomatic history, Holl awakened his interest in the history of German Protestantism.

Holborn's dissertation and his first book dealt with Bismarckian diplomacy and still stood in the shadow of Meinecke's work. They did not depart very markedly from the kind of historiography then current in Germany. His *Habilitation,* soon to be issued as a book (1929), on

Luther's friend, the humanist Ulrich von Hutten, came close to a revision of received wisdom. There Holborn adumbrated the view that it had been a mistake of previous scholarship to conceive of the Reformation and humanism as essentially parallel intellectual movements. Such a view had political implications. Under the monarchy the intimate connection of the Protestant church and the Prussian state had been a key determinant of cultural life. The received historical judgments posited the unity of throne and altar. In the book on Hutten, and much more explicitly in an article in the *Historische Zeitschrift* published two years later, "Protestantism and the History of Political Ideas," Holborn challenged the view of those who sought to glorify conservative nationalism by linking it to the Protestant tradition. Whereas the traditionalists had seen the Bismarckian Reich as the historical product of Protestant religiosity, Holborn argued that the time had come to reexamine German political developments and to show that Protestantism was only one of the intellectual forces that had conditioned them. In pointing to the conservative political bias of most of historical scholarship, Holborn now consciously took his stand on the left.

Despite his deviant political views, Holborn's career ran smoothly. In 1926, at the age of twenty-four, he was called to a privatdozent position at Heidelberg, and was probably the youngest lecturer in any German university at that time. He served in that position until 1931, when he accepted an appointment to one of the most liberal academic institutions, the Berlin Hochschule fuer Politik, where he remained until his emigration in 1934. During that time he was also a lecturer in history at the University of Berlin.

After his Heidelberg days, Holborn turned away from the Reformation and renewed his earlier interests in diplomatic history and the historical study of twentieth-century developments. His chair at the Hochschule fuer Politik required that he teach international affairs as well as history, but the turbulent events on the international scene in the last years of the Weimar Republic were probably more potent stimuli for Holborn's turning away from Reformation studies than were formal teaching requirements. Much like Max Weber, Holborn was throughout his career powerfully attracted to playing a role in the political arena. When he was only twenty-two years old, he wrote to his friend the historian Dietrich Gerhard, who later also emigrated to America and taught for many years at Washington University: "I believe in my historical calling and will never abandon it. But next to it I am always tempted by the idea of direct participation in the common weal. This desire often makes me lose any inner balance."[3] Although in his teachings and writings he valiantly participated in efforts to stem the Nazi tide in the last years of the Weimar Republic, and though he had intimate contacts with Democratic and Social Democratic political and governmental circles, Holborn did not manage in Germany to play the large-scale political role he dreamed of. That was to come much later in his adopted country. In his acceptance speech for the Internationes Prize, which he received in postwar Germany and accepted a few hours before his death, Holborn said, "As a very young man, I told myself that when I had got a certain security in my job—that is, had become more or less a professor—I would get involved in politics. The year 1933 saw to it that this political commitment came to me, and it has since never left me. In that sense, I only kept doing what I started out to do; kept doing . . . what it was in my blood to do."[4]

In his last years in Germany, Holborn pursued his earlier dual interests in contemporary history and the period of the Reformation. Upon Meinecke's recommendation he was chosen to edit and publish a collection of documents on the birth of the Weimar Republic when it was already in its death throes. Just before leaving Germany, Holborn, in collaboration with his wife, Annemarie, published an edition of and commentary on Erasmus's works on Christian philosophy.

When he was barely thirty Holborn accepted a positon at Yale. He seems to have managed the transition from Germany to America in an unusually smooth manner. Even though his interests were wide indeed, ranging from the history of ideas to the history of historiography, from classical studies to philosophy, his main concern continued to be German history after the Reformation and contemporary international relations. He wrote essays on, inter alia, "The Social Basis of the German Reformation" and "Power Politics and Christian Ethics in Early German Protestantism," but also on "Jakob Burckhardt as Historical Thinker" and "The Greek and Modern Concepts of History."[5]

Holborn's most important work was his magisterial three-volume *A History of Modern Germany*.[6] The first volume appeared in 1959; the final volume was completed shortly before his death in 1969. This monumental achievement has become the standard work in modern German history. Even though he stood on the shoulders of Ranke and Meinecke, Holborn here showed how sensitivity to the complex strands of social and political history can illuminate the history of culture and ideas. Although he was aware of the roots of much of his thought in the tradition of German idealism, Holborn indicated that this tradition had become obsolete to the extent that it was incapable of linking concern with ideas to their sociopolitical context.

Holborn's other major work, *The Political Collapse of Europe* (1951), which he published at the suggestion of Walter Lippmann, deals with the breakdown of the system of European states in the recent past and ends with suggestions for the rebuilding of a European comity of nations, of which a democratic Germany should be a constituent part.[7] The book was widely read not only by scholars but also by political decision-makers and seems to have had a considerable impact on American foreign policy in the 1950s and after.

In 1967, Holborn was elected president of the American Historical Association, the only refugee historian so honored. His standing and prestige among historians came not only from his abundant publications but also from the fact that he was a superb teacher who had trained some of the major historians of the next generation. During his years at Yale, Holborn directed the dissertations of over fifty students—most of them in history but some also in international relations. Among his prominent students were Leonard Krieger, the historian of ideas now at the University of Chicago; Theodore S. Hamerow, the social historian and student of revolutions at the University of Wisconsin; and the diplomatic historian Arno J. Mayer, now at Princeton University. There are probably few departments of history in major universities in which one does not find a former student of Hajo Holborn.

Holborn was devoted to the historian's craft, and he seems to have enjoyed the influence he had on professional historians in America. Yet not all of his satisfactions came to him in the halls of academe. During the war years and after, Holborn was finally granted his long-held wish to become a major political actor devoted to the res publica.

From 1942 to 1945, Holborn was a key member of the brilliant group of refugee scholars and native American social scientists and historians in the Office of Strategic Services. There he served as chief of the Research and Analysis Branch and was largely responsible for its scrutiny of Nazi policies and the elaboration of blueprints for postwar Germany. After 1946, Holborn became adviser to the U.S. Department of State on German and European affairs, which gave him an opportunity to voice his views to the highest levels of American policymakers. A crystallization of Holborn's ideas on postwar Germany, the book *American Military Government: Its Organization and Policies* (1947) had a major influence on decision-makers in German affairs, especially the American commander-in-chief in Germany, General Lucius D. Clay.[8] Together with others who had served with him in the OSS and later in the State Department, Holborn helped bring about major revisions in U.S. policy in Germany that culminated in Secretary of State James F. Byrnes's Stuttgart speech of 1946. That speech laid the foundations for the policy of reintegration of a democratic Germany in the European concert of nations and for the close German-American collaboration in the 1950s and after.

Without having any official assignment after 1946, Holborn became in the postwar years a mediator between the United States and the Federal Republic of Germany, interpreting American policy to Germany and German policies to the United States. John J. McCloy, the first U.S. High Commissioner in Germany, listened to Holborn's advice, and so did Theodor Heuss, the first president of the Federal Republic, who had once been a colleague of Holborn at the Hochschule fuer Politik. Holborn lectured to German audiences in universities and in practically every Amerika-Haus in Germany. He consulted with politicians and foreign ministry officials in Germany and, upon his return to America, reported to the State Department and the Pentagon on his German conversations. Just as he introduced many younger German historians to American colleagues, so he helped to introduce many younger German diplomats and politicians to their American counterparts. Even though he was firmly committed to remaining an American and never seems to have been tempted to return to Germany permanently, he became in the last period of his life a wanderer between two worlds. He had finally realized his youthful ambition of combining the scholar's domain with action in the public arena. He may well have felt that he would not only leave a major imprint on American historiography but would also be remembered as an architect of postwar democratic Germany.

Felix Gilbert

Like Hajo Holborn, Felix Gilbert was a student of Friedrich Meinecke at the University of Berlin.[9] The lifelong friendship of Gilbert and Holborn dates from these student years, and their intellectual concerns and careers in America have a good deal in common. Yet they also differed significantly. Holborn was older than Gilbert and therefore belonged to a somewhat earlier generation of Meinecke students. Gilbert's generation was more radical. Moreover, Holborn worked mainly on diplomatic history and primarily on German political and institutional history; Gilbert, by contrast, with the exception of a handbook on German history which he wrote for the American occupation forces, did not work on German but rather on Italian and American history. Even though both men were interested in contributing to intellectual history, this interest was more pronounced with Gilbert than with Holborn. As has been seen, Holborn worked closely in the tradition of German political history and was strongly attracted by political activity. Gilbert, by contrast, though highly interested in politics and sometimes expressing his political concerns in articles, "never had the slightest interest in taking an active part in politics."[10]

Alongside such differences, these scholars had much in common. Both developed a continuing interest in the history of international relations, and both made their knowledge bear upon concrete policy issues of the day by serving during the war years on the staff of the Office of Strategic Services in Washington. In addition, both centered much of their attention on an approach to the history of ideas and on the history of historiography grounded in the notion that ideas can be fully understood only if they are explicated in the context of social and political conditions. They were both heirs of the German historical tradition, and they both aimed at transcending it critically.

Gilbert was born in Baden-Baden, in the south of Germany, in 1905, but he was mainly educated in Berlin. His paternal grandfather, who had been a British officer, lived after his retirement in Germany, and his father consequently grew up in Germany and went to German universities, although he became a naturalized German citizen only fairly late in life. Gilbert was born in Baden-Baden because his father directed a sanitorium there; but he never knew his father, who died when Felix was nine months old. His mother, who was Jewish, then moved to Berlin to be with her mother, who was the daughter-in-law of the composer Felix Mendelssohn Bartholdy. Thus Gilbert had mixed Jewish and Christian roots in the patrician upper class of Berlin. He himself rejects the idea that this combined ancestry might have contributed to his cosmopolitan cast of mind and his liberal outlook, but he has said that the tradition of the Mendelssohn family might indeed lie at the roots of his cosmopolitanism and liberalism.[11]

Gilbert chose to work with Meinecke rather than with the more nationalist professors who taught at the University of Berlin principally because of Meinecke's scholarly standing. One may nevertheless surmise that the fact that he was a politically progressive figure may also have had some importance. But even during his apprenticeship with Meinecke, Gilbert situated himself to the left of his teacher. He remembers that Meinecke once asked him to do some work for the German Democratic party and was astonished to learn that Gilbert was in fact a Socialist.[12] Gilbert later registered surprise that Meinecke could have argued, in one of his best-known works, that the emergence of German nineteenth-century nationalism should be seen as "progress" from the emphasis on *Weltbuergertum* (world citizenship) that had been the prevalent German intellectual stance in the preceding century.

Gilbert published his doctoral dissertation on the German nineteenth-century historian Johann Droysen, as well as an edited collection of Droysen's political writing in Germany; but unlike those of Holborn, who already had an abundant publication record when he came here, almost all his other writings were conceived in America.

While Gilbert shared with Holborn historiographical interests and a concern for international affairs, he also had a passionate interest in Italian Renaissance thought in general, and Machiavelli and his contemporaries in particular. This interest led him to stay in Italy from 1931 to 1933 to work in Florentine archives. When Hitler came to power, he decided not to return to Germany and, after a few years' stay in England, came to this country in 1936.

For sixteen years, Gilbert was a member of the faculty of Bryn Mawr College. One may assume that, as in the case of Hans Rosenberg (see pp. 289–91), heavy teaching responsibilities accounted for a publication record which, even though quite impressive, is lower than that of Holborn. But unlike Brooklyn College, where Rosenberg taught, Bryn Mawr had a small graduate school, so that Gilbert was given a chance to teach some brilliant women scholars who later went on to teach at, among other institutions, Washington University and Yeshiva University. It remains true that Holborn, mainly a teacher of graduate students at Yale, found more time to pursue his research interests. When, after the long Bryn Mawr years, Gilbert was offered a chair in Renaissance Studies at the Princeton Institute for Advanced Study, from which he has recently retired, his intellectual productivity seems to have increased. It was probably not only the lack of teaching responsibilities but also the stimulating effect of interaction with a group of like-minded fellow historians that account for this. One may also surmise that his earlier stay in wartime Washington with a congenial group of both central European refugees and native-born historians may have been intellectually stimulating for Gilbert. Gilbert himself, by the way, seems unconvinced by the "sociological" argument as to the stimulating influence of colleagues at Princeton and in Washington.[13] I nevertheless feel that contact with such eminent historians and social scientists as Franz Neumann, Herbert Marcuse, H. Stuart Hughes, Franklin Ford, Leonard Krieger, and Carl Schorske probably left permanent marks on Gilbert's mind, even though Ford, Krieger, and Schorske were only graduate students at the time and were then known as Gilbert's "young men."

Gilbert's essays in the history of ideas and the history of historiography are all marked by his prepotent concern to understand ideas in a sociopolitical context. Whether he is writing on great German historians such as Droysen, Hintze, or Meinecke or on Machiavelli and other Italian Renaissance thinkers, Gilbert insists on showing the influence of ideas on politics as well as the influence of politics on ideas. When he was working on Machiavelli, for example, he found, to quote Peter Burke, "that he understood [him] better by locating him in a group of friends who met at the beginning of the sixteenth century to discuss politics in the Rucellai Gardens in Florence."[14] He also found that the French invasion of Italy led the Florentine ruling class to lose faith in rational thought as a political force. Hence he saw Machiavelli's ruthless disregard for previous rationalistic assumptions in political thinking largely as a distillation of upper-class opinion in an era of breakdown and ca-lamity.[15]

While concern with placing men of ideas in their social context can thus be seen as one of the distinguishing characteristics of Gilbert as a historian, close attention to archival sources, which had previously often been neglected in American scholarship, is another. His study of Amer-ican eighteenth-century ideas on foreign policy in *To the Farewell Address* (1961) or his history of modern international relations in *The End of the European Era* (1970) are based on close scrutiny of archival sources. But, above all, a series of his books and essays on early sixteenth-century Florence and Venice, of which *The Pope, His Banker, and Venice* (1980),[16] is the latest, testify to immersion in often quite obscure archival records.

Concentration on Gilbert's main published works risks obscuring his long-standing concern with improving the status of historical scholar-ship in America. He was largely responsible for bringing both Italian and American Renaissance historians to the Princeton Institute, making it a major locus of Renaissance studies in America. He was instrumental in organizing a conference at the Princeton Institute which resulted in two *Daedalus* volumes assessing "Historical Studies Today," and he pub-lished an influential report on the international historical conference of 1960. Through most of his career in America, Gilbert has dedicated himself to upgrading the historical profession through a variety of or-ganizational initiatives, as well as through the power of his own exem-plary work.

Gilbert's preferred medium seems to be the essay rather than a full-length study.[17] This probably acocunts for the fact that his work has not reached as wide an audience as that of his friend Holborn. Holborn wished to be a historian with an impact on public life; Gilbert, by con-trast, wanted to be, and is, a historian's historian, an impeccable crafts-man who through his archival research, as well as through his persistent concern with the social and political roots of ideas, influenced several generations of American historians. His thought was originally rooted in the "Prussian school" of German historical scholarship, but his almost fifty years as a professional historian in America have been as conse-quential for the flowering of his ideas as his German background. He did not have a chance to supervise as many graduate dissertations as Holborn because he spent sixteen years at a primarily undergraduate college and later held a chair in a research institute that offered no reg-ular graduate instruction. But his intellectual influence on younger his-torians remains considerable. When I mentioned to historian friends that I planned to devote a few pages to Gilbert and his work, their eyes lit up.

Hans Rosenberg

Born in February 1904 to a middle-class family in Hanover, Hans Rosenberg grew up in Cologne, where the family moved in 1910.[18] As an adolescent, Rosenberg experienced the war, the subsequent revolution, and the beginnings of the Weimar Republic in the relatively liberal and open atmosphere of the Rhineland. After graduating from gymnasium, the seventeen-year-old Rosenberg went to the University of Berlin in 1917 to devote himself to the study of history. He soon fell under Friedrich Meinecke's spell. He wrote his doctoral dissertation under Meinecke's supervision, and his early concern with the history of German liberalism in the first half of the nineteenth century was due to Meinecke's guidance. His book on *Rudolf Haym and the Beginnings of Classical Liberalism* (1933), which served as his *Habilitation,* was attacked by conservative critics, who resented his attempt to understand the causes of the differing orientations of Prussian and West European liberalism and of the alienation of German liberalism from its Western European counterparts.

While his early work was developed on the model of Meinecke's exclusive emphasis on the history of ideas, Rosenberg's subsequent work departed from his teacher's by emphasizing the social and economic matrix of systems of ideas. From now on he wanted to develop a social history of ideas and lay the foundations of a "history of mental groupings." In the early years of his career he was concerned with such topics as the spread of ideas from elite strata to the mass, the role of ideas in political contests, the changing structures of public life before the revolution of 1848, the social carriers of political processes of mass mobilization. Some of these concerns seem to be precursors of those that Karl Mannheim developed roughly at the same time.

While engaged in a kind of protosociology of knowledge, Rosenberg pursued parallel inquiries in a wholly different area: the economic history of the nineteenth and twentieth centuries. His book on *The World Economic Crisis of 1857 to 1859* (1934), broke almost entirely new ground, since only Werner Sombert had earlier attempted to undertake historical studies of world economic trends and their repercussions in Germany.

After his academic studies, Rosenberg at first worked for a research institute. It was only in the winter of 1932–33 that he received an academic appointment as a lecturer at the University of Cologne. Hitler came to power before Rosenberg's first year as an instructor ended, and he left for London in the spring of 1933. At first he believed, like many others, that the Hitler regime would soon collapse, and he apparently made no effort to secure a permanent position in England.

The World Economic Crisis was published in Germany in 1934, and a two-volume collection of German national political pamphlets and journals between 1858 and 1866 appeared in 1935. Even though these works were reviewed in some German publications, it became clear to Rosenberg that from now on he had to find an audience elsewhere. Meinecke had managed to channel royalties for Rosenberg's work to London, and Rosenberg had secured a modest stipend from the London Institute for Historical Research, but this allowed only precarious living. In 1935 Rosenberg decided to emigrate to America.

His early years in America proved to be difficult. He was able to secure a teaching position only in an undergraduate institution, Brooklyn College, where much of his time and most of his energies were consumed by routine lectures, leaving him little time for research. (He often taught twenty hours a week and felt compelled to teach night school to supplement his meager salary.) In addition, Rosenberg had to deal with five centuries of German history instead of concentrating on his beloved nineteenth century. Despite these impediments, he seems to have enjoyed his stay in New York and to have valued the intellectual stimulation the city provided in abundance.

In the years at Brooklyn College, Rosenberg mainly pursued two interrelated programs of research. In the first place he explored the social functions of the agrarian policies of the German Reich after 1871 and related problems of modernization. In a series of articles in the *Journal of Economic History* and the *Economic History Review,* Rosenberg attempted to provide clues to the "exceptionalism" of German economic developments due to the impact of the Junkers on the polity of the Reich. Such concerns were rare at the time but recently have been in the center of sociological and historical attention, for example, in the work of Barrington Moore.

Rosenberg's second line of research bore even more abundant fruit. His *Bureaucracy, Aristocracy and Autocracy: The Prussian Experience 1660 to 1915* (1958)[19] was a pathbreaking attempt to understand the complex ways in which Prussian bureaucratization, combined with the continuing influence of the Prussian Junker aristocracy, prevented the development of a self-conscious liberal bourgeois politics in Prussia and thus laid some of the foundations for the "exceptional" development of the Prussian modernizing state. The book, borrowing heavily from sociology, especially from Max Weber, has come to be seen as an exceptionally fine exemplar of modern social history. It continues to exert considerable influence not only in America but also in postwar Germany.

From 1959 to his retirement in 1972 Rosenberg taught at Berkeley, where for the first time he had the opportunity to teach graduate students and to direct dissertations. He succeeded in guiding a number of his students in the direction of the social history of bureaucracies, aristocracies, and other social formations. He emphasized to his students that the history of industrial developments should not be divorced from the study of agrarian trends and sociopolitical developments. Rosenberg's capacity to synthesize research results in areas that, before him, were mainly considered in isolation has been greatly admired not only by specialists in German history but by many others who have seen how his research applies to comparative studies in other geographic and historical contexts. The harvest of his work might have been more abundant had he not been obliged to devote so much time and energy to undergraduate instruction during much of his career in America. But, as it is, he will be remembered for a long time as one of the grand masters of social history as well as a scholar who has thrown revealing light on some of the causes of Germany's "exceptional" development.

Paul Oskar Kristeller[20]

It is a tribute to Paul Kristeller's breadth of learning that I might have dealt with him in at least three different sections of this book. He was trained as a philosopher and taught for many years in Columbia's philosophy department; he was a classical philologist who had been a student of Werner Jaeger; he was a historian whose contributions to the study of medieval and Renaissance thought are highly valued by students of Italian humanistic ideas.

Paul Kristeller was largely a scholar's scholar. Most of his abundant, erudite, painstaking work did not resonate among a wider audience but caught the attention of specialists. Yet several generations of Columbia students profited from his courses in philosophy. A textbook, *The Renaissance Philosophy of Man* (1948), which he edited with the philosophers Ernst Cassirer and John H. Randall, Jr., soon after its publication became the most influential volume on Renaissance thought used in American colleges and universities.

Kristeller was born to well-to-do Jewish parents in Berlin in May 1905. While a student at the Mommsen gymnasium of his native city he concentrated on the classics, studying Latin for nine years and Greek for six. One of his teachers, Ernst Hoffman, with whom he studied Plato, also became his first philosophy teacher at the University of Heidelberg in the spring of 1923. At Heidelberg, where he concentrated on philosophy, Kristeller followed an unusually broad program, studying not only medieval history but also mathematics and taking courses in musicology, literature, linguistics, as well as in physics and art history. Hoffman and the existential philosopher Karl Jaspers had the greatest impact on him at Heidelberg.

Kristeller's doctoral dissertation on aspects of the ethics of Plotinus, which he published in 1929 when only twenty-four years old, was recognized by scholars as one of the most important monographs on the founder of Neoplatonic philosophy. But rather than prepare for a position in a department of philosophy, Kristeller decided, after receiving his doctorate, to study classical philology with Werner Jaeger at the University of Berlin. He remained a member of Jaeger's famous seminar for two years and then moved to Freiburg to study under Martin Heidegger and to prepare his *Habilitation*—a study on the Renaissance Neoplatonist Marsilio Ficino—under Heidegger's supervision. This work, though begun in Freiburg, was never finished in Germany because Kristeller decided after Hitler's rise to power to emigrate to Italy, with which he was already familiar because of his work on Ficino done in various Italian libraries and archives.

He supported himself at first by teaching at a high school for German-Jewish students in Florence and lecturing in German at a Florentine school. In 1935 Kristeller secured a lectureship in German at the University of Pisa owing to the support of the philosopher Giovanni Gentile. Gentile, who had made his peace with Mussolini's regime and therefore enjoyed a great deal of power in Italy's academic system, supported the publication of Kristeller's major book on Ficino and wrote a preface to a supplementary volume of his Ficino studies. When Kristeller lost his position in Pisa in 1938, after the Fascist anti-Semitic laws were passed, Gentile helped him to emigrate to America.

Kristeller's five years in Italy were highly productive. Even though his later interchanges with American scholars, especially with colleagues at Columbia University, proved to have considerable influence on Kristeller's ideas and program of study, it would nevertheless seem that his mature work in America was largely an outgrowth of his work in Italy and during his student days in Germany.

When Kristeller arrived in the United States in February 1939, he was already known to a number of American scholars, especially Albrecht Goetze and Roland H. Bainton of Yale University. At their suggestion, he spent the spring term at Yale as a Fellow in Philosophy. In the fall of that year, the philosophy department of Columbia University made him an offer to join its ranks as an adjunct faculty member. He held this "temporary" position for nine years. In 1948 he was finally appointed to a regular faculty position with the rank of associate professor. Apparently Kristeller's support at Columbia came at first mainly from its Italian department, whose chairperson, Dino Bigongiari, he had met in Italy. Subsequently his close association and friendship with two key members of Columbia's philosophy department, John H. Randall, Jr., and Ernest A. Moody, helped to integrate him into the Department of Philosophy.

He gave joint seminars with both of these philosophers and collaborated with Randall on the widely read *The Renaissance Philosophy of Man*.

Despite Kristeller's continued interest in Medieval and Renaissance thought, and despite the fact that he published a great variety of studies on Italian humanism, Ficino studies remained at the center of his interests. The English version of his book on the philosophy of Marsilio Ficino, which appeared here in 1944, is likely to be considered his major work and his most important single contribution to the study of Italian Renaissance philosophy.[21] Numerous other studies—on Renaissance Platonism, on the Renaissance philosopher Pico della Mirandola, on the relations between *The Classics and Renaissance Thought* (1955)—followed his work on Ficino. Most of these were published in America, but others appeared in Italy, where Kristeller had many friends and admirers and where he lectured frequently after the end of the war. In addition to his individual studies, Kristeller also became editor-in-chief of two monumental publication projects: a catalogue and systematic listing of all the Latin translations and commentaries on Greek and Latin works written before 600 A.D.; and a multivolume listing of previously uncatalogued or incompletely catalogued humanistic manuscripts of the Renaissance in Italian and other libraries. The latter publication, *Iter Italicum* (1963),[22] became a scholarly resource which, so Renaissance students have testified, might be compared with the search for manuscripts of classical authors that Italy's classical humanists undertook after the fall of Byzantium.

As distinct from scholars such as Werner Jaeger, who adopted a withdrawn style in their years in America, Kristeller threw himself into various public activities in his chosen fields of study. He served as president of the Renaissance Society of America, as secretary of the International Federation of Renaissance Studies, and as president of the Medieval Academy of America. Together with Randall, he organized the Columbia University Seminar on the Renaissance, which has flourished for over thirty years. He served on the editorial board or as book editor of various scholarly publications in philosophy, the history of ideas, and related areas.

At Columbia, Kristeller over the years offered courses and seminars not only on Italian thinkers and Renaissance philosophy but also on Plato, Aristotle, Plotinus, Descartes, Kant, Hegel, Spinoza, and others. Attracting graduate students not only in the philosophy department but in other departments as well and supervising a considerable number of doctoral dissertations, Kristeller became a vital focal point of the intellectual life of Columbia, an indispensable living link between European scholarship and the American mind. He is a Fellow of the British Academy and of the American Academy of Arts and Sciences. He has received honorary degrees from the University of Padua, Columbia University, and Middlebury College. To list all the honors he has received from various learned bodies both here and in Europe would fill a page. As his friend John H. Randall, Jr., once remarked, "He is a living witness to the creative fruits when the best German and the best American thought and scholarship find happy and fruitful union."[23]

The German refugee historians who came to America cannot be said to have revolutionized the writing of history in America. Their impact was not as profound as, say, that of refugee psychoanalysts. Yet, perhaps especially in the history of ideas and in political, social, and diplomatic history, they left an inheritance that will be lasting. By reacting against, or by modifying, the assumptions of the "Prussian historiography" in which most of them had been trained, they brought to American and postwar German audiences the idea that whatever was exceptional in German thought might not have been as wholly admirable as their teachers had given them to believe. Because they were wanderers between two worlds, they found it easier to bridge those worlds while demystifying some of the core assumptions of their traditionalist teachers.

VIII
Philosophy and Theology

Introduction

The reception and fate of European philosophers on the American scene illustrates in particularly graphic fashion a theme that informs much of this book. Philosophers who worked in a tradition that had some affinity with the philosophical world of America found fairly rapid acceptance here and were able to make a major contribution to American philosophical studies. On the other hand, those who came from philosophical orientations that were largely alien to American trends of the 1930s had to accept relatively marginal positions in the academic world and exerted only limited influence, at least during their lifetimes. The logical positivists of the Vienna Circle almost all gained stellar positions in the American philosophical world, while phenomenologists and existentialists (who would come into their own only after their deaths) were reduced to academic marginality.

Still others, such as the philosopher-theologian Paul Tillich, played a commanding role on the American cultural scene, but largely because they managed to shed much of their earlier radical philosophical and theological orientation and to adopt a new skin more readily acceptable to their new American audience. By watering down the heavy, largely Marxist rhetoric of his younger days and substituting an uplifting moral and religious rhetoric more in tune with the demands of his American audience, Tillich became for a while a leader of "progressive," liberal theology in America—thus illustrating the fact that creative adjustment to prevailing trends of thought can bring big dividends.

Rudolf Carnap (1891–1970) and The Vienna Circle in America: A Success Story

The members of the Vienna Circle and their close associates from Berlin came to America as refugees in the 1930s in quest of teaching positions in philosophy and eager to spread the message of logical positivism. They were largely successful. They faced obstacles, to be sure, yet most of them in due time obtained leading positions in prominent philosophy departments all over the United States. They became active participants in the professional meetings of philosophers, were honored in a variety of ways, and influenced many of their fellow philosophers. They also had students who continue to hold eminent positions in American philosophy departments. Almost all of them worked in the philosophy of science, but their impact on American philosophy went beyond that area to epistemology and the philosophy of language.

The logical positivists attempted to lay the foundations for a philosophy to end all previous philosophy, especially metaphysics. In this they did not succeed. But they continue to have a very wide influence in epistemology and the philosophical analysis of language. The current formal approach to linguistics, in particular, owes much to the pioneering work of the members of the Vienna Circle. Even philosophers not directly linked to the circle, such as the great Harvard pragmatist logician W. V. Quine, treat problems of knowledge in a way that differs but little from the Vienna Circle approach. They are at one in contending that knowledge in general is to be sought on the model of scientific knowledge.

The reception in America of the members of the Vienna Circle can be accounted for, at least in part, by a number of features of the American scene in philosophy at the time of their arrival that provided them with a ready audience. Whereas the Gestalt psychologists, as has been noted, found it difficult to get a hearing because American psychology was dominated by the behaviorists, philosophy in the 1930s was not dominated by any particular school. Idealists and pragmatists, critical realists and empiricists, all contended with each other, so there was no united opposition. Even though positivism might have horrified philosophers reared in an idealistic tradition, it was largely seen as one more voice among the many that struggled for a hearing.

Another reason for the refugee philosophers' relatively easy acceptance was the fact that they had many affinities with the British philosophical tradition of Bertrand Russell, A. J. Ayer, and the early Wittgenstein, all of whom were already well known in American philosophical circles and served, as it were, as the pathmakers for the newcomers from Vienna and Berlin. In addition, a number of influential natural scientists and psychologists with philosophical interests provided a willing audience and became active supporters of the members of the Vienna Circle, who had largely been trained in mathematics and the natural sciences, often before they turned to philosophy. Finally, one of them, Herbert Feigl, had come to America as early as 1930, before the others arrived here as refugees, and hence had occasion to prepare the terrain.[1]

The most eminent member of the Vienna Circle was the German-born philosopher Rudolf Carnap. Although the group had no leader in any formal sense, there seems to have been agreement that he was preeminent, at least since Moritz Schlick, the founder of the circle, had been assassinated by a crazed student in 1936. When Feigl was introduced to Bertrand Russell in 1935, Russell asked him: "Who is your [intellectual] father?" Feigl replied: "We have three of them: Schlick, Carnap, and Wittgenstein."[2] In his later works Wittgenstein took a direction uncongenial to the members of the Vienna Circle; and Schlick was dead. Hence Carnap came to be seen in America as the unquestioned "father" of the whole group.

Rudolf Carnap was born in northwestern Germany in a small town near the city of Barmen. His family were weavers who, by adhering to the strict demands of the Protestant ethic, had forged ahead in the world.[3] Both of his parents were deeply religious. Their faith, Carnap says, "dominated their whole lives." Carnap's father died when the young boy was only seven years old. His mother, who had previously been a schoolteacher, taught him herself for several years. After the family had moved to the provincial capital of Barmen, Carnap studied at the local gymnasium. The curriculum was based on classical languages, but Carnap was fascinated by mathematics, which, so he says, "attracted [him] by the exactness of its concepts and the possibility of proving results by mere thinking."[4]

From 1910 to 1914 Carnap studied at the universities of Jena and Freiburg, concentrating on philosophy, mathematics, and physics. In the field of logic, which soon assumed pride of place in his interests, the greatest influence on Carnap came from the teachings of the mathematician Gottlob Frege. Frege, now generally recognized as one of the greatest mathematician-logicians of the century, was hardly known at the time, and even though already past sixty, was still only a Professor Extraordinarius at Jena. It seems characteristic of Carnap, even at a young age, to be attracted by innovators who had the capacity to hack their own path through the wilderness of an emerging field. The new logic of mathematics that Frege had introduced in his *Begriffschrift* and *Fundamentals of Arithmetic* (which he had privately printed since no publishing house was willing to bring it out), even though it later was supplemented by the influence of Bertrand Russell, Wittgenstein, and others, came to be the foundation stone of Carnap's way of thinking. His dissertation on the notion of space (1921) was largely based on Frege's and Russell's symbolic logic.

Carnap lost the religious beliefs that had been so ingrained in his family tradition during his student days. As is so often the case, he turned to the militant atheism represented by the Society of Monists, in sharp reaction against the theology and metaphysics of the idealist tradition in which he had been reared. When the war broke out, Carnap was drafted and served in the front lines until he was transferred to Berlin in the summer of 1917. The revolution that broke out a year later was greeted with enthusiasm by Carnap and his friends, who now became self-conscious radicals and militant adherents of the left-wing socialists. Other German scholars who later came to America—Karl August Wittfogel, Hans Reichenbach, and Max Wertheimer, among others—belonged to the same left-wing Berlin student movement as Carnap. But he, unlike most of the others, retained his socialist beliefs throughout his life.

From the early to the middle 1920s, Carnap developed the essential elements of the philosophical approach that characterized his work thereafter. He was intent, so he said, on applying the new logical instruments that had become available in the work of Frege and Russell "for the purpose of analyzing scientific concepts and clarifying philosophical problems." Most of Carnap's work in this early period dealt with the logical foundations of physics and concept formation in the physical sciences. Much of his thought in these years was influenced by close intellectual interchanges with his lifelong friend Hans Reichenbach, to whose chair in philosophy at UCLA he succeeded toward the end of his career. While their interests largely overlapped, Carnap was primarily concerned with formal-logical problems while Reichenbach was mainly a philosopher of physics. Carnap's best-known work, *The Logical Structure of the World* (1928), was partly written during the 1920s in Germany, but was brought to completion only after he moved to Vienna in 1926. His *Logical Syntax of Language* (1937) was written in Vienna.

Carnap was offered a lectureship at the University of Vienna in 1926.

Moritz Schlick had been impressed with the quality of his mind, and there was a close resemblance of his thought with that of the Vienna Circle, which was then in the process of formation. Although Reichenbach and Carnap were now geographically separated, they continued to collaborate closely. Reichenbach had become a lecturer in physics at the University of Berlin in 1928, where he formed the Society for Scientific Philosophy, which was closely patterned after the Vienna Circle. In 1929 Carnap and Reichenbach joined their efforts and became coeditors of the periodical *Erkenntnis,* which for ten years was the house organ of the German and Austrian logical positivists.[6]

The Vienna Circle, led by Schlick, attracted a group of unusually gifted young scholars. I can only mention a few: the mathematicians Richard von Mises, Hans Hahn, Gustav Bergmann, Kurt Goedel, and Karl Menger; the economist-sociologist Otto Neurath; the physicist Philipp G. Frank; and the philosophers Friedrich Waisman and Herbert Feigl. Others on the periphery of the circle, though never full members, were the philosopher Ludwig Wittgenstein, who lived in Vienna in the 1920s, the philosopher Karl Popper, and the legal philosopher Felix Kaufmann. Many of these were young men barely out of university who plunged with the enthusiasm of youth into the propagation of the new gospel of radical philosophical reconstruction which came to be named logical positivism. The Vienna Circle aimed at nothing less than the final overthrow of all metaphysical speculation, all references to transcendent entities, and their replacement by resolutely this-worldly empiricism informed by the symbolic logic of Frege and Russell.

The logical positivists not only opposed all metaphysical thought, they also offended a tradition deeply entrenched in the German world of scholarship which saw a fundamental difference between the natural sciences and the *Geisteswissenschaften*—that is, the social sciences and the humanities. The positivists held that all the different branches of the empirical sciences are separated only in terms of a practical division of labor and are fundamentally parts of a comprehensive, unified science. This unified science, so Carnap and his associates argued, must be expressed in physicalist language so that the events described are in principle observable by all users of the language. The Vienna Circle considered it axiomatic that only two types of knowledge exist: the purely formal and the empirical. In the latter realm, only statements that can, at least in principle, be put to scientific tests have philosophical validity. Any reference to transcendent metaphysical notions is without meaning since it can never be tested.[7]

The Vienna Circle was permitted to function for only a little over a decade. It was disbanded after Hitler's invasion of Austria in 1938. But in the few years of its existence, it exerted a powerful influence not only in Austria and Germany but also in Poland, Czechoslovakia, and, above all, England. I know of few other philosophical movements that attained such eminence in a comparably short period of time.

When the members of the Vienna Circle, most of whom were Jewish, were forced to become exiles, almost all decided to make their new home in America. Some of the more peripherally involved, Wittgenstein and Popper in particular, chose Great Britain. Most members of Reichenbach's Berlin group, including Reichenbach himself and his star pupil, Carl Hempel, also came here.

When the Vienna Circle's main proponents came to America, its intellectual landscape was for them largely unknown territory, although some of them had been here on visits and had met American scholars in Europe. Feigl seems to be correct when he writes: "Most of us . . . were largely ignorant of American philosophy. We had, of course, read some of the work of William James and John Dewey. But we had only a very vague idea of Charles S. Peirce. . . . Our ignorance was vast."[8] Yet some American philosophers, in particular those reared in the pragmatic tradition, were eager to assist the newcomers in their attempts to find a hearing in America.

The University of Chicago philosopher Charles Morris, a follower of George Herbert Mead and a pragmatic philosopher of note, became Carnap's academic sponsor soon after his arrival in America in 1935. (He had previously spent several years at the German University of Prague.) Another major sponsor was the Harvard logician W. V. Quine, who also worked largely in a pragmatic tradition. At the urging of Quine and Morris, Carnap was invited soon after his arrival to participate in Harvard's Tercentenary Celebration in September 1936 and to teach at the University of Chicago in the winter quarter of 1936. Soon thereafter he was offered a permanent position at the University of Chicago, where he taught until 1952. Unlike most of his fellow refugees, Carnap hence faced no difficulties in securing a position. Most other members of the Vienna Circle also had relatively little trouble finding academic appointments.

In Vienna, the members of the circle had kept mainly to themselves. They had few discussions with philosophers outside their own ranks. Only in the United States did Carnap have frequent occasions to engage in scholarly discussions with philosophers of other persuasions. Participating in various seminars and conferences at the University of Chicago as well as at Harvard and Princeton, Carnap developed fruitful exchanges of ideas with scholars as diverse as the logicians Alfred Tarski and W. V. Quine, the British philosophers Bertrand Russell and J. H. Woodger, Albert Einstein, and John V. Neumann, as well as several younger American philosophers, such as Nelson Goodman and the mathematician-philosopher John G. Kemeny. The regular faculty seminars at the University of Chicago served to familiarize Carnap with proponents of still other currents of philosophical thought. There were also many opportunities to reestablish contact with old associates from Vienna and Prague, such as Philipp G. Frank, Richard von Mises, and Herbert Feigl. It would be presumptuous for a non-philosopher to pronounce on such matters, but one gets the impression from Carnap's autobiographical essay, as well as from his reply to his critics in the book devoted to discussions of his work edited by Paul Schilpp, that his wide network of associates and partners in intellectual exchange in America contributed to a broadening of Carnap's outlook and philosophical sympathies, and perhaps also to a toning down of the dogmatic stance he and his Vienna associates had taken previously. They were now no longer an embattled saving remnant. They could afford to become more flexible in the way they defended their main tenets.

Carnap has remarked that modern logic, still almost unknown in his native Germany, was at the time he arrived already regarded by many in America as an important field of philosophy. What is more, a number of other philosophical tendencies such as pragmatism, critical realism, and sets of ideas stemming from the British tradition of G. E. Moore and the early Wittgenstein, while diverging from the ideas of the Vienna Circle, still shared a concern with the development of symbolic logic and the rejection of metaphysics. But Carnap also has remarked that at the University of Chicago he was often made uncomfortable by colleagues, such as the Thomist philosopher Mortimer Adler, who stubbornly defended the age-old tradition of transcendental philosophy. "In some philosophical discussion meetings, " Carnap has written, "I had the weird feeling that I was sitting among a group of medieval learned men with long beards and solemn robes."[9] Although he had been able to bring two younger former colleagues, Carl Hempel and Olaf Helmer, from Europe to the University of Chicago as his research associates, one still has the feeling that Carnap was somewhat isolated at Chicago, where many considered him a great scholar in the formal study of language and in the logic and philosophy of science but thought that he was naively unaware of those philosophical problems that did not lend themselves to his physicalist criteria of verifiability.

Carnap continued to be highly productive in his years in America. His *Introduction to Semantics* (1942) and his pathbreaking *Logical Foundations of Probability* (1950),[10] as well as many other writings, brought him fame and recognition both here and abroad. Carnap had a number of influential students and younger associates among native Americans, of which

Nelson Goodman and Hilary Putnam are perhaps the best known. His influence was pervasive. Quine said in 1971 that Carnap was "the dominant figure in philosophy from the 1930s onward."

After teaching for many years at the University of Chicago, Carnap in 1953 accepted the chair at UCLA that his lifelong friend Hans Reichenbach had occupied until his premature death. Carnap himself died in 1970. He was regarded, during his lifetime and after, as one of the great masters of the logic of science. His application of the logical tools of Frege, Tarski, and Russell to problems in semantics and the philosophy of language were outstanding achievements. His ready acceptance and relatively unproblematic career in America surely helped to sustain his continued creativity and productivity until the end. The fact that symbolic logic and formal methods in linguistics and the philosophy of science have now become essential parts of the curriculum in nearly all departments of philosophy owes a great deal to the pioneering efforts of Carnap and his associates. But in general philosophy, though the impact of the Vienna Circle has been strongly felt, certain older traditions, such as pragmatism and newer phenomenological trends still find their defenders here. Carnap and his associates established a powerful stronghold *in partibus infidelium*, but they did not conquer, as they had perhaps hoped, the whole territory.

Turning briefly to the careers of other members of the Vienna Circle, one notes that almost all of them found secure niches in the American academy and were able to attract students who continued their tradition in this country. The Hamburg-born Hans Reichenbach, after having spent five years as a refugee scholar at the University of Istanbul, came to this country in 1938 at the invitation of UCLA, where he taught until his death in 1953. He was scheduled to give the prestigious William James lectures at Harvard in that year but died shortly before. His books on the philosophy of physics and related matters such as *The Philosophical Foundations of Quantum Mechanics, Philosophical Problems of Space and Time* and *The Rise of Scientific Philosophy*[11] have become influential contributions to the philosophy of science even though they are no longer as eagerly consulted as a few decades ago. Like Carnap, Reichenbach never wanted for receptive students, and his continued influence on a younger generation of philosophers of science seems assured.

Herbert Feigl, after first teaching at the University of Iowa (where he was succeeded by another member of the Vienna Circle, Gustav Bergmann), moved to the University of Minnesota, where, in association with some of his native-born colleagues, he helped to found the Minnesota Center for Philosophy of Science as a research department within the university. Its many publications served for many years as effective propagators of the philosophy of science in America and elsewhere.[12]

Carl Hempel, who originally belonged to the Berlin branch of logical positivism under Reichenbach, arrived in this country in 1937. After serving for a while as Carnap's research associate at the University of Chicago, he moved to Queens College but soon thereafter went to Yale and finally to Princeton, where he became an influential teacher who made Princeton into one of the most outstanding centers of instruction and research in the philosophy of science. Among his distinguished students are Jaegwan Kin at the University of Michigan and Adolf Gruenbaum at the University of Pittsburgh. In contrast to most other members of the Vienna Circle, who were mainly concerned with the natural sciences, Hempel wrote searchingly on the social sciences and on the logic of historical inquiry. His 1942 paper on "The Functions of General Laws in History,"[13] in which he proposed that historical explanation should rely on "covering laws" so that the occurrence of historical events could be deduced from general laws and statements of antecedent conditions, has been debated at great length among historians and social scientists. Hempel's *Fundamentals of Concept Formation in Empirical Science* (1952), as well as his writing on typology in the social sciences, have been influential among sociologists—Paul F. Lazarsfeld and Robert K. Merton, for example. It would seem that Hempel almost alone among logical positivists has succeeded in reaching an audience of social scientists and historians which has otherwise been unreceptive to their message.[14]

Kurt Goedel, of the Princeton Institute for Advanced Study, is perhaps the most influential of all the refugee members of the Vienna Circle, but since almost all his work is in mathematics rather than in philosophy, he will not be discussed here. A more extended study would have to deal, inter alia, with University of California psychologist Egon Brunswik, Harvard professor of physics Philipp Frank, and philosopher Paul Schilpp of Northwestern University, who is best known as the devoted editor of the widely acclaimed Library of Living Philosophers.

On the present scene, Vienna Circle philosophy is no longer a distinctive doctrine, but its diffuse influence continues to be pervasive. The assessment by the well-known Australian philosopher John Passmore, a scholar by no means hostile to the Vienna Circle, seems balanced enough to be quoted at some length:

Logical Positivism, considered as the doctrine of a sect, has disintegrated. In various ways it has been absorbed into the international movement of contemporary empiricism, within which the disputes which divided it are still being fought out. . . . Logical positivism, then, is dead, or as dead as a philosophical movement ever becomes. But it has left a legacy behind. . . . Insofar as it is widely agreed that transcendental metaphysics, if not meaningless, is at least otiose, that philosophers ought to set an example of precision and clarity, that philosophy should make us use technical devices, deriving from logic, in order to solve problems relating to the philosophy of science, that philosophy is not about 'the world' but about the language through which men speak about the world, we can detect in contemporary philosophy at least, the persistence of the spirit which inspired the Vienna Circle.[15]

Even if they did not conquer it, the members of the Vienna Circle left a substantial imprint on American philosophy. By becoming deeply absorbed in the general philosophy of empiricism, the Vienna Circle philosophers were not able to maintain their earlier distinctiveness. The circle died of its members' success. Most of these one-time outsiders became insiders in America and hence found it impossible to maintain their separateness. But though their influence was more diffuse than they might have expected, it was still consequential and widespread. The readiness of many American philosophers to receive the newcomers from Vienna and Berlin paid splendid dividends. If Anglo-Saxon philosophy of science and of language is now the most sophisticated and developed in the world, much of the credit belongs to the members of the Vienna Circle.

Aron Gurwitsch (1901–1973) and the Early Phenomenological Movement in America

The followers of Edmund Husserl's phenomenological approach and their allies among existential philosophers did not find a favorable environment upon their arrival in America. This was in contrast to the reception of the Vienna Circle's logical positivists, who, it will be remembered, found an audience in America immediately after coming here because they shared major philosophical assumptions with a significant number of their native-born colleagues. They arrived at the right time for their message to be heard, whereas the phenomenologists and existential philosophers came here several decades too early from the point of view of their careers.

Unlike the Vienna Circle philosophers, who soon moved into prestigious chairs in major universities, those of their colleagues who followed in the footsteps of Husserl or Martin Heidegger had to be content with positions in relatively minor university departments or at the New School for Social Research, that bastion of Continental approaches to the social sciences and philosophy. Very few of the phenomenologists' native-born colleagues in philosophy had been influenced by Husserl or Heidegger before World War II or knew much about their work. The phenomenologists hence did not find the support that comes from networks of congenial thinkers and remained isolated on the American philosophical scene. Only several decades after their arrival, partly under the influence of a handful of students trained by Continental refugees, would phenomenology and existential philosophy grow to major stature on the American intellectual scene. I shall take the career of Aron Gurwitsch as a typical example of the career of phenomenologists in America. (Alfred Schutz, Gurwitsch's close friend, is dealt with in pp. 121-25.)

If one wishes to illustrate the notion of "marginal man," Aron Gurwitsch's life provides a prototypical example.[1] He was born in Vilna, Lithuania, then part of czarist Russia, in 1901, to Jewish parents. He attended gymnasium in the German city of Danzig, where he was treated as an "enemy alien" during World War I. Soon after the war, Gurwitsch left Danzig to pursue a university education. He studied mathematics and philosophy at the universities of Berlin and Freiburg and psychology at Frankfurt, and received his Ph.D. in philosophy summa cum laude under Moritz Geiger at Goettingen in 1927. He had a number of eminent teachers, such as Geiger, Kurt Goldstein, and Carl Stumpf, but when he came under the profound influence of Edmund Husserl at Freiburg he resolved that he would thenceforth devote himself, as he put it much later, to "the service of Husserlian phenomenology," "intending to advance and to develop [it] further rather than merely expound."[2] "It was the style of Husserl's philosophizing," Gurwitsch wrote in an autobiographical aside, "that made the young student take the decision to devote his life and work to the continuation and expansion of Husserl's phenomenology—in a word to become a disciple forever, faithful to Husserl's spirit and general orientation, but at the same time prepared to depart from particular theories."[3] Gurwitsch never wavered from this devotion to Husserl's general philosophical approach throughout the trials and tribulations of his career.

Husserl's phenomenological approach can hardly be dealt with adequately here. It must suffice to say that Husserl attempted to develop the phenomenological method as a way of elucidating the features of the world as they appear to the intentionally oriented consciousness. "Constitutive phenomenology," as Gurwitsch puts it, "can well be characterized as the consistent and radical development of [the] privilege of consciousness into its last ramifications and consequences."[4] The phenomenological method attempts to reach the pure essences of objects of inquiry through the phenomenological reduction whereby all existential belief is bracketed or suspended. Thus, to quote Gurwitsch again, "the pre-eminent task of philosophy may be defined as accounting for objects of every type and kind and for objectivity in every conceivable sense in subjective terms—i.e., in terms of acts of consciousness."[5]

As a Russian emigré, Gurwitsch did not manage to attain a teaching position in Germany, although he published several philosophical articles after the completion of his dissertation. When Hitler came to power in 1933, Gurwitsch fled to France. He was later to remark that he was a practiced emigré, wise in the ways of passports, visas, and cartes d'identité, collecting and discarding nationalities like so many pieces of clothing.

The French academy proved somewhat more receptive to Gurwitsch than the Germans had been. He served as a lecturer at the Institut d'Histoire des Sciences of the Sorbonne between 1933 and 1940. His sponsors were the philosophers Léon Brunschwicg and Alexandre Koyré as well as the anthropologist Lucien Lévy-Bruhl. One has the impression that the Paris years were among the happiest in Gurwitsch's life, as they allowed him to come into contact with young philosophers, such as Merleau-Ponty and Sartre, who also were at the beginning of their careers and were intent upon freeing French philosophizing from its Cartesian and Kantian allegiances in the image of the work of Husserl and Heidegger.

Soon after the beginning of World War II, in 1940, Gurwitsch decided to leave France and come to the United States, his third country of refuge. His early years here were difficult indeed. During the first eight years in this country he managed to receive only temporary academic appointments. He was a visiting lecturer at Johns Hopkins from 1940 to 1942, moved to Harvard in 1943, and stayed there as an instructor until 1946. But he taught physics at Harvard rather than philosophy. He was a visiting lecturer at Wheaton College from 1947 to 1948; but it was only in 1948 that Gurwitsch, then approaching his fifties, received a regular faculty appointment at the as yet little-known Brandeis University, where he was for many years the chairperson of the department of philosophy and had a hand in shaping it. Gurwitsch had no graduate students, as in those years Brandeis did not offer graduate instruction in philosophy.

It was only in 1959, when he was nearing his sixties, that Gurwitsch finally moved to a full professorial position in a graduate department—at The New School for Social Research. I remember him remarking wryly that, although he welcomed the new appointment and the prospect of helping to train graduate students, he also felt that, given the Continental character of the New School, he was subtly being "put into his place." Nevertheless, it was in the next fourteen years at the New School that Gurwitsch came fully into his own.

From 1929 on, he had brought out roughly one philosophical article per year, first in German, then in French, then in English. He published his first book, *Théorie du champ de la conscience*, in 1957 at the age of fifty-six. It is worth noting that he wrote the book in French, even though by then he had already lived and taught for seventeen years in the United States. Only seven years later did he publish an English version.[6] But with Gurwitsch's coming to the New School his rate of publication increased rapidly. Having found an audience not only there but among many younger colleagues who from the 1960s on made their appearance in the philosophy departments of a number of universities, Gurwitsch became considerably more productive than during his years of relative isolation. His *Studies in Phenomenology and Psychology* (a collection of papers published earlier both here and abroad) appeared in 1966. Shortly before his death he completed a major treatise on Leibniz's Panlogism (1974).[7] His *Phenomenology and the Theory of Science* (1974)[8] was published posthumously. When death struck, Gurwitsch was at work on still another work, *Logic and Reality*.

Gurwitsch's remarkable spurt in productivity at an age when many scholars begin to slow down was at least partly motivated by the new audience he had found in America in the 1960s. When he arrived here, there were few philosophical publications receptive to phenomenological research. *Philosophy and Phenomenological Research*, founded in 1941, was the only major outlet for work in the Husserlian tradition, and Gurwitsch contributed several major articles to that journal from 1941 to 1957. But apart from these papers, one article in *The Journal of Philosophy*, and a few contributions to collections of essays, Gurwitsch wrote mainly for French and German publications until the early 1960s.

In the 1960s interest in phenomemological and related approaches in America increased rapidly.[9] A number of major scholarly publishers, such as Northwestern University Press, Ohio University Press, Indiana University Press, Humanities Press, and the Press of Duquesne University eagerly sought manuscripts on phenomenological themes and published translations of the works of Continental phenomenologists and existentialists. In addition, a variety of philosophical journals such as *Research in Phenomenology* and the *Journal of the British Society for Phenomenology* now vied for significant contributions. While at an earlier stage only the New School had a philosophical faculty that was devoted to phenomenological research, now a number of other universities, from Yale to Northwestern, from the State University of New York at Stony Brook to Duquesne, Pennsylvania State, Boston College, and Purdue, had faculty members belonging to the phenomenological movement. Many of these young teachers had been trained at the New School. Gurwitsch's own students, however, largely teach in colleges rather than in universities. Only two of them are in doctorate-granting institutions, M. Natanson at Yale and Lester Embree at Duquesne. Thus Gurwitsch's fate continues with his students.

Not only in philosophy but also in sociology, largely due to the influence of Gurwitsch's close personal friend and comrade-in-arms Alfred Schutz, phenomenological approaches began to enjoy a rapidly growing attention from the 1960s on. Gurwitsch was a bit bewildered by these sociological approaches, especially as applied by some of the disciples of Harold Garfinkel, the founder of "ethnomethodology," but he must nevertheless have rejoiced in the fact that phenomenology had spread well beyond its earlier narrow confines. The newfound audience, he seems to have noted with satisfaction, was eager to learn from one of the last philosophers who had sat at the feet of Edmund Husserl, and it thus behooved him, Gurwitsch, to bring the fruits of his many years of philosophical reflection to the eyes and minds of an eager audience. When his friends and former students published a festschrift for him (*Life-World and Consciousness: Essays for Dr. Aron Gurwitsch*) in 1972,[10] he must have realized that, despite all his wanderings and the lack of recognition that had been his lot for many years, he had finally achieved the supreme satisfaction of reaching a stable audience of scholars for whom his work was consequential.

Gurwitsch remained throughout his life in the United States only peripherally and inorganically connected with American cultural trends and the life of the American mind. He stressed in many conversations I had with him that he was not really at home in America. While Alfred Schutz made a major effort to engage himself with native American philosophical trends, Gurwitsch did not. He published one article on William James but otherwise remained detached from American mainline philosophy. While he made efforts to integrate into his phenomenology the theories of, inter alia, Jean Piaget, Kurt Goldstein, and Gestalt psychology, he made no such efforts in regard to American psychology or philosophy. The index to his *Studies in Phenomenology and Psychology* has many entries under Bergson, Merleau-Ponty, Sartre, and various German scholars, but there are no references to American authors except William James. The other major pragmatists, John Dewey and George Herbert Mead, do not seem to have attracted Gurwitsch's interest. He admired Charles Peirce but did not comment on him in his writings.

There is no record that Gurwitsch had connections with other than phenomenological societies or journals. He served on the editorial board of several philosophical journals and was an active member of several philosophical societies, but these were all parts of the phenomenological movement.

His private life also, it seems, was largely based on close friendships with European refugees, such as Alfred Schutz, or with native-born American phenomenologists. The fact that Aron Gurwitsch and his wife, Alice, a talented painter, had no children may also have contributed to the tenuousness of their ties to American society. Children were often the intermediaries that linked their refugee parents to closer associations with native-born Americans.

The Gurwitsches lived quiet lives in their apartments in Cambridge and later on New York's West Side. Warm, hospitable, ever attentive to their guests, both lovely human beings, they were devoted to their friends and visitors. Their home reminded one instantly of the homes of European professors. Throughout his life in America, Gurwitsch lived in American society and the American academy, but he was never fully a part of it. He remained a European scholar through the more than thirty years he dwelt in America. It is perhaps symbolic that he died while vacationing in Switzerland. Yet his impact is likely to persist for a long time in the now well-established American phenomenological movement.[11]

Paul Tillich (1886–1965): Refugee Theologian à la Mode Américaine

Paul Tillich entitled one of the several autobiographical sketches he published in this country *On the Boundary*. This title and some of the chapter headings of the book—"Between City and Country," "Between Social Classes," "Between Theory and Practice," "Between Theology and Philosophy," "Between Lutheranism and Socialism," "Between Idealism and Marxism"—convey that throughout his life he located himself in a marginal position. He was truly a marginal man in Germany and remained so in his life-style after he came to America. Yet, while his marginality had led him to take a pronounced radical stance in German theology, philosophy, and politics, his encounter with American culture soon made him abandon most of the radical visions that had animated his youth. As in the case of several other previously radical thinkers, such as the painter Georg Grosz, the composer Kurt Weill, and the psychiatrist Alfred Adler, Tillich's gradual immersion in American culture took the sting out of his previous radical beliefs and helped to make him in a few years one of the exemplars of American New Deal–type liberal culture. While he had had only a small audience among fellow radical intellectuals in Germany, he gained a very large audience among both lay readers and professionals in America. In America the would-be outsider became an intellectual insider.[1]

Tillich was born on August 20, 1886, in a town near the border between the Prussian provinces of Brandenburg and Silesia. His father was a stern, authoritarian, and self-righteous minister of the Lutheran church. When Paul was four years old his father was appointed to a diocese in eastern Brandenburg. The young Tillich grew up in a small town that was still largely medieval in character. He went to the humanistic gymnasium in a neighboring town. He seems to have relished the romantic glow of the medieval atmosphere of the small towns in which he grew up, but he also resented what he experienced as the constrictions of small-town life. Hence he felt "extreme joy" when in 1900 his father was called to an important position in the Lutheran establishment in Berlin. The freer atmosphere of Berlin allowed the young man to escape, at least in part, from the authoritarianism and Lutheran paternalism, not only of his father's household, but of his previous schools as well. Discipline and authority permeated the atmosphere in which Tillich grew up, and it was largely in a spirit of revolt against this intellectually and morally stultifying milieu that Tillich slowly developed his own libertarian style of life and thought.

These tendencies toward revolt and radical rejection did not emerge at the outset of Tillich's career. In fact, his life plan at first seemed thoroughly conventional. After finishing his gymnasium studies in Berlin, he followed in the footsteps of his father by embarking on a career that would prepare him for the Lutheran ministry. After studying in the theological faculties of Berlin, Tuebingen, and Halle, he acquired a Ph.D. from Breslau in 1911 and a license in theology from Halle a year later. Soon thereafter he was ordained into the Evangelical Lutheran church.

When World War I broke out, Tillich volunteered to join the German army as a war chaplain. This war experience proved to be the turning point in his life. He had been a proud German patriot, politically naive, embued with romantic idealism. When he returned to Berlin four years later he was utterly transformed. He had become a radical Christian socialist and a cultural pessimist deeply influenced by Nietzsche and the existentialist thinkers. The repressed, puritanical young man now assumed a Bohemian life-style in which a variety of erotic adventures played a considerable part.

First as a privatdozent of theology at the University of Berlin (from 1919 to 1924), later as a professor of philosophy of religion and social philosophy at the universities of Marburg, Dresden, and Leipzig, and finally as a professor of philosophy at the University of Frankfurt (1929–33), Tillich developed a radical political and moral outlook that was congenial to many young men and women of his generation who felt that they had liberated themselves from the constraints of orthodox Lutheran doctrine.

Upon his return to Berlin at the end of the war, Tillich joined the Independent Socialist party (USPD), a left-wing breakaway from the Social Democratic party (SPD). In Berlin, Tillich also joined a group of religious radical socialists, including such men as Adolf Loewe, Eduard Heimann, and Arnold Wolfers, who would later follow him as refugees to America. The group became known as the "Kairos Circle" (hinting at the notion that the "right time" for a revolutionary transformation of the bourgeois world was close). The group published a small journal, the *Blaetter fuer religioesen Sozialismus,* in which many of Tillich's radical political and religious essays were first published.

In the interwar years, Tillich considered himself an unorthodox Marxist. Even though he wanted to be regarded as a member of the Marxist movement, his religious socialism was largely an amalgam of specifically Marxist tenets and humanitarian and ethical themes that were foreign to the orthodox Marxist vision. He conceived of socialism as a "restructuring of the world according to love and justice." Belief in the class struggle went side by side with appeals to a new Christian community based on love and charity.[2]

After Tillich moved to the University of Frankfurt, where he became a close intellectual companion of Max Horkheimer and other members of the Frankfurt school as well as of Karl Mannheim, Tillich's radical Marxist vision became even more pronounced. When some of Marx's early writings became available for the first time, Tillich welcomed them enthusiastically since they seemed to bolster his own humanistic and antimechanistic socialist stance.

Despite his close association with radical Marxist thinkers who were atheists, Tillich insisted that he remained a religious thinker. The religious socialism he preached "seeks to overcome the static opposition of the concepts of religion and socialism by demonstrating their dialectical relationship." For him, socialism was a prophetic movement because it broke the powers of blood, soil, tribe, and nation in the expectation of an imminent transformation, and because it presented a promise of future fulfillment.[3]

Tillich's tenacity in clinging to a religious vision separated him to some extent from his Frankfurt friends. But his religion was resolutely non-supernatural. All sorts of experiences and attitudes—whether esthetic, moral, or political—could be seen, so he preached, as religious, provided that they were embued with what Tillich variously called "unconditional" or "ultimate" concern.

In an early polemic between Karl Barth, the great Protestant theologian, and Tillich, Barth accused Tillich of still fighting "against the Grand Inquisitor."[4] By this he meant that Tillich was constantly in revolt against any authoritarian system based on heteronomy. Tillich readily granted that this was indeed the case. "History has shown," he wrote, "that the Grand Inquisitor is always ready to appear in different disguises, political as well as theological."[5]

Yet, as will be shown below, soon after coming to America, Tillich dropped almost all of his previous rebelliousness. As he himself wrote, "The fight against the Grand Inquisitor could lapse [in America], at least before the beginning of the second half of this century."[6] Preoccupation with the "ultimate concern" was to remain in the forefront of Tillich's preaching and writing, but socialist commitment and prophetic Marxist visions did not survive the transatlantic passage.

In Germany, publication of the *Neue Blaetter fuer religioesen Sozialismus* was forbidden soon after Hitler came to power. Most of the academic members of its editorial board were suspended or dismissed from their professorships. Tillich wondered for a while whether he should withdraw from membership in the Social Democratic party as a defense against possible reprisals, but he did not do so. Tillich's name is on the first list of those suspended from university teaching, dated April 13, 1933. The names of his friends Max Horkheimer and Adolf Loewe appeared on the same list, along with those of such major figures as Paul Klee and Alfred Weber. While many of the persons on this list decided almost immediately to leave Germany, Tillich hesitated, hoping against hope that his post in Frankfurt would be restored. He accepted an invitation from the Union Theological Seminary in New York to lecture there for a year, but only after seeking and gaining permission to leave from the relevant Nazi authorities. When he was informed by the Nazi minister of culture at the end of December 1933 that he would not be permitted to hold an official position in Germany, he protested in terms that were, to say the least, curious. He argued, for example, in a letter to the Nazi minister that, "As a theoretician of religious socialism I have fought throughout the years against the dogmatic marxism of the German labor movement, and thereby I have supplied a number of concepts to the National Socialist theoreticians."[7] The less said about this painful letter the better. Only after he had abandoned hope of receiving a reply did Tillich finally decide to cast his lot with America.

The initial invitation to lecture at Union Theological Seminary came from its president, Henry Sloane Coffin, who had seen Tillich's name on a list of persecuted German academics in need of help. Coffin asked Reinhold Niebuhr to provide him with background information about Tillich. It so happened that Niebuhr's younger brother, H. Richard Niebuhr, had translated and written an introduction to Tillich's book *The Religious Situation* (1932). Both Niebuhrs considered themselves radical theologians at that time, and they probably saw Tillich as a kindred spirit. It was largely at their prodding that Union Seminary extended its invitation to Tillich.

When Tillich and his wife arrived in New York in November 1933, they hardly knew the country and its culture. They spoke almost no English. Even after he had studied diligently, so one is told, Tillich's first lecture was hardly understandable. He retained a pronounced German accent to the end of his life, and his linguistic lapses gave rise to a series of affectionate and funny stories that continue to circulate about him up to this day.

From 1933 to 1937, Tillich was reappointed from year to year as a visiting professor at Union Theological Seminary. His salary was low indeed—no more than $3,500 a year—for several years, even though it was subsidized by the Rockefeller Foundation and the Emergency Committee for Displaced Persons. But in compensation the Tillichs were given a large and comfortable apartment in a building belonging to the seminary. Only in 1937 was Tillich, largely owing to a petition circulated by his students, finally appointed associate professor of philosophical theology for three years at a salary of $4,500 and with the promise of a larger apartment. His elevation to the status of full professor was postponed for another three years because of the protests of some conservative members of the faculty. From 1940 to 1955 he served as professor of philosophical theology.

Tillich does not seem to have been particularly perturbed about starting his career all over again at the bottom of the ladder. He had originally hoped to secure a position in a philosophy department of a major university, but that hope was soon dispelled. Philosophy departments were staffed by pragmatists or logical positivists who had no use for what they considered Teutonic obscurantism. So Tillich, who was in any case fascinated and attracted by the cosmopolitan cultural life of New York, decided that he would patiently wait for a permanent position at the seminary.

His close friendship with Reinhold Niebuhr allowed Tillich to have a secure anchorage at the seminary as well as a reliable guide to American academic mores. He never showed particular interest in the complications of administrative and committee work. He was reticent about expressing his opinions when it came to curricular changes or faculty promotions, but he lectured and preached conscientiously. Tillich's social relations with his colleagues were friendly but formal. Except for Niebuhr, he largely associated with old friends from Europe rather than with his American colleagues. His students sometimes found it hard to follow the intricacies of his thought, but they loved him nevertheless. He was a beloved figure, and, as the years went by and his name became more widely known in the philosophical and the theological community, he became an intensely admired exemplar.

Soon after his arrival in America, Tillich began to publish in a variety of publications ranging from *The American Scholar* to *Christianity and Crisis* and *Commentary*. In the later 1940s and in the 1950s, he wrote a number of major works that spread his renown well beyond narrow philosophical or theological circles. His *The Protestant Era* (1948), *Systematic Theology*, vol. 1 (1951), and, above all, *The Courage to Be* (1952) were widely reviewed and discussed by critics who were not usually attracted by theological thought. Only his close friend Reinhold Niebuhr could boast a comparable audience.

One cannot help but feel that the immense success of Tillich's writings had something to do with the studied vagueness and ambiguity of his theological pronouncements. When he told his audiences that God is that which unconditionally and ultimately concerns us, this might have appealed even to listeners who would have had great difficulty accepting supernatural religious imagery. In the 1940s and 1950s, many American intellectuals who had become disillusioned with Marxism, especially in its Communist manifestation, and who felt vaguely uneasy in a secular world that seemed to be largely devoid of meaning, Tillich's thought seemed appealing, just like that of Reinhold Niebuhr. Arthur Schlesinger, Jr., once proposed laughingly that what was needed was an association of "Atheists for Niebuhr"; he might have said the same for Tillich. Tillich in theology, just like Erich Fromm in psychology, proposed a spiritual cure for uneasy souls vaguely perturbed about the spiritual desolation of America amid unprecedented material prosperity.

Tillich made no great effort to acquaint himself with indigenous theological or philosophical thought in this country. His mind was essentially fixed before he came here. Apart from a short period during the war, when he chaired the Council for a Democratic Germany, a stillborn attempt to create an umbrella organization for all German refugee factions, Tillich did not concern himself with political affairs. His socialist convictions, if they existed at all, had been put on a back burner. What he embraced with genuine enthusiasm was America's democratic and, as he saw it, antiauthoritarian spirit. A nation in which schools and families were governed in a nonauthoritarian manner, where there was no authoritarianism in religion or in administration—so Tillich saw the matter—no longer needed to fight the Grand Inquisitor. Tillich's restless and rebellious spirit had come to rest in the America of the New Deal.

After his retirement from the Union Theological Seminary in 1955, Tillich became a university professor at Harvard, where he served until 1962. In the last three years of his life he occupied a chair in theology at the University of Chicago. Tillich's faithful disciple and translator, his apostle to the American gentiles, theologian James Luther Adams, seems to have had a large hand in securing both these positions for him. In both of them, Tillich was treated with great reverence. He had become a kind of totem animal.

In the last few years, the erstwhile rebellious firebrand from Germany became an American institution, a revered and highly respected voice that, far from being critical of things American, provided soothing relief from the anxieties and the spiritual unease of the times. When the "socialist decision" of yore became the "courage to be," America had managed to domesticate a rebellious mind and rendered innocuous what had once been a spirit of revolt from things as they are.

In Tillich's vocabulary, *sin* became separation; *grace,* reunion; *God,* the ground and aim of being; and *faith,* ultimate concern. Traditional religious terms and notions were transmuted into vaguely existentialist language that suited modern men and women who would have been embarrassed by old theological language. What could be more soothing than to learn that instead of Christ one might better speak of "New Being," and instead of the "Holy Spirit," of "spiritual presence"? A nay-sayer from Germany had become a yea-sayer in his adopted land.[8]

Notes

Preface

1. Cf. Jennifer Platt, "Stouffer and Lazarsfeld: Patterns of Influence," paper given at the 1983 meeting of the American Sociological Association in Detroit.

2. Cf. Mark Granovetter, "The Strength of Weak Ties," *American Journal of Sociology* 78, no. 6 (May 1973): 1360–81.

Part I: Introduction

1. Francis Bacon, *History of the Reign of King Henry VII,* in *Works,* ed. J. Spedding et al., 14 vols. (Boston, 1900), 11:363.

2. Karl Marx, *The Eighteenth Brumaire of Louis Bonaparte* (New York: International Publishers, 1963), p. 13.

3. Cf. Franz Neumann, "The Social Sciences," in Rex Crawford, ed., *The Cultural Migration: The European Scholar in America* (Philadelphia: University of Pennsylvania Press, 1953), pp. 4–26, and Hans Speier, "The Social Conditions of the Exile Intellectual," in Hans Speier, *Social Order and the Risks of War* (Cambridge: MIT Press, 1969), chapter 7.

4. There were, to be sure, also cases in which refugees inflated their previous status in order to gain preferment here.

5. Neumann, "The Social Sciences."

6. William J. Goode, *The Celebration of Heroes: Prestige as a Control System* (Berkeley: University of California Press, 1978), p. 56.

7. After the death of the Cornell classicist Harry Caplan in 1980, the following letter from several of his former teachers was found in his desk:

> My dear Caplan: I want to second Professor Bristol's advice and urge you to get into secondary teaching. The opportunities for college positions, never too many, are at present few and likely to be fewer. I can encourage no one to look forward to securing a college post. There is, moreover, a very real prejudice against the Jew. Personally, I do not share this, and I am sure the same is true of all our staff here. But we have seen so many well-equipped Jews fail to secure appointments that this fact has been forced upon us. I recall Alfred Gudeman, E. A. Loew—both brilliant scholars of international reputation—and yet unable to obtain a college position. I feel it wrong to encourage anyone to devote himself to the higher walks of learning to whom the path is barred by an undeniable racial prejudice. In this I am joined by all my classical colleagues, who have authorized me to append their signatures with my own to this letter. [Signed] Charles E. Bennet, C. L. Durham, George S. Bristol, E. P. Andrews. [Dated] Ithaca, March 27, 1919.

Cornell Alumni News 84 (July 1981): 7. Comment seems superfluous. Caplan did not follow this advice. For a general treatment of anti-Semitism in the American academy, cf. E. Digby Baltzell, *The Protestant Establishment* (New York: Vintage, 1966).

8. H. Stuart Hughes, "Social Theory in a New Context," paper delivered at a lecture series at the Smithsonian Institution, spring 1980. Cf. also his printed version in Jarrell C. Jackman and Carla M. Borden, *The Muses Flee Hitler* (Washington, D.C.: Smithsonian Institution Press, 1983), pp. 111–22.

9. Erwin Panofsky, "The History of Art," in Crawford, ed., *The Cultural Migration* pp. 82–111.

10. Cf. Alexander Weinstock, "Some Factors that Retard or Accelerate the Rate of Acculturation," *Human Relations* 17 (1964): 321–40.

11. H. Stuart Hughes, "Social Theory in a New Context."

12. Mary McCarthy, "Exiles, Expatriates and Internal Emigrés," *The Listener* 86, no. 2226 (Nov. 25, 1971): 2.

13. Arnold Brecht, *Mit der Kraft des Geistes: Lebenserinnerungen, Zweite Haelfte* (Stuttgart: Deutsche Verlagsanstalt), p. 383.

14. Henry Pachter, "A Memoir," *Salamagundi*, nos. 10–11 (Fall 1969–Winter 1970), pp. 12–51.

15. Ibid.

16. Ibid.

17. Neumann, "The Social Sciences," p. 20.

18. Rose Laub Coser, "The Complexity of Roles as a Seedbed of Individual Autonomy," in Lewis A. Coser, ed., *The Idea of Social Structure: Papers in Honor of Robert K. Merton* (New York: Harcourt Brace Jovanovich, 1975), pp. 237–63. Quote on p. 254.

19. Ibid, p. 247.

20. H. Stuart Hughes, "Social Theory in a New Context."

21. Georg Simmel, "The Stranger," in Kurt H. Wolff, ed., *The Sociology of Georg Simmel* (New York: The Free Press, 1950), pp. 402–08.

22. Alfred Schutz, "The Stranger," in his *Collected Papers*, vol. 2 (The Hague: Nijhoff), pp. 91–105. See also similar observations by Karl Mannheim and Thorstein Veblen.

23. Maurice Halbwachs, *The Collective Memory* (New York: Harper, Colophon, 1980).

24. Schutz, "The Stranger," p. 96.

Part II: Psychology and Psychoanalysis

Kurt Lewin

1. For biographical and bibliographical details on Lewin, I have chiefly relied on Alfred J. Marrow's *The Practical Theorist: The Life and Work of Kurt Lewin* (New York: Basic Books, 1969). Cf. the following for detailed discussion of Lewin's work and that of his disciples: Dorwin Cartwright, "Lewinian Theory as a Contemporary Systematic Framework," in Sigmund Koch, ed., *Psychology: A Study of a Science* (New York: McGraw-Hill, 1959), 2:7ff.; and Morton Deutsch, "Field Theory in Social Psychology," in Gardner Lindzey and Elliot Aronson, eds., *The Handbook of Social Psychology,* 2d ed. (Reading, Mass.: Addison-Wesley, 1968), 1:412ff. For a current assessment of Lewin's work, see the July 1978 issue of *The Journal of the History of the Behavioral Sciences* vol. 14, no. 3, with contributions by Jerome Frank, Erling Eng, Mary Henle, Steve Heims, and Ralph K. White. For a recent assessment of Lewin's continued impact on social psychology, see Leon Festinger, ed., *Retrospections on Social Psychology* (New York: Oxford University Press, 1980).

2. Terman to Boring, August 13, 1931, Boring Papers. Cited in Michael M. Sokal, "The Gestalt Psychologists in Behaviorist America," presented at the symposium "The Muses Flee Hitler I," Smithsonian Institution, February, 1980.

3. New York: McGraw-Hill.

4. New York: McGraw-Hill.

5. Kurt Lewin, "Forces behind Food Habits and Methods of Changes," National Research Council Bulletin, no. 108 (1943): pp. 35–65.

6. Edwin Boring, *A History of Experimental Psychology,* 2d ed. (New York: Appleton-Century, 1957), p. 724.

7. Marrow, *The Practical Theorist,* p. 229.

8. Ibid., p. 235.

Wolfgang Koehler, Kurt Koffka, and Max Wertheimer

1. Grace M. Heider, "Kurt Koffka," *International Encyclopedia of the Social Sciences* (New York: Macmillan, 1968), hereafter cited as *IESS.*

2. See Jean Matter Mandler and George Mandler, "The Diaspora of Experimental Psychology: The Gestaltists and Others," in Donald Fleming and Bernard Bailyn, eds., *The Intellectual Migration* (Cambridge, Mass.: Harvard University Press, 1969). I have used this fine paper throughout this section.

3. Cf. Harry Helson, "Why Did Their Precursors Fail and the Gestaltist Psychologists Succeed?" *American Psychologist* 24 (1969): 1006–11.

4. Mary Henle, "Wolfgang Koehler," *Year Book of the American Philosophical Society,* 1968, p. 143. Hereafter cited as *YAPS.*

5. Mary Henle, "The Influence of Gestalt Psychology in America," *Annals of the New York Academy of Science* 291 (April 18, 1977): 3–12. I have used this fine paper throughout these pages.

6. For biographical information on Wertheimer, see, in addition to the above, Abraham Luchins, "Max Wertheimer," *IESS;* Edwin B. Newman, "Max Wertheimer," *The American Journal of Psychology* 57, 20.3 (July 1944): 429–35; and an as yet unpublished paper by Wertheimer's son, the psychologist Michael Wertheimer, entitled "Max Wertheimer, Gestalt Prophet," read before the Nebraska Wesleyan Symposium on Gestalt Psychology in April 1978 and later given as Michael Wertheimer's Presidential Address for the Division of the History of Psychology of the American Psychological Association.

7. See Mary Henle, "Wolfgang Koehler," *YAPS;* Hans Wallach, "Wolfgang Koehler," *IESS;* for an overall appreciation of Koehler's work, see W. C. H. Prentice, "The Systematic Psychology of Wolfgang Koehler," in Sigmund Koch, ed., *Psychology: A Study of a Science,* vol. 1 (New York: McGraw-Hill, 1959), pp. 427ff.

8. Wolfgang Koehler, *Mentality of the Apes,* 2d ed., trans. from the German by Ella Winter, International Library of Psychology (Boston: Routledge & Kegan Paul, 1973).

9. *Die Physischen Gestalten in Ruhe und in Stationaeren Zustand.*

10. Cf. Mary Henle, "One Man against the Nazis—Wolfgang Koehler," *American Psychologist* 33, no. 10 (October 1978): 939–44.

11. For biographical information on Koffka, see Grace M. Heider, "Kurt Koffka," *IESS;* M. R. Harrower-Erikson, "Kurt Koffka," *The American Journal of Psychology* 4, no. 2 (April 1942): 278–81.

12. Harrower-Erikson, p. 278.

13. London: Routledge.

14. New York: Harcourt Brace, 1935.

15. Mandler and Mandler, "The Diaspora of Experimental Psychology," p. 389. A more detailed account can be found in Michael M. Sokal, "The Gestalt Psychologists in Behaviorist America," a paper presented to the symposium "The Muses Flee Hitler I," Smithsonian Institution, February, 1980.

16. Cf. Frank S. Freeman, "The Beginnings of Gestalt Psychology in the United States," *Journal of the History of the Behavioral Sciences* 13 (1977): 352–53.

17. See the detailed, though largely unedited, record of Wertheimer's seminars by Abraham Luchins and Edith Luchins, *Wertheimer's Seminars Revisited: Problem Solving and Thinking*, 3 vols. (Albany, N.Y.: Faculty-Student Association, State University of New York, 1970); and *Revisiting Wertheimer's Seminars*, 2 vols. (Lewisburg, Pa.: Bucknell University Press, 1978).

18. Mandler and Mandler, p. 395.

19. Meyer Schapiro, personal communication, April 20, 1981.

20. Mitchell G. Ash, "Gestalt Psychology as a Case Study in the Social History of Science," paper presented to the 22d International Congress of Psychology, Leipzig, G.D.R., July 19, 1980.

21. Mandler and Mandler, p. 389.

22. See Helson, "Why Did Their Precursors Fail and the Gestaltist Psychologists Succeed?" p. 1006. See also Wolfgang Koehler, "The Scientists from Europe and Their New Environment," in W. Rex Crawford, ed., *The Cultural Migration* (Philadelphia: The University of Pennsylvania Press, 1953).

23. Mary Henle, "The Influence of Gestalt Psychology in America."

24. See Helson, n. 22 above.

25. Edwin Boring, "A History of Experimental Psychology, 2d ed. (New York: Appleton-Century, 1957), p. 600.

26. Cf. Mandler and Mandler, p. 398.

27. Quoted in Molly Harrower, "A Note on the Koffka Papers," *Journal of the History of the Behavioral Sciences* 7, no. 2 (April 1971): 151.

28. The following persons were kind enough to give me details on the history of the Gestalt movement in personal communications: Mary Henle, The New School for Social Research; Grace Heider, University of Kansas; Barbara Ross, editor of *The Journal of the History of the Behavioral Sciences;* Robert I. Watson, University of Florida; Eileen A. Gavin, Secretary-Treasurer, Division of the History of Psychology, American Psychological Association; John A. Popplestone, Director, Archives of the History of American Psychology, The University of Akron; and Mitchell G. Ash, who is writing a dissertation on the history of Gestalt psychology. I am most grateful to all of them. The information they provided was so abundant that much of it could not be included in the above few pages. I propose to return to a more detailed study of the Gestalt movement at a later time.

Charlotte Buehler and Karl Buehler

1. For biographical data on Karl Buehler, I have largely relied on Albert Wellek, "Karl Buehler," *Archiv fuer Gesamte Psychologie* 116 (1964): 3–8. A shorter version of this paper can be found in the *IESS*. For biographical data on Charlotte Buehler, I have chiefly relied on her autobiographical paper in Ludwig J. Pongrantz et al., eds., *Psychologie in Selbstdarstellungen* (Bern/Stuttgart/Vienna: Hans Huber, 1972); and on her paper, "Die Wiener Psychologische Schule in der Emigration," *Psychologische Rundschau* 16, no. 3 (1965): 187–96. Albert Wellek's "The Impact of the German Immigration on the Development of American Psychology," *Journal of the History of the Behavioral Sciences* 4, no. 3 (July 1968): 207–29 also proved helpful.

2. Charlotte Buehler, "Die Wiener Psychologische Schule," p. 188.

3. See Charlotte Buehler and Hildegard Hetzer, *Testing Children's Development from Birth to School Age*, translated from the first German edition (1932) (New York: Farrar and Rinehart, 1935).

4. Albert Wellek, "The Impact," p. 220.

European Psychoanalysts in America

1. This section is deeply indebted to the superb historical work of Nathan G. Hale, Jr., *Freud and the Americans: The Beginnings of Psychoanalysis in the United States, 1876–1917* (New

York: Oxford University Press, 1971), and its sequel, "From Berggasse XIX to Central Park West: The Americanization of Psychoanalysis, 1919–1940," *Journal of the History of the Behavioral Sciences* 14 (1978): 219–315, which were indispensable to me in the writing of this section. Unless otherwise noted, all data cited here come from these publications. I have also consulted and profited from the following: Stanford Gifford, "Psychoanalysis in Boston," in George E. Gifford, Jr., ed., *Psychoanalysis, Psychotherapy and the New England Medical Scene, 1894–1944* (New York: Science History Publications/USA, 1978); C. P. Oberndorf, *A History of Psychoanalysis in America* (New York: Grune and Stratton, 1953); Reuben Fine, *A History of Psychoanalysis* (New York: Columbia University Press, 1979). On the domestication and medicalization of psychoanalysis in America, see Russell Jacoby, *The Repression of Psychoanalysis: Otto Fenichel and the Political Freudians* (New York: Basic Books, 1983).

2. Karl Menninger, *A Guide to Psychiatric Books with Some Suggested Reading Lists*, 2d rev. ed. (New York: Grune and Stratton, 1956).

3. Otto Fenichel, oral communication to Rose Laub Coser, Los Angeles, 1940.

4. Hale, *Freud and the Americans*, p. 434.

5. Hale, "From Berggasse XIX," passim, and Fine, *A History*, p. 130.

6. Dr. Charles Brenner, personal communication, New York, January 23, 1980.

7. Ibid.

8. Arnold A. Rogow, *The Psychiatrists* (New York: Putnam's, 1970), p. 38.

9. Dr. Charles Brenner, personal communication, New York, January 23, 1980.

10. Rogow, *The Psychiatrists*, pp. 105–09.

11. See Walter C. Langer and Sanford Gifford, "An American Analyst in Vienna during the Anschluss, 1936–1938," *Journal of the History of the Behavioral Sciences* 14 (1978): 42 and 53.

12. Cf. H. Stuart Hughes, *The Sea Change: The Migration of Social Thought* (New York: Harper & Row, 1975), chap. 5.

13. Hale, "From Berggasse XIX," p. 308.

14. This questionnaire was constructed and analyzed by Rose Laub Coser. All the tabulations are hers. I am most grateful for her contribution in an area in which I lack qualifications which she possesses in ample measure. For consultation I am grateful to Karen Oppenheimer Mason. Judith and Robert Wallerstein were most helpful in locating and identifying many of the respondents.

Erik Homburger Erikson and Wilhelm Reich

1. For the theoretical background of these notions, cf. Rose Laub Coser, "The Complexity of Roles as a Seedbed of Individual Autonomy," in Lewis A Coser, ed., *The Idea of Social Structure* (New York: Harcourt Brace, 1975), pp. 237–63. For Erikson's own analysis of refugee experience, see his "Identity and Uprootedness in Our Time," in *Insight and Responsibility* (New York: Norton, 1964).

2. For biographical data on Erikson, I have largely relied on Robert Coles, *Erik H. Erikson: The Growth of His Work* (Boston: Little, Brown, 1970). See also Maria Piers and Genevieve Landow(?) "Erikson, Erik H.," in *Biographical Supplement to the International Encyclopedia of the Social Sciences* (New York: Macmillan, 1979).

3. New York: Norton, 1950.

4. Cf. Paul Roazen, *Erik Erikson* (New York: The Free Press, 1976).

5. See Mark Granovetter, "The Strength of Weak Ties," *American Journal of Sociology* 78, no. 6 (May 1973): 1360–81.

6. My biographical data are based on *Wilhelm Reich: A Personal Biography*, by Ilse Ollendorf Reich, his former wife (New York: St. Martin's Press, 1969). Myron Sharaf's admiring

yet fair biography, *Fury on Earth: A Biography of Wilhelm Reich* (New York: St. Martin's Press, 1983), appeared too late for me to consult it in detail.

7. Jerome Greenfield's *Wilhelm Reich vs. U.S.A.* (New York: Norton, 1974), contains a detailed account of the investigation and the subsequent trials but is heavily biased in Reich's favor.

8. For detailed discussions of Reich's psychoanalytic work, see Paul Robinson, *The Freudian Left* (New York: Harper & Row, 1969), and Philip Rieff, *The Triumph of the Therapeutic* (New York: Harper Torchbooks, 1968).

Bruno Bettelheim

1. My biographical information is largely based on Morris Janowitz, "Bettelheim, Bruno," in *Biographical Supplement to International Encyclopedia of the Social Sciences* (New York: Macmillan, 1979).

2. Bruno Bettelheim, "Individual and Mass Behavior in Extreme Situations," *Journal of Abnormal and Social Psychology* 38 (1943): 417–52.

3. Eugene L. Hartley et al., eds., *Readings in Social Psychology*, 3d ed. (New York: Holt, Rinehart & Winston, 1958).

4. Cf. Terrence Des Pres, "The Bettelheim Problem," *Social Research* 46, no. 4 (Winter 1979): 619–47.

5. Bruno Bettelheim, *Love Is Not Enough: The Treatment of Emotionally Disturbed Children* (New York: The Free Press, 1950).

6. Bruno Bettelheim and Morris Janowitz, *Dynamics of Prejudice* (New York: The Free Press, 1950).

7. Bruno Bettelheim, *Symbolic Wounds: Puberty Rights and the Envious Male* (New York: The Free Press, 1954).

8. Bruno Bettelheim, *Truants from Life: The Rehabilitation of Emotionally Disturbed Children* (New York: The Free Press, 1955).

9. Bruno Bettelheim, *A Home for the Heart* (New York: The Free Press, 1955).

10. Bruno Bettelheim, *The Informed Heart: Autonomy in a Mass Age* (New York: The Free Press, 1960).

11. Bruno Bettelheim, *The Empty Fortress* (New York: The Free Press, 1967).

12. Bruno Bettelheim, *The Children of the Dream* (New York: Macmillan, 1969).

13. Bruno Bettelheim, *The Uses of Enchantment: The Meaning and Importance of Fairy Tales* (New York: Knopf, 1976).

14. Bruno Bettelheim, *Freud and Man's Soul* (New York: Knopf, 1983).

15. Frank Kermode, "Freud Is Better in German," *The New York Times Book Review*, February 6, 1983, pp. 9 and 25.

Erich Fromm

1. My biographical information comes from Bernard Landis and Edward S. Tauber, "Erich Fromm: Some Biographical Notes," in Bernard Landis and Edward S. Tauber, eds., *In the Name of Life* (New York: Holt, Rinehart and Winston, 1971), and from Michael Maccoby, "Fromm, Erich," in *Bibliographical Supplement to the International Encyclopedia of the Social Sciences* (New York: Macmillan, 1979), as well as from personal recollections. See also Martin Jay, *The Dialectical Imagination* (Boston: Little, Brown, 1973), chap. 3.

2. Gershom Scholem, "How I Came to Kabbalah," *Commentary* 69, no. 5 (May 1980): 39–53.

3. Erich Fromm, "Theoretische Entwuerfe ueber Autoritaet und Familie," in Max Horkheimer, ed., *Studien ueber Autoritaet und Familie* (Paris: Alcan, 1936). See also Fromm's related contributions to Horkheimer's *Zeitschrift fuer Sozialforschung* for 1932, 1933, 1934, 1935, and 1937.

4. Erich Fromm, *Escape From Freedom* (New York: Holt, 1941).

5. Erich Fromm, *The Dogma of Christ and Other Essays on Religion, Psychology and Culture* (New York: Holt, 1963).

6. New York: Holt; New York: Harper; New York: Harper.

7. For a critical view on Fromm's overall stance, see John H. Schaar, *Escape from Authority; The Perspectives of Erich Fromm* (New York: Basic Books, 1961).

Karen Horney

1. For biographical information, I have relied on the following: Martin Birnbach, "Horney, Karen," in *IESS;* Harold Kelman's "Introduction" to Karen Horney, *Feminine Psychology* (New York: Norton, 1967); "In Memoriam—Karen Horney," in the Horney Memorial Issue of *The American Journal of Psychoanalysis* 14, no. 1 (1954). See also Jack Rubins, *Karen Horney* (New York: Dial, 1978).

2. *The Adolescent Diaries of Karen Horney* (New York: Basic Books, 1980).

3. Karen Horney, *The Neurotic Personality of Our Time* (New York: Norton, 1937); and Karen Horney, *New Ways in Psychoanalysis* (New York: Norton, 1939).

4. Cf. Jack Rubins, *Karen Horney.*

5. Karen Horney's *Feminine Psychology* contains translations of many, though not all, of her German writings on this topic.

6. Ibid., pp. 60–61.

7. Ibid., pp. 29–30.

8. Franz Alexander, "Psychoanalysis Revised," *The Psychoanalytical Quarterly* 9 (1940): 1–36. For another more sympathetic yet also critical assessment of Horney's work, see Clara Thompson, *Psychoanalysis: Evolution and Development* (New York: Hermitage, 1950).

9. Robert K. Merton, "Insiders and Outsiders: A Chapter in the Sociology of Knowledge," *American Journal of Sociology* (July 1972), pp. 9–47.

Part III: Sociology and Social Thought

Introduction

1. Rainer Lepsius, "Die Soziologie der Zwischenkriegszeit" in *Soziologie in Deutschland und Oesterreich 1918–1945, Koelner Zeitschrift fuer Soziologie und Sozialpsychologie* (Sonderheft 23/1981), p. 17.

2. Rainer Lepsius, "Die Soziologie nach dem Zweiten Weltkrieg" in *Deutsche Soziologie seit 1945, Koelner Zeitschrift fuer Soziologie und Sozialpsychologie* (Sonderheft 21/1979), p. 26.

3. Edward Shils, *The Calling of Sociology and Other Essays on the Pursuit of Learning* (Chicago: Chicago University Press, 1980), p. 110.

4. Cf. Svend Riemer, "Die Emigration der deutschen Soziologen nach den Vereinigten Staaten," *Koelner Zeitschrift fuer Soziologie und Sozialpsychologie* 11 (1959): 100–12. Riemer himself was a refugee scholar.

5. H. H. Gerth and C. Wright Mills, *From Max Weber: Essays in Sociology* (London: Kegan Paul, 1947;) and Hans Gerth and C. Wright Mills, *Character and Social Structure* (New York: Harcourt Brace, 1953). Cf. also Joseph Bensman and Arthur J. Vidich, eds., *Politics, Character and Culture: Perspectives from Hans Gerth* (Westport, Conn.: Greenwood, 1982).

6. Kurt H. Wolff, ed., *The Sociology of Georg Simmel* (New York: The Free Press, 1950); and *Trying Sociology* (New York: Wiley, 1974). See especially the extensive bibliography on the sociology of knowledge in America. See also *From Karl Mannheim*, edited and with an introduction by Kurt H. Wolff (New York: Oxford University Press, 1971); and Kurt H. Wolff, ed., *The Sociology of Knowledge in the United States of America* (The Hague: Mouton, 1967).

7. J. W. *Sociology of Religion* (Chicago: University of Chicago Press, 1944).

8. Rudolf Heberle, *Social Movements* (New York: Appleton-Century, 1951), esp. chapter 4. See esp. Rudolf Heberle, *From Democracy to Nazism* (New York: Fertig, 1970); (orig. ed. 1945).

9.Werner Stark, *The Sociology of Knowledge* (London: Routledge & Kegan Paul, 1967).

The Institute for Social Research

1. This section relies very heavily on Martin Jay's superb history of the Institute, *The Dialectical Imagination: A History of the Frankfurt School and The Institute of Social Research 1923–1950* (Boston: Little, Brown, 1973). I am greatly indebted to this work. I have known almost all the core members of the Institute, and several were personal friends; I have hence drawn on personal recollections in a number of places. A number of other writings on members of the Frankfurt School have also been consulted: see especially Susan Buck-Morse, *The Origins of Negative Dialectics, Theodor W. Adorno, Walter Benjamin and the Frankfurt School* (New York: The Free Press, 1977), and Gillian Ross, *An Introduction to the Thought of Theodor W. Adorno* (New York: Columbia University Press, 1978). Cf. also Barry Katz, *Herbert Marcuse and the Art of Liberation* (London: Verso, 1982). This is an uncritical but informative book.

2. Cf. also parallel remarks by Leo Lowenthal in his *Mitmachen Wollte Ich Nie: Ein Autobiographisches Gespraech* (Frankfurt: Suhrkamp, 1980), pp. 225–26.

3. Edward Shils, in his *The Calling of Sociology and Other Essays on the Pursuit of Learning* (Chicago: Chicago University Press, 1980), pp. 189ff., shows in instructive ways how Karl Mannheim's lack of entrepreneurial abilities prevented him from institutionalizing the sociology of knowledge, while Horkheimer's skills enhanced the institutionalization of critical theory.

4. Lowenthal, *Mitmachen Wollte Ich Nie*, p. 81.

5. Theodor W. Adorno et al. (New York: Harper).

6. Lowenthal, p. 128.

7. Leo Lowenthal, "Wir haben nie im Leben diesen Ruhm erwartet," in Martin Greffrath, ed., *Die Zerstoerung einer Zukunft: Gespraeche mit emigrierten Sozialwissenschaftlern* (Reinbeck: Rowohlt, 1979), pp. 215–17.

8. Many of the members of the Horkheimer group were prolific writers. While in America, some of them, especially Horkheimer and Adorno, wrote mainly for their drawer but then published a good deal of this material after returning to Germany. Among Adorno's major works, now available in English translations, are the following: (with Horkheimer) *Dialectic of Enlightenment* (New York: Herder and Herder, 1972); *Maxima Moralia* (London: NLB, 1974); *Introduction to the Sociology of Music* (New York: Seabury, 1976); *Negative Dialectics* (New York: Seabury, 1973). Horkheimer's major ideas, in addition to his collaborative work with Adorno, can be found in his *Eclipse of Reason* (New York: Herder and Herder, 1972). Lowenthal's two major books in English are: *Literature and the Image of Man* (Boston: Beacon, 1957); and *Literature, Popular Culture and Society*, new ed. (Palo Alto: Pacific Books, 1968). Pollock's major contributions can be found in the pages of the Institute journal rather than in book form.

9. 2d ed. (New York: Humanistic Press, 1968).

10. 2d ed. (Boston: Beacon Press, 1966).

11. 2d ed. (Boston: Beacon Press, 1968).

The New School for Social Research

1. Cf. Alvin Johnson's autobiography, *Pioneer's Progress* (New York: Viking, 1952).

2. I have profited a great deal from Charles S. Lachman's "The University in Exile," *Discourse, Stony Brook Working Papers in the Social Sciences and Philosophy* 2, no. 1 (Fall 1976):

25–37. The then editor of *Discourse,* Chris Bernert, was also kind enough to let me consult a longer paper by Mr. Lachman from which the *Discourse* article was excerpted. I have also learned from a proposal for "An Intellectual History of the New School for Social Research" by William B. Scott and Peter Rutkoff, which the authors kindly brought to my attention. In addition, I have consulted a variety of memoirs, as well as biographical and autobiographical materials on members of the New School Graduate Faculty. Obituaries in *Social Research* often proved especially helpful. Cf. also Benita Luckmann, "Eine deutsche Universitaet in Exil: Die 'Graduate Faculty' der 'New School for Social Research'" in Rainer Lepsius, ed., *Soziologie in Deutschland und Oesterreich 1918–1945,* Sonderheft 23/1981, *Koelner Zeitschrift fuer Soziologie und Sozialpsychologie,* pp. 427–41.

3. Personal communications 12/6/1980 and ca. 1960.

4. Interview with Hans Speier, May 9, 1981.

5. Henry Pachter, "A Memoir," *Salamagundi* 10–11 (Fall 1969–Winter 1970): 12–51; esp. 34–35.

6. Ibid.

7. Cf. *Contributions to Scholarship: Doctoral Dissertations of the Graduate Faculty of Political and Social Science* (New York: The New School for Social Research, published on its fortieth anniversary).

8. While the members of the Graduate Faculty never adhered to a common ideological viewpoint like the Horkheimer group, it is nevertheless worthy of note that at least the economists among them had a great deal in common. They all rejected the laissez-faire model of liberal economics and advocated an interventionist governmental stance to smooth and correct the swings of the market. In a sense, many of them were Keynesians before Keynes. See Claus-Dieter Krohn, "An Overlooked Chapter of Economic Thought: The New School's Effort to Salvage Weimar's Economy," *Social Research* 50, no. 2 (Summer 1983): 452–68.

9. Emil Lederer, *State of the Masses* (New York: Norton, 1940); Hans Jonas, *The Gnostic Religion* (Boston: Beacon, 1963); Felix Kaufmann, *Methodology of the Social Sciences* (New York: Humanities Press, 1958); Arnold Brecht, *Political Theory: The Foundations of Twentieth-Century Political Thought* (Princeton: Princeton University Press, 1967).

Paul F. Lazarsfeld

1. My biographical data on Lazarsfeld derive mainly from two sources: his "An Episode in the History of Social Research: A Memoir," in Donald Fleming and Bernard Bailyn, eds., *The Intellectual Migration: Europe and America, 1930–1960* (Cambridge, Mass.: Harvard University Press, 1969), pp. 270–3371 and David Edward Morrison, "Paul Lazarsfeld: The Biography of an Institutional Innovator" (Ph.D. diss., Leicester University, 1976). See also David L. Sills, "Lazarsfeld, Paul F.," in *Biographical Supplement to the International Encyclopedia of the Social Sciences* (New York: Macmillan, 1979), esp. the full bibliography; James Coleman's paper on Lazarsfeld in Robert K. Merton and Matilda White Riley, eds., *Sociological Tradition from Generation to Generation* (Norwood, N.J.: Ablex, 1980); the biographical essays and reminiscences in Robert K. Merton, James S. Coleman, and Peter Rossi, eds., *Qualitative and Quantitative Social Research: Papers in Honor of Paul F. Lazarsfeld* (New York: The Free Press, 1979); see also papers by Glock, Barton, Zeisel, and others listed in Sill's bibliography.

2. Lazarsfeld, "A Memoir," p. 272.

3. Marie Jahoda et al., *Marienthal: The Sociography of the Unemployed Community* (Chicago: Aldine, 1971).

4. See the log of Lazarsfeld's travels in appendix to Morrison, "Paul Lazarsfeld."

5. Lazarsfeld, "A Memoir," p. 298.

6. See Charles Kadushin, "Reason Analysis," in *IESS*, and Paul F. Lazarsfeld, "Historical Notes on the Empirical Study of Action: An Intellectual Odyssey," in Paul F. Lazarsfeld, *Qualitative Analysis: Historical and Critical Essays* (Boston: Allyn and Bacon, 1972).

7. Paul F. Lazarsfeld, *Radio and the Printed Page* (New York: Duell, Pearce and Sloan, 1940); Paul F. Lazarsfeld and Frank Stanton, eds., *Radio Research, 1941* (New York: Duell, Pearce and Sloan); idem, *Radio Research 1942–1943* (New York: Duell, Pearce and Sloan, 1944); idem, *Communications Research 1948–1949* (New York: Harper, 1949); Paul F. Lazarsfeld and Patricia Kendall, *Radio Listening in America* (Englewood Cliffs, N.J.: Prentice-Hall, 1948).

8. Paul F. Lazarsfeld et al., *The People's Choice* (New York: Columbia University Press, 1944); Bernard Berenson et al., *Voting* (Chicago: Chicago University Press, 1944); Paul F. Lazarsfeld and W. Thielens, *The Academic Mind* (New York: The Free Press, 1958); Elihu Katz and Paul F. Lazarsfeld, *Personal Influence* (New York: The Free Press, 1958).

9. Paul F. Lazarsfeld, "A Memoir," p. 271, 299.

10. See Morrison, "Paul Lazarsfeld."

11. Ibid., p. 127.

12. Ibid.

Alfred Schutz

1. My biographical information is largely derived from Maurice Natanson's introduction to *Phenomenology and Social Reality, Essays in Memory of Alfred Schutz* (The Hague: Martinus Nijhoff, 1970); and H. L. Van Breda's preface to volume 1 of Alfred Schutz's *Collected Papers* (The Hague: Martinus Nijhoff, 1962). For an excellent overview of Schutz's phenomenological approach to sociology, see Helmut Wagner's introduction to *Alfred Schutz on Phenomenology and Social Relations* (Chicago: University of Chicago Press, 1972). Cf. also Helmut Wagner, "Die Soziologie der Lebenswelt: Umriss einer intellektuellen Biographie von Alfred Schuetz," *Koelner Zeitschrift fuer Soziologie und Sozialpsychologie*, Sonderheft 23/1981 (Opladen: Westdeutscher Verlag), pp. 379–94. Wagner will soon publish a full "intellectual biography" of Schutz that will be published by the University of Chicago Press.

2. Natanson, *Phenomenology and Social Reality*, p. x.

3. Among Schutz's American works, the following seem most important: *Collected Papers*, ed. Maurice Natanson, 3 vols. (The Hague: Martinus Nijhoff, 1962–1966); *On Phenomenology and Social Relations*, ed. Helmut Wagner, see n. 1 above; and the translation of his earlier work *The Phenomenology of the Social World* (Evanston, Ill.: Northwestern University Press, 1967).

4. Cf. Richard Grathoff, ed., *The Correspondence of Alfred Schutz and Talcott Parsons* (Bloomington: Indiana University Press, 1978). See also my review of this volume in *Contemporary Sociology* 8 (1979): 680–82.

5. Hugh Mehan and Houston Wood, "De-Secting Ethnomethodology," *The American Sociologist* 11, no. 1 (February 1976): 15.

Karl August Wittfogel

1. New Haven: Yale University Press, 1957.

2. Most of my biographical information comes from G. L. Ulmen's *The Science of Society: Toward an Understanding of the Life and Work of Karl August Wittfogel* (The Hague/New York: Mouton, 1978). This is a most detailed account and an admirable source of documentation. It is, however, flawed by the author's hagiographic approach to his subject.

3. *Die Wissenschaft der Buergerlichen Gesellschaft* (Berlin: Malik, 1922).

4. *Das Erwachende China* (Vienna: Agis, 1926).

5. *Wirtschaft und Gesellschaft in China* (Leipzig: Hirschfeld, 1931).

6. Ulmen, *The Science of Society*, p. 139.

7. With Feng Chia-Shong (Philadelphia: American Philosophical Society, 1949).

8. Ulmen, p. 294. See the preceding pages for an account of the McCarran hearings. For balanced accounts of these hearings, cf. Earl Latham, *The Communist Controversy in Washington* (Cambridge, Mass.: Harvard University Press, 1966), and John N. Thomas, *The Institute of Pacific Relations: Asian Scholars and American Politics* (Seattle: University of Washington Press, 1974).

9. See G. L. Ulmen, *Society and History: Essays in Honor of Karl August Wittfogel* (The Hague/New York, 1979), for the continued impact of Wittfogel's thought on a variety of American and European scholars.

Part IV: Economics and Economic History

Ludwig von Mises, Oskar Morgenstern, Fritz Machlup, and Gottfried von Haberler

1. Cf. J. R. Hicks and W. Weber, *Carl Menger and the Austrian School of Economics* (Oxford: The Clarendon Press, 1973), especially the final chapter by Weber and Streissler.

2. My biographical information and most of my account of Mises's theories are based on the following: Murray N. Rothbard, "von Mises, Ludwig," in *IESS;* Laurence S. Moss, ed., *The Economics of Ludwig von Mises,* (Kansas City: Sheed and Ward, 1976); Mary Sennholz, ed., *On Freedom and Free Enterprise: Essays in Honor of Ludwig von Mises* (Princeton: Van Nostrand, 1956); *Toward Liberty: Essays in Honor of Ludwig von Mises,* 2 vols. (Menlo Park, Calif.: Institute for Human Studies, 1971). Mises also wrote an autobiographical book, *Notes and Recollections* (South Holland, Ill.: Libertarian Press, 1978). See also his wife's recollections, Margit von Mises, *My Years with Ludwig von Mises* (New Rochelle, N.Y.: Arlington, 1976). For a detailed and sharply critical discussion of Mises and other members of the Austrian school, see Ben B. Seligman, *Main Currents in Modern Economics* (New York: The Free Press, 1962).

3. *Theorie des Geldes* (Munich: Duncker und Humblot).

4. *Die Ursachen der Wirtschaftskrise* (Tuebingen: Mohr, 1931).

5. Trans. W. M. MacMillan, 1936.

6. It may be of some interest to point out that von Mises, the great defender of liberal free enterprise, at an earlier point in his career expressed his admiration for fascism. He wrote in 1927 that fascism had saved European culture: "The honor that fascism has thus gained will live on in history forever," Ludwig Mises, *Liberalismus* (Jena: Gustav Fischer, 1927), pp. 43 and 45, cited in Claus-Dieter Krohn, "An Overlooked Chapter of Economic Thought: The New School's Effort to Salvage Weimar's Economy," *Social Research* 50, no. 2 (Summer 1983): 455.

7. New Haven: Yale University Press, 1940.

8. *Wirtschaftsprognose* (Vienna: Springer, 1928).

9. Biographical information and my account of Morgenstern's theoretical work are based on: Martin Shubik, "Morgenstern, Oskar," in *Biographical Supplement to the International Encyclopedia of the Social Sciences* (New York: Macmillan 1979); Martin Shubik, "Oskar Morgenstern: Mentor and Friend," *International Journal of Game Theory,* vol. 7, issue 3/4, pp. 131–35; and two festschriften for Morgenstern: Martin Shubik, ed., *Essays in Mathematical Economics* (Princeton: Princeton University Press, 1967); and Rudolph Henn and Otto Moeschlin, eds., *Mathematical Economics and Game Theory* (Berlin/New York: Springer, 1977).

10. John von Neumann and Oskar Morgenstern, *Theory of Games and Economic Behavior* (Princeton: Princeton University Press, 1944).

11. Shubik, "Oskar Morgenstern," p. 131.

12. Oskar Morgenstern, "Game Theory: Theoretical Aspects,: *IESS.*

13. Most of my biographical information comes from John S. Chipman, "Machlup, Fritz," in *Biographical Supplement to the International Encyclopedia of the Social Sciences* (New York: Macmillan, 1979); and from Jacob S. Dreyer, ed., *Breadth and Depth in Economics: Fritz Machlup—The Man and His Ideas* (Lexington, Mass.: Heath, 1978). See esp. the preface and the papers by Eisner and Malkiel in that volume. Professor Machlup was also kind enough to send me his vita and a complete list of his contributions.

14. Fritz Machlup, *The Production and Distribution of Knowledge* (Princeton: Princeton University Press, 1962).

15. Cf. Eisner in Dreyer, *Breadth and Depth in Economics*, p. 5.

16. Fritz Machlup, *The Political Economy of Monopoly* (Baltimore: Johns Hopkins Press, 1952).

17. Fritz Machlup, *Methodology of Economics and Other Social Sciences* (New York: Academic Press, 1978).

18. Biographic and bibliographic information on Gottfried Haberler comes mainly from an address by the rector of the University of Vienna upon the conferral of an honorary doctoral degree to him.

19. Gottfried Haberler, *Theory of International Trade* (Fairfield, N.J.: Augustus M. Kelley, Publishers, 1968; rpt. of 1936 ed.)

20. 4th ed. (Cambridge, Mass.: Harvard University Press, 1964).

21. Joseph Schumpeter, *History of Economic Analysis* (New York: Oxford University Press, 1954).

Jacob Marschak

1. My information on Marschak's biography and on his contributions is based on the following: Kenneth Arrow, "Marschak, Jacob," in *Bibliographic Supplement to the International Encyclopedia of the Social Sciences* (New York: Macmillan, 1968); Kenneth Arrow, "Jacob Marschak's Contributions to the Economics of Decision and Information," *The American Economic Review* 68, no. 2 (May 1978): xii–xix; Tjalling C. Koopmans's "Jacob Marschak," *The American Economic Review* 68, no. 2 (May 1978): ix–xi; Roy Radner, "Jacob Marschak," *Behavioral Science* 23, no. 2 (March 1978): 63–66; Kenneth Arrow, "Jacob Marschak," *Challenge* (March/April 1978), pp. 69–71.

2. "Der Neue Mittelstand," *Grundriss der Nationaloekonomik* 9, no. 1 (1926): 120–41.

3. Koopmans, "Jacob Marschak," p. x.

4. Arrow in *Challenge*, p. 71.

5. *Economic Information, Decision and Prediction*, 3 vols. (Dordrecht: D. Reidel, 1974).

6. Radner, "Jacob Marschak," p. 65.

7. Arrow in *Challenge*, p. 71.

Alexander Gerschenkron and Albert O. Hirschman

1. Charles Gulick, *Austria from Hapsburg to Hitler*, 2 vols. (Berkeley: University of California Press, 1948).

2. My biographical information, as well as some of my knowledge of the finer points of Gerschenkron's teaching, derive from the following essays: Alexander Erlich, "Gerschenkron, Alexander," in *Biographical Supplement to the International Encyclopedia of the Social Sciences* (New York: Macmillan, 1979); and Henry Rosovsky, "Alexander Gerschenkron: A Personal and Fond Recollection," *Journal of Economic History* 39, no. 4 (December 1979): 1009–13. See also Gottfried Haberler's splendid essay "Alexander Gerschenkron," which appeared in the American Philosophical Society's *Yearbook* in 1981.

3. New ed. (New York: Fertig, 1966).

4. Howard S. Ellis, *Exchange Control in Central Europe* (Westport, Conn.: Greenwood, 1969; rpt. of 1941 ed.).

5. Alexander Gerschenkron, *Economic Backwardness in Historical Perspective* (Cambridge, Mass.: Harvard University Press, 1962), and *Continuity in History* (Cambridge, Mass.: Harvard University Press, 1968).

6. Henry Rosovsky, *Capital Formation in Japan, 1868–1940* (New York: Free Press, 1961); A. Eckstein, *China's Economic Revolution* (New York: Cambridge University Press, 1977); Alexander Erlich, *The Soviet Industrialization Debate* (Cambridge, Mass: Harvard University Press, 1960); and Joseph Berliner, *Factory and Manager in the USSR* (Cambridge, Mass: Harvard University Press, 1957).

7. 1st ed. (New York: McGraw-Hill, 1948).

8. For biographical information I have largely relied on materials kindly provided me by Professor Hirschman. I am most grateful to him for a close critical reading of a first draft of this section and for many valuable suggestions for improvement. For Hirschman's work in Marseilles, see Varian Fry, *Surrender on Demand* (New York: Random House, 1943).

9. Albert Hirschman, *National Power and the Structure of Foreign Trade* (Berkeley: University of California Press, 1945).

10. Albert Hirschman, *The Strategy of Economic Development* (New Haven: Yale University Press, 1958).

11. Ibid.

12. In addition to *The Strategy of Economic Development*, see also Hirschman's *Journeys toward Progress* (New York: The Twentieth Century Fund, 1963), and *Development Projects Observed* (Washington, D.C.: Brookings, 1967).

13. Albert Hirschman, *Exit, Voice, and Loyalty: Responses to Decline in Firms, Organizations, and States* (Cambridge, Mass.: Harvard University Press, 1970).

14. Albert Hirschman, *The Passions and the Interests: Political Arguments for Capitalism Before its Triumph* (Princeton: Princeton University Press, 1977).

15. Princeton: Princeton University Press, 1982.

Karl Polanyi and Paul Baran

1. For biographical information I have relied on Hans Zeisel, "Polanyi, Karl," *IESS* (New York, Macmillan, 1967), and on Paul Bohannan and George Dalton, "Karl Polanyi," *The American Anthropologist* 67 (1965): 1508–11.

2. Karl Polanyi, *The Great Transformation* (New York: Farrar and Rinehart, 1944).

3. Karl Polanyi et al., *Trade and Markets in the Early Empires* (New York: Free Press, 1957).

4. Professor Hans Zeisel, in a personal communication (June 4, 1980), disagrees with this characterization and disputes my interpretation of Polanyi's marginality. I am constrained, however, not to accept his optimistic interpretation. Professor Zeisel was also good enough to send me valuable critical comments by Dr. Kari Polanyi, Karl Polanyi's daughter, from which I have profited.

5. Karl Polanyi, "Our Obsolete Market Mentality," *Commentary*, February 1947.

6. Zeisel, p. 173.

7. I base my biographical data on Paul Sweezy, "Paul Alexander Baran: A Personal Memoir," in Paul M. Sweezy and Leo Huberman, eds., *Paul Baran: A Collective Portrait* (New York: Monthly Review Press, 1965); and on Melvin W. Reder, Lorie Tarshis, and Thomas C. Smith, "Memorial Resolution: Paul Alexander Baran, 1909–1964," mimeo, Stanford Department of Economics, 1964.

8. Paul Baran, *Die planwirtschaftlichen Versuche in der Sovietunion* (Leipzig: C. L. Hirschfeld, 1929).

9. Letter of May 27, 1956, in Paul Sweezy and Leo Huberman, *Paul Baran*, p. 53; letter of January 13, 1962, in ibid., pp. 57–58; letter of May 26, 1963, in ibid., p. 60.

10. Personal communication from Professor Moses Abramovitz, June 6, 1980.

11. Ibid.

12. See " A Preliminary Bibliography of Paul A. Baran," in Sweezy and Huberman, pp. 132–35.

13. Paul Sweezy, "Paul A. Baran," *Monthly Review* 16 (May 1964): 25–26.

14. Paul A. Baran and Paul Sweezy, *Monopoly Capital* (New York: Monthly Review Press, 1966).

15. Paul A. Baran, *The Longer View.*

George Katona, Peter Drucker, and Fritz Redlich

1. George Katona, *Organizing and Memorizing* (New York: Columbia University Press, 1940). Among Katona's many works the following seem most noteworthy: *Psychological Analysis of Economic Behavior* (New York: McGraw-Hill, 1951); *The Powerful Consumer* (New York: McGraw-Hill, 1960); and *Consumer Responses to Income Increases* (Washington D.C.: Brookings, 1968).

2. Cf. Herbert E. Krugman, "Consumer Behavior," *IESS* (New York: The Free Press, 1968), 3: 351.

3. New York: John Day; New York: John Day; New York: John Day; New York: Harper & Row; New York: Harper & Row;

4. The following is largely based on a loving memoir by Kenneth E. Carpenter and Alfred D. Chandler, Jr., "Fritz Redlich: Scholar and Friend," *Journal of Economic History* 39, no. 4 (December 1979): 1005–07.

5. Fritz Redlich, *History of American Business Leaders: A Series of Studies* vol. 1: *Theory, Iron and Steel, Iron and Ore Mining* (Ann Arbor: Edwards, 1940).

6. Fritz Redlich, *The Molding of American Banking: Men and Ideas,* pt. 1, *1781–1840;* pt. 2, *1840–1910* (New York: Hafner, 1947 and 1951).

Part V: Political Science and Political Theory

Hannah Arendt

1. My biographical information is mainly based on Elisabeth Young-Bruehl's *Hannah Arendt: For Love of the World* (New Haven: Yale University Press, 1982). See also George Kateb, "Arendt, Hannah," in *Biographical Supplement to the International Encyclopedia of the Social Sciences,* (New York: Macmillan, 1979).

2. Young-Bruehl, *For Love of the World.*

3. Hannah Arendt, *Rahel Varnhagen: The Life of a Jewish Woman* (New York: Harcourt Brace, 1974).

4. See, for example, the essay "We Refugees," in Hannah Arendt, *The Jew as a Pariah* (New York: Grove Press, 1978).

5. See, among others, *The Human Condition* (Chicago, University of Chicago Press, 1958); *On Revolution* (New York: Viking, 1963); *Eichmann in Jerusalem* (New York: Viking, 1963); *On Violence* (New York: Harcourt Brace, 1970); *Men in Dark Times* (New York: Harcourt Brace, 1968); and *Crisis of the Republic* (New York: Harcourt Brace, 1972).

6. George Kateb, "Freedom and Worldliness in the Thought of Hannah Arendt," *Political Theory* 2 (May 1977): 141–82.

7. See, among others, Benjamin Schwartz, "The Religion of Politics," *Dissent* 17 (March-April 1970): 144–61.

8. For an overall assessment of Arendt's thought, see a special issue of *Social Research* devoted to her, vol. 44, no. 1 (Spring 1977). Cf. also "Hannah Arendt," by Patrick Levy and Robert Davren, in *Les Etudes Philosophiques 2,* 1976 (April-June), pp. 237–42; and Margaret Lanovan, *The Political Theory of Hannah Arendt* (New York: Harcourt Brace, 1974).

Franz Neumann

1. I owe my biographical information, and much more, to H. Stuart Hughes's loving and brilliant portrait of Franz Neumann in his *The Sea Change* (New York: Harper & Row, 1975), pp. 100–19. See also the twin essays on Neumann by Otto Kirchheimer and David Kettler in *Dissent* 4 (Autumn 1957).

2. Franz Neumann, *Behemoth: The Structure and Practice of National Socialism* (New York: Oxford University Press, 1942).

3. Franz Neumann, *The Democratic and the Authoritarian State: Essays in Political and Legal Theory*, ed. Herbert Marcuse (New York: The Free Press, 1957).

4. Franz Neumann, "The Social Sciences," in W. Rex Crawford, ed., *The Cultural Migration* (Philadelphia: University of Pennsylvania Press, 1953), pp. 4–26.

5. Twenty-five years after his death, the annual social science citation index still lists roughly ten sources per year that quote from Neumann's work.

Leo Strauss

1. For information on the major Straussians in the contemporary academic scene, I am indebted to personal communications from Werner J. Dannhauser of Cornell and Michael Walzer of the Institute for Advanced Study, Princeton.

2. Werner J. Dannhauser, "Leo Strauss: Becoming Naive Again," *The American Scholar* 44, no. 4 (Autumn 1975): 638. For an overall evaluation of Strauss's life and work, I have found an essay by his disciple Allan Bloom most helpful: "Leo Strauss," *Political Theory* 2, no. 4 (November 1974): 372–91. See also Milton Himmelfarb, "On Leo Strauss," *Commentary* 58, no. 2 (August 1974): 60–65; and Joseph Cropsey, "Strauss, Leo," *Biographical Supplement to the International Encyclopedia of the Social Sciences* (New York: Macmillan, 1979).

3. Cf. Peter Gay, *Freud, Jews and Other Germans* (New York: Oxford University Press, 1978).

4. Leo Strauss, *Political Philosophy* (New York: Pegasus, 1975), p. 18.

5. Leo Strauss, *Natural Right and History* (Chicago: University of Chicago Press, 1953), pp. 41, 42.

6. *Political Philosophy*, p. 128.

7. Ibid., pp. 22–23.

8. Leo Strauss, *On Tyranny* (New York: The Free Press, 1950); Leo Strauss, *Thoughts on Machiavelli* (New York: The Free Press 1958); Leo Strauss, *The Political Philosophy of Hobbes* (Chicago: University of Chicago Press, 1962; 1st ed., 1936); Leo Strauss, *Spinoza's Critique of Religion* (New York: Schocken, 1964); the clearest exposition of Strauss's exegetical method is found in his *Persecution and the Art of Writing* (New York: The Free Press, 1952). A good sample of the writings of Strauss's disciples can be found in Joseph Cropsey's Festschrift for Strauss, *Ancients and Moderns* (New York: Basic Books, 1964).

9. J. G. A. Pocock, "Prophet and Inquisitor," *Political Theory* 3, no. 4, (November 1975): 391.

10. Allan Bloom, "Leo Strauss," p. 381.

Karl W. Deutsch

1. Bruce M. Russett, "Methodological and Theoretical Schools in International Relations," in *A Design for International Relations Research: Scope, Theory, Methods and Relevance*, Monograph no. 10 of the American Academy of Political and Social Science, Philadelphia (October 1970), pp. 87–105.

2. Biographical data and much else are largely based on Richard L. Merritt and Bruce M. Russett, "Karl W. Deutsch and the Scientific Analysis of World Politics," in *From National Development to Global Community*, ed. Russett and Merritt (London: Allen and Unwin, 1980).

3. Karl W. Deutsch, *Nationalism and Social Communication: An Inquiry into the Foundations of Nationalism* (Cambridge, Mass.: The Technology Press of MIT; and New York: Wiley, 1953).

4. Karl W. Deutsch et al., *Political Community and the North Atlantic Area: International Organization in the Light of Historical Experience* (Princeton, Princeton University Press, 1957).

5. Karl W. Deutsch, *The Nerves of Government: Models of Political Communication and Control* (New York: The Free Press, 1963).

6. Karl W. Deutsch and Lewis Edinger, *Germany Rejoins the Powers: Mass Opinion, Interest Groups, and Elites in Contemporary German Foreign Policy* (Stanford: Stanford University Press, 1959).

7. Bruce M. Russett, Hayward Alker, Jr., Karl W. Deutsch, and Harold Lasswell, *World Handbook of Political and Social Indicators* (New Haven: Yale University Press, 1964).

8. Personal communication, Berlin, February 13, 1980.

Eric Voegelin

1. My biographical information is mainly based on an interview with Professor Voegelin on December 17, 1979 in Stanford, California, and on William C. Havard's "Voegelin's Changing Conception of History and Consciousness," in Stephen A. McKnight, ed., *Eric Voegelin's Search for Order in History,* (Baton Rouge: Louisiana State University Press, 1978). For commentaries on Voegelin's thought, I have largely relied on other contributions to the McKnight volume, as well as on the chapter devoted to Voegelin in Dante Germino's *The Revival of Political Theory* (New York: Harper & Row, 1967).

2. Quoted in Havard, p. 4.

3. Eric Voegelin, *The New Science of Politics* (Chicago: Chicago University Press, 1952).

4. Eric Voegelin, *Order and History (vol. 1, Israel and Revelation; vol. 2, The World of the Polis; vol. 3, Plato and Aristotle; vol. 4, The Ecumenic Age)* (Baton Rouge: Louisiana State University Press, 1956–75).

5. Both these judgments can be found on the back cover of McKnight's book.

6. *Eric Voegelin: Philosopher of History* (Seattle: University of Washington Press, 1981).

Hans Morgenthau

1. Hans Morgenthau, "Fragments of an Intellectual Autobiography: 1904–1932," in Kenneth Thompson and Robert J. Myers, eds., *A Tribute to Hans Morgenthau* (Washington, D.C.: The New Republic Book Company, 1977), p. 9. Most of my biographical information is based on Morgenthau's fragment and other contributions to this volume. See also Kenneth Thompson, "Morgenthau, Hans," in *Biographical Supplement to the International Encyclopedia of the Social Sciences* (New York: Macmillan, 1979). The bulk of the Winter 1981 issue of *Social Research* (vol. 48, no. 4), is devoted to Hans Morgenthau. See especially the papers by George Eckstein, Richard Rosecrance, and Michael Joseph Smith.

2. Kenneth W. Thompson, "Hans J. Morgenthau," *The New Yorker,* August 11, 1980.

3. The above information comes from Laura Fermi's *Illustrious Immigrants* (Chicago: Chicago University Press, 1968), pp. 28–29 and 347–48.

4. For all of the above, see Kenneth Thompson's "The Two Commitments of Hans J. Morgenthau," in Kenneth Thompson and Robert J. Myers, *Tribute.* Thompson lists the following junior colleagues of Morgenthau as having been influenced by his teaching: Charles M. Hardin, Milton Rakove, Gerald Stourzh, George Liska, Tang Tsou, and Robert Osgood. The Thompson and Myers volume contains essays by a number of other scholars who at one time or another were either students of Morgenthau or among his colleagues and associates: Louis J. Halle, Norman A. Graebner, Richard Falk, Marcus Raskin, Roger L. Shinn, Robert J. Myers, Kenneth Thompson, Michael Selzer, Richard J. Barnet, Erich Hula,

Herbert Butterfield, Leo Gross, John G. Stoessinger, Peter Jankowitsch, Harold P. Ford, Jacques Freymond, Adam Watson, Alfred J. Hotz, Francisco Cuevas Cancino. Henry Kissinger considers himself Morgenthau's student. Helen Danner, Morgenthau's former secretary, has been kind enough to provide me with an additional list of names of students and associates of Morgenthau. A high proportion of these persons occupy prestigious chairs in major universities. There can be no doubt that they will continue in one form or another to help diffuse Morgenthau's philosophical and political message.

5. *Scientific Man vs. Power Politics* (Chicago: Chicago University Press, 1946); *In Defense of the National Interest* (New York: Knopf, 1951); *Politics among Nations: The Struggle for Power and Peace*, 5th ed. (New York: Knopf, 1973).

6. Hans Morgenthau, *Scientific Man vs. Power Politics*, pp. 202–03.

7. Hans Morgenthau, "The Purpose of Political Science," in James C. Charlesworth, ed., *A Design for Political Science: Scope, Objectives, and Methods*, Monograph 6 (Philadelphia: The Academy of Political and Social Science, December 1966), p. 72.

8. Ibid., p. 67.

9. At the Center for Advanced Study in the Behavioral Sciences.

10. On the influence of Morgenthau and other refugee social scientists had on America's policy in regard to Europe, see Joachim Radkau *Die deutsche Emigration in der U.S.A. Ihr Einfluss auf die amerikanische Europapolitik 1933–1945* (Duesseldorf, 1971).

Part VI: Writers

Exiled Writers in New York and Hollywood

1. Quoted by Egbert Krispyn, *Anti-Nazi Writers in Exile* (Athens, The University of Georgia Press, 1979), p. 1.

2. Elias Canetti, *Aufzeichnungen 1942–1948* (Munich: Hausen, 1965), p. 70, as quoted in Manfred Durzak, "From Dialect Play to Philosophical Parable: Elias Canetti in Exile," in Joseph P. Strelka et al., eds., *Protest-Form in Tradition* (University, Ala.: University of Alabama Press, 1979), p. 40.

3. Krispyn, *Anti-Nazi Writers*, pp. 118–19.

4. This information and much that follows is largely based on Erna M. Moore's "Exil in Hollywood: Leben und Haltung deutscher Exilautoren nach ihren autobiographischen Berichten," pp. 21–39, in John M. Spalek and Joseph Strelka, eds., *Deutsche Exilliteratur seit 1933*, vol. 1, pt. 1 (Bern and Munich: Francke Verlag, 1976).

5. Quoted in Robert E. Cazden, *German Exile Literature in America: 1933–1950* (Chicago: American Library Association, 1970), p. 148. This book has a good general discussion of the plight of the emigré author on pp. 137–62.

6. Quoted in Klaus Weissenberger, "Alfred Doeblin," in *Deutsche Exilliteratur*, p. 304.

7. Bertolt Brecht, *Poems 1913–1956*, ed. John Willett and Ralph Manheim (New York: Methuen, 1980).

8. Quoted in Erna M. Moore, "Exil in Hollywood," p. 29.

9. Quoted in James K. Lyon and John B. Fuegi, "Bertolt Brecht," in *Deutsche Exilliteratur*, p. 270.

10. Quoted in Moore, p. 28.

11. Ibid., pp. 26–27.

12. Ibid., p. 22.

13. For additional material on Hollywood writers, see two contributions to the Smithsonian symposium, The Muses Flee Hitler, February 1980: Hans-Bernard Mueller, "German Hollywood Presence and Parnassus: Central European Exile and American Filmmaking," and Jarrell C. Jackman, "German Emigrés in Southern California in the 1930s and

1940s." The latter is included in Jarrell C. Jackman and Carla M. Borden, eds., *The Muses Flee Hitler* (Washington, D.C.: Smithsonian Institution Press, 1983).

Hermann Broch

1. I have largely used Thomas Koebner's, *Hermann Broch* (Bern and Munich: Francke Verlag, 1965), for biographical and bibliographical information. Cf. also Hannah Arendt, "The Achievement of Hermann Broch," *Kenyon Review* 11, no. 3 (Summer 1949): 476–483.

2. André Schiffrin, now editor-in-chief of Pantheon Books, wrote to me (November 8, 1979): "Your impression of [The Death of Virgil] is quite right and it is safe to say that Broch made no impression at all on American life during his time here. . . . I have to rely on memory, but if mine serves me, we sold the 1500 copies of *The Death of Virgil* in English very very slowly. It took some twenty years. . . . The paperback, by the way, didn't do all that much better."

3. Hermann Broch, *Briefe von 1929 bis 1951*, Zurich: Rhein Verlag, 1957), p. 265. The Yale Library has a collection of 866 manuscript letters by Broch, most of them to refugee or European recipients. See John M. Spalek, *Guide to the Archival Materials of the German-Speaking Migration to the United States* (Charlottesville: University Press of Virginia, 1978).

4. Ibid., p. 359.

5. Ibid., pp. 404–06.

Thomas Mann

1. Cf. Thomas Mann, *Die Entstehung des Doktor Faustus: Roman eines Romans* (Stockholm: Berman-Fischer, 1949); Thomas Mann, *Briefe 1937-1947* (Frankfurt: S. Fischer, 1963); Katia Mann, *Meine Ungeschriebenen Memoiren* (Frankfurt: S. Fischer, 1974). For a full list of published and unpublished letters, see John M. Spalik et al., *Deutsche Exilliteratur seit 1933* 1, pt 2 (Bern/Munich: A. Francke, 1976), pp. 85–86. In some of these letters American recipients are somewhat more frequent than in the published letters, but they are still a decided minority.

2. Roman Karst, *Thomas Mann: Oder der Deutsche Zwiespalt* (Vienna, Munich, Zuerich: Fritz Molden, 1977), p. 155.

3. Nigel Hamilton, *The Brothers Mann* (New Haven: Yale University Press, 1979).

4. Mann, *Briefe*, p. 459.

5. See Spalik et al., *Deutsche Exilliteratur seit 1933* 1, pt. 1, 513–15 and 525–26.

6. Alfred Kazin, "The European Writer in Exile," *The New Republic*, April 12, 1980.

Vladimir Nabokov

1. This account of Nabokov's career in America is largely based on two works by Andrew Field, *Nabokov: His Life in Art* (Boston: Little, Brown, 1967), and *Nabokov: His Life in Part* (New York: Viking, 1977).

2. *Life in Part*, pp. 249–50.

3. For the relations between Nabokov and Wilson, their *Correspondence* (New York: Harper & Row, 1978), ed. Simon Karlinsky, is indispensable.

4. *Life in Part*, p. 235.

5. *Life in Art*, pp. 64–65.

6. *New York Review of Books*, Sept. 25, 1980, p. 20.

7. *Life in Art,* p. 328.

8. *New York Review of Books,* Aug. 14, 1980, n. 24.

Part VII: The Humanities

Roman Jakobson

1. Ved Mehta, *John Is Easy to Please* (New York: Farrar, Straus and Giroux, 1971), p. 232.

2. My biographical information is largely based on Morris Halle, "Jakobson, Roman," in *Biographical Supplement to the International Encyclopedia of the Social Sciences* (New York: Macmillan, 1979), as well as on Mehta, *John Is Easy to Please,* and Thomas A. Sebeok, "Roman Jakobson's Teaching in America," in Daniel Armstrong and C. H. Van Schooneveld, eds. *Roman Jakobson: Echoes of His Scholarship* (Lisse, The Netherlands: Peter de Ridder, 1977).

3. Halle, p. 338. See also Sebeok p. 416.

4. Mehta, p. 232.

5. Ibid., pp. 229; 231; 192.

6. Sebeok, p. 417.

7. My account of the key elements in Jakobson's linguistics is largely built on Morris Halle, (see n. 2) and various contributions to *Roman Jakobson: Echoes of His Scholarship.* Of Jakobson's own writings, "Efforts toward a Means–Ends Model of Language in Interwar Continental Linguistics," in *Trends in Modern Linguistics,* ed. Christine Mohrmann, F. Norman, and Alf Sommerfelt (Utrecht, The Netherlands: Spectrum, 1963), has proved most helpful.

8. Quoted in Morris Halle, p. 340.

Erwin Panofsky

1. Erwin Panofsky, "Three Decades of Art History in the United States: Impressions of a Transplanted European," in his *Meaning in the Visual Arts* (Woodstock, N.Y.: Overlook Press, 1974), p. 326.

2. I have profited a great deal from what is by far the most comprehensive account of the contributions of refugees to American art history: Colin Eisler, "*Kunstgeschichte* American Style: A Study in Migration," in Donald Fleming and Bernard Bailyn, eds. *The Intellectual Migration: Europe and America, 1930–1960* (Cambridge, Mass.: Harvard University Press, 1969). Professor Eisler was perhaps especially well equipped to do this study, since he himself is the son of refugees but grew up in America. This origin may have created an optimum balance between nearness and distance to his topic. Cf. also Eisler's "American Art History," *Art News,* May 1976.

W. Eugene Kleinbauer's introduction to his anthology, *Modern Perspectives in Western Art History* (New York: Holt, Rinehart and Winston, 1971), provides an overview of various trends in art history here and in Europe that has been most helpful to me.

A long conversation with Meyer Schapiro (April 20, 1981) provided me with many guidelines and permitted me to profit from his unparalleled knowledge of the subject.

3. Erwin Panofsky, "Three Decades of Art History in the United States," in his *Meaning in the Visual Arts,* p. 326.

4. Eisler, *Kunstgeschichte,* p. 559.

5. Panofsky, p. 332.

6. On Panofsky's career and impact the following have been most helpful: Creighton Gilbert, "The Man Who Asks about Ideas," *Arts Magazine,* October 1961, pp. 62–63; and E. H. Gombrich, "Obituary—Erwin Panofsky," *Burlington Magazine,* June 1968, pp. 357–60.

7. On Panofsky's helpfulness and generosity in regard to younger scholars, see W. McAllister Johnson, "Working with Panofsky," *Gazette des Beaux Arts*, May-June 1968, pp. 263–64.

8. Erwin Panofsky, *The Life and Art of Albrecht Duerer* (Princeton: Princeton University Press, 1943).

9. Max J. Friedlaender, *Die Altniederlaendische Malerei*, 14 vols. (Berlin, 1924-37).

10. Ernst Kris, *Psychoanalytical Explorations in Art* (New York: International Universities Press, 1952).

11. See Rudolf Arnheim, *Art and Visual Perception: A Psychology of the Creative Eye* (Berkeley: University of California Press, 1966).

12. Quoted in Eisler, *Kunstgeschichte*, p. 628.

Erich Auerbach, Leo Spitzer, and René Wellek

1. I owe a great debt to Harry Levin's splendid essay "Two Romanisten in America: Spitzer and Auerbach," in Donald Fleming and Bernard Bailyn, eds., *The Intellectual Migration: Europe and America, 1930–1960*, (Cambridge, Mass.: Harvard University Press, 1969), pp. 463–84. On Auerbach I have also profited from the following: R. W. (René Wellek), "Erich Auerbach," *Comparative Literature* 10 (1958): 93–94; Wolfgang Bernard Fleischmann, "Auerbach's Critical Theory and Practice: An Appraisal," *Modern Language Notes* 81, no. 5 (December 1966): 535–41; Lowry Nelson, Jr., "Erich Auerbach: Memoir of a Scholar," *The Yale Review* 69, no. 2 (Winter 1980): 312–20; and Arthur R. Evans, "Erich Auerbach as European Critic," *Romance Philology* 25, no. 5 (November 1971): 193–215. My main source on Spitzer, in addition to Harry Levin, has been René Wellek, "Leo Spitzer," *Comparative Literature* 12, no. 1 (Fall 1960): 310–31. My main source on Wellek has been his autobiographical essay "Prospect and Retrospect," *The Yale Review* 69, no. 2 (Winter 1980): 301–12.

2. On the Turkish exile of a significant number of German academics, cf. Horst Widmann, *Exil und Bildungshilfe: Die deutschsprachige akademische Emigration in die Tuerkei nach 1933* (Bern and Frankfurt: Herbert Lang, 1973.)

3. Harry Levin, "Two Romanisten," pp. 466–67.

4. R. W. (René Wellek) "Erich Auerbach," p. 94.

5. Cf. Y. M. (Yakov Malkiel) "Leo Spitzer," *Romance Philology* 41, (1960–61) pp. 362–64.

6. Levin, p. 475.

7. Wellek, "Prospect and Retrospect," p. 305.

8. Ibid., pp. 309–10.

9. Ibid., p. 311.

Werner Jaeger

1. These pages could not have been written without the help and guidance of William M. Calder III of the University of Colorado. The clues and interpretative guidelines that he provided in personal communications (April 21, 1981, May 3, 1981, and May 5, 1982) were invaluable to me. His published work proved likewise indispensable. I especially profited from the following: "Die Geschichte der Klassischen Philologie in den Vereinigten Staaten" in *Jahrbuch fuer Amerikastudien*, vol. 11; "Jaeger, Werner Wilhelm," *Dictionary of American Biography*, Supplement 7, pp. 387–89, "The Correspondence of Ulrich von Wilamowitz-Moellendorff with Werner Jaeger," *Harvard Studies in Classical Philology* 28 (1978): 303–47; "Ulrich von Wilamowitz-Moellendorff to James Loeb: Two Unpublished Letters," *Illinois Clasical Studies* 2 (1977): 315–32; review of Volker Losemann, "Nationalsozialismus and Antike: Studien zur Entwicklung des Faches Alte Geschichte 1933–1945," Hamburg, 1977, in *Classical Philology* 76, no. 2 (1981): 166–68.

2. Thorstein Veblen, *The Theory of the Leisure Class* (New York: Mentor Books—New American Library, 1953), p. 256.

3. Cf. Jaeger's autobiographical comments in the introduction to his *Scripta Minora* (Rome: Edizioni di Storia e Litteratura, 1960): ix–xxviii.

4. Werner Jaeger, *Paideia:The Ideals of Greek Culture,,* trans. by Gilbert Highet, 3 vols. (New York: Oxford University Press, 1939, 1943, 1944).

5. *Scripta Minora*, p. xvi.

6. The above paragraph is largely based on a personal communication from Charles P. Segal of Brown University (May 5, 1981). See also Clara Claiborne Park's loving memoir of Jaeger as a teacher, "At Home in History: Werner Jaeger's Paideia" in *The American Scholar* 52, no. 3 (Summer 1983): 378–85.

7. Werner Jaeger, *Scripta Minora* p. xxvi.

Hajo Holborn, Felix Gilbert, Hans Rosenberg, and Paul Oskar Kristeller

1. For the overall account of the background of German refugee historians and their impact on American scholarship I am deeply indebted to Georg G. Iggers, "Die Deutschen Historiker in der Emigration," in Bernard Faulenbach, ed., *Geschichtswissenschaft in Deutschland* (Munich: C. H. Beck, 1974), pp. 97–111. Hans-Ulrich Wehler's *Historische Sozialwissenschaft und Geschichtsschreibung* (Goettingen: Vendenhoeck and Ruprecht, 1980), especially the section on "Aussenseiter der Deutschen Geschichtswissenschaft," proved most helpful.

2. Most of my information on Holborn is based on two special issues of *Central European History* 3, nos. 1, 2 (March, June 1970), published in his memory. The papers by Felix Gilbert and Dietrich Gerhard proved especially helpful. I have also profited from Leonard Krieger's introduction to a collection of Holborn's papers, *History and the Humanities* (New York: Doubleday, 1972); the introduction by Leonard Krieger and Fritz Stern to *The Responsibility of Power: Historical Essays in Honor of Hajo Holborn* (New York, Doubleday, 1967), also proved helpful. Lastly, *Hajo Holborn: Internationes Prize* (Bonn/Bad Godesberg: Internationes, 1969) provided valuable information.

3. Quoted in Gerhard p. 9.

4. *Internationes Prize* p. 21.

5. Many of these essays can be found in Holborn's *History and the Humanities.*

6. Hajo Holborn, *A History of Modern Germany,* 3 vols. (New York, Knopf, 1959, 1964, 1968).

7. Hajo Holborn, *The Political Collapse of Europe* (New York: Knopf, 1951).

8. Hajo Holborn, *American Military Government: Its Organization and Policies* (Washington, D.C.: Infantry Journal Press, 1947).

9. I have learned much from Franklin L. Ford's introduction to Felix Gilbert, *History: Choice and Commitment* (Cambridge, Mass.: Harvard University Press, 1977), as well as from Peter Burke's review of Gilbert's, *The Pope, His Banker, and Venice* (Cambridge, Mass.: Harvard University Press, 1980), in *The New York Review of Books,* March 5, 1981, pp. 33–34.

10. Felix Gilbert, personal communication, June 23, 1982.

11. Ibid.

12. Ibid.

13. Ibid.

14. See Burke's review of Gilbert, *The Pope, His Banker, and Venice.*

15. Felix Gilbert, *Machiavelli and Guicciardini: Politics and History in Sixteenth-Century Florence* (Princeton: Princeton University Press, 1965).

16. Felix Gilbert, *To the Farewell Address: Ideas of Early American Foreign Policy* (Princeton: Princeton University Press, 1961); idem, *The End of the European Era: 1890 to the Present* (New York, Norton, 1970); idem, *The Pope, His Banker, and Venice.*

17. Felix Gilbert, *History: Choice and Commitment.*

18. I owe most of my data on Rosenberg to Hans-Ulrich Wehler's fine portrait of him in *Historische Sozialwissenschaft.* Wehler uses a number of autobiographical sketches that Rosenberg published in Germany.

19. Hans Rosenberg, *Bureaucracy, Aristocracy, and Autocracy: The Prussian Experience 1660–1815* (Cambridge, Mass.: Harvard University Press, 1958).

20. This section is largely based on "Paul Oskar Kristeller and His Contribution to Scholarship," in Edward P. Mahoney, ed., *Philosophy and Humanism: Renaissance Essays in Honor of Paul Oskar Kristeller* (Leiden: E. J. Brill, 1976).

21. Paul Oskar Kristeller, *The Philosophy of Marsilio Ficino* (New York: Columbia University Press, 1944).

22. Paul Oskar Kristeller, ed., *Inter Italicum* (Leiden: E. J. Brill, 1963).

23. *Philosophy and Humanism* p. 16.

Part VIII: Philosophy and Theology

Rudolf Carnap and the Vienna Circle

1. My account of the Vienna Circle in America is largely based on Herbert Feigl's "The Wiener Kreis in America," in Donald Fleming and Bernard Bailyn, eds., *The Intellectual Migration: Europe and America, 1930–1960* (Cambridge, Mass.: Harvard University Press, 1969). I have also benefited from converstations with Paul Benacerraf of Princeton University, at the Center for Advanced Study in Behavioral Sciences, where we were both Fellows in 1979–1980. Cf. also Albert E. Blumberg, "Carnap, Rudolf," in *Biographical Supplement to the International Encyclopedia of the Social Sciences* (New York: Macmillan, 1979).

2. Feigl, "The Wiener Kreis," p. 659.

3. Most of my biographical information on Carnap comes from his "Intellectual Autobiography," in Paul A. Schilpp, *The Philosophy of Rudolf Carnap* (La Salle, Ill.: Open Court, 1963).

4. Ibid., p. 3.

5. Rudolf Carnap, *Der Logische Aufbau der Welt* (Berlin: Weltkreis Verlag, 1928); *Logical Syntax of Language* (London, 1937).

6. See Peter Achinstein, "Reichenbach, Hans" in *Encyclopedia of Philosophy* (New York, Macmillan, 1967).

7. See Carnap, "Intellectual Autobiography," p. 52 and Feigl, p. 654.

8. Feigl, p. 644.

9. Carnap, "Intellectual Autobiography," p. 42.

10. Rudolf Carnap, *Introduction to Semantics* (Cambridge, Mass.: Harvard University Press, 1942); Rudolf Carnap, *Logical Foundations of Probability* (Chicago, Chicago University Press, 1950).

11. See the bibliography in Achinstein.

12. See Feigl.

13. *The Journal of Philosophy* 39 (1942): 35–48.

14. For an overall appreciation of Hempel's work and a full bibliography, see Jaegwon Kim, "Hempel, Carl Gustav," in *Encyclopedia of Philosophy* (New York, Macmillan, 1967); and Philip Quinn, "Hempel, Carl Gustav," in *Biographical Supplement to International Encyclopedia of the Social Sciences* (New York: Macmillan, 1979).

15. John Passmore, "Logical Positivism," in *Encyclopedia of Philosophy* (New York: Macmillan, 1967).

Aron Gurwitsch

1. For biographical information on Gurwitsch, I have mainly relied on Hans Jonas, "Aron Gurwitsch," *Social Research* 40, no. 4 (Winter, 1973): 567–69, and Lester Embree "Aron Gurwitsch," *Philosophy and Phenomenological Research* 33 (September 1973): 141–42.

2. Aron Gurwitsch, *Studies in Phenomemology and Psychology* (Evanston, Ill.: Northwestern University Press, 1966), p. xv.

3. Ibid., p. xvi.

4. Ibid., p. xix.

5. Ibid., p. 93.

6. Aron Gurwitsch, *The Field of Consciousness* (Pittsburgh: Duquesne University Press, 1964).

7. Aron Gurwitsch, *Leibniz: Philosophie des Panlogismus* (Berlin and New York: de Gruyter, 1974).

8. Aron Gurwitsch, *Phenomenology and the Theory of Science* (Evanston, Ill.: Northwestern University Press, 1974.) See also, a posthumously translated work of Gurwitsch's youth, *Human Encounters in the Social World*, ed. Alexandre Métraux (Pittsburgh: Duquesne University Press, 1979).

9. Cf. Hugh J. Silverman, "Phenomenology," *Social Research* 47, no. 4 (Winter 1980): 704–20.

10. Northwestern University Press, 1972.

11. For an authoritative history of the phenomenological movement, see Herbert Spiegelberg, *The Phenomenological Movement: A Historical Introduction*, 2d ed. (The Hague: Nijhoff, 1962).

Paul Tillich

1. The following pages are largely based on Wilhelm Pauck and Marion Pauck, *Paul Tillich: His Life and Thought*, vol. 1 (New York: Harper & Row, 1976); Paul Tillich, *On the Boundary: An Autobiographical Sketch* (New York: Scribner's, 1966); Paul Tillich, *Ein Lebensbild in Dokumenten* (Stuttgart: Evangelisches Verlagswerk, 1980); Charles W. Kegley and Robert W. Bretall, *The Theology of Paul Tillich* (New York: Macmillan, 1964).

2. Cf. Terence M. O'Keefe, "Paul Tillich's Marxism," *Social Research* 48, no. 3 (Autumn 1981): 472–99.

3. Ibid., p. 493.

4. Paul Tillich "Autobiographical Reflections" in Kegley and Bretall, *Theology of Paul Tillich*, p. 8.

5. Ibid.

6. Ibid., p. 20.

7. Pauck and Pauck, p. 149.

8. Ibid., p. 229.

Index of Persons
and Institutions